SECOND
EDITION
2016

CHARITY LAW

A GLOBAL GUIDE FROM PRACTICAL LAW

General Editor:
Anne-Marie Piper
FARRER & CO

General Editor
Anne-Marie Piper
Farrer & Co

Commissioning Editor
Emily Kyriacou
emily.kyriacou@thomsonreuters.com

Commercial Director
Katie Burrington
katie.burrington@thomsonreuters.com

Publishing Editor
Anisha Radia
anisha.radia@thomsonreuters.com

Editor
Helen Clarke
helen.clarke@thomsonreuters.com

Published in October 2016 by Thomson Reuters (Professional) UK Limited
Friars House, 160 Blackfriars Road, London, SE1 8EZ
(Registered in England & Wales, Company No 1679046.
Registered Office and address for service:
2nd floor, 1 Mark Square, Leonard Street, London EC2A 4EG)
A CIP catalogue record for this book is available from the British Library.

Printed and bound by CPI Group (UK) Ltd, Croydon, CR0 4YY.

ISBN: 9780414057340

Thomson Reuters and the Thomson Reuters logo are trade marks of Thomson Reuters.

Crown copyright material is reproduced with the permission of the Controller of HMSO
and the Queen's Printer for Scotland.

CONTENTS

FOREWORD

Anne-Marie Piper, FARRER & CO

Charitable and philanthropic endeavours have a long and honourable tradition in many countries. However, in recent decades charitable activity, like economic activity, has become increasingly globalised, with more charities working internationally either alone or within federations and partnerships. Also, with the rise of the ideal of good corporate citizenship, many multi-national businesses want to contribute to the wellbeing of the countries in which they have operations. Having acted for such clients I am keenly aware of how complex the legal issues can be. The philanthropic urge may be common throughout the world, but the way in which it is translated into a legal and regulatory framework most certainly isn't. Moreover, as countries become increasingly aware of the need to combat financial fraud, money laundering and terrorist financing, many jurisdictions have stepped up control and supervision of their not-for-profit sectors, creating tighter legislative frameworks and appointing greater regulation. For any organisation planning cross-border charitable or not-for-profit activities, putting the right arrangements in place can be like wandering through a minefield.

The first edition of this book (published as part of the European Lawyer Reference Series) was a welcome addition to the bookshelves of charities, not-for-profits, legal professionals and corporations wanting to understand how charities could operate in different countries.

This second edition covers 20 jurisdictions (including all those in the United Kingdom), and follows a similar format with each chapter outlining the history of its charitable/not-for-profit sector, the legal framework governing it, the structures used by not-for-profit organisations, the advantages and disadvantages of operating as a charity in that country, and how overseas bodies can operate and fundraise there. Although this book cannot take the place of bespoke advice, it will at least give charities and their advisers a basic roadmap through that cross-jurisdictional minefield.

Again, I am grateful to Thomson Reuters for the opportunity to help compile this book. It has been hard work, but educational. I cannot adequately express my thanks to my colleagues in the Charity & Community Team at Farrers and, in particular, for his exceptional contribution to my colleague Philip Reed without whom it simply would not have been possible. I would also give particular thanks to the team at Thomson Reuters for co-ordinating the project.

Anne-Marie Piper, Partner
Farrer & Co
October 2016

AUSTRALIA

Vera Visevic, MILLS OAKLEY

OVERVIEW AND MAIN TRENDS

1.   WHAT IS THE HISTORICAL BACKGROUND TO CHARITY LAW AND CHARITABLE ORGANISATIONS IN YOUR JURISDICTION?

Australian legal system

The Australian legal system consists of both federal laws and state and territory laws. The Australian Constitution of 1901 established a federal system of government, the Commonwealth, which clearly sets out the division of power between the Commonwealth and state and territory governments. In effect, Australia has nine sources of legislation - the eight state and territory systems, and the federal Commonwealth system.

The Constitution vests exclusive powers in the Commonwealth in sections 51 and 52 to make laws on certain matters such as trade and commerce, taxation, external powers, defence and immigration, which apply to the whole of Australia. Powers which are not exclusively vested in the Commonwealth government remain with the states and territories.

The Constitution also gives states and territories independent legislative power, known as concurrent or shared power, to make laws in the areas where the Commonwealth government has power, provided that the state laws do not conflict with those of the Commonwealth. Where there is inconsistency between Commonwealth and state or territory law, section 109 of the Constitution provides that Commonwealth law will prevail, and the state or territory law, to the extent that it is inconsistent, will be invalid.

The history and development of charity law

The origins of Australian settlement by Europeans occurred just over 200 years ago. After initially being established as a penal colony, "free settlers" (mostly from lower or middle class Britain) followed the convicts who had been sent to Australia. As the new colony began to grow, it quickly became apparent that not all the needs of the poorest in the community were being met by the government. Providing for the poor and the sick soon became the domain of the leading colonists and their wives, who were encouraged to form and support not-for-profit organisations to provide these much needed services. Initially, the government subsidised these public charities, mostly on a dollar-for-dollar basis, which increased at a higher rate, especially into the 20th century, and with the increase in government subsidisation there developed an increase in government regulation.

Up until recently, charity law in Australia was essentially treated as a subset of the law of trusts. This is primarily because trusts were the traditional vehicle through which charitable purposes were given effect. This is no longer an appropriate classification in modern times, as trusts have been replaced by other legal vehicles such as incorporated associations and public companies limited by guarantee. Further, characteristics exist within charity law which are foreign to much of the law of trusts (Gino E Dal Pont, *Law of Charity (LexisNexis Butterworths, 2010)*, 3-4). An example is that currently, and over the past 80 years, the existence of charities owes a considerable debt of gratitude to revenue-related exemptions and concessions, resulting in the general law of charity being an artificial construct, driven more by statutory concession rather than pure altruism (*Law of Charity, 9*).

In recent years, there has been a dramatic overhaul of charity law in Australia. The Charities Act 2013 (Cth) (Charities Act) has introduced a new statutory federal definition of a charity, and provides a legal federal framework for the operation of charity law in Australia. Prior to the statute's commencement, the common law contained a complicated collection of definitions and categories which the Charities Act has sought to simplify. The Charities Act has reformulated a large portion of the former law as it existed, and restated it in modern language which is easier to understand and reflects a contemporary understanding of the meaning of "charity".

A further significant reform has been the establishment of the Australian Charities and Not-for-profits Commission (ACNC). Established by the Australian Charities and Not-for-profits Commission Act 2012 (Cth) (ACNC Act), the ACNC is the sole regulator of charities in Australia, and is responsible for their registration, the maintenance of a register of details of registered charities and the enforcement of regulation reform. The introduction of the ACNC represents a shift in Australian charity law towards a centralised system of regulation and control.

2. ARE INDEPENDENT CHARITABLE ORGANISATIONS COMMON AND SIGNIFICANT IN YOUR JURISDICTION? WHAT IS THE CURRENT SIZE AND SCOPE OF THE SECTOR AND THE MAIN TRENDS?

In Australia, there are roughly 600,000 not-for-profit organisations. The majority of these organisations are small bodies which do not employ many people; instead they rely on volunteers and the participation of members. At the time of writing, there were about 53,668 charities registered with the Australian Charities and Not-for-profits Commission (ACNC) in Australia (source: *ACNC Charities Register, 2016 (based on data provided in June 2016)*). In December 2015, the ACNC released a report which laid out important quantitative data, providing a snapshot of the charity sector in Australia (Cortis, N and others, *Australian Charities Report 2014*, Centre for Social Impact and Social Policy Research Centre, UNSW Australia). At the time, charities employed 1,005,694 people, 475,777 in a full time capacity and 529,917 persons in a part time capacity. In 2014, 47.7% of charities had at least one paid employee and one volunteer in their service.

Charities range significantly in their size and make up. Around two-thirds (64.1%) of Australian charities are small, with an annual income of less than A$250,000. Large charities with a turnover exceeding A$1 million comprise about one-fifth (19.2%) of charities in Australia, and medium-sized charities, those with a turnover between A$250,000 and A$1 million, comprise the remainder, at 16.6%.

Australian charities mostly operate in only one state or territory, with only 3.9% of charities operating nationally, and 9.3% of charities operating in at least more than one state or territory. About two-thirds of charities are located in metropolitan areas and about one-third (31.2%) are located in rural areas, with the remainder in remote areas. A small number (7.7%) of charities have operations which extend overseas, although 16.9% of charities have involvement with other overseas parties and organisations. These figures demonstrate that a large number of charities have a local focus, and do not operate interstate or overseas.

Charities in Australia have a diverse range of activities and functions. About one-third of charities are religious, although they are typically small in size. The second major type of activity undertaken by Australian charities is education and research, which accounts for 18.4% of all registered charities.

Australian charities seek to assist a wide range of people and groups. Almost half of existing charities (47.6%) benefit members of the general public. 40.9% of charities state that they assist women, 38.3% assist men and 37.6% assist children.

LEGAL FRAMEWORK

Charities Act

The Charities Act provides the framework for the operation of charity law at a federal level in Australia. It is important to note that not all non-profit organisations are charities; charities are essentially a subset of not-for-profit organisations in Australia. There is no consistent definition of a charity at a state/territory level.

The Charities Act defines a "charity" as a not-for-profit entity which exists for a "charitable purpose" and for a "public benefit". The Act further defines a public benefit as something which is available to the general public or a sufficient section of the general public. If a not-for-profit exists for any of the following purposes, it is deemed to be for the public benefit:

- Preventing and relieving sickness, disease or human suffering.
- Advancing education.
- Relieving the poverty, distress or disadvantage of individuals or families.
- Caring for and supporting the aged or individuals with disabilities.
- Advancing religion.

A not-for-profit has a charitable purpose if it exists for one of the following purposes:

- Advancing health.
- Advancing education.
- Advancing social or public welfare.
- Advancing religion.
- Advancing culture.
- Promoting reconciliation, mutual respect and tolerance between groups of individuals that are in Australia.
- Promoting or protecting human rights.
- Advancing the security or safety of Australia or the Australian public.
- Preventing or relieving the suffering of animals.
- Advancing the natural environment.

- Any other purpose beneficial to the general public that may reasonably be regarded as analogous to, or within the spirit of, any of the above purposes.
- Advancing public debate (promoting or opposing a change to any matter established by law, policy or practice in Australia or another country).

For the purposes of the legal definition of a charity, it does not matter if a charitable purpose is intended to be advanced in Australia or overseas.

A charity will be disqualified from being a charity if its purpose is either:

- Engaging in or promoting activities that are unlawful or contrary to public policy.
- Promoting or opposing a political party or a candidate for political office.

Importantly, it is still permissible for a charity to advocate for policy change in carrying out its purpose. However, it cannot exist for the sole purpose of supporting a political candidate or party.

Australian Charities and Not-for-profits Commission (ACNC) legislation

The establishment of the ACNC has dramatically altered the way in which charities operate in Australia. As the ACNC is a large, sophisticated body, there are several pieces of legislation which govern how it functions, what its role is, and the nature of its powers.

The ACNC Act established the ACNC and lays out its objects and functions. The legislation contains the framework for how charities are to be registered and regulated. In addition, the Australian Charities and Not-for-profits Commission Regulation 2013 (Cth) lays out the practical requirements as to how the ACNC itself functions. For example, it oversees the ACNC Register which contains the details of all registered charities in Australia. The Regulations also set out how charities are to comply with financial reporting requirements and governance standards.

LEGAL BODIES

4. WHAT ARE THE FORMS OF ORGANISATIONS THAT ARE USED FOR CHARITABLE PURPOSES? WHAT ARE THEIR ADVANTAGES/DISADVANTAGES?

Charities

Public company limited by guarantee. Increasingly in Australia, charities are established as public companies limited by guarantee. The structure is similar to a company limited by shares, but instead of shareholders, a company limited by guarantee has members, who guarantee the payment of a fixed contribution in the event the company is wound up and cannot pay its creditors.

The members of a public company limited by guarantee have no right to receive a share of the company's profits, which must be applied only for its charitable purposes. If a company is wound up, any surplus assets must be applied to another organisation for similar charitable purposes (often this means its assets are transferred to another charity). If the company is also endorsed as a deductible gift recipient (*see Question 9, Deductible gift recipients (DGR)*), any surplus assets arising from deductible monies must be transferred to another deductible gift recipient.

Public companies limited by guarantee must comply with company law provisions set out in the Corporations Act 2001 (Cth), although section 111L does provide exemptions for charities. These entities are also regulated by the Australian Securities and Investments Commission (ASIC).

A public company limited by guarantee also has its own legal personality, meaning that it can hold land, enter into contracts in its own name, sue and be sued. Such a company can also carry on activities anywhere in Australia and is not limited to one particular state or territory. This makes the public company limited by guarantee structure quite popular and the most suitable for larger charities.

A public company limited by guarantee can either be wound up under insolvency proceedings (in the same way a for-profit company can be), or it can be dissolved and an application can be made for it to be removed from the register of companies held by ASIC. Once the company has been wound up or dissolved, the Australian Securities and Investments Commission (ACNC) must be notified so that it can be removed from the register of charities.

Incorporated association. For small charities operating in only one jurisdiction, it may be more appropriate that they operate as incorporated associations. If an incorporated association eventually wishes to carry on activities in more than one jurisdiction, it is legally possible in most states and territories for it to convert into a public company limited by guarantee. An alternative route which is quicker and cheaper is for an incorporated association to register itself with ASIC as a Registered Australian Body.

Each state and territory in Australia has its own Associations Incorporation Act, which is administered by the relevant authority. An incorporated association is a legal entity separate from its individual members, can hold property, and can sue and be sued.

Once the incorporated association has been wound up or has had its incorporation cancelled, the ACNC must be notified so that it can be removed from the register of charities.

On a wind-up or cancellation of incorporation, any remaining assets of the charity must be passed to another charity with similar purposes. It is important to note that under no circumstances can the assets of an incorporated association be divided among its members.

Charitable trust. Historically, the trust was the legal structure of choice for many charities. This has changed in recent years, primarily because of the advantages for trustees of incorporating as a company or an incorporated association.

A charitable trust is formed by a trustee or trustees agreeing to hold assets on trust to be applied for the purposes of the charity. The trustee can be an individual or a body corporate (such as a company or incorporated association). The charitable trust has no separate legal identity from the trustee, and cannot own land or sign documents in its own name. Everything must be done by and in the name of the trustee.

A charitable trust does not need to comply with company law or the law applying to incorporated associations (unless and to the extent that trustee is a company or an incorporated association), and can therefore be more flexible than a public company limited by guarantee or an incorporated association. However, it will be governed by trust law which can be a complex area requiring specialist advice. The trust itself (as distinct from the trustee) does not need to report on its affairs and accounts to ASIC, although it may still have reporting obligations to the ACNC.

The main disadvantage of a charitable trust is the absence of limited liability for the trustees, who are jointly and severally liable for the debts and liabilities of the charity. If the liabilities do not result from a breach of trust by the trustees, the trustees are entitled to be reimbursed from the assets of the charity, but this indemnity is of little value if the charity has insufficient assets to cover its debts and liabilities. Many potential trustees are uncomfortable about entering an agreement which would require them to personally be named as employer, buyer and so on, on behalf of the charity.

The trust deed usually sets out the procedure under which a charitable trust can be dissolved. If there is no procedure, a charitable trust can be dissolved when all of its assets have been applied in furtherance of its objects. Once all of the liabilities of the trust have been settled and its assets spent, the trustees can apply to the ACNC to have the trust removed from the register of charities.

Unincorporated association. The largest proportion of not-for-profit organisations in Australia are unincorporated. Any number of persons who wish to associate together as a group for any lawful non-commercial purpose, which does not involve a personal pecuniary profit, may agree to form an unincorporated association. The founding members will normally give the association a name and adopt suitable rules. The elected members of the executive committee are in a fiduciary position and as such have a duty to act in the best interests of the members of the association.

The advantage of an unincorporated association is that it is relatively simple to create and flexible to run and, in most cases, professional legal advice can be kept to a minimum. It can also provide a structure whereby all of the members can play a role in carrying out its objects.

As with a charitable trust, the disadvantage of an unincorporated association is that it will have no separate legal personality. The members and executive committee will also not be protected from liability and so may be personally liable for the association's debts. This personal liability extends to any damages payable by the unincorporated association as a result of a successful action against the association in contract or tort.

Unincorporated associations can be dissolved subject to any procedure or restrictions set out in their governing documents. The procedure is generally the same as for a charitable trust (*see above, Charitable trust*).

An unincorporated association is the simplest form of charity to establish, but provides the least protection for its members and its executive committee. Unincorporated associations are generally more suitable for small, membership based charities that hold few or no assets and employ no staff.

Other types of charitable structure. Most charities in Australia are public companies limited by guarantee, incorporated associations, charitable trusts or unincorporated associations.

However, there are a number of other legal forms that charities can adopt. The particular circumstances in which these would be appropriate are outside the scope of this guide, but charities may also be:

- Royal Charter bodies (which are incorporated by way of a charter from the Queen). There are only a few of these remaining and they are generally no longer granted.
- Incorporated by federal or state parliament by a special Act of Parliament (such as religious denominations).
- Co-operatives.
- Aboriginal companies (which are regulated by the Office of the Registrar of Indigenous Corporations).

Other non-profit organisations

Public company limited by guarantee. Most non-charitable not-for-profits which carry on activities in more than one state or territory are incorporated as public companies limited by guarantee, with a prohibition on the members sharing in any profits of the company.

Non-charitable public companies limited by guarantee are only subject to company law and do not need to comply with charity law. However, if they enjoy any tax exemptions or concessions, then they must also comply with the state and federal laws granting them the exceptions or concessions.

Incorporated associations. Incorporated associations are also a popular vehicle for other not-for-profits, especially the smaller entities which only operate in one state or territory. These entities are still subject to the laws governing incorporated associations. Further, if they enjoy any tax concessions or exemptions, then the incorporated associations must also comply with the relevant federal and state/territory laws which grant them the exemptions or concessions.

Other types of non-profit structure. As with charities, non-profits can also take the form of Royal Charter bodies, bodies which have been incorporated pursuant to a special Act of Parliament, or Aboriginal companies.

Another structure which is typical for a not-for-profit (but not a charity) is that of the co-operative society. This is a non-profit organisation formed or carried on for the mutual benefit of its members and is quite common in industries as diverse as publishing, tourism, catering, dairy produce, taxis, housing, recycling and childcare. Co-operatives are different from other forms of incorporation because of their membership ownership and democratic structure.

5. WHAT ARE THE QUALIFICATION REQUIREMENTS/FORMALITIES TO SET UP THESE ORGANISATIONS?

Charities

Public companies limited by guarantee. The first task when establishing a public company limited by guarantee is to prepare the company's constitution (its governing document).

The constitution is a formal document used to incorporate and govern the company. This document:

- Contains the charity's objects.
- Sets out what must happen to any surplus assets if the charity is dissolved.
- Contains procedural rules governing matters such as membership, and the appointment and retirement of directors.
- Contains the procedures to be followed at meetings.

It is largely up to the founders of the charity to decide how the company will operate by deciding what should and should not be included in its constitution. There are some provisions, however, that will need to be included, such as restrictions on director benefits and on members receiving any share of the charity's profits.

Relevant details about the company's registered office and directors must be collected. The first members and directors then complete the necessary incorporation documentation and lodge it with the relevant fee at the Australian Securities and Investments Commission (ASIC). The incorporation process is usually fairly straightforward and should take only about one week with ASIC.

Once incorporated as a public company limited by guarantee, the company must apply for an Australian Business Number (ABN) with the Australian Tax Office (ATO). Once the ABN has been obtained, the company must then apply to the Australian Charities and Not-for-profits Commission (ACNC) to be registered as a charity, as set out above.

Incorporated associations. The first step is to prepare a constitution which complies with the relevant state/territory legislation. Once the constitution is prepared and the committee members and members of the proposed incorporated association have been identified, the committee members can apply for incorporation as an incorporated association with the relevant state/territory authority by lodging the appropriate forms. There is also a fee to be paid with the lodgement of the forms. There is a further fee payable to ASIC if the incorporated association subsequently applies to become a Registered Australian Body, enabling it to operate in more than one jurisdiction.

Once incorporated, which usually only takes a few days, it must then apply to the ATO for an ABN. The incorporated association must then apply to the ACNC to be registered as a charity, as set out above.

Charitable trusts. In order to establish a charitable trust, a trust deed must be drawn up. This is the document which governs how the trust will be operated: it explains how the trustees determine which causes the trust will support, and may outline any limits on the way that assets can be disbursed. It also sets out who the trustees are and includes provisions setting out how they should govern the trust. It is important that this document satisfies the legal requirements for the creation of a trust and includes clauses that satisfy the ACNC and ATO requirements for a charitable trust. Stamp duty may be payable on the trust deed (depending on its jurisdiction) and the deed may also need to be registered with the local Department of Lands (again, depending on its jurisdiction).

The trust can be funded either through the founders transferring assets to the trust or by soliciting donations. The process of drafting a charitable trust deed depends on the complexity of the trusts involved, but should not take long.

Application must then be made to the ATO for an ABN. The trust must then apply to the ACNC to be registered as a charity, as set out above.

Unincorporated associations. An unincorporated association's governing document is usually known as its constitution or its rules. There is no prescribed format, but it usually specifies:

- The objects of the association.
- How the members and management committee of the association are appointed.
- How the association will be operated.
- The restrictions on the distribution of the association's assets.

Once the governing document has been drawn up, the members and management committee of the association can be appointed.

The association must then apply to the ATO for an ABN. The unincorporated association must then apply to the ACNC to be registered as a charity, as set out above.

Not-for-profit organisations

Public company limited by guarantee. The procedure is identical to that for a charitable public company limited by guarantee, save that there is more flexibility in the drawing up of the constitution. Nevertheless, the constitution must contain certain clauses to be able to legally classify itself as a not-for-profit. These include a:

- Special dissolution clause.
- Prohibition on the distribution of income and assets to directors or members.

It may not be necessary for the company to apply to the ATO for an ABN, but it is still advisable to do so. As opposed to charities, it is not necessary for not-for-profits to register with the ACNC.

Incorporated and unincorporated associations. Setting up an incorporated or unincorporated association which is a not-for-profit is similar to the processes outlined above for public charitable incorporated and unincorporated associations. The main differences are:

- There is greater flexibility with the drafting of the constitution, so long as the requisite clauses (those outlined for charitable public companies limited by guarantee above) are included.
- There is no requirement to be registered with the ACNC.

Registration of charities and not-for-profits

If a charity wishes to obtain charity status in Australia, it must be registered with the ACNC. The ACNC Act sets out the conditions for registration as the following:

- Being a not-for-profit entity.
- Compliance with the governance and external conduct standards set out in Part 3-1 of the ACNC Act. In short, these standards require the open, accountable, transparent, effective and efficient governance of entities seeking registration.
- Having an ABN.
- Not being covered by a decision in writing made by a government agency that characterises the entity as engaging in or supporting terrorist or other criminal activities.
- Meeting the criteria of a charity or not-for-profit subtype (*see Question 3, Charities Act*).

In addition to these conditions, in the application for registration, the ACNC requires certain details about the organisation seeking registration including:

- A statement of charitable purpose and description of activities.
- The beneficiaries of the organisation.
- Financial information for the current and previous financial year.

The ACNC aims to process applications for registration within 28 days.

ACNC Register. The ACNC must keep a publicly accessible register containing information about each registered and formerly registered charity. This register is published on the ACNC website at *www.acnc.gov.au/findacharity*. In addition to the name and contact details of each charity, the register includes the subtype of charity, copies of governing documents and financial records disclosed to the ACNC, information about the beneficiaries of the charity and any enforcement orders made by the ACNC Commissioner against the charity.

ONGOING REGULATORY REQUIREMENTS

6.   WHAT ARE THE MAIN REGULATORY AUTHORITIES FOR CHARITABLE ORGANISATIONS? WHAT ARE THEIR POWERS OF INVESTIGATION/AUDIT/SANCTIONS?

Australian Charities and Not-for-profits Commission (ACNC)

The ACNC is the sole regulator of charities in Australia in their capacity as charities. It is responsible for the registration of charities, maintenance of a register of organisation details and enforcement of charities' regulations.

ACNC regulatory and enforcement powers. The ACNC Act grants the ACNC limited powers to monitor charities' compliance with regulations and subsequent enforcement.

Regulatory requirements. Charities are required to satisfy certain areas of compliance to fulfil their ongoing regulatory requirements. Charities must:

- Remain a not-for-profit organisation, maintain a charitable purpose for the public benefit and comply with the governance standards that apply to them.
- Update the ACNC when they change their legal name, address, "responsible persons" and governing documents (constitution, rules or trust deed).
- Keep records.
- Keep accurate financial and operational records for at least seven years.
- Report their financial information to the ACNC annually. The stringency of these requirements varies depending of the size of the revenue of the organisation (*see Question 8*).

Enforcement and regulatory powers. The ACNC typically uses its enforcement powers as a final measure following provision of guidance and support to charities to meet their obligations. Where compliance does not result from this approach, formal powers of enforcement may be used. These powers include:

- Warnings.
- Directions.
- Enforceable undertakings.
- Seeking injunctions.
- Suspension or removal of a "responsible person" (such as a committee or board member or trustee) of a charity.
- Disqualification of a responsible person from being a responsible person of any charity.
- Revocation of registration.
- Imposition of administrative penalties for the making of false or misleading statements or failure to lodge documents on time. For example, at the time of writing, administrative penalties ranged from A$170 to A$4,260 for failure to lodge an annual information statement on time.

The ACNC has the power to gather information and documents necessary to monitor compliance with the regulations and assess ongoing entitlement to registration. ACNC officers also have the power to monitor the activities of a charity to verify the accuracy of information provided, and to ensure compliance with regulations. These monitoring powers extend to the search and examination of premises for which a monitoring warrant is granted.

Other regulators

At a federal level, the ATO also has a role in regulating charities. The ATO ultimately grants tax exemptions to charities, in most cases on the basis of endorsement by the ACNC. Applications for tax exemptions are usually forwarded to the ATO by the ACNC, allowing charities to mostly deal with a single federal regulator. At a state or territory level, the relevant Associations Incorporation Act may impose additional financial reporting or governance requirements on incorporated associations that are charities.

7.   WHICH BODIES OR PERSONS MANAGE CHARITABLE ORGANISATIONS AND WHAT GENERAL REQUIREMENTS MUST THEY MEET?

Responsible persons

There are a variety of structures which charitable organisations adopt in Australia (*see Question 4*). Each structure has different types of persons who manage these organisations depending on their construct. The Australian Charities and Not-for-profits Commission (ACNC) Act refers to these persons as "responsible persons":

- **Public company limited by guarantee.** The directors of the company are the responsible persons. Directors' duties include:
  - avoiding conflicts of interest;
  - acting with due care and diligence;
  - acting in good faith.
- **Incorporated associations.** Members of the committee of management of the association are the responsible persons. Incorporated association management committee members' responsibilities will be determined by the relevant state or territory legislation. However, their obligations may include:
  - maintaining the association's financial viability; and
  - ensuring the association's purposes are being achieved.
- **Unincorporated associations.** The governing body of an unincorporated association is not always clear. The responsible persons may be members of the association, in particular, members who direct or provide guidance for the association, and those who monitor its solvency. Responsible members of an unincorporated association are bound by obligations placed on them by the constitution of the association.
- **Trust.** The trustees and, in the case of a corporate trustee, the directors of that corporation, are the responsible persons. Trustees must exercise reasonable care and know the terms of the trust.
- **Co-operative.** The directors of the co-operative are the responsible persons. Co-operative directors' responsibilities are determined by the relevant state or territory legislation, but may include:
  - acting in good faith in the interests of the co-operative;
  - acting with reasonable care;
  - acting for a proper purpose;
  - making decisions independently; and
  - avoiding conflicts of interest.
- **Insolvent charity.** When an organisation can no longer pay its debts as they fall due, a person is appointed to administer the organisation's liabilities. This appointed person is deemed to be the responsible person. Depending on the legal structure of the charity that has become insolvent, the appointed person may be a "trustee in bankruptcy", "receiver", "administrator" or "liquidator". The responsibilities of such a person usually include the duty to act with due care and in good faith for the benefit of the creditors of the charity.

Obligations of responsible persons

Generally, the ACNC Act requires that charities meet certain governance standards. Charities must ensure that the responsible persons who manage or govern the organisation are suitable, and that each person is fully aware of their duties. Generally, the duties of responsible persons are as follows:

- Act with reasonable care and diligence.
- Act honestly and fairly in the best interests of the charity in the pursuit of its purposes.
- Not misuse their positions or information they receive because of their positions.
- Disclose all actual or potential conflicts of interest.
- Not to operate the charity if it is insolvent.
- Manage the financial affairs of the charity responsibly.

Further obligations may be placed on responsible persons depending on the construct of the charity (*see above, Responsible persons*). There may be further obligations that responsible persons must meet under state and territory legislation.

8.   WHAT ARE THE ACCOUNTING/FINANCIAL REPORTING REQUIREMENTS?

The accounting/financial reporting requirements of a not-for-profit organisation will depend largely on:

- Its tax status, that is, whether it is a charity, an income exempt not-for-profit or a tax paying not-for-profit.
- Its structure, that is, whether it is a public company limited by guarantee, an incorporated association or some other structure.

Australian Charities and Not-for-profits Commission (ACNC)

All charities must report to the ACNC, regardless of structure.

Small charities (those with an annual revenue less than A$250,000) must submit an "Annual Information Statement" which includes basic financial questions such as overall figures for income, expenditure, assets and liabilities.

Medium-sized charities (those with annual revenue between A$250,000 and A$1 million) must submit an Annual Information Statement, requiring more detailed income, expenditure, asset and liabilities information.

Large charities (those with annual revenue above A$1 million) have the same obligations as medium-sized charities, but must also submit an independently audited financial report.

Basic religious charities are exempt from financial reporting entirely.

Australian Tax Office (ATO)

Every type of charity and not-for-profit is accountable to the ATO (and some are required to report, depending on their tax concessions or exemptions).

Australian Securities and Investments Commission (ASIC)

The following are accountable to ASIC:

- Public companies limited by guarantee which are not charities.
- Incorporated associations that are registered Australian bodies and are not charities.

Office of the Registrar of Indigenous Corporations

Indigenous corporations that are not charities must report to the Office of the Registrar of Indigenous Corporations.

State or territory regulator

Incorporated associations (unless exceptions apply) and co-operatives must report to state or territory regulators.

TAX

9.   HOW ARE CHARITIES TAXED, AND WHAT (IF ANY) ARE THE PRINCIPAL EXEMPTIONS AND/OR RELIEFS FROM TAXATION THAT THEY ENJOY?

General tax concessions

There are multiple tax exemptions and concessions available to charities in Australia. In order to gain an exemption or concession, a charity must first be registered with the Australian Charities and Not-for-profits Commission (ACNC). After this, the charity must then apply to the Australian Tax Office (ATO) to obtain the benefit of the taxation exemptions and concessions. Generally, the tax concessions and exemptions that are available to charities are as follows:

- **Income tax exemption.** Any taxable income (including capital gains tax) received by the charity is not taxed; therefore, they are not required to lodge tax returns with the ATO.
- **Refunds on franking credits.** This applies if the charity holds shares in a company that provides franked dividends.
- **Goods and services tax (GST).** GST operates similarly to a value added tax. In Australia the GST rate is 10%. When goods and services are sold, the amount which the seller receives for the sale usually carries GST. When goods and services are purchased, the purchaser may be able to claim a GST credit for the GST included in the amount paid. Charities are granted significant GST concessions.
- **Fringe benefit tax rebate.** Fringe benefits tax is a tax placed on benefits which an employee receives in addition to their salary. For example, a company car, or phone. Charities may be granted a rebate of up 47% until 31 March 2016, and up to 49% from 31 March 2017.

Further tax concessions

In addition to the purposes listed in the Charities Act, there are two further types of charities, which entitle an organisation to tax concessions in addition to those listed above. These are public benevolent institutions and health promotion charities. These charities are entitled to a fringe benefit tax exemption and deductible gift recipient status (*see below, Deductible gift recipients (DGR)*).

Deductible gift recipients (DGR)

Some charities can also apply for DGR status when they register with the ACNC. If a charity has DGR status, donations which are made to the charity may be tax deductible to the donor (meaning that when donors lodge their tax returns with the ATO, they may deduct any donation made to a DGR from their taxable income).

State and territory tax concessions

Charities may also be eligible for certain state and territory tax exemptions or concessions. These include:

- Payroll tax exemptions.
- Stamp duty on property, insurance and motor vehicle duty.
- Council rates.
- Water rates.
- Land tax.

For each of these duties and taxes, the relevant legislation in each state or territory will determine which organisations are entitled to the tax exemptions and concessions. It must also be noted the organisations entitled to these exemptions and concessions are defined differently in each state and territory legislation.

10.   WHAT, IF ANY, ARE THE TAXATION BENEFITS FOR DONORS TO CHARITIES?

The key taxation benefit for donors arises from donating to charities which have deductible gift recipient (DGR) status (*see Question 9, Deductible gift recipients (DGR)*) as it generally entitles donors to a tax deduction. This applies whether the donor is an individual or a corporate entity. There are special rules as to:

- The sort of donated property that can entitle the donor to a tax deduction.
- The amount of the tax deduction available to the donor.

Organisations which are endorsed as DGRs find fundraising easier, given that donations generally entitle the donor to a tax deduction. However, having DGR endorsement places additional statutory reporting requirements on the charity, such as the requirement of having their accounts audited, even if the charity is small or medium sized.

DISADVANTAGES

11.   WHAT ARE THE MAIN DISADVANTAGES OF CHARITABLE STATUS?

The principal disadvantage for organisations with charitable status is the on-going regulation and public scrutiny required for the tax advantages they receive.

As a charity registered with the Australian Charities and Not-for-profits Commission (ACNC), there are several on-going responsibilities that may strain a charity's time and resources. Most notably, charities must maintain clear financial records, submit Annual Information Statements and abide by strict corporate governance standards. For small organisations, these tasks may be difficult to complete without diverting significant amounts of time away from their original charitable purpose. In addition, charities may find it difficult to comply with legislative changes if they operate across multiple jurisdictions. This is why the ACNC imposes reduced reporting requirements on smaller charities.

OVERSEAS CHARITIES

For an overseas charity to operate within Australia, it must be registered with the Australian Charities and Not-for-profits Commission (ACNC). It will be able to do so if it:

- Satisfies the legal meaning of charity.
- Identifies its charitable purpose.
- Has an Australian Business Number (ABN).
- Meets the governance standards.
- Is not a type of organisation that cannot be registered, such as an organisation included in a written decision made by an Australian government agency or judge that lists it as engaging in or supporting terrorist or other criminal activities.

To benefit from tax concessions available from the Australian Tax Office (ATO), the charity must satisfy one of the following three:

- Physical presence in Australia test.
- The deductible gift recipient test.
- The "prescribed by law" test. Essentially, this test refers to when an Australian statute names a specific charity and allows it to operate in Australia.

Many overseas charities struggle to satisfy the physical presence in Australia test, which has two elements:

- The charity must have a physical presence in Australia.
- To the extent that the charity has a physical presence in Australia, if it pursues its objectives and incurs its expenditure principally in Australia.

An overseas charity that does not have some form of legal operating structure in Australia:

- Will find it difficult to be registered with the ACNC.
- Will find it difficult to receive charity tax concessions from the ATO (as registration with the ACNC is a precondition).
- May struggle to gain public support, secure leases or employ staff.

Therefore, an overseas charity that is planning to undertake significant operations in Australia, or which wishes to raise funds from Australian donors, should consider:

- Creating a separate Australian legal entity.
- Registering with Australian Securities and Investments Commission (ASIC) as a foreign company.

Importantly, overseas charities and domestic charities operating overseas must engage in risk minimisation with regard to whom the charitable funds are ultimately benefitting. Concerns have been raised with regard to funds being misused or re-directed to inappropriate purposes, including terrorism funding and money laundering. As such, these charities must take reasonable steps to ensure that:

- Their activities outside Australia are carried out in a way that is consistent with their purpose and character as a charity.
- The resources (including funds) given to third parties outside Australia are applied in accordance with their purpose and character as a charity, and with proper controls and risk management processes in place.

13. IS IT POSSIBLE TO REGISTER A DOMESTIC CHARITY ABROAD, AND HAS YOUR JURISDICTION ENTERED INTO ANY INTERNATIONAL AGREEMENTS OR TREATIES IN THIS AREA?

There is no specific Australian law which prohibits an Australian charity from registering overseas. However, certain organisational structures, such as incorporated associations, do not permit activity outside of a particular State of Territory. At the time of writing, Australia is a not a member to any treaty which governs the ability of domestic charities registering overseas. Importantly, as mentioned in *Question 12*, a charity must maintain a physical presence in Australia; therefore, an Australian charity should take this into account when any it considers activity overseas.

The charity must also consider the domestic law of the foreign country in which it seeks to operate.

REFORM

14. ARE THERE ANY PROPOSALS FOR REFORM IN THE AREA OF CHARITY LAW?

Given there has been significant reform in this area in the past few years, it is unlikely that any policy reform will occur in the near future. The Australian Charities and Not-for-profits Commission (ACNC) has been fully funded until 2019, after which the Federal Government may decide to de-fund the Commission. If this were to occur, it would significantly change the regulations and operations surrounding the charities sector.

At the time of writing, there have been no significant proposals to reform the area of charity law; however, the ACNC does periodically publish guidance regarding the conduct of charities.

The multi-layered regulatory framework for charities in Australia has given rise to suggestions of a need to create greater uniformity across states and territories by replacing state and territory regulations with further Commonwealth regulations, enforced by the ACNC. This would consolidate regulation and reduce the compliance burden for charities. (See also Deloitte Access Economics, *Cutting Red Tape: Options to align state, territory and Commonwealth charity regulation Final Report (23 February 2016) Australian Charities and Not-for-profits Commission, 35-38)*.)

REGULATORY AUTHORITIES/ONLINE RESOURCES

AUSTRALIAN CHARITIES AND NOT-FOR-PROFITS COMMISSION (ACNC)

W www.acnc.gov.au

E advice@acnc.gov.au

Description. The ACNC is the primary regulator of charities in Australia. It is constituted under the Australian Charities and Not-for-profits Commission Act 2012 (Cth).

The official ACNC website contains up-to-date information about registering and managing charities. It contains information for charities as well as the general public. It also contains the Australian charities register.

AUSTRALIAN SECURITIES AND INVESTMENTS COMMISSION (ASIC)

W www.asic.gov.au

T +61 3 5177 3988

Description. ASIC is the primary corporate regulator in Australia. It enforces and regulates Australian company law, seeking to protect consumers, investors and creditors.

The official ASIC website contains current information about establishing, running and closing public companies.

AUSTRALIAN TAXATION OFFICE (ATO) – NOT-FOR-PROFIT

W www.ato.gov.au/Non-profit

T +61 2 6216 1111

Description. The ATO is the federal Australian taxation authority. It collects company tax and the goods and services tax among others. The ATO also maintains the Australian Business Register on which Australian Business Numbers are recorded.

The ATO not-for-profit website contains information about the federal taxation requirements for not-for-profit organisations and the tax concessions available to them. This website also provides for online lodgement of activity statements.

BELGIUM

Philippe Malherbe, LIEDEKERKE WOLTERS WAELBROECK KIRKPATRICK

OVERVIEW AND MAIN TRENDS

1.   WHAT IS THE HISTORICAL BACKGROUND TO CHARITY LAW AND CHARITABLE ORGANISATIONS IN YOUR JURISDICTION?

Under the *Ancien Régime*, charity (*caritas*, meaning "love thy neighbour") was provided by the Catholic Church. The French Revolution, which was imported into Belgium, confiscated Church property and proclaimed freedom of enterprise. Not for profit activity was looked on with distrust, all the more because it could freeze property out of the economic circuit. Some acts gradually relaxed that view, for:

*   Specific purposes, like the 1898 act on "professional unions".
*   Specific persons, like the 1911 act granting legal personality to the universities of Louvain and Brussels.

In 1921, after World War I, the spirit had changed and a new statute allowed for non-profit associations at large.

Belgian law offers various possibilities to conduct a business of a non-profit nature. The law recognises four different forms of non-profit organisation. The majority of Belgian non-profit organisations take the form of a "regular" non-profit association (*see Question 4, Non-profit association*), which enjoys legal personality under a re-enacted version of the 1921 act.

2.   ARE INDEPENDENT CHARITABLE ORGANISATIONS COMMON AND SIGNIFICANT IN YOUR JURISDICTION? WHAT IS THE CURRENT SIZE AND SCOPE OF THE SECTOR AND THE MAIN TRENDS?

Non-profit organisations occupy a key role in Belgium, particularly with regard to education, hospitals, culture and leisure ("non-trading" sector). Employment in that sector represents more than one-fifth of the total employment in Belgium.

LEGAL FRAMEWORK

Definition of charity

Charity is not defined as such, but the common trait of various types of organisations is the lack of lucrative purpose. The non-profit association does not engage in industrial or commercial transactions and does not seek to secure a material gain for its members. The foundation is the dedication of assets to a specified disinterested purpose.

Principal sources of law

Non-profit organisations are governed by the law of 27 June 1921 on non-profit associations, international non-profit associations and foundations (as modified by the laws of 2 May 2002, 27 December 2004 and 23 March 2007) (Non-Profit Organisations Law).

LEGAL BODIES

The law recognises four legal forms of non-profit organisation:

- Non-profit association (*association sans but lucrative (ASBL); vereniging zonder winstoogmerk (VZW)*).
- International non-profit association (*association internationale sans but lucrative (AISBL); internationale vereniging zonder winstoogmerk (IVZW)*).
- Private foundation (*fondation privée; private stichting*).
- Foundation of public interest (*fondation d'utilité publique; stichting van openbaar nut*).

The non-profit association is the simplest vehicle.

The law also provides for the possibility to set up a Belgian centre of operations of a foreign non-profit organisation (*see Question 12*).

Non-profit association

A non-profit association is an association that does not conduct industrial or commercial operations, and does not aim to generate any tangible profit for its members (*Article 1, Non-Profit Organisations Law*). The second condition is clear: the proceeds of its activities must not be directly or indirectly distributed to its members; they can only be used for the activities of the association. However, the interpretation of the first condition is subject to discussion. For civil (as opposed to tax) law purposes, it can be considered as a minimal position that a non-profit association can conduct commercial or industrial operations if both:

- They are ancillary.

• The profits they generate are allocated to the realisation of the purpose of the association.

A non-profit association has legal personality.

The founding members and the members who join the association after its creation do not have to bring contributions to the association.

The registered office must be located in Belgium (but additional offices can be opened elsewhere in Belgium and/or abroad).

International non-profit association

An international non-profit association is largely the same as a non-profit association, and the same conditions and basic requirements apply as in relation to non-profit associations (*see above, Non-profit association*) (except that incorporation requires a notarial deed and an approval by Royal Decree, and organisational freedom is broader).

A non-profit association is international if it is meant to further the realisation of a non-lucrative purpose of international relevance, provided that its purpose or activities do not contravene the law or public policy (*Article 46, Non-Profit Organisations Law*). The association itself need not be international in its constitution.

Private foundation

A private foundation is a legal entity created by the allocation by one or several founders of personal or real assets to the implementation of a selfless aim. It must not provide tangible benefits to the founder(s), the directors or other third persons, except when the distribution of funds to third persons is precisely the purpose for which the foundation has been created (*Article 27, Non-Profit Organisations Law*). There is no minimum capital to be contributed on incorporation.

Contrary to the non-profit association (including international), a private foundation can conduct commercial operations without distinction between principal and ancillary activities. The profits generated by the activities of the foundation must be allocated to the implementation of the aim of the foundation, and not distributed to the founder(s) or directors.

The registered office of the private foundation must be located in Belgium (but additional offices can be opened elsewhere in Belgium and/or abroad).

Foundation of public interest

The rules relating to private foundations also apply to foundations of public interest, apart from:

• A foundation of public interest must necessarily be intended to implement a purpose of a philanthropic, philosophical, religious, scientific, artistic, educational or cultural character (*Article 27, Non-Profit Organisations Law*).

• The incorporation under that status or transformation of a private foundation into a foundation of public interest is subject to authorisation by Royal Decree. In addition, some subsequent modifications of the articles of association require approval by Royal Decree. This procedure usually takes two to four months.

As the relevant rules are largely the same as for private foundations, this Q&A will not further specifically consider foundations of public interest.

5. WHAT ARE THE QUALIFICATION REQUIREMENTS/FORMALITIES TO SET UP THESE ORGANISATIONS?

Non-profit association

A non-profit association can be created by all the founding members signing the articles of association. These are then filed (together with all related documents) with the clerk of the Commercial Court, and published in the Annexes to the Belgian State Gazette (*Moniteur belge; Belgisch Staatsblad*). Publication is made automatically within 15 days from filing and makes the existence of the non-profit association enforceable towards third parties.

The articles of association must be drafted in French, Dutch or German (depending on the location of the non-profit association's registered office) and must include at least the following information (*Article 2, Non-Profit Organisations Law*):

- Identification of the members.
- Name and address of the association.
- Minimum number of members (not less than three).
- Description of the association's purposes.
- Conditions and procedures for the admission and exclusion of members.
- Powers, convening formalities and decision-making process of the general meeting, as well as the manner of communicating the resolutions to the members.
- Rules relating to the appointment and dismissal of directors (as well as daily managers and persons entrusted with the representation of the association), and a description of their powers (including representation powers) and duration of their mandate.
- Maximum amount of the members' financial contributions.
- Allocation of the net assets of the non-profit association in the case of dissolution and liquidation.
- Duration of the non-profit association (if not unlimited).

The association obtains legal personality at the time of this filing (*Article 3, Non-Profit Organisations Law*).

Considering these steps, the creation of a non-profit association takes a minimum of 15 to 20 days. Contracts and commitments towards third parties can be taken on behalf of the association in the process of incorporation.

A register of the members must be kept at the registered office of the non-profit association. The board of directors must update the register to reflect the admission of new members, and the dismissal and exclusion of existing members (*Article 10, Non-Profit Organisations Law*).

For each non-profit association, a file is kept at the office of the clerk of the competent Commercial Court. That file includes the main corporate documents (*Article 26novies, Non-Profit Organisations Law*):

- Articles of association.
- Documentation of appointment or termination of directors.
- Documents relating to statutory auditors and proxyholders.
- Any decision to dissolve and liquidate the association.
- Yearly accounts.
- Any modifications of the above.
- Re-stated amended articles, if applicable.

Excerpts of decisions appointing or removing directors, liquidators and auditors, or amending the articles and so on, must be published.

International non-profit association

An international non-profit association must be created by notarial deed (*Article 46, Non-Profit Organisations Law*). The notary must verify that the conditions provided by law are fulfilled and to attest to this fulfilment. The articles must be detailed and must state:

- The name and address of the association.
- The association's purpose and activities.
- The conditions for joining and departing as members (possibly including specific rules for various categories of members).
- The rights and obligations of the members.
- The convening and decision making competence of the "general direction body" (typically the general meeting).
- The competence, convening and decision making of the "management body" (typically the board of directors) and the appointment and termination of directors and proxyholders as well as revocation of their powers.
- The conditions for amending the articles of association, and dissolving and winding up the association (*Article 48, Non-Profit Organisations Law*).

The articles of association (and related documents) must be filed with the clerk of the Commercial Court, in order to be published in the Annexes to the Belgian State Gazette.

The creation of an international non-profit association must be authorised by Royal Decree. That authorisation is required for the recognition of its legal personality. The notary who enacted the deed submits a certified copy of the deed to the Ministry of Justice, together with a request for legal personality (*Article 50, Non-Profit Organisations Law*). The Ministry of Justice verifies that the purposes of the international non-profit association satisfy the test of Article 46 (supra, No.) (this verification is repeated in the case of amendment of the purpose). This process usually takes two to three months. Contracts and commitments can be taken on behalf of the association in the process of incorporation, like renting premises.

For each international non-profit association, a file is kept at the office of the clerk of the competent Commercial Court. That file includes the main corporate documents (*Article 51, Non-Profit Organisations Law*):

- Articles of association (and re-stated amended articles, if applicable).
- Documentation of appointment of directors and proxyholders.
- Any decision to dissolve and liquidate the association.
- Yearly accounts.

Excerpts of decisions to appoint or remove directors, liquidators and auditors, to amend the articles or to dissolve the association must be published.

Private foundation

The creation of a foundation is a unilateral act that must be done by notarised deed (which can be a last will). The notary must verify that all the conditions and requirements provided by law are fulfilled. The articles of association (and all related documents) are filed with the clerk of the Commercial Court, and published in the Annexes to the Belgian State Gazette. The creation of a private foundation takes at least 15 to 20 days.

For each private foundation, a file is kept by the Clerk of the competent Commercial Court. This file contains the main corporate documents (that is, the deed of incorporation and amendments, appointment or termination of directors, statutory auditors and proxyholders, the decision to become a foundation of public interest (*see below*), the decision to dissolve and liquidate the foundation, and yearly accounts) (*Article 31, Non-Profit Organisations Law*). Excerpts of decisions on those matters must be published.

ONGOING REGULATORY REQUIREMENTS

6.   WHAT ARE THE MAIN REGULATORY AUTHORITIES FOR CHARITABLE ORGANISATIONS? WHAT ARE THEIR POWERS OF INVESTIGATION/AUDIT/SANCTIONS?

Regulatory authorities

There is no general regulatory authority.

For certain activities, like education or childcare, or co-operation with developing countries, an administrative agreement is required to evidence satisfaction of certain conditions and can be withdrawn.

Operations can be scrutinised by the King's prosecutor.

Powers

On application of a member, an interested person or the King's prosecutor, the court can dissolve a non-profit association that:

- Is insolvent.
- Uses its assets or income for a purpose other than specified in its articles.
- Seriously breaches its articles, the law or public policy.
- Fails for three years to file its accounts and does not do so before the end of the arguments in front of the court.
- Does not have three members (*Article 18, Non-Profit Organisations Law*).

Similar rules apply to international associations. On application of a member, an interested person or the King's prosecutor, the court can dissolve an association that:

- Is insolvent.
- Uses its assets or income for a purpose other than specified in its articles.
- Is not managed.
- Seriously breaches its articles, the law or public policy (*Article 55, Non-Profit Organisations Law*).

Again, similar rules apply to foundations. On application of a founder, a founder's successor, a director or the King's prosecutor, the court can dissolve a foundation that:

- Has realised its purpose.
- Is no longer able to further its purpose.
- Uses its assets or income for a purpose other than specified in its articles.
- Seriously breaches its articles, the law or public policy.

- Fails for three years to file its accounts and does not do so before the end of the arguments in front of the court.
- Has run its duration (*Article 39, Non-Profit Organisations Law*).

7.   WHICH BODIES OR PERSONS MANAGE CHARITABLE ORGANISATIONS AND WHAT GENERAL REQUIREMENTS MUST THEY MEET?

Non-profit association

There are two main bodies in a non-profit association.

General meeting. This consists of the members (including the founding members). There must be at least three founding members, irrespective of their nationality. A legal entity can also be a (founding) member.

Some powers are expressly reserved to the general meeting (*Article 4, Non-Profit Organisations Law*):

- Amendments to the articles of association.
- Appointment and dismissal of the directors and, if applicable, the statutory auditor.
- Release from liability to be granted annually to the directors and to the statutory auditor.
- Approval of the annual accounts and the budget.
- Dissolution/winding-up of the association.
- Exclusion of a member.
- Transformation of the association into a social purpose company (that is, a company engaging in non-ancillary industrial or commercial activities, such as a construction company employing handicapped workers, without seeking to distribute profits to its shareholders).

The articles of association may add to that list of reserved powers.

The register of members is kept at the head office. Each member has one vote. Decisions are usually taken by a majority of the votes (although the articles of association may provide differently).

Members joining or exiting does not have any financial consequences for the assets of the association, as the members do not bring in any contribution on incorporation or later. The members only pay annual dues, if any.

Dissolution of a non-profit association is usually decided by the general meeting, but can also be decided by the court.

On dissolution, the proceeds or the assets of the association must not be shared between the members, but must be allocated to a similar selfless aim (*Article 2, 9°, Non-profit Organisations Law*).

Board of directors. Management of the association is vested with the board of directors, appointed by the general meeting. The board of directors is a collegiate body that includes at least three directors (two if there are only three members), irrespective of their nationality. It exercises all the powers not expressly reserved to the general meeting by law or by the articles of association. A legal entity can also be appointed as a director of the association.

The board of directors represents the association. The representation of the association and the day-to-day management can be granted to particular persons (or a person), who need not be directors, and who can act alone, jointly or as a college (*Article 13bis, Non-Profit Organisations Law*). The appointment and dismissal of those persons must be filed with the clerk of the Commercial Court and published in the Annexes to the Belgian State Gazette.

International non-profit association

The administration and corporate structure of an international non-profit association are more flexible than in a regular non-profit association, to facilitate the implementation of alternative governance schemes. Articles 49 and 53 of the Non-Profit Organisations Law refer to a "general body of direction" and a "management body" for the corporate governance of an international non-profit association. However, very few competences are expressly attributed to either body. These bodies usually take the form of a general meeting (general body of direction) and a board of directors (management body), but this dual corporate structure is not mandatory. The members can decide on the corporate organisation of the international non-profit association on incorporation or by amending the articles.

The Non-Profit Organisations Law does not impose any requirement related to the nationality of the members of the association or the members of the administration body.

The rules relating to dissolution of non-profit associations also apply to international non-profit associations.

Private foundation

A private foundation has no members. A board of directors manages and represents the foundation (*Article 34, Non-Profit Organisations Law*). The directors appoint new directors. The articles of association can create a protector or protection board for certain purposes (for example, appointing or screening future directors to ensure that their actions remain within the stated purpose and policy).

The board of directors is a collegiate body with at least three members. There is no nationality requirement. Legal entities can be appointed as directors (but must designate an individual as permanent representative to perform the management duties on their behalf). Decisions to appoint or dismiss directors must be filed with the clerk of the Commercial Court and published in the Annexes to the Belgian State Gazette (*Article 35, Non-Profit Organisations Law*).

The board of directors can grant particular persons (who must not be directors) day-to-day management responsibility to particular persons, to act jointly or alone. Decisions to appoint or dismiss these persons must be filed with the clerk of the Commercial Court and published in the Annexes to the Belgian State Gazette.

The management of a private foundation cannot resolve to dissolve the foundation. This can only be decided by the Civil Court (*Article 39, Non-profit Organisations Law*). In principle, the assets of the foundation must be allocated to the furtherance of a similar selfless aim. However, it is possible for the deed of incorporation to provide that the founders or their entitled beneficiaries are entitled to get back the assets put in upon incorporation of the foundation, if the selfless aim has been achieved (*Article 28, 6°, Non-profit Organisations Law*).

8. WHAT ARE THE ACCOUNTING/FINANCIAL REPORTING REQUIREMENTS?

Non-profit association

Each year, the board of directors must prepare the annual accounts for the previous financial year and the budget for the next year, and submit these documents for the general meeting's approval.

The form and content of these accounts, and the publication formalities, depend on the size of the non-profit association (*Article 17, Non-Profit Organisations Law*):

- **Small associations.** These must file their annual accounts with the clerk of the competent commercial court. A small non-profit association is an association that does not exceed more than one of the following thresholds (subject to consumer price index (CPI) adaptation):
  - average number of employees over the year: five;
  - annual receipts: EUR250,000 (excluding VAT);
  - balance sheet total: EUR1 million (excluding VAT).

- **Large and very large associations.** These must file their annual accounts with the National Bank of Belgium. When certain thresholds are met (employment headcount, balance sheet and turnover), the annual accounts must be controlled by a statutory auditor.

  A large non-profit association is an association that reaches at least two of the following thresholds (subject to CPI adaptation):
  - average number of employees over the year: five;
  - annual receipts: EUR250,000 (excluding VAT);
  - balance sheet total: EUR1 million (excluding VAT).

  A very large non-profit association is an association that has more than 100 employees or exceeds at least two of the following thresholds (subject to CPI adaptation):
  - average number of employees over the year: 50;
  - receipts on an annual basis: EUR6,250,000 (excluding VAT);
  - balance sheet total: EUR 3,125,000 (excluding VAT).

International non-profit association

The same rules apply as for a non-profit association, but the relevant provision of the Non-Profit Organisations Law is Article 53 (*see above, Non-profit association*).

Private foundation

The same rules apply as for a non-profit association, but the relevant provision of the Non-Profit Organisations Law is Article 37 (*see above, Non-profit association*).

TAX

9. HOW ARE CHARITIES TAXED, AND WHAT (IF ANY) ARE THE PRINCIPAL EXEMPTIONS AND/OR RELIEFS FROM TAXATION THAT THEY ENJOY?

Tax on income

Non-profit organisations are usually exempt from corporate tax and only subject to the "tax on legal entities" (*see below*). To qualify for this exemption, they must not carry out profit making operations or transactions (*Article 220, Code of Income Taxes*). The following are not considered as profit making transactions:

- Isolated or exceptional transactions.

- Portfolio investments.
- Transactions in an activity that entails industrial, commercial or agricultural transactions only on an ancillary basis, or does not implement industrial or commercial methods (*Article 182, Code of Income Taxes*).

Further, certain non-profit associations and "other non-profit legal persons" are not liable to corporate income tax, even if they carry out operations that could be characterised as profit-making operations (*Article 181, Code of Income Taxes*):

- Associations only or mainly aimed at studying, protecting and furthering professional or inter-professional interests of their members.
- Associations that, in addition to the above, fulfil in the name and for the account of their members all or part of the members' obligations with regard to social security, tax or labour law, or assist their members in complying with these obligations.
- Associations that are responsible for the collection, centralisation, capitalisation and division of funds used for the granting of benefits under social security laws.
- Associations only or mainly involved in providing or supporting education.
- Associations only or mainly involved in organising commodity exchanges or exhibitions.
- Associations that by the competent institutions of the regions are recognised as services to assist families or elderly people.
- Associations recognised under Article 145/33 of the Code of income taxes as acting for the general interest, or entities which on request would be recognised as such if they applied or which meet all the conditions for recognition (except the condition on the development of nation-wide or region-wide or community-wide activities).
- Associations whose sole purpose is the certification in compliance with Article 13 of the law of 15 July 1998 of securities issued by commercial companies.

Non-profit organisations subject to the tax on legal entities are subject to limited tax liability. Taxable income is limited to (but see also below, *Tax on capital gains and Tax on property used by the organisation*):

- Domestic or foreign income from portfolio investments (*Article 221, 2°, Belgian Code of Income Taxes*):
  - dividends at a rate of 27% (*Article 269, Code of Income Taxes*). Certain reduced rates apply depending on the issuer of the shares;
  - interest and royalties at a rate of 27%. However, under certain conditions, the first EUR1,250 per year of income derived from a savings account is exempt (*Articles 221, 2°, and 21, 5°, Belgian Code of Income Taxes*);
  - income from the rental or licensing of movable assets at a rate of 15%;
  - annuity income (other than pension income) vested after 1 January 1962 due from legal entities or enterprises at a rate of 27%;
  - income derived from the cession or concession of copyright and related rights at a rate of 27%.
- Commissions, rebates and fees that are not reported on individual and summing up statements are taxed as secret commissions at a flat rate of 100% (103% including the surcharge of 3%) (*Articles 223, 1°, and 225, 4°, Code of Income Taxes*).
- Certain types of compensation benefits that would be disallowed for a corporation are subject to tax at the corporate income tax rate.

Therefore, the tax on legal entities applies only to clearly determined income, which is only subject to a withholding tax or a specific contribution (but in most cases without deduction of any charges). If the non-profit organisation is subject to corporate income tax, its profits from commercial activities are taxable at the corporate tax rate of 33.99%. Business expenses are deductible.

Tax on capital gains

Certain short to medium term capital gains realised on land and buildings located in Belgium are taxed at a rate of 16.995% or 33.99%.

Capital gains tax is also charged on a substantial holding (more than 25%) in a resident corporation sold to a company or an association that does not have its registered seat or principal place of business in a member state of the European Economic Area (*Articles 222, 5° and 90, 9°, Code of Income Taxes*). In the case of successive transfers during the 12 month period preceding a taxable transfer, each transfer is taxable if the required 25% holding existed at the time of the first assignment (*Article 94, Code of Income Taxes*). Those capital gains are taxed separately at a rate of 16.995%.

Tax on property used by the organisation

Tax on legal entities also applies to:

* Income from real estate owned by the non-profit organisation (*Article 221, 1° and Article 222, 1° to 3°, Code of Income Taxes*). Determination of the taxable income depends on the use made of the property and the location of the property:
  - in respect of immovable property located in Belgium and not rented out, the tax is the immovable prepayment tax. It is assessed on the indexed cadastral income, a fixed notional rental income. The rate varies depending on the region and the municipality: 1.25% in the Walloon or Brussels Region, and 2.5% in the Flemish Region. Added to municipal surcharges, the total rate is about 25% to 30% (*Article 464, 1°, Code of Income Taxes*);
  - in respect of rented-out immovable property located in Belgium, the part of the net total of the rent (reduced by 40% for buildings or 10% for land) that exceeds the indexed cadastral income is taxed at 20.6%. This is unless the immovable property is rented to a natural person not using the immovable property (or part of it) for the execution of their professional activity, or the immovable property is rented out and used by the tenant for agricultural and horticultural purposes;
  - when immovable property located in Belgium is rented out to an association and that association has rented it out to one or more natural persons to be used exclusively for residential purposes, the indexed cadastral income increased by 40% is taxed at a rate of 20.6%;
  - in respect of immovable property located abroad, the basis of assessment is determined on the basis of the rental value if the property is not rented, or the actual rent and rental charges received if the property is rented. However, the gross amount of the rental value or actual rent and rental charges received is reduced by 40% (for buildings) or 10% (for land) to cover maintenance and repair expenses. This amount is taxed at a rate of 20.6%.

  Various exemptions apply. For example, the cadastral income is tax exempt if the real property is used for a charitable or non-profit purpose, such as a church, school or hospital (*Article 12, Belgian Code of Income Taxes*).
* Income derived from the sublease or the transfer of a lease of real property located in Belgium or abroad, whether furnished or not, or from the rental of billboards, at a rate of 27% (*Articles 221, 2° and 90, 5°, Code of Income Taxes*).

Value added tax (VAT)

General. A non-profit organisation is not considered to be a Belgian VAT taxpayer unless it carries out economic activities in Belgium (*Article 4, VAT Code*). If a non-profit organisation supplies goods or renders services for a price within the meaning of the VAT laws, it is ordinarily liable to VAT. Therefore, it is important to verify how an organisation obtains its income. For example, a non-profit organisation that only receives contributions from its members (for example, donations and subsidies) is not liable to VAT.

Rates. The applicable VAT tariff is determined by the nature of the delivery or service. The standard VAT rate is 21% (*Article 37, VAT Code* and *Article 1, Royal Decree No. 20 of 20 July 1970*). It applies to all supplies of goods and services, and imports and intra- EU acquisitions of goods, unless the VAT Code explicitly provides otherwise.

A reduced rate of 12% applies, for example, to restaurant and catering services (excluding drinks) (*Table B, Royal Decree No. 20 of 20 July 1970 (entered into force on 1 January 2010)*).

A reduced rate of 6% applies, *inter alia*, to the following, among other things (*Table A, Royal Decree Nr. 20 of 20 July 1970*):

- Construction and transfer of dwellings in the framework of public housing, and cars for disabled persons and related equipment.
- Renovation, improvement or maintenance of buildings that are at least 15 years old.

Rights and obligations of a taxable person for VAT purposes. The standard VAT rights and obligations apply to a non-profit organisation that is liable to VAT. For example:

- The right to deduct any VAT charged by the vendors on the organisation's purchases (*Article 45, Code of Income Taxes*). The normal conditions for deduction are that the input tax must have been incurred in the current tax period (or earlier) and the taxable person must hold a valid tax invoice to support the claim. In addition, the right to deduct input VAT must be exercised within three years of the period in which the right has arisen.
- The obligations concerning the:
  - issue of invoices (*Articles 53, § 2 and 53octies, Code of Income Taxes*). The invoice must be issued, at the latest, on the fifth working day of the month following that during which the VAT became due on the price or on a part of the price (*Article 4, § 1, Royal Decree No. 1 of 29 December 1992*);
  - making of returns at the start, during and on termination of the activity that is subject to VAT (*Article 53, § 1, 1° and 2°, Code of Income Taxes*);
  - payment of the VAT due (*Article 53, § 1, 3°, Code of Income Taxes*).

Exemptions. A non-profit organisation is exempt in Belgium if it does not carry out economic activities in Belgium. It does not have to charge any Belgian VAT to its members and it is not entitled to deduct the VAT charges by the Belgian vendors on its purchases, or ask the Belgian vendors not to charge VAT on its purchases.

Certain activities carried on by non-profit organisations are exempt (*Article 44, VAT Code*):

- Services provided by physical education or sport facilities to people who practise physical culture or sport activities.
- Providing food and drink when it is performed in combination with some other particular activity, such as a charity party.
- Services of medical practitioners and other listed healthcare professionals.

European Court of Justice case law has established that these exemptions are interpreted strictly.

Other

Tax in lieu of inheritance tax. Non-profit organisations are subject in Belgium to a wealth tax called a duty in lieu of inheritance tax. It is calculated on the value of all the assets of the organisation, without deduction for debts, and charged at the rate of 0.17% (*Articles 147 to 160, Belgian Inheritance Tax Code*).

Organisations whose assets do not exceed EUR25,000 are exempt from this duty.

Registration duty on gifts. There is no gift tax in the strict sense, but a gift must usually be made by a notarised deed, which must be registered. If a gift is made to a non-profit organisation by way of a notarised deed, it is subject to a registration duty amounting to 7% of the gift's amount, depending on the region. Gifts given by hand, including notably bank transfers of cash, are not liable to registration duty. However, it is necessary to document the date of the gift, to prove that it was made more than three years before the death of the donor, to avoid it being included in the donor's estate and liable to inheritance tax.

10. WHAT, IF ANY, ARE THE TAXATION BENEFITS FOR DONORS TO CHARITIES?

Income tax deductibility of donors

Donations in cash to approved institutions (*see below*) entitle donors to tax benefits, for personal or corporate income tax purposes, provided they amount to at least EUR40 and can be substantiated by receipts from the beneficiaries (*Article 107, Code of Income Taxes*).

Tax treatment of donors

Individual donors are entitled to a tax reduction of 45% of the amount of their donations up to a maximum of 10% of their global taxable income, with an absolute maximum of EUR376,350 (*Article 145/33, Code of Income Taxes*).

Corporate donors can deduct the amount of their donations up to a maximum limit of 5% of their gross revenue, with an absolute maximum of EUR500,000 (*Article 200, Code of Income Taxes*).

(With the exception of gifts given by hand, gifts received by a non-profit organisation and individually exceeding EUR100,000 must be approved by the government by means of a Royal Decree (*Article 16, Non-Profit Organisations Law*).)

Approved institutions

Article 145/33 of the Income Tax Code lists the institutions that can be taken into consideration for possible approval and that can issue receipts to their donors for the tax deductibility of donations. This include institutions that operate in:

- Scientific research.
- Dissemination of culture.
- Assistance to certain groups of people (for example, disabled, elderly or poor people, or victims of war or natural disasters).
- Environmental protection.
- Preservation or protection of monuments and sites.
- Management of licensed animal shelters.

- Assistance to third world countries.
- Assistance to victims of major industrial accidents.

Conditions for approval

To qualify for approval, any institutions must comply with the following conditions (*Articles 58 to 59sexies, Royal Decree implementing the Code of Income Taxes*):

- It must enjoy legal personality under Belgian law. It must not pursue any profit-making purpose, either for itself or for its members.
- It must not dedicate more than 20% of its resources to general administrative expenses.

In addition, specific conditions apply, depending on the field the institution operates in.

Approval is given for six years maximum, but often for three years.

Formalities for obtaining approval

Applications for approval, and the related file (*see below*), must be filed exclusively with the Ministry of Finance no later than 31 December of the year preceding the period for which the licence or renewal is sought.

The file must allow the administration to verify that the applicant meets the requirements.

It is preferable to provide the following documents:

- A copy of the articles of association and deeds concerning the appointment or termination of directors, managing directors, persons authorised to represent the institution, and a copy of any amendments to these documents (as filed with the Court of Commerce).
- A calendar of activities and the activities report of the year, a detailed statement of pending projects and all other documents in connection with the operation of the institution (for example, publications and programmes).
- A copy of :
  - the profit and loss account of the last financial year ended;
  - the budget of the current financial year.

Applications are made by way of a simple letter. They can be sent by regular or registered mail.

DISADVANTAGES

11.   WHAT ARE THE MAIN DISADVANTAGES OF CHARITABLE STATUS?

The main disadvantages are the possibility of court ordered dissolution and the constraints linked to maintaining the recognition procuring tax benefits for donors.

Some (notably trade unions) view the obligation to publish accounts as a disadvantage and elect not to incorporate and enjoy legal personality.

OVERSEAS CHARITIES

Definition and purpose

A foreign non-profit association can open and establish a centre of operations in Belgium (*Article 26octies, § 1, Non-profit Organisations Law*). This also applies to foreign foundations (*Article 45, Non-profit Organisations Law*).

A Belgian centre of operations is an extension of the entity validly incorporated and existing in a foreign country, without separate legal personality. The foreign entity remains governed by the laws of its country of origin. However, some publication formalities are necessary to entitle it to conduct operations in Belgium.

Establishment and incorporation

The foreign entity must have been created according to the legal provisions of its home jurisdiction. The corporate body empowered to resolve on the setting up of a Belgian centre of operations must make a resolution to that effect. The resolution must include the address of the centre of operations and the designation of the persons empowered to represent the foreign association within the scope of its Belgian operations.

The resolution and the articles of association or bye-laws must be legalised and translated into French, Dutch or German (depending on the location of the registered office of the foreign non-profit association), by a sworn translator, before being filed with the clerk of the competent Commercial Court (so it can be published in the Annexes to the Belgian State Gazette).

The length of the process depends on how difficult it is to obtain and translate legalised documents.

Annual accounts

Foreign non-profit associations or foundations having one or more centres of operation in Belgium are subject to certain obligations with regard to the preparation, filing and publication of annual accounts. The relevant annual accounts are those of all the Belgian centres of operation of the foreign entity, not just the accounts of the foreign head office or of any other foreign branches (*Article 26octies, § 3, Non-profit Organisations Law*).

The exact scope of the accounting and filing obligations vary depending on whether the centre of operations is regarded as large, very large or small. When certain thresholds are met (that is, employment headcount, balance sheet and turnover amount) the annual accounts must be controlled by a Statutory Auditor.

Tax treatment on donations to foreign non-profit associations

Institutions or non-profit organisations located in any of the EEA countries are eligible to procure tax benefits in connection with donations from Belgian donors, provided that these institutions are similar to Belgian eligible ones and are recognised in their jurisdiction in an analogous manner.

13.   IS IT POSSIBLE TO REGISTER A DOMESTIC CHARITY ABROAD, AND HAS YOUR JURISDICTION ENTERED INTO ANY INTERNATIONAL AGREEMENTS OR TREATIES IN THIS AREA?

The possibility of registering a Belgian charity abroad depends on applicable foreign law. Belgium has not entered into specific treaties on the subject. EU/EEA law and other general treaties may be relevant.

REFORM

14.   ARE THERE ANY PROPOSALS FOR REFORM IN THE AREA OF CHARITY LAW?

There are no current government sponsored proposals for reform.

ONLINE RESOURCES

W www.ejustice.just.fgov.be/loi/loi2.htm

Description. Official website, publishing laws and decrees in French and Dutch.

BRAZIL

Flavia Regina de Souza Oliveira and Michelle Baldi Ballon Sanches,
MATTOS FILHO, VEIGA FILHO, MARREY JR. E QUIROGA

OVERVIEW AND MAIN TRENDS

1.   WHAT IS THE HISTORICAL BACKGROUND TO CHARITY LAW AND CHARITABLE ORGANISATIONS IN YOUR JURISDICTION?

The non-profit sector in Brazil is governed by a large and complex system of laws.

Brazilian non-profit organisations originate from the acts of philanthropy and religious charity. The Holy Houses of Mercy (*Santas Casas de Misericórdia*) started their social activities in the mid-16th century and some are still active. Throughout the colonial period until the end of the 19th century, new organisations emerged with a common religious origin and welfare practice in underprivileged communities.

In 1916, such organisations were legally recognised as associations, foundations and civil societies without economic purposes by the Civil Code (*Law No. 3, 071/1916*).

In 1935, the Ministry of Justice granted these entities public utility status (*Law No. 91/1935*), which provided that they "selflessly served the community". However, this did not grant any real advantages or benefits.

In 1959, recognition of these organisations was expanded by creation of the Entity Certificate of Philanthropic Purposes Entity (*Law No. 3, 577/1959*). This allowed exemption from social security employer's contribution for entities with philanthropic purposes, recognised as federal public service, and whose board members did not receive remuneration.

With the 1988 Federal Constitution, which recognised the importance of involving civil society in ensuring basic social rights, the legal evolution of non-profit organisations began to show more significant developments.

The Social Organisation and Public Interest Civil Society Organisation was created in the 1990s (*see Question 3*). The Voluntary Law was also enacted, recognising the relationship between non-profit organisations and their volunteers.

Reform of the Civil Code in 2002 (*Law No. 10, 406/2002*) defined associations and foundations as legal forms in the charity sector, and excluded civil societies without economic purposes from the list of private law legal entities.

In 2009, Law No. 12,101 made many changes to rules for non-profit organisations granted with a Certificate of Beneficent Social Assistance Entity (CEBAS). Known as the new philanthropy law, this special designation qualifies entities for an exemption from the social security employer's contribution.

Recently, the relationship between non-profit organisations and the government has changed. Law No.13.019/2014 promotes more transparency in the use of public resources, better control and evaluation systems, to verify projects carried out in partnership. This law, referred to as the New Regulatory Framework for Civil Society Organisations, has created new legal instruments for partnerships between government and non-profit entities.

2. ARE INDEPENDENT CHARITABLE ORGANISATIONS COMMON AND SIGNIFICANT IN YOUR JURISDICTION? WHAT IS THE CURRENT SIZE AND SCOPE OF THE SECTOR AND THE MAIN TRENDS?

According to the latest data from the Brazilian Institute of Geography and Statistics (IBGE), in 2010 Brazil had 290,700 private foundations and non-profit associations. The methodology follows the guidelines of the Handbook of Non-profit Institutions in the System of National Accounts, prepared by the Statistics Division of the United Nations. It refers to organisations that meet five criteria:

- Organisations.
- Not-for-profit and non-profit distributing.
- Institutionally separate from government.
- Self-governing.
- Non-compulsory (can be set up freely by any group of people).

In Brazil, these criteria correspond to two legal entities in the new Civil Code: associations and foundations.

Using the criteria adopted by IBGE, non-profit entities carrying out activities relating to the development and defence of citizens' rights and interests account for 30% of all organisations in Brazil. These are followed by non-profit organisations relating to:

- Religion (28%).
- Culture and recreation (12.7%).
- Social assistance (10.5%).
- Education and research (6.1%).

According to incorporation date, 40% of non-profit organisations were created between 2001 and 2010 (half of them in 2006). Most organisations were founded between 1981 and 2000 (46.5%), with the highest concentration from 1991 to 2000 (31%).

Regarding the labour market, in 2010 the Brazilian non-profit sector employed 2.1 million formal salaried workers (4.9% of all Brazilian formal workers).

LEGAL FRAMEWORK

3. IS THERE A LEGAL DEFINITION OF A "CHARITY"? WHAT ARE THE PRINCIPAL SOURCES OF LAW AND REGULATIONS RELATING TO CHARITABLE ORGANISATIONS AND ACTIVITIES?

Definition of charity

There is no single definition of charity in Brazil as such. There is a parallel between UK charities and Brazilian tax exempt non-profit entities, that is, social assistance, health and education organisations. Under the Civil Code, charitable foundations must be incorporated exclusively for the development of certain public activities (*see Question 5*).

An entity is often recognised as charitable due to a designation granted by public authorities. Currently, the main designations are:

- Public interest civil society organisation (OSCIP).
- Certificate of Beneficent Social Assistance Entity (CEBAS).
- Social organisation (OS).

The OSCIP designation is granted by the Ministry of Justice to non-profit legal entities that pursue public interest purposes, which cannot be exclusively for the benefit of or directed to a specific group of people.

To be designated as an OSCIP, the non-profit entity cannot have public employees in its management bodies, must have an audit committee, and must abide by certain restrictive rules regarding transparency, accountability and conflict of interest (*Law No. 9,790/1999*). Further, the entity must develop activities in at least one of the following areas:

- Promotion of social welfare.
- Promotion of culture, protection and preservation of historical and artistic heritage.
- Free promotion of education.
- Free promotion of health.
- Promotion of food security and nutrition.
- Protection, preservation and conservation of the environment and promotion of sustainable development.
- Promotion of volunteering.
- Promotion of economic and social development and poverty reduction.
- Experimentation, in a non-profit manner, of new social productive sectors and alternative systems of production, sale, employment and credit.
- Promotion of established rights and construction of new rights and access to free legal services.
- Promotion of ethics, peace, human rights, democracy and other universal values.
- Promotion or performance of studies and research, as well as the development of alternative technologies, production and dissemination of information and technical and scientific knowledge relating to these activities.
- Studies and research for the development, delivery and implementation of technologies related to the mobility of persons, by any means of transport.

OSCIP designation can only be granted to non-profit legal entities incorporated at least three years before the application (*Federal Law No.13,019/2014, amending Law No. 9,790/1999*).

CEBAS designation is granted exclusively to non-profit entities that develop activities related to social assistance, health and education. It is granted respectively by the Ministry of Social and Agrarian Development, the Ministry of Health or the Ministry of Education, depending on the main activities of the entity.

The main requirements to obtain CEBAS designation are, broadly:

- To be incorporated as a non-profit legal entity in Brazil for at least 12 months, and provide evidence of activities developed relating to social assistance, health and/or education during the fiscal year before the application.
- Provide evidence that its resources, income, profits and operational results are invested exclusively in Brazil, for development of activities related to social assistance, health and/or education.

- To maintain its accounting records in accordance with the legal requirements.
- Not to pay dividends or distribute any part of its assets.
- To be registered with the state or local social assistance council and perform its activities at no cost for its beneficiaries, if the entity has social assistance activities.
- To provide a certain amount of scholarships, if the entity has education activities.
- To provide a certain amount of hospital beds or develop strategic health projects, if the entity has health activities.

OS designation can be granted by public authorities, at their discretion, to non-profit entities able to operate public facilities related to health, culture, technology research, education and others. A designated non-profit entity establishes a contract called a management agreement (*contrato de gestão*) with the public authority.

Principal sources of law

These are:

- Federal Constitution: regulates the right of association and tax regimes.
- Civil Code: regulates the incorporation, legal requirements and functioning of associations and foundations.
- Tax Code: regulates the requirements for income tax immunity.
- Law No. 9,532/1997: regulates the requirements for income tax exemption.
- Law No. 9,790/1999: regulates the requirements and procedures for the designation as a Public Interest Civil Society Organisation (OSCIP).
- Law No. 12,101/2009: regulates the requirements and procedures for the Certificate of Beneficent Social Assistance Entity (CEBAS).
- Law No. 9,637/1998: regulates the requirements and procedures for designation as social organisation (OS).
- Law No. 13,019/2014: regulates partnerships between non-profit entities and public authorities.

LEGAL BODIES

4.   WHAT ARE THE FORMS OF ORGANISATIONS THAT ARE USED FOR CHARITABLE PURPOSES? WHAT ARE THEIR ADVANTAGES/DISADVANTAGES?

Under the Civil Code, non-profit organisations can be incorporated in Brazil as an association or a foundation. Associations and foundations are corporate entities with procedures and requirements set out in the Civil Code.

Unlike other corporate entities (such as limited companies or corporations), associations and foundations:

- Cannot pay dividends to their members.
- Can obtain federal, state and local government designations allowing, for example, access to further tax benefits, contracts with public authorities to manage public assets, or to grant benefits to their donors.

Both corporate types have advantages and disadvantages, depending on the intent of the founding members. A foundation is generally used to create a legacy, subject to more control to ensure perpetuity. An association is usually a more dynamic entity, with no regulation by public authorities.

Association

An association is a non-profit legal entity formed by a group of people with a common purpose. An association must have at least two members to be incorporated.

Associations are not subject to the oversight of public authorities, nor to prior approval of strategic decisions.

The incorporation of an association is less time consuming and sometimes more cost effective than the incorporation of a foundation.

The purpose of an association can be freely amended at any time, whereas the social purposes of a foundation cannot be radically amended.

Foundation

A foundation is a collection of assets with legal personality that must achieve an aim serving a public interest.

Even though trusts are not recognised under Brazilian law, foundations are similar to UK charitable trusts, to the extent they must have a charitable purpose and develop activities for public benefit. Foundations are managed by a special body called the curators' counsel. It is subject to the oversight and prior approval of its strategic decisions by the state public prosecutor, in the jurisdiction in which it operates.

In contrast to an association, a foundation requires the existence and allocation of assets for its incorporation. Further, the assets conveyed for incorporation of a foundation cannot be reclaimed by the grantor.

The social purposes of a foundation cannot be radically amended. This can restrict its activities, but can also ensure more stability regarding the grantor's legacy.

Since foundations are subject to the oversight of the state public prosecutor, their management is more bureaucratic.

5. WHAT ARE THE QUALIFICATION REQUIREMENTS/FORMALITIES TO SET UP THESE ORGANISATIONS?

The social purposes of a non-profit entity dictate the applicable tax regime and access to tax exemptions. For example, entities that develop activities related to education, health or social assistance can benefit from tax immunity (*see Question 9*). These entities can apply for the Certificate of Beneficent Social Assistance Entity (CEBAS) (*see Question 3*).

Associations

The social purposes of associations, as a rule, are not subject to legal restrictions.

To incorporate an association, the first step is to draw up its bye-laws. The bye-laws are the internal rules of the association, with contractual clauses establishing the purpose, rights and duties of the association and its members.

The Civil Code establishes that association bye-laws must set out:

- The name and institutional purpose of the association.
- Requirements to admit, dismiss, and exclude members.
- Members' rights and duties.
- Sources of income of the association.
- Constitution and functioning of the management body.
- Conditions for amendment of the bye-laws and winding up of the association.

To incorporate an association, its bye-laws must be filed with the Civil Registry and it must be registered with the Corporate Taxpayers' Registry of the Ministry of Finance. The association is then a legal entity with legal capacity.

Foundations

The Civil Code establishes that foundations must be incorporated exclusively for the development of activities related to:

- Social assistance.
- Culture, defence and preservation of historical and artistic heritage.
- Education.
- Health.
- Food and nutrition security.
- Defence, preservation and conservation of the environment and promoting sustainable development.
- Scientific research, development of alternative technologies, modernisation of management systems, production and dissemination of information and technical and scientific knowledge.
- Promotion of ethics, citizenship, democracy and human rights.
- Religious activities.

Foundations are created through either:

- A testamentary instrument, which is a unilateral disposition of last wishes.
- A public writ, which is a public declaration of will.

A public writ or testament that intends to incorporate a foundation must include:

- Information about the grantor(s).
- The grantor's intentions to create the foundation.
- The aim of the foundation.
- The grantor's disposition of his/her unencumbered personal property or real estate.

A foundation only acquires legal status after its bye-laws are filed with the Civil Registry.

Representatives designated by the grantor in his/her testament or public writ must prepare the foundation's bye-laws. In certain cases, the bye-laws are set out in the testament or public writ.

To file the bye-laws, it is first necessary to obtain the approval of the public prosecutor's office, which ensures that the legal rules relating to the organisation of the foundation are respected.

ONGOING REGULATORY REQUIREMENTS

6.   WHAT ARE THE MAIN REGULATORY AUTHORITIES FOR CHARITABLE
ORGANISATIONS? WHAT ARE THEIR POWERS OF INVESTIGATION/AUDIT/SANCTIONS?

Regulatory authorities

The main regulatory authorities are:

- Ministry of Justice: responsible for granting the title Organisation of Civil Society of Public Interest (OSCIP) and Foreign Organisation (*Organização Estrangeira, OE*).
- Ministry of Health Issues: responsible for granting the Certificate of Beneficent Social Assistance Entity (CEBAS) to organisations developing health activities.
- Ministry of Education: responsible for granting the Certificate of Beneficent Social Assistance Entity (CEBAS) to organisations developing education activities.
- Ministry of Social Development: responsible for granting the Certificate of Beneficent Social Assistance Entity (CEBAS) to organisations developing social assistance activities.
- Courts of accounts (Federal and State): audits the accounts of administrators and persons responsible for public funds, assets, and other monies. The courts are also responsible for the accounts of any person or organisation that causes loss, misapplication or other irregularities resulting in damage to public funds. There are also municipal courts of accounts in the states of São Paulo and Rio de Janeiro.
- Office of the Attorney General (State Prosecutor): responsible for monitoring and supervising foundations to meet the purposes intended by the grantor, and to achieve their full potential.
- Secretariat of the Federal Revenue of Brazil: responsible for the administration of federal taxes. It controls and audits entities to verify compliance with tax immunity and exemptions.
- Federal Supreme Court: this is the highest body of the judiciary. It is responsible for upholding the Federal Constitution, and establishes precedents for the constitutionality of non-profit legislation.

Powers

See above, *Regulatory authorities*.

7.   WHICH BODIES OR PERSONS MANAGE CHARITABLE ORGANISATIONS AND WHAT
GENERAL REQUIREMENTS MUST THEY MEET?

Associations

Under the Civil Code, an association is a non-profit legal entity formed by at least two individuals or legal entities, either Brazilian or foreign, pursuing a common purpose. Foreign members are represented by powers of attorneys, with specific authority to act for the association.

The minimum governance and management required by law for associations are:

- The general meeting (the deliberation body, composed of its members).
- At least one executive officer (or a board of officers), who is the legal representative of the association with executive administrative functions. The executive officer must be a Brazilian citizen or a foreign person with a permanent visa for Brazil.

The mandatory and non-transferable powers of the general meeting are (*section 59, Civil Code*):

- Dismissal of the administrators (for example, members of the board of officers).
- Amendments to the bye-laws.

The bye-laws can expand the powers of the general meeting.

Associations can also create a non-mandatory board, such as a board of directors and audit committees.

Foundations

In contrast to associations, foundations are formed by assets, so there is no requirement for a minimum number of individuals to form a foundation. Foundations are created by testamentary instrument or public writ (*see Question 5*).

The governance body of a foundation is the curators' council, composed of individuals not subject to a judgment in criminal or civil proceedings. The curators' council must follow the directions set out in the foundation's charter documents, as stated by the grantor.

The minimum governance requirements for a foundation are:

- The curators' council.
- At least one executive officer (or a board of officers), who is the legal representative of the foundation with executive administrative functions. The executive officer must be a Brazilian citizen or a foreign person with a permanent Brazilian visa.

Foundations can also create a non-mandatory board, such as a board of directors and audit committees.

8.   WHAT ARE THE ACCOUNTING/FINANCIAL REPORTING REQUIREMENTS?

Non-profit organisations (associations and foundations) must prepare annual accounts and comply with filing deadlines to avoid cancellation of their designations.

They must follow Brazilian Accounting Standards (ITG 2002), which impose criteria and procedures for:

- Evaluation.
- Recognition of transactions and changes in equity.
- Structuring of financial statements.
- Minimum information to be disclosed in the accounts.

In particular, the following is required:

- Activities report.
- Financial statements.
- Legal entities income tax report (ECF).
- Social security annual report relating to employees (E-Social).
- Audit committee report (depending on the administrative structure of the non-profit entity).
- Opinion and independent audit report (might be required by the government or donors).

TAX

Non-profit organisations, incorporated as associations or foundations under Brazilian law, that pursue public interest purposes, can be entitled to tax and other legal benefits according to their social purposes, on meeting certain conditions.

Tax immunity

The Federal Constitution sets out limitations on the government's powers to tax, also known as tax immunity. Under section 150(VI)(c) of the Federal Constitution the union, states, federal district and municipalities cannot tax educational, health, and social assistance non-profit private organisations. Tax immunity covers the organisation's assets, income and services relating to essential activities (social purposes) of the legal entity.

To receive tax immunity, the entity must meet the following requirements (*section 14, Tax Code*):

- No distribution of its assets and profits among its members.
- Maintenance of accounting books and registers, to ensure transparency of its activities and accounts.
- Use of its resources is limited to Brazil and the maintenance and development of its social purposes.

If tax immunity is not possible, the legal entity can be granted specific exemptions.

Tax exemptions

In contrast to tax immunity, which is set out in the Federal Constitution, tax exemptions are set out in federal, state or municipal law.

Exemptions are available under specific laws for each tax. For example, under section 12 and 15 of Law No. 9.532/1997, philanthropic, recreational, cultural or scientific non-profit organisations and/or civil associations are exempted from income tax and social contribution on net profits, if they comply with the following:

- If its officers receive compensation for their services, the amount must be limited to up to 70% of the highest compensation paid to an executive officer (except for non-profit entities performing at least one activity listed in Article 3 of Law No. 9,790/1999, that are not involved in political party or electoral interest campaigns, in which case the executive officer can receive market practice compensation).
- Apply all of their resources to the maintenance and development of their social purposes.
- Maintain full accounting registers, in compliance with formal/legal requirements.
- Maintain over five years' of documents that support the accounting registers.
- File annual income tax returns, in compliance with tax authority requirements.

To verify if a non-profit entity can obtain a tax exemption, it is necessary to analyse the relevant law and verify whether the organisation meets all its requirements. Depending on the tax, a formal recognition from public authorities may also be required.

Tax on income

See above, *Tax immunity* and *tax exemptions*.

Tax on capital gains

See above, *Tax immunity* and *tax exemptions*. As a general rule, capital gains earned by non-Brazilian residents in transactions involving the disposal of Brazilian assets are subject to tax in Brazil at a rate of 15% or 25%, if the beneficiary is domiciled in a low tax jurisdiction.

Tax on capital gains is not payable by tax immune entities (under an injunction granted in a direct action of unconstitutionality, No. 1802-3).

Tax on property used by the organisation

Generally, tax on urban property (IPTU) is payable on the ownership, control, or possession of urban land or buildings, based on the assessed value of the real estate. The rate varies according to the city and type of real estate involved. Non-profit social assistance, health and education entity properties are immune to this tax, even if the core activity does not take place at the property or it is rented or used for commercial purposes. However, all money received from the leased property must be used for the development of the entity's social assistance, health and educational activities.

Value added tax (VAT)

The equivalent to VAT in Brazil is the state value added tax (ICMS), imposed on:

- Sales of goods.
- Inter-municipal and interstate transport services.
- Communications services.

It is generally calculated on the amount of the transaction, or on the price of goods and services. ICMS rates vary depending on the goods or services, and specific regulations in each state (the average rate is 18%).

ICMS is currently paid by non-profit entities, but the Supreme Court has decided that ICMS levied on products sold by non-profit social assistance entities is not payable, if the economic result obtained is used for the development of the entity's social purposes (*RE No. 540,725*).

National Institute of Social Security Tax (INSS)

The National Institute of Social Security Tax (INSS) is a social security tax paid by both employers and workers, levied on payroll and on remuneration. For employees, directors, and independent workers, it is calculated on gross remuneration, including certain benefits. The tax base is limited to an amount determined by the government. For the employer, INSS tax is levied on total remuneration paid to employees, directors, and independent workers, including indirect benefits.

This tax is not paid by tax immune entities with the CEBAS designation.

Contribution for the Social Integration Program (PIS)

PIS is levied at a different rate for associations and foundations (tax immune or exempted) (1% of the payroll).

This tax is not paid by tax immune entities with the CEBAS designation.

Social security financing (COFINS)

COFINS is not due on inherent revenues of tax immune and exempted entities. The tax authorities hold that inherent revenues are from contributions, donations, fees or annuities, fixed by law, statute or the general meeting, received from members or supporters, that are not a payment of consideration.

This tax is not paid by immune entities with the CEBAS designation.

Tax on donations (ITCMD)

Inheritance and donations are subject to a state tax on donations, at a rate varying from 4% to 8% of the total amount donated. Some states have full or partial tax exemptions for non-profit entities.

10. WHAT, IF ANY, ARE THE TAXATION BENEFITS FOR DONORS TO CHARITIES?

Under Federal Law No. 9,249/95, donations to non-profit organisations by companies meeting certain requirements are deductible from the corporate entity's operational income, up to 2% of the income.

Only donors that calculate income tax through the "real profit system" can make these deductions. Operational income is the basis for calculating their income tax and social contribution obligations. This deductibility generally provides the donor with a 34% return on the amount donated, meaning that for each BRL100 donated, the donor has a reduction of about R$34 from its income tax and social contribution obligations.

Law No.13,204/2015 has extended this benefit to all non-profit entities, regardless of their designation, provided that they both:

• Perform at least one of the activities listed in Article 3 of Law No. 9,790/1999.

• Are not involved in political party or electoral interest campaigns, under any means or form.

Companies donating to educational or research institutions can also tax deduct up to 1.5% of their operational income, calculated before any deduction.

At federal level, there are also tax benefits for cultural, sports, and health projects, and projects targeted at children, adolescents, and the elderly.

The most well-known tax incentive for businesses in Brazil relates to cultural projects. Under the Rouanet Statute (*Federal Law No. 8.313/91*), legal entities can deduct sums contributed through donations or sponsorship to cultural projects approved by the Ministry of Culture. A legal entity can deduct part of the amount it donates from its income tax payable (30% for sponsorship, and 40% for donations), up to 4% of the income tax payable.

In specific sectors such as the visual arts and preservation of cultural heritage, amounts donated to cultural projects can be tax deducted, up to 4% of income tax due from the taxpayer. However, donations in these sectors cannot be deducted from taxable income.

States and municipalities can also establish their own tax incentives, which typically benefit cultural and sports projects. For example, both the State and Municipality of São Paulo have incentives for companies that donate to cultural projects.

DISADVANTAGES

11.   WHAT ARE THE MAIN DISADVANTAGES OF CHARITABLE STATUS?

An entity is often recognised as charitable through a designation by the public authorities (*see Question 3*). The main disadvantages of this are the bureaucracy involved in renewing the designations, and having to provide accounts to public authorities.

OVERSEAS CHARITIES

12.   IS IT POSSIBLE TO OPERATE AN OVERSEAS CHARITY IN YOUR JURISDICTION? WHAT ARE THE REGISTRATION FORMALITIES? HOW (IF AT ALL) ARE OVERSEAS CHARITIES TREATED DIFFERENTLY IN YOUR JURISDICTION FROM CHARITIES SET UP UNDER DOMESTIC LAW?

The Law of Introduction to Brazilian Law Rules (Decree Law 4.657/42, as amended) allows foreign legal entities to carry out their activities in Brazil. The legal personality of these entities is recognised, provided they have been duly incorporated according to their own country's legislation.

Therefore, foreign associations, civil societies and foundations incorporated in accordance with the laws of their own countries can have legal status and capacity to operate in Brazil, on granting of authorisation by the Brazilian government.

An authorisation request must be sent to the Co-ordination of Social Entities of the Ministry of Justice, and addressed to the President of the Federative Republic of Brazil with the following documents:

- Complete copy of the bye-laws.
- Evidence that the non-profit entity was duly incorporated (certificate of incorporation).
- Copy of the minute of the general meeting that authorised the operation of the non-profit entity as a foreign organisation in Brazil.
- Power of attorney, granting powers for the grantee to accept the conditions under which the authorisation will be granted, as well as receiving judicial notices.
- Copy of the minutes of the general meeting, by which the current members of the board of directors and governing councils were appointed.
- List of the members of the board of directors and governing councils, specifying their job titles and contact information.
- Statement of whether there are foreign persons working in the organisation in Brazil. If yes, documentation evidencing their Brazilian visas is required.
- Detailed report specifying in which areas it will operate in Brazil. It must state if it intends to operate in the Amazon area (states of Acre, Amapá, Amazonas, Pará, Rondônia, Roraima, Mato Grosso, Tocantins, and Maranhão).
- A qualitative specification of the social purposes and activities.
- Balance sheet for the previous fiscal year.

Once the Ministry of Justice has approved the application, it is forwarded for the approval of the President, with a later decree granting authorisation to operate.

After this decree is enacted in the Official Gazette of the Federal Executive, it must be registered with the Civil Registry of Legal Entities. On registration, the entity can request its corporate taxpayers' registration with the Ministry of Finance (CNPJ/MF), as a foreign non-profit association authorised to operate in Brazil.

To operate, a foreign organisation must evidence that it is duly incorporated and that the individual (officer or representative) acting on its behalf has powers to do so in its bye-laws. Even when translated into Portuguese, the bye-laws are usually in a format unfamiliar to the Brazilian authorities and third parties. Since foreign organisations are not as common as local associations, they can face challenges in evidencing their legal existence and functioning, such as when opening and closing bank accounts, executing agreements, and leasing real estate.

13. IS IT POSSIBLE TO REGISTER A DOMESTIC CHARITY ABROAD, AND HAS YOUR JURISDICTION ENTERED INTO ANY INTERNATIONAL AGREEMENTS OR TREATIES IN THIS AREA?

There is no Brazilian legal prohibition on Brazilian non-profit entities registering a branch or operating abroad. In addition, there are no applicable international agreements or treaties which Brazil has entered into.

A tax immune entity (*see Question 9*) is legally obliged to apply its resources, income, profits and operational results exclusively in Brazil, for its social purposes.

REFORM

14. ARE THERE ANY PROPOSALS FOR REFORM IN THE AREA OF CHARITY LAW?

The economic sustainability of civil society organisations is a challenge that requires legal reform. Donations must be encouraged and tax barriers reduced and simplified.

The main tax related to donations is the state tax on donations (ITCMD) (*see Question 9*). Even though some states provide exemptions for non-profit entities, the procedures are very bureaucratic.

There is an ongoing debate about non-profit organisations being financed with their own resources, through the creation of an endowment fund.

In 2015 a bill that includes non-profit organisations to simplify taxes and reduce tax rates was discussed at the national congress. This should be implemented, once it has the potential to contribute to their sustainability and decrease bureaucracy regarding the payment of taxes.

The abolition of the public utility designation, by Federal Law No. 13,204/2015, may lead to possible reform. This designation previously allowed non-profit organisations to grant benefits to donors, and was a requirement for establishing partnerships with some government authorities.

ONLINE RESOURCES

LEGISLATION PORTAL, BRAZILIAN FEDERAL GOVERNMENT

W www4.planalto.gov.br/legislacao

Description. Official website that contains acts of all Brazilian federal legislation, since 1889. Available in Portuguese only.

CIVIL SOCIETY ORGANISATIONS MAP

W https://mapaosc.ipea.gov.br

Description. Official website of the Brazilian Institute of Applied Economic Research. It offers a geo-referenced data platform for organisations operating in Brazil, with a large volume of continuously updated information. Available in Portuguese only.

CANADA

Robert B Hayhoe and Sarah G Fitzpatrick, MILLER THOMSON LLP

OVERVIEW AND MAIN TRENDS

1. WHAT IS THE HISTORICAL BACKGROUND TO CHARITY LAW AND CHARITABLE ORGANISATIONS IN YOUR JURISDICTION?

Canadian Charity law is shaped by federal tax regulation which contains the most extensive regime of supervision and regulation for charitable organisations in Canada. Before 1967 there were limited tax legislation and administrative practices governing charitable organisations, and what existed was predominantly focused on tax collection. The goal during this period was to protect the public treasury against abuse and fraud, or to subsidise the sector with tax expenditures.

The first attempt at regulating charitable organisations on a federal level was made under the War Charities Act 1917. Its purpose was to control fraudulent appeals and to encourage the efficient operation of legitimate war charities. The Act established a registration system for war charities that entailed complying with onerous requirements on banking and organisation. If organisations were not registered or did not have a ministerial exemption from registration, they were not allowed to solicit the public for donations. The federal government took a step back in regulating and supervising charities when the Act was repealed in 1927.

At the start of the 20th century, the government generally viewed tax deductions for charitable donations as a wasteful tax expenditure. Under the Income War Tax Act 1917, the Minister of Finance allowed an exemption and deduction without limit for amounts donated by taxpayers to ministry-approved patriotic and war funds. The intention was to reduce government support of charitable objects and to encourage volunteers to enlist in the war effort. In 1920, this legislation was repealed.

The Great Depression of the 1930s prompted the government to bring in the first general tax deduction for donations. The deduction was available to corporate and individual taxpayers. During this period, minor changes were made to create consistency among the three parts of the Income War Tax Act.

In 1948, the Income War Tax Act was replaced by the Income Tax Act (ITA) to become the main federal taxation statute. Similar to the old Act, the ITA had provisions governing deductibility of gifts, tax exemptions for certain organisations and exemptions from gift tax. The ITA brought further consistency to the governance of charitable organisations by referring to organisations operating "exclusively for charitable purposes".

The first income tax act exempted the income of religious, charitable, agricultural and educational institutions. The tax exemption for "charitable organisation" and "foundation" later included charitable trusts, corporations and all organisations that were charitable under a common law definition. There was no requirement in 1917 that charitable institutions file an annual tax return to prove their eligibility for this exemption. However, "war charities" were required to file financial returns under the War Charities Act 1917. In 1922, legislation implemented this filing requirement for all tax-exempt institutions.

In 1950, charities were divided into "charitable organisations", "charitable trusts" and "charitable corporations". Each classification had its own thresholds to meet in order to qualify for tax-exempt status. A more stringent regime was enacted for trusts and corporations as a reaction to certain abuses. It contained general prohibitions against carrying on a business and against financing programmes with debt, and a rudimentary disbursement regime, all of which still apply to charitable organisations.

Since major tax reform in 1967, the dominant legislation governing charities has been the ITA. The tax reform marked a watershed in Canadian legal regulation of charitable organisations by requiring charities to register in a central registry and report annually on their finances and operations. Charitable donations were deductible only if they were to entities registered as Canadian charities. The government's intention was to regulate this sector as a response to abuses of the receipting system and to replace the other legislative regimes governing charities in Canada.

Legislation in 1976 established the framework on which the current law is based. Charitable organisations and charitable foundations were distinguished and charitable foundations were further divided into public and private.

In the 1980s, opinion swung back to the perception that tax deductions for charitable donations were an unjustifiable tax expenditure. The Canada Revenue Agency (CRA), the federal agency that regulates tax laws, became more aggressive in deciding what would be deemed charitable and prohibited activity. In response to heated debates on the role of charities, amendments were made to the ITA in 1986 that set out what was acceptable political activity for charities to be involved in.

Throughout the 1970s and 1980s, the Department of Finance continued to be pre-occupied with the potential abuses of the disbursement system. As a result, legislation in 1984 established a disbursement regime for public foundations and penalty taxes for charities whose registration was revoked.

In the 1990s there were several technical changes that encouraged charitable donations. The 1996 federal budget introduced a series of major tax breaks for charitable donations by increasing tax recognition for donors. The trend of increasing tax incentives continued, but the government began to address perceived charity abuses, such as loan-back schemes. There were also several provisions designed to make transactions between the CRA and registered charities more transparent.

The 2004 federal budget implemented the most significant changes since 1980. They included intermediate sanctions, a new tax appeal process and new disbursement quota spending requirements.

2. ARE INDEPENDENT CHARITABLE ORGANISATIONS COMMON AND SIGNIFICANT IN YOUR JURISDICTION? WHAT IS THE CURRENT SIZE AND SCOPE OF THE SECTOR AND THE MAIN TRENDS?

There are more than 86,000 registered charities in Canada according to the Charities Directorate, the department of the Canada Revenue Agency that oversees registered charities. There is no general registry of tax exempt non-charitable non-profit organisations.

In 2014, the total value of donations reported by Canadian taxpayers to registered charities was Can$8.8 billion. This money was donated by over 5.5 million donors.

Registered charities are engaged in all activities permitted by the traditional common law definition of charitable purposes, which include:

- Cultural activities and the promotion of arts.
- Religious congregations or parishes.
- Missionary organisations and propagation of gospel.
- Teaching institutions or institutions of learning.
- Support of schools and education.
- Libraries, museums and other repositories.
- Preservation of sites, both of beauty and historical.
- Animal welfare.
- Recreation, playgrounds and vacation camps.
- Health organisations.
- Organisations providing care other than treatment.

Non-profit organisations range from very high-profile groups such as national political parties to small and informal groups of people linked by a common interest or cause. There are also sporting organisations, such as golf and curling clubs, professional groups, trade groups, social clubs and fraternal organisations.

LEGAL FRAMEWORK

3.   IS THERE A LEGAL DEFINITION OF A "CHARITY"? WHAT ARE THE PRINCIPAL SOURCES OF LAW AND REGULATIONS RELATING TO CHARITABLE ORGANISATIONS AND ACTIVITIES?

Definition of charity

Charities are governed by the Income Tax Act (ITA) and the common law. The ITA grants tax exemptions to a number of third-sector organisations, such as registered charities and non-profit organisations. The ITA defines a registered charity as a "charitable organisation, private foundation or public foundation...that has applied to the Minister in prescribed form for registration and that is at the time registered" (*subsection 248(1), ITA*).

An organisation is only eligible to register under subsection 248(1) if it has exclusively charitable purposes. "Charitable purpose", however, is not defined in the ITA, so courts rely on the common law definition of charity, as amended by the ITA. These amendments relate to an organisation's involvement in political activities and unrelated business activities.

A charitable activity has two essential attributes:

- Subject matter.
- Public benefit.

Subject matter refers to diverse charitable purposes that can be grouped into four categories recognised by English common law:

- The relief of poverty.
- The advancement of religion.

- The advancement of education.
- Other purposes of a charitable nature beneficial to the community.

"Public benefit" is any activity falling within the four categories that is concerned with the benefit of the public, or a large section of the public, and is not harmful.

The fourth category, "other purposes of a charitable nature", is very diverse and there are two requirements that must be met to fall under it:

- The organisation must have a public or community benefit.
- The organisation must have a purpose that is recognised by the law as charitable.

The courts have recognised several types of charitable purposes, including:

- The relief of distress and suffering.
- The support and care of ex-service personnel.
- The advancement of social and recreational purposes.
- The advancement of animal welfare.
- The benefit of the community at large.

The test of public benefit varies between the four categories of charity. Generally, the beneficiaries of a charitable organisation must form a sizeable portion of the community or be the community at large. Satisfying the public benefit requirement under the category of relief of poverty is usually not problematic, since poverty trusts affect sizeable classes, such as the old and widowed women.

Public benefit is still generally presumed in Canadian law in the context of the advancement of education and the advancement of religion.

However, under the heads of education and "other purposes beneficial to the community", there will be no finding of public benefit where the beneficiaries are associated by common employment. For example, a non-contributory pension set up by an employer for its employees is a fringe benefit and does not qualify as a public benefit. Public benefit under the head of religion is determined by a test of whether the religious activities are open to, or otherwise demonstrably for the benefit of, the public or a sufficient section of the public.

Principal sources of law

Canada is a federal state with a federal parliament and ten provinces. Although the provinces have the power to regulate charities as a matter of property law, they have largely abdicated this power as a matter of pro-active regulation and have in essence allowed the federal government to regulate charities through the ITA. The ITA deals with the:

- Deductibility of charitable donations.
- Tax-exempt status of charitable organisations and non-profit organisations.
- Regime of tax supervision and regulation.

Other non-profit organisations

Non-profit organisations are defined as "a club, society or association that, in the opinion of the Minister, was not a charity.., and that was organised and operated exclusively for social welfare, civic improvement, pleasure or recreation, or for any other purpose except profit, or was otherwise available for the personal benefit of any proprietor, member or shareholder thereof unless the proprietor, member or shareholder was a club, society or association the primary purpose and function of which was the promotion of amateur athletics in Canada" (*subsection 149(1)(l), ITA*).

These terms "club, society, or association" are not to be read technically. An organisation in any form can qualify as a non-profit organisation. For example, a corporation, unincorporated association, or a trust can be considered a "club, society or association".

A non-profit organisation must be, in the opinion of the Minister of National Revenue, not a charity. This appears to mean that an organisation cannot be charitable at law (regardless of charitable registration status) in order to be a non-profit organisation. There is no need for an organisation to obtain a prior decision from the Minister of National Revenue as to whether it is a charity.

Although a non-profit organisation can have virtually any purpose, it must be both organised and operated for a purpose other than profit. Being "organised" for a purpose other than profit requires that the corporate objects and/or other statements of purpose of the organisation are drafted so that profit-making is not a proper purpose of the organisation.

The definition of non-profit organisation prohibits paying income to members. "Income" refers to current year income, not contributed capital or capitalised income.

Recently, the Canada Revenue Agency (CRA) has taken a stricter stance than the courts in defining the requirements of non-profit organisations. For example, if any activity, examined in isolation, appears to have been budgeted to earn net income, it will endanger the organisation's tax exemption. While the position of the CRA is unsupported by jurisprudence, the federal government in the 2014 federal budget announced its intention to carry out a consultation project to review whether the non-profit exemption is properly targeted and not subject to abuse.

There are also a number of quasi-charities that can receive gifts and issue official donation receipts under the ITA, but are not registered charities. Quasi-charities fall into the following categories:

- Registered Canadian amateur athletic associations.
- Housing corporations that provide low-cost housing accommodation for the aged that have registered with the CRA.
- Canadian municipalities.
- The United Nations, or its agencies.
- Prescribed universities outside of Canada.
- Foreign charities that have received a gift from Her Majesty in right of Canada (the federal government) in the current or immediately previous taxation year.
- Institutions designated under the Cultural Property Export and Import Act to receive cultural property.

LEGAL BODIES

Corporation

The most common legal form for voluntary sector organisations is the corporation. Most Canadian charities are organised as non-share capital corporations under provincial or federal corporate statutes of general application. Some larger and/or older organisations are created under special acts of the federal parliament or a provincial legislature. On rare occasions, charities and non-profits are created under share capital corporate statutes of general application.

Advantages. A corporation has a separate legal entity from its members. The model provides limited liability to its members and, to a lesser extent, its directors.

Disadvantages. A corporation is subject to statutory corporate governance requirements and must file annual returns with its regulatory body to maintain its incorporated status.

Charitable trusts

Charitable trusts are recognised in Canada. However, as a result of legal concerns about trustee liability, charitable trusts are now used rarely for charities other than grant-making foundations. A trust is created when one or more persons hold legal title to property, but another person or group of persons has the right to enjoyment of or to benefit from that property.

Charitable trusts receive certain benefits that other types of trusts do not, such as exemption from the rules against perpetuities (provided that any gifts vest in the charity within the appropriate time period) and against inalienability.

Advantages. Unlike corporations, charitable trusts are not required to file annual returns with any provincial or federal agencies that regulate trusts.

Disadvantages. A trust may not be the most useful structure if the intention is to own or lease real estate or enter into a number of contractual relationships. Additionally, this may not be the best model if the organisation will likely be exposed to tort or regulatory liability from its activities.

Unincorporated associations

The unincorporated organisation was once the dominant form of legal entity for charitable and non-profit organisations in Canada. In particular, virtually all individual congregations of non-episcopal religious traditions were once organised as unincorporated associations. As a result of liability concerns, more and more unincorporated religious organisations have transformed themselves into non-share capital organisations. Despite these changes, there remains a significant number of smaller unincorporated non-profit organisations that are organised (usually by groups of individual members of a local community without the assistance of legal advisers) as unincorporated associations.

Advantages. Unincorporated organisations are relatively easy to organise and their governance is infinitely flexible.

Disadvantages. An unincorporated organisation is not a separate legal entity from its members. Members and directors or other decision makers could be held liable for the actions of the unincorporated organisation. If the organisation plans to hold real property, it is necessary to operate as a corporation or trust.

5. WHAT ARE THE QUALIFICATION REQUIREMENTS/FORMALITIES TO SET UP THESE ORGANISATIONS?

Corporation

A corporation is established when a non-share capital corporation is incorporated. Incorporation under the Canada Not-for-Profit Corporations Act is appropriate where the organisation will operate nationally or in more than one province, or if the objects and activities fall within federal constitutional jurisdiction. If the objects and activities fall within provincial jurisdiction, it can be incorporated under the provincial statute of the province in which it will primarily operate.

Incorporation generally involves filing an application for incorporation or for letters patent. The application sets out the objects of the corporation (whether or not charitable) and the recipient of the assets on the dissolution of the corporation. After incorporation, the corporation will typically pass bye-laws to provide governance rules.

Charitable trust

A charitable trust is most often created through a declaration of trust. Although it is possible in theory to have an oral declaration of trust, most charitable trusts are created either through an *inter vivos* trust indenture or by a will. The Canada Revenue Agency (CRA) does not in practice accept an oral declaration of trust when registering a charitable trust as a charity.

All trusts must have three certainties to be created:

- Intention to create a trust.
- Subject matter (the trust property).
- Objects of the trust.

Courts have modified the certainty of objects to accommodate charitable activities. Rather than identifying beneficiaries by name or class, a charitable trust can have a charitable purpose as its object. However, the charitable purpose must be specific and certain, and enable the trustees to determine how the charitable activities must be carried out.

Unincorporated associations

It is relatively easy to establish an unincorporated association. The mere coming together of like-minded people to carry on activities will suffice. More sophisticated unincorporated associations record this agreement in a memorandum of association or similar document. Religious congregations that are unincorporated associations often rely on religious rules of general application to form the bulk of their contractual provisions. Many smaller unincorporated associations have no written memorandum of association and, instead, rely on an informal understanding between members. To register as a charity, the CRA will need documentation to prove the existence of an unincorporated association.

ONGOING REGULATORY REQUIREMENTS

Regulatory authorities

Due to the practical abdication of provincial responsibility for charities, the *de facto* regulator of charities and the voluntary sector in Canada is the Canada Revenue Agency (CRA). The CRA is the federal tax regulatory agency and regulates charities under the Income Tax Act (ITA).

Registered charities

An organisation must be a registered charity to enjoy privileges under the ITA, such as exemption from income tax. Entities with exclusively charitable purposes do not need to register with the CRA, but unregistered charities will not be exempt from income tax. Due to this advantage, most Canadian charities register with the CRA.

The following is the process to register a charity:

- An Application to Register a Charity under the Income Tax Act (Form T2050) must be completed.
- The completed application, including all supplementary materials such as the nature of charitable activities, expected financial data, and governing documents are sent to the CRA Charities Directorate. The goal of the form is to show the aims, goals and purposes of the potential charity to the examiner.
- Often an examiner will contact the applicant's authorised representative for additional information on the application.
- If the application is approved, the CRA will send the applicant a "notification of registration", which will include information about the rights and obligations of a registered charity.
- If the organisation is denied charitable registration, the charity can appeal the decision by filing a notice of objection within 90 days after the day on which the Minister of National Revenue's decision was mailed. An organisation can file a notice of objection with the Minister by sending a written response with the reasons for the objection and all relevant facts to the Assistant Commissioner Appeals Branch.
- If the appeal to the Assistant Commissioner Appeals Branch is denied, the organisation can ask for judicial review of the objection by the Federal Court of Appeal.

The CRA has limited resources to check on charities' compliance. Often the only opportunity the CRA has to scrutinise the activities of a charity is at the time of registration. Consequently, the registration procedure is lengthy and rigorous. The CRA is very particular about the wording used by the charity in the registration application and seeks to ensure that the activities the charity is proposing to carry out are neither too broad nor vague.

Over the years, registration has become increasingly difficult and many more applications are rejected or returned to be amended. A major reason for rejection is that the CRA has taken a narrower position on definitional questions, such as whether the organisation has "exclusively charitable" objectives.

Other non-profit organisations

There is no registration system for non-profit organisations. So, unlike a registered charity, a non-profit entity cannot face the threat of losing its registration. Non-profit organisations are exempt from income tax simply by meeting the legal definition of a non-profit organisation under subsection 149(1)(l) of the ITA.

While gifts made to quasi-charities are creditable or deductible for tax purposes, these organisations are not registered charities and are not subject to the regulatory rules that apply to registered charities (except the rules on issuing receipts under Regulation 3500). The only quasi-charity that is subject to the full tax regulatory controls under the ITA provisions on charities is the registered Canadian amateur athletic association (RCAAA). RCAAAs must file an annual return and keep books and records in Canada.

Powers

CRA auditors have extensive powers when auditing registered charities. Through audits, the CRA will determine whether a charity is compliant both financially and in its activities. The auditors will examine whether a charity properly:

- Issues donation receipts.
- Spends its resources.
- Conducts activities in furtherance of its charitable purposes.

The ITA provides the CRA with a series of information-gathering tools. The CRA has authority to inspect any records that the ITA requires a charity to keep. Under subsection 230(2)(a) of the ITA, registered charities must keep sufficient records to enable the Minister of National Revenue to determine whether there are any grounds to revoke its registration. CRA policy states that, subject to solicitor-client privilege, it has power to access any documents which may be relevant, including third party documents. Section 231.2 of the ITA gives the CRA power to issue a "requirement", which is an order for information or documents to be provided to the CRA. If a registered charity does not comply with a requirement, its registration can be revoked. The CRA can also obtain court-issued search warrants if it suspects that an offence under the ITA has been committed (*section 231.3, ITA*).

Until 2004, the only compliance tool the CRA had was to revoke registrations. The CRA now has several compliance tools at its disposal that offer a sliding scale of punishment. Minor infractions can result in specific and/or general education for charities about the ITA requirements. For serious cases of non-compliance, the CRA can enter into a compliance agreement with the charity, impose financial penalties or suspend a charity's right to issue income tax donation receipts for a year. Sanctions will become more serious if offences are repeated within a five-year period.

Revocation of registration is reserved for repeat offences or serious violations such as fraud or other deliberate misbehaviour. The CRA's guidelines provide that sanctions are intended to encourage compliance. Increasingly, however, CRA auditors are taking more aggressive approaches that do not follow the guidelines. In some situations, the CRA has proposed to revoke registration where the error was an inadvertent first time offence.

Other non-profit organisations

The CRA has the power to audit non-profit organisations. If the CRA determines that an organisation no longer qualifies as a non-profit organisation, it can advise the organisation of its determination, or issue a tax assessment. There has been a dramatic increase in non-profit organisation audit activity in recent years.

7.   WHICH BODIES OR PERSONS MANAGE CHARITABLE ORGANISATIONS AND WHAT GENERAL REQUIREMENTS MUST THEY MEET?

Charitable and non-profit corporations are managed by boards of directors. The qualification and governance requirements for the boards depend on the statute under which the corporation is incorporated.

Charitable trusts are managed by trustees. Trustees must meet duties prescribed by common law and legislation in the provincial jurisdiction of the trust.

The 2011 federal budget gave the Canada Revenue Agency the power to refuse or revoke registration where the charity has a director or manager who:

• Has been convicted of a financial crime or other crime relevant to the charity's mission.

• Has been convicted of a similar regulatory offence in the last five years.

• Was a director or manager of another charity revoked for cause.

• Was a promoter of a tax shelter for which another charity had registration revoked.

These conditions are onerous and may discourage people from serving on more than one charity board at a time.

8.   WHAT ARE THE ACCOUNTING/FINANCIAL REPORTING REQUIREMENTS?

Registered charities

A registered charity must file a T3010 information return with the Canada Revenue Agency (CRA) within six months of its year end, along with its most recent financial statement. Failure to file can result in de-registration of the charity and penalty taxes.

At a minimum, the financial statement must include:

• A statement of assets and liabilities.

• A statement of revenue and expenditures.

• Any prepared notes.

There is no requirement under the Income Tax Act (ITA) for audited financial statements. However, if the charity is an incorporated entity, the statute under which it is incorporated may require audited financial statements.

Non-profit organisations

If the non-profit organisation is a Canadian resident or carries on a business in Canada as a corporation, it is required by the ITA to file an ordinary income tax return that indicates it is a non-profit organisation. In addition, subsection 149(12) of the ITA requires non-profit organisations to file a T1044 information return if they have annual property income (interest, rental income, or royalties) in excess of Can$10,000 or assets in excess of Can$200,000. There is no requirement to file financial statements.

The only quasi-charities required to file annual information returns with the CRA are registered Canadian amateur athletic associations.

TAX

Tax categories

The Income Tax Act (ITA) provides an exemption from paying income tax for a number of participants in the voluntary sector, including:

• Provincial governments and quasi-governmental organisations such as municipal authorities.
• Various specific types of voluntary sector organisations such as agricultural organisations.
• Non-profit scientific research corporations.
• Homes for the aged.

In addition to these specific voluntary organisations listed above, there are two major categories of voluntary organisations that are the most common:

• Non-profit organisations.
• Registered charities.

Non-profit organisations

Non-profit organisations are exempt from income tax, including tax on capital gains. If an organisation ceases to meet the definition of non-profit organisation under subsection 149(1)(l) of the ITA at any time, it will cease to qualify for the exemption. The definition of non-profit organisation constitutes virtually the entire income tax legislative system for such organisations. As a result, there have been a number of issues that have required interpretation by Canadian courts.

In Canada, the goods and services tax (GST) is a federal value added tax that applies to most supplies of goods, services, real property and intangible property. The provinces have their own provincial sales tax (PST). In some cases, this has been harmonised with the GST to form the harmonised sales tax (HST). GST/HST applies to most property and services that are supplied by non-profit organisations. However, there are exemptions available to non-profit organisations for certain supplies under specific conditions. Whether there are exemptions available to non-profit organisations from PST will depend on the provincial tax statutes.

Registered charities

The ITA provides an income tax exemption for a registered charity, including tax on capital gains. Charities can also be unregistered, but if they are they will not receive the special income tax exemption. For registered charities, most property and services they supply are exempt from GST/HST. However, if no exemption applies, the registered charity must register for GST/HST and collect and remit it on the registered charity's taxable property and services.

There are three types of designations for charities, depending on their board governance and mode of operation:

• Charitable organisation.
• Public foundation.
• Private foundation.

Charitable organisation

To qualify as a charitable organisation under subsection 149.1(1) of the ITA, the organisation must both:

- Devote all its resources to its own charitable activities and ensure that no part of its income is available for the benefit of a proprietor, member, shareholder, trustee, or settlor of the charity.
- Be governed at arm's length.

An activity is considered charitable based on its purpose. The relevant test will examine:

- Whether the activity is voluntary.
- Intent to benefit the public in an objectively measurable way.
- Identification of a sufficiently large and identifiable social group that the activity is intended to benefit.

A charitable organisation must not allow any part of its income to be given to any proprietor, member, shareholder, trustee, or settlor of the charity. This limitation applies only to income and the requirement is not breached where payment is made for a legitimate expense of the organisation.

Under the common law definition of charity, an organisation with exclusively charitable purposes must not engage in political activity. However, registered charities can carry on limited political activities that are ancillary or incidental to the charity's purposes (*subsection 149.1(6.2), ITA*). This requirement has become problematic, as the boundary between permissible charitable activities and prohibited political purposes is not always clear. The policy rationale supporting this distinction is that a court cannot determine whether a proposed change in the law is necessarily for the benefit of the public.

The common law definition has also been amended by the ITA with respect to business activity. The ITA permits charitable organisations to engage in and devote resources to "related businesses". Business is related if it advances the goals of the charity. "Related business" can also include a business that is unrelated to the charity's purpose if substantially all of the persons employed in it are volunteers.

Charitable foundations (including public foundations and private foundations)

"Charitable foundation" is defined as a corporation or trust that is constituted and operated exclusively for charitable purposes and is not a charitable organisation (*subsection 149.1(1), ITA*). Charitable purpose has a broad meaning and includes the distribution of funds to other registered charities involved in charitable activities. Additionally, none of the income should be available for the benefit of any proprietor, member, shareholder, trustee or settlor of the foundation.

The essential difference between a charitable organisation and a public foundation is that a charitable organisation focuses on carrying on its own charitable activities and a public foundation funds (primarily, but not exclusively) qualified donees such as registered charities. Additionally, a foundation must take the legal form of a corporation or a trust.

The definition of charitable foundation applies to both private and public foundations. An organisation will be considered a private foundation if it is a corporation or a trust constituted and operated exclusively for charitable purposes, but does not meet the arm's length governance requirements for charitable organisations and public foundations. Private foundations can carry on their own charitable activities and/or can fund other qualified donees.

A private foundation is a registered charity that is not a public foundation or charitable organisation because it is either controlled by one person or a non-arm's length group of persons or because it received over 50% of its capital from one person or non-arm's length group of persons who control the foundation after making the gift *(subsection 149.1(1), ITA)*.

10. WHAT, IF ANY, ARE THE TAXATION BENEFITS FOR DONORS TO CHARITIES?

Tax relief

The ITA recognises individuals who donate to qualified donees (registered charities and quasi-charities) through a tax credit. The first Can$200 is credited at the lowest general marginal rate. Before 2016, the excess over $200 was credited at the highest general marginal rate. In 2016, the federal government introduced a new income tax bracket applicable to income in excess of Can$200,000. Now, if the donor has income over Can$200,000, the excess donations over Can$200 will be credited at the new highest general marginal rate, to the extent that the individual has income taxed at that rate. The remainder of the excess donations over Can$200 is credited at the second highest marginal rate. If the individual does not have income above Can$200,000, the excess over Can$200 is credited at the second highest general marginal rate.

The annual limit on the amount an individual can claim is 75% of his or her income for that year. The donation does not need to be claimed in the year it was made. Any donations in excess of the annual limit can be carried forward for a maximum of five years.

With gifts of capital property, special rules in the ITA allow the donor to opt out of the recognition of a capital gain. Where an individual or corporation makes a gift of capital property to a qualified donee (and provided that the fair market value of the property is greater than its adjusted cost base), the donor can elect as proceeds of disposition an amount between the adjusted cost base of the property and its fair market value. This amount is also used for the purpose of calculating the tax credit.

The ITA also provides benefits for gifts of certain types of capital property, exempting such gifts from capital gains and providing a credit for the full fair market value of the gift. The types of gift that qualify for this treatment are:

- Gifts of publicly-traded shares and stock options.
- Gifts of certified ecologically sensitive land to the Crown in right of Canada, a province, a municipality, or a registered charity certified by the Minister of the Environment in conservation and preservation.
- Gifts of certified Canadian cultural property given to an institution or public authority designated under the Cultural Property Export and Import Act.

Where the gift is ecologically sensitive land or certified Canadian cultural property, there is no annual limit on the tax relief that a donor can claim.

Gift planning

The CRA permits some flexibility in claiming tax relief within a household. Where a charitable donation is made by way of cheque from an account held jointly by spouses, either or both can claim the donation, regardless of who actually endorsed the cheque. As a result of the tax credit system, the lower-income earning spouse should make the claim because this may generate a tax refund. The Canada Revenue Agency also permits the transfer of receipts between family members.

From 2016, a charitable donation made in a will is considered made at the time the property is actually transferred to the registered charity by the estate. Estates are now provided with flexible rules as to which taxation year a charitable donation can be applied to if the estate qualifies as a "graduated rate estate" (GRE) under subsection 248(1) of the ITA. A gift made by a GRE can be used by:

- The deceased in his terminal return for his last taxation year (up to 100% of income).
- The deceased for his taxation year preceding the taxation year of death (up to 100% of income).
- The GRE for the year in which the donation is made (up to 75% of income).
- The GRE for its prior tax years (up to 75% of income).
- The GRE for the five subsequent taxation years (up to 75% of income).

Estates that do not qualify as GREs will be able to claim a charitable donation tax credit in the year in which the gift was made or in the five subsequent tax years, up to 75% of income. For an estate to be able to offset the deemed realisation of any capital assets at the death of the deceased, the estate must qualify as a graduated rate estate.

DISADVANTAGES

11.   WHAT ARE THE MAIN DISADVANTAGES OF CHARITABLE STATUS?

The principal disadvantage for charities is the regulation that results from registration and receiving tax advantages, such as the filings with the Canada Revenue Agency (CRA).

Disbursement regimes

Registered charities are required by the ITA to disburse 3.5% of their investments and other assets not used directly in their operations (disbursement quota) (*subsection 149.1(1), ITA*). The disbursement quota was designed to ensure that a significant portion of a registered charity's resources are devoted to charitable programmes and services, rather than fundraising, management or administration. A charity's registration can be revoked if it fails to meet its annual disbursement quota (*subsection 149.1(2)(b), ITA*).

Receipting privileges

Although issuing receipts is generally an advantage to becoming a registered charity, it can be administratively onerous and costly. Charities often try to avoid official donation receipts for small gifts. Failure to properly receipt can result in progressive penalties, such as a 5% penalty on the amount stated on the receipt and eventually de-registration. Charities operate with limited resources and despite genuine efforts to comply with receipting requirements, oversights in preparing receipts do occur.

Anti-avoidance provisions

In response to the proliferation of charitable donations with tax shelter schemes, the CRA, the Department of Finance and the courts have all played a role in trying to close these programmes.

If Canadian-registered charities are found participating in tax shelters, they can have their registration revoked, be subject to penalty taxes or have their receipting privileges suspended.

OVERSEAS CHARITIES

12. IS IT POSSIBLE TO OPERATE AN OVERSEAS CHARITY IN YOUR JURISDICTION? WHAT ARE THE REGISTRATION FORMALITIES? HOW (IF AT ALL) ARE OVERSEAS CHARITIES TREATED DIFFERENTLY IN YOUR JURISDICTION FROM CHARITIES SET UP UNDER DOMESTIC LAW?

Foreign charities that operate directly in Canada cannot register as charities with the Canada Revenue Agency. Registration requires a charity to be resident and established in Canada. If a foreign charity intends to be exempt from income tax in Canada and to provide Canadian donors with donation receipts, they must establish a separate Canadian-registered charity.

Non-profit organisations are not required to be resident and established in Canada in order to qualify under the Income Tax Act. Accordingly, foreign non-profit organisations can be exempt from tax under it.

13. IS IT POSSIBLE TO REGISTER A DOMESTIC CHARITY ABROAD, AND HAS YOUR JURISDICTION ENTERED INTO ANY INTERNATIONAL AGREEMENTS OR TREATIES IN THIS AREA?

Canadian charities operating overseas

There are very restrictive rules on Canadian charities funding activities abroad. A registered charity can only use its funds to further its own activities or to make grants to "qualified donees" (other registered charities or qualified charities). In a cross-border situation, there are limited organisations that a registered charity can make grants to, including:

- Canadian-registered charities operating abroad.
- The Crown in right of Canada or a province.
- The United Nations and its agencies.
- Foreign universities customarily attended by Canadians.
- Foreign charities that have received a gift from the Federal Crown in the current or immediately previous tax year.

The Income Tax Act permits a Canadian-registered charity to carry on activities anywhere in the world, provided that it carries on its own charitable activities and does not merely fund the charitable activities of another. However, a Canadian-registered charity cannot carry out foreign activities that violate Canadian public policy.

The Canada Revenue Agency (CRA) also allows Canadian-registered charities to carry on their own activities through a foreign agent or joint venture with a foreign charity. The Canadian-registered charity must maintain "direction and control" over a foreign agent's activities. The CRA now requires that all intermediaries, including foreign charities, be listed on a Canadian-registered charity's annual information return.

While a Canadian-registered charity should insist on retaining ownership and control over all capital assets it funds, the CRA recognises that the empowerment of foreign communities may involve the transfer of ownership of the registered charity's assets. Ownership of real property by foreign entities is prohibited in some parts of the world and the CRA allows the Canadian-registered charity to enter into a title-holding arrangement with a local charity or government body as long as the property will be used for charitable purposes.

Over the years, the CRA has taken a strict stance on arrangements between Canadian-registered charities and foreign entities. Recent decisions by the Federal Court of Appeal have denied revocation of registration appeals brought by charities involved in foreign activities.

International treaties

The Canada-US Tax Treaty exempts US charities from tax on their non-business income from Canada and vice versa for Canadian charities operating in the US. This provision is not duplicated in other Canadian tax treaties.

REFORM

14. ARE THERE ANY PROPOSALS FOR REFORM IN THE AREA OF CHARITY LAW?

The Canadian legislative and regulatory regime for charities and the broader voluntary sector is seen overall as lagging behind the modernisation of the non-profit networks of other developed nations. Some positive developments have occurred, for example, in the 2016 federal budget, the federal government made a commitment to review and modernise the rules on the involvement of charities in political activities. This commitment follows the winding-down of a Canada Revenue Agency political activities audit programme which had revealed that registered charities were substantially compliant with the existing rules on political activities.

In addition, over the last decade, there has been an increase in interest in social enterprises in Canada. While there are a variety of available options under which social enterprises in Canada can be structured, Canada has seen a considerable effort to establish legislation and financing in support of social enterprise and social purpose business.

ONLINE RESOURCES

GOVERNMENT OF CANADA, JUSTICE LAWS WEBSITE

W www.laws-lois.justice.gc.ca

Description. Justice Laws is maintained by the government of Canada and contains up to date legislation and regulations that have been enacted by the federal government. All legislation and regulations are available in both the official English and French versions.

REGULATORY AUTHORITIES

CANADA REVENUE AGENCY

W www.cra-arc.gc.ca

Description. The Canada Revenue Agency (CRA) is the federal agency that administers tax laws for the government of Canada. The Charities Directorate of the Canada Revenue Agency regulates the registration and compliance of registered charities.

GERMANY

Dr Andreas Richter and Dr Anna Katharina Gollan,
P+P PÖLLATH + PARTNERS

OVERVIEW AND MAIN TRENDS

1. WHAT IS THE HISTORICAL BACKGROUND TO CHARITY LAW AND CHARITABLE ORGANISATIONS IN YOUR JURISDICTION?

The first charitable organisations in Germany were established as foundations in the Middle Ages, under the control of the church. During the 13th century, the appearance of foundations independent of the church increased, administered by laymen and supervised by public authorities. They pursued religious and social purposes by providing hospitals and hostels. During the 17th and 18th centuries, the foundations became more secular and focused, for example, on education and science.

Charitable objectives were considered to be an original function of the state, so private foundations were subject to very strict public regulation. Private foundations reached their prime before the First World War. In particular, industrialists supported art and science through donations and foundations. The foundation laws of the federal states have been revised since 2002. Today, they emphasise the will of the founder and the discretion of the board of directors.

In the mid-19th century, people were allowed to form associations without any public authorisation and to pursue charitable, benevolent, social, scientific and artistic purposes. Today, charitable organisations have become major economic forces and are some of the most significant contributors to social life and its improvement. These organisations serve important human needs, ranging from supporting the arts to combating poverty. In 2007 the sector was strengthened by an improved donation law, allowing tax deductions of a considerable part of charitable contributions.

The charitable sector is quite complex, including very different institutions. It is divided into two parts, which has hindered the development of a unified sector identity. Organisations are active in:

- Areas such as culture, recreation and sports, and the environment. They show a remarkable degree of civic participation and rely heavily on membership dues and volunteer input to finance their activities.

- Health and social services, which are an integral part of the German welfare state, where the principle of subsidiarity is strongest. Health and social service organisations are highly professionalised and perceived as less civic, relying primarily on income from social insurance payments and direct state subsidies.

2. ARE INDEPENDENT CHARITABLE ORGANISATIONS COMMON AND SIGNIFICANT IN YOUR JURISDICTION? WHAT IS THE CURRENT SIZE AND SCOPE OF THE SECTOR AND THE MAIN TRENDS?

There are about 21,500 independent foundations, about 20,000 to 40,000 charitable corporations and non-independent foundations, and about 600,000 associations. The charitable sector is therefore a significant economic and social factor in Germany.

With 64.3% as opposed to the international average of 42.7%, public financing bears the biggest portion of the costs, while receipts from donors are at the lower level in Europe. However, the volume of donations increased to EUR5.5 billion in 2015.

LEGAL FRAMEWORK

3. IS THERE A LEGAL DEFINITION OF A "CHARITY"? WHAT ARE THE PRINCIPAL SOURCES OF LAW AND REGULATIONS RELATING TO CHARITABLE ORGANISATIONS AND ACTIVITIES?

Definition of charity

In Germany, charity (*Gemeinnützigkeit*) as a legal term is only relevant in tax law. In particular, there is no separate body of law for charities.

Charity in terms of the Fiscal Code (*Abgabenordnung*, *AO*) means to pursue aims that benefit the public (*gemeinnützige Zwecke*), benevolent aims (*mildtätige Zwecke*), or religious aims (*kirchliche Zwecke*). The list of public benefit purposes includes (*section 52(2)(1 to 25), Fiscal Code*):

- The advancement of science, religion, art and culture.
- Education.
- Protection of the environment.
- Public welfare.
- Support for persons persecuted for political, racial, or religious reasons.
- Internationalism.
- Protection of animals.
- Foreign aid.
- Consumer advice.
- Sport.

Recognition as a tax-privileged organisation does not depend solely on the pursuit of charitable purposes in accordance with the Fiscal Code. Charitable organisations have to pursue such aims selflessly (*selbstlos*), exclusively (*ausschließlich*) and directly (*unmittelbar*). In addition, a charitable organisation is not allowed to accumulate income (*Gebot der zeitnahen Mittelverwendung*).

The rule of altruistic activity (*Gebot der Selbstlosigkeit*) is stipulated in section 55(1) of the Fiscal Code:

- The legislature's definition of altruism is based mainly on a negative description: an organisation acts altruistically if it does not primarily serve the corporation's own economic purposes.

- A charity is subject to a non-distribution constraint: it is a violation of the altruistic nature of a charitable organisation if its employees or third parties are given unreasonably high remuneration. Salaries or payments in the commercial sector are used as a standard in determining a reasonable level of remuneration, so that the permissible level varies depending on the particular case.

- If the corporation is dissolved or liquidated, or where its former purpose ceases to apply, the corporation's assets that exceed the members' paid-up capital shares and the fair market value of their contributions in kind can only be used for tax-privileged purposes (dedication of assets).

Charities gain legal recognition as tax-exempt entities (*see Question 9*) from recognition of the charitable nature of their objectives, as stated in their statutes. Charities can only pursue those objectives (*section 56, Fiscal Code*), unless the law permits certain exceptions (for example, a restricted possibility to maintain the founder and his relatives). If an organisation carries out other activities, it can lose tax benefits.

In addition, a charitable organisation must carry out its activities as stated in its statute directly (*Grundsatz der Unmittelbarkeit*). According to section 57(1) of the Fiscal Code, an organisation pursues its tax-privileged statutory purposes directly if it serves those purposes itself. Depending on the circumstances, the requirement can still be met even if an auxiliary person (*Hilfspersonen*), for example an individual or another charitable or non-charitable organisation, is in charge of pursuing the charity's goals. In this case, all actions undertaken by the auxiliary person are deemed to be the actions of the charity itself. Several exceptions to the principle of directness are in section 58 of the Fiscal Code, especially the possibility to procure funds for other charities.

A charitable organisation must use its funds in a timely manner for the tax-privileged purposes stipulated in its articles (*Grundsatz der zeitnahen Mittelverwendung*) (*section 55(1) (5), Fiscal Code*). This is fulfilled if the funds are disbursed for the tax-privileged purposes in its articles by the end of the second year following receipt of the funds (for example, funds received in 2016 must be spent by the end of 2018). However, the tax law also grants exemptions, especially the possibility of allocating to reserved capital (*section 62, Fiscal Code*).

Principal sources of law

Charities are regulated by the Fiscal Code and special tax rules. Under the heading of tax-privileged purposes (*steuerbegünstigte Zwecke*), the Fiscal Code clarifies the concept of charity (*Gemeinnützigkeit*) in sections 51 to 68.

In contrast, there are no specific rules for the variety of charitable (that is, tax-exempt) legal forms in the law relating to foundations, associations and corporations. While there is no uniform tax law for charities, the recognition that an organisation is pursuing charitable purposes is reflected in individual tax laws, for example:

- Section 5(1)(9) of the Corporate Income Tax Act (*Körperschaftsteuergesetz, KStG*).

- Section 13(1)(16b) of the Inheritance and Gift Tax Act (*Erbschaftsteuer- und Schenkungsteuergesetz, ErbStG*).

LEGAL BODIES

4.   WHAT ARE THE FORMS OF ORGANISATIONS THAT ARE USED FOR CHARITABLE PURPOSES? WHAT ARE THEIR ADVANTAGES/DISADVANTAGES?

According to tax law, all charitable organisations are considered corporate bodies (*Körperschaften*) regardless of the organisations' definition according to civil law and their membership and legal capacity. Partnerships (for example, *Gesellschaften bürgerlichen Rechts*, *Offene Handelsgesellschaften* and *Kommanditgesellschaften*) are excluded from tax-exempt status. Individual persons as receivers of donations are also excluded from the tax advantages.

In the charitable sector, there are three principle organisational forms:

- Registered association (*Verein* or *e.V.*).
- Foundation (*Stiftung*).
- Limited company (*GmbH*).

Charitable purposes can also be achieved by donations as specific purpose funds, which are not legal persons. The funds must be entrusted to another individual or legal person. This trust-like device is often called a non-independent foundation (*unselbstständige Stiftung*).

The choice of legal form is also influenced by subjective preferences. In particular, the foundation is associated by the public with positive aspects such as benevolence, welfare and doing good deeds. Because of the different needs and requirements, for example the influence of the executive director, it is not possible to recommend a specific legal form in every case.

Associations

A registered association is regulated at federal level by sections 21 to 70 of the Civil Code (*Bürgerliches Gesetzbuch, BGB*). It is described as a coalition of several natural or legal subjects organised in a corporative way, to act over a certain period of time to reach a common purpose. Both public benefit and mutual benefit associations are permitted.

The Civil Code distinguishes between a non-profit incorporated association (*Idealverein*) and an economic association (*wirtschaftlicher Verein*) with a business purpose. The latter is not relevant to charitable organisations. The non-profit incorporated association is the main form for civic activities, and there are several hundred thousand in Germany.

The association has at least two institutions: the general meeting and the management board. A supervisory board is optional.

The general meeting is the decision-making body. It can change the purpose and statutes of the association and elect the management board. The management board is the legal representative of the association. Its power of representation in relation to third persons cannot be restricted.

There is no external regulatory body for associations. The main reason for this is that the members in the general meeting make the fundamental decisions and the association is not intended for extensive economic activities. Due to this open self-regulatory structure, the association can be recommended if an organisation expects a many members and a frequent change in membership.

Foundations

There is no legal definition of a foundation in the Civil Code. They are characterised by having no shareholders, a permanent object and a need to have endowment property. Generally, a foundation must preserve its endowment property. However, the possibility of spend-down foundations has been legally clarified. A spend-down foundation can use its endowment property, in addition to its earnings, to further its purpose.

In the past, other legal forms of organisations such as associations, stock companies and limited companies were allowed to bear the name *Stiftung*. Currently, the local association or commercial register determines whether the name *Stiftung* is accepted, whereas there are generally no objections to the name foundation.

The term foundation in tax law, with privileges primarily concerning tax deductibility, only covers a foundation in the sense of sections 80 et seq. of the Civil Code and the non-independent foundation (*unselbstständige Stiftung*). Certain tax-privileges for foundations do not apply to other charities, such as associations or corporations (*see Question 9*).

Companies

The limited company (*Gesellschaft mit beschränkter Haftung, GmbH*) is a legal person and liable for its obligations to third parties. It can be founded for any purpose permitted by law (*section 1, Limited Companies Act*) and can therefore be used for business purposes and charitable purposes.

The main difference between a limited company for a typical business and a charitable company is its purpose and permitted adaptations of the corporate structure to tax law requirements for non-distribution of profits. There are no general legal requirements for charitable companies, but tax privileges are only available if the purpose and company are set up according to tax law (*see Question 9*).

The law on companies and directors' duties is well settled. Due to its flexible structure, the limited company is often used by charitable entities. However, given the need to notarise each assignment of shares, the limited company can be more suitable for an organisation with a stable membership.

Charitable limited companies can use the abbreviation gGmbH instead of GmbH. The "g" means *gemeinnützig* (tax-exempt).

5.   WHAT ARE THE QUALIFICATION REQUIREMENTS/FORMALITIES TO SET UP THESE ORGANISATIONS?

Associations

A non-profit incorporated association, whose main aim and activity cannot involve the conduct of business, becomes a separate legal person on registration with the federal register of associations (*Vereinsregister*). When registered, it puts eV (*eingetragener Verein*) at the end of its name. To register, an association must have at least seven members. A copy of the articles of association signed by at least seven members and a copy of the appointment of the board members must be enclosed with the application for registration.

Associations can also be unincorporated and unregistered, without legal personality (*nichtrechtsfähiger Verein*) (*section 54, Civil Code*). An unincorporated association is mainly used by political parties.

Foundations

A foundation under the Civil Code (*sections 80 to 88, Civil Code*) has legal personality, which it receives on recognition by the competent authority in the state (*Bundesland*) in which the foundation will have its headquarters.

The authority will recognise the foundation if the (*sections 80(2) and 81(1), Civil Code*):

- Declaration of the settlor (*Stiftungsgeschäft*) meets certain legal requirements (that is, certainty of name, domicile, purpose, assets, and organisational structure).
- Purpose can be pursued permanently.
- Purpose does not breach the public interest.

In most cases, it takes two to four weeks until a foundation is recognised. Before recognition, the supervisory authority can be asked if the draft articles meet the legal requirements or if there is a need for clarification.

Although the law does not specify a minimum capital amount, the authorities usually require at least EUR50,000 to EUR100,000.

While the law permits both public benefit and private purpose foundations, private purpose foundations are not tax-exempt.

Federal legislation in the Civil Code is complemented by laws in the 16 states, which deal with issues such as state supervision.

Foundations without legal personality are called *nichtrechtsfähige* or *unselbstständige Stiftungen*. Their establishment is subject to general contract law. The contract between the settlor and the trustee (individual or legal person) can be compared with a common law trust. As they are not registered, their total number is unknown. However, they have become more popular and are often administered by other charities seeking additional funds.

Companies

To establish a limited company, the memorandum and articles of association must be signed and notarised and the first managing directors must be appointed by the signatories. The notary then submits an application for registering the company with the local commercial register.

Further:

- The articles of association must comply with the minimum content requirements of the Limited Companies Act.
- At least 50% of the statutory capital must be paid in before filing the registration.
- The limited company is deemed to exist on registration.
- The limited liability company must have a minimum capital of EUR25,000.
- In a tax-privileged limited company, the tax-authorities must provide an opinion stating that there are no objections to the tax privilege.

ONGOING REGULATORY REQUIREMENTS

Associations, charitable companies, and foundations each require the approval of a public authority to become established (*see Question 5*).

A foundation is subject to ongoing supervision by the state authority that decides on its recognition. The state authority has power to enforce compliance with the rules without requiring a court order. As its main task, state supervision must ensure that the original intention of the founder is protected. A decision of the board of directors cannot contradict the founder's intention, as recorded in the statute. The state authority is only allowed to examine whether the requirements made by the foundation law and the statute are met. It cannot make its own decisions concerning the administration of the foundation.

All tax-exempt charitable organisations are supervised by the regional tax authorities. They monitor compliance with the tax exemption requirements.

Association and foundation

A foundation and an association must have a board of directors. It can consist of one or more persons. Board members can be both individuals and legal persons. Additionally, it is possible to provide for further bodies in the statutes, for example a supervisory board.

Board members of an association or a foundation can only be remunerated if the statutes provide for remuneration exceeding reimbursement of expenses. Statutory board members receiving remuneration of up to EUR720 per year are only liable to the association or the foundation for wilful intent or gross negligence (*sections 31a and 86, Civil Code*).

Companies

The mandatory corporate bodies of a limited company are the shareholder's meeting (*Gesellschafterversammlung*) and management (*Geschäftsführung*). There must be at least one managing director (*Geschäftsführer*). The responsibility for administration and management of the company is delegated to the managing director(s) by the shareholders, subject to company law and the company's articles. Managing directors can only be individuals, including foreign persons.

There is no case law on whether a legal person can be a member of a supervisory board of a limited company. Most commentators think that a legal person cannot be so.

Any individual or legal person, including foreign persons with legal personality, can be a shareholder of the company.

Tax-exempt entities must file a report on their activities, their accounts on the use of funds, and reports on the accumulation of reserves with the tax authorities. Generally, accounts must be filed annually. On approval by the tax authorities and depending on the extent of business activities, charitable associations and foundations can file accounts every third year.

Associations and foundations

A foundation or an association can prepare a cash accounting scheme with an inventory, or a commercial annual financial statement with a balance sheet and profit and loss account. They generally do not have to be published.

Companies

For charitable companies, the requirements for publishing annual accounts vary depending on the size of the company. Small companies only need to publish their annual accounts. The bookkeeping, annual accounts and business report of large and medium-sized companies must be audited by qualified auditors or, in the case of medium-sized companies, by certified accountants:

- Small companies do not exceed two of the following: EUR6 million balance sheet total, EUR12 million turnover in the last 12 months, and 50 employees per year on average.
- Medium-sized companies exceed at least two of the above criteria, but do not exceed two of the following: EUR20 million balance sheet total, EUR40 million turnover in the last 12 months, and 250 employees per year on average.
- Large companies exceed at least two of the following: EUR20 million balance sheet total, EUR40 million turnover in the last 12 months, and 250 employees per year on average.

TAX

9.   HOW ARE CHARITIES TAXED, AND WHAT (IF ANY) ARE THE PRINCIPAL EXEMPTIONS AND/OR RELIEFS FROM TAXATION THAT THEY ENJOY?

There are two significant tax benefits for organisations that pursue a charitable purpose in an altruistic manner:

- No inheritance and gift tax, and basically no corporate income tax.
- Donations and endowments can be deducted from the taxable income of donors.

Tax on income

All "corporations, associations, and endowments" can be exempt from corporate income tax if they are organised and operated exclusively for public benefit, benevolent or religious purposes, in terms of sections 51 to 68 of the Civil Code (*section 5(1)(9), Corporate Income Tax Act*). This tax exemption applies to income in the "ideal" sphere of a charity (for example, membership dues or donations) or income from capital investments (sphere of *Vermögensverwaltung*). In contrast, income from unrelated business activities (*wirtschaftlicher Geschäftsbetrieb*) is basically taxable (currently at 15%) (*section 64, Fiscal Code*).

Income from related business activities (*Zweckbetriebe*) is tax-exempt, and includes the following (*sections 65 to 68, Fiscal Code*):

- Operating homes for the elderly, orphans or young people, people with disabilities, and so on.

- Hospitals.
- Schools, colleges and universities.
- Museums and art institutions.
- Workshops for the disabled.
- Joint service businesses of charities (for example, laundries serving only charitable hospitals).

To facilitate small unrelated business activities, section 64(3) of the Fiscal Code assumes that annual turnover up to EUR35,000 does not produce any taxable income.

In addition to corporate income tax, trade tax (*Gewerbesteuer*) applies at a rate of about 15%. Basically, charities do not pay trade tax. However, this tax exemption does not apply to unrelated business activities.

Tax on capital gains

Capital gains as income are tax exempt, if the criteria are met (*see above, Tax on income*).

Tax on property used by the organisation

The organisation is exempt from property tax (*Grundsteuer*), provided that the property is used for tax-exempt purposes.

Value added tax (VAT)

Generally, sales of goods and services are subject to VAT (*Umsatzsteuer*). However, many charitable activities are exempt from VAT, including health-related, educational, cultural and scientific activities. Charitable status is not usually required for this exemption. A certificate from the state authorities is sometimes required.

If an activity is subject to VAT, charities are allowed to apply a reduced VAT rate (7%), except for unrelated business income to which the general VAT rate (19%) applies. Grants are generally not subject to VAT.

Other

Charities are exempt from inheritance and gift tax, provided that their tax-exempt status lasts for at least ten years after the inheritance or the transfer between living persons (*section 13(1)(16b), Inheritance and Gift Tax Act*).

10. WHAT, IF ANY, ARE THE TAXATION BENEFITS FOR DONORS TO CHARITIES?

The Income Tax Act (*Einkommensteuergesetz, EStG*) and the Corporate Income Tax Act give special tax treatment to donations for tax-exempt purposes (as defined in the Fiscal Code) (*see Question 3*).

Individual donors and corporate donors receive similar tax benefits for their charitable contributions.

Donations

The general rule for tax benefits is that the deductibility of a donation is limited to a maximum of 20% of total income (*section 10b(1)(1), Income Tax Act,* and *section 9(1) (2)1, Corporate Income*

Tax Act). In other words, instead of being taxed on 100% of his income, a donor can make the maximum donation of 20% and be taxed on 80% of his income.

Alternatively, an entrepreneur or a self-employed professional who produces turnover can deduct up to 0.4% of turnover, plus wages and salaries as special expenses, under the VAT Act (*Umsatzsteuergesetz, UStG*).

Endowments to charitable foundations

Donations to foundations enjoy greater tax relief than donations to associations or corporations. The term foundation in tax law covers both a foundation under sections 80 et seq of the Civil Code (*rechtsfähige Stiftung bürgerlichen Rechts*) and a non-independent foundation (*unselbstständige Stiftung*). However, this additional tax relief does not apply to the endowment of a spend-down foundation.

In addition to general tax deductibility (*see above, Donations*), an individual donor can deduct up to EUR1 million if the contribution endows a charitable foundation (*section 10b(1a), Income Tax Act*). There is no similar provision in the Corporate Income Tax Act, so corporate donors do not receive additional tax benefits for donations to foundations.

An endowment to a foundation can be spread over ten years for income tax purposes. It is therefore up to the donor to ask the tax authority to apply an amount in any given year in the most beneficial way.

The main justifications for this unequal treatment based on legal form are specific to foundations. They are characterised by not having any members, a permanent object, government supervision (but not for non-independent foundations) and the need to have endowment property.

Certificate of tax deductibility (*Zuwendungsbescheinigung*)

Charitable organisations can receive tax-deductible donations directly, and can independently confirm receipt of donations to the donor. Special regulations on the recipient certifying donations are in section 50 of the Regulations on the Income Tax Act (*Einkommensteuerdurchführungsverordnung, EStDV*).

For donations of up to EUR200, tax laws provide an abridged system of obtaining a deduction. In certain cases, a bank receipt is sufficient proof that a donation was made.

Those donating in good faith can rely on certificates of deductibility issued to them. Negligence or deliberate abuse incurs, for the person in charge at the charity's office, liability to pay of 30% of the amount donated as compensation for tax evaded (*section 10b(4) 2, 3, Income Tax Act*).

Exemption from inheritance and gift tax

Heirs to assets are exempt from inheritance and gift tax if they wholly or partly donate the assets to a charitable foundation (*section 29(1)4, Inheritance and Gift Tax Act*). They must donate the assets within 24 months of receiving the inheritance or gift, to obtain the tax exemption. However, they cannot both reduce their inheritance and gift tax and deduct the amount from their taxable income, so a choice must be made between the two reliefs.

DISADVANTAGES

The principal disadvantage for charities is the difficulty in giving up charitable status. In case of an exit, a charity is subject to tax for the previous ten years, which makes it practically impossible in most cases.

The level of remuneration of directors and other charity staff is still under the level of for-profit organisations of a comparable size. However, if the remuneration is at an appropriate level, it may approximate to the compensation of for-profit managers.

OVERSEAS CHARITIES

Foreign charities operating in Germany

Generally, to be tax-exempt in Germany, a foreign charity must meet the same conditions as a German entity. The Court of Justice of the European Union (ECJ) has held that, if a charity recognised in one EU member state also satisfies the charitable requirements of another EU member state, and its object is to promote the same public interest (which is for the national authorities of the other state, including its courts, to determine), the authorities of that member state cannot deny the foundation the right to equal treatment solely because it is not established in its territory (*Stauffer, Case C-386/04, 14 September 2006, available at http://curia. europa.eu/juris/liste.jsf?language=en&jur=C,T,F&num=C-386/04&td=ALL*).

Accordingly, foreign organisations subject to limited tax liability can generally be tax-exempt in Germany, under section 5(2)2 of the Corporate Income Tax Act, which was adopted in response to this ECJ ruling.

However, foreign organisations applying for tax exemption in Germany still have practical difficulties. For example, it has not been determined which German tax authority is competent to recognise the tax exemption of a foreign charitable organisation that has no German income.

An organisation which furthers tax-exempt purposes abroad must assist persons resident or domiciled in Germany or, among other things, make some contribution to the prestige of the German state abroad (*section 51(2), Fiscal Code*). These criteria must be generally fulfilled by a domestic entity or a foreign entity promoting charitable purposes in Germany. In practice, this provision only becomes relevant if a foreign organisation is subject to limited tax liability in Germany without carrying out charitable purposes in Germany.

Donors giving to foreign charities

In the past, German tax law did not generally allow donations to a charity in a foreign country to be tax-deductible in Germany. This was because the German tax authority cannot verify whether a foreign charity fulfils its charitable purposes, and has no control over amendments to the charity's purposes. Misuse of funds cannot be sanctioned according to German tax law.

To overcome these restrictions, a domestic charity had to be set up and the annual proceeds of the invested capital then transferred to foreign recipients (*section 58(1), Fiscal Code*). Due to some recent rulings by the ECJ, options for tax deducting cross-border donations in the EU have improved and German legislation has been amended. However in practice, the new rules have no significant impact.

Cross-border donations to charitable organisations in other EU member states or a state in the European Economic Area (EEA) that are subject to limited tax liability in Germany are tax deductible (*section 10b, Income Tax Act, in conjunction with section 5(2)2, Corporate Income Tax Act*). However in practice, the German taxpayer must prove that the foreign organisation meets the conditions for charity (*Gemeinnützigkeit*) (*see Question 3*), so the provision has practically no impact.

The ECJ has ruled that donations by a taxpayer to charitable entities resident in another EU member state must generally be tax deductible under the law of the donor's jurisdiction. The taxpayer must have the opportunity to show that a donation made to an entity established in another EU member state satisfies the requirements imposed by the other member state for tax deductibility (*Case C-316/07, Persche, available at http://curia.europa.eu/juris/liste.jsf?language=en&jur=C,T,F&num=C-316/07&td=ALL*). If a charity recognised in one member state satisfies the charitable requirements imposed by another member state, and its object is to promote the same public interest, equal treatment must not be denied solely because it is not established in the other member state. Further, the need to safeguard fiscal supervision cannot justify a restriction on the tax deductibility of donations. However, the tax authorities can ask the taxpayer to provide such proof as they consider necessary, to determine whether the conditions for tax deductibility have been met.

Further to this ECJ ruling, in 2010 the German parliament adopted provisions enabling the deduction of cross-border donations. Donations for charitable, benevolent or religious purposes to EU corporate bodies under public law are deductible, if individuals resident or domiciled in Germany benefit from the entity's activities, or the activities contribute to the prestige of Germany. Donations for charitable, benevolent or religious purposes to EU tax-exempt entities are deductible if both:

- The entity would be tax exempt if it was subject to tax liability in Germany.
- The member state provides administrative assistance (*Directive 77/799/EEC on mutual assistance by the competent authorities of the member states in the field of direct taxation and taxation of insurance premiums*) and assistance in the collection of taxes (*Directive 2008/55/EC on mutual assistance for the recovery of claims relating to certain levies, duties, taxes and other measures*) (*sections 10b(1)1(1 and 3), Income Tax Act*).

Given the increased requirements for taxpayer co-operation under the ECJ ruling, and the procedure for recognising foreign tax-exempt entities under the new section 10b of the Income Tax Act, the ECJ judgment and the new legislative provision only have a small practical impact.

Donations by a German taxpayer to foreign charities can be exempt from inheritance and gift tax if the beneficiary's country of residence has entered into a reciprocity agreement (*Gegenseitigkeitserklärung*) with Germany (*section 13(1) 16c, Inheritance and Gift Tax Act*). Such an agreement is contained, for example, in Article 10 of the Convention for the Avoidance of

Double Taxation between Germany and the US with respect to taxes on estates, inheritance and gifts. Under this agreement, property transferred to an organisation pursuing public benefit purposes, which is resident and tax-exempt in one state, is exempt from inheritance and gift tax in the other contracting state, if that property transfer would be tax-exempt if made to a domestic organisation.

13. IS IT POSSIBLE TO REGISTER A DOMESTIC CHARITY ABROAD, AND HAS YOUR JURISDICTION ENTERED INTO ANY INTERNATIONAL AGREEMENTS OR TREATIES IN THIS AREA?

Gemeinnützigkeit or German tax law is not opposed to the idea of charities operating abroad. In other words, charities do not lose their tax-exempt status if they pursue their purposes outside Germany. The US-German Double Taxation Treaty contains a provision regarding the mutual recognition of the tax-exemption in the respective other country.

REFORM

14. ARE THERE ANY PROPOSALS FOR REFORM IN THE AREA OF CHARITY LAW?

A working group consisting of representatives from the federation and the federal states is currently discussing reforms to the law relating to foundations. Topics include, among others:

- Protection of the name *Stiftung*.
- A legal framework for the capital preservation of foundations.
- Increased transparency and publicity requirements.
- Legal amendments relating to fundamental changes of foundations.

ONLINE RESOURCES

GERMAN MINISTRY OF JUSTICE

W www.gesetze-im-internet.de/Teilliste_translations.html

Description. The site is maintained by the German Ministry of Justice, and provides some translations of important German legal acts such as the Fiscal Code, the Civil Code and the Limited Companies Act. English translations are for guidance only and may be out of date.

REGULATORY AUTHORITY

GERMAN FEDERAL ASSOCIATION OF FOUNDATIONS

W www.stiftungen.org/en/association-of-german-foundations.html

T +49 30 89 79 47 63

Description. The site is maintained by the German Federal Association of Foundations, a charitable association, and provides the contact details of Foundation authorities in the 16 German states.

GIBRALTAR

Peter Montegriffo, HASSANS INTERNATIONAL LAW FIRM

OVERVIEW AND MAIN TRENDS

1.   WHAT IS THE HISTORICAL BACKGROUND TO CHARITY LAW AND CHARITABLE ORGANISATIONS IN YOUR JURISDICTION?

There is a long and established tradition of charitable giving and philanthropy in Gibraltar.

Various local merchants and religious institutions have historically provided for and promoted charitable purposes and causes.

Many longstanding local charities (for example, the John Mackintosh Trust) have endowed the community, with the benefit of wealth created through trading and mercantile activities connected with Gibraltar.

The position prior to the early 1960s is that charities were organised in accordance with the applicable English common law and rules of equity. Gibraltar law is based entirely on English law and (subject to amendment arising from local statutes and/or case law) the general position is the application of English common law and rules of equity.

2.   ARE INDEPENDENT CHARITABLE ORGANISATIONS COMMON AND SIGNIFICANT IN YOUR JURISDICTION? WHAT IS THE CURRENT SIZE AND SCOPE OF THE SECTOR AND THE MAIN TRENDS?

There are numerous independent charitable organisations established in Gibraltar. They cover a wide variety of activities. They range from small and very targeted charitable organisations, through to significantly endowed charities (often set up in recent times by international entrepreneurs established in Gibraltar).

While there continues to be a strong and (given Gibraltar's size) small domestic sector, there is an increasing trend involving international charity and philanthropy. This arises primarily from the presence in Gibraltar of international business entrepreneurs. Gibraltar's legal, fiscal, geographical and cultural features tend to encourage the establishment of such organisations.

LEGAL FRAMEWORK

Definition of charity

Gibraltar's charity law is primarily contained in the Charities Act. This is largely modelled on the UK Charities Act 1960.

The Charities Act defines charitable purposes as meaning purposes which are exclusively charitable according to the law of England.

The result of this definition is effectively to keep updated (and applicable to Gibraltar) the definition of a charity as such evolves and is applied under the law of England.

Principal sources of law

The Charities Act forms the basic legal framework. Under section 40 of the Charities Act all matters with reference to a new charity, for which no specific provision is made in the Charities Act, are to be determined according to the principles of equity in force at the time in England and Wales.

LEGAL BODIES

The Charities Act does not prescribe the forms of organisations that can be used for charitable purposes. The usual form is either a trust (fully adopted in Gibraltar, since local law is entirely based on that of England and Wales) or a company (usually limited by guarantee).

The advantages and disadvantages of each structure are those that arise from the main features of trusts and companies. There is, of course, a developed jurisprudence in relation to both trusts and companies. In Gibraltar this will follow both Gibraltar case law and UK cases. In the absence of a Gibraltar authority a decision of the Privy Council is binding. It may often be the case that charitable trusts are set up and then incorporate companies to better insulate (through limited liability) various projects or initiatives undertaken by the charity.

At a practical level, there is no material difference in administration, registration, taxation or management. Both forms have been successfully used in Gibraltar over the years.

Some arrangements (primarily of a broadly philanthropic but not exclusively charitable type, and therefore outside the definition in the Charities Act) have been established as both trusts and corporate vehicles. There is a debate developing locally as to whether our charities/philanthropic law should be amended, to provide a wider base and definition for the registration of such activities.

5.   WHAT ARE THE QUALIFICATION REQUIREMENTS/FORMALITIES TO SET UP THESE ORGANISATIONS?

The Charities Act establishes a register of charities which is maintained by the Charity Commissioners, and sets out the formal requirements for registration. Every charity (that is, a charity established exclusively for charitable purposes) can apply for registration.

The only charities that are not required to be registered are either:

- Exempt charities (essentially, any registered building used exclusively as a place of meeting for religious purposes, or any friendly or benefits society or saving bank).
- Any charity otherwise accepted as such by order or regulations.

An application for registration must be accompanied with copies of the charity's trust, or such other documents or information as prescribed by the Charity Commissioners.

It is very simple to establish a trust or company in Gibraltar. A charitable trust is usually established by way of written instrument which requires registration as a charity with the Charity Commissioners. The trust deed will need to have regard to the requirements of the Charities Act in respect of governance and obligations arising from registration as a charity. The incorporation of companies is regulated by the Companies Act. This provides for the incorporation for a number of different types of companies including companies limited by guarantee with or without a share capital. Full information in relation to registration of companies can be found on the Companies House website, *www.companieshouse.gi*.

ONGOING REGULATORY REQUIREMENTS

6.   WHAT ARE THE MAIN REGULATORY AUTHORITIES FOR CHARITABLE ORGANISATIONS? WHAT ARE THEIR POWERS OF INVESTIGATION/AUDIT/SANCTIONS?

Regulatory authorities

The Charities Act appoints a Board of Charity Commissioners headed by a Chief Charity Commissioner, who must be legally qualified.

Schedule 1 of the Charities Act sets out the basic constitutional requirements relating to the Charity Commissioners. This allows them to regulate their own proceedings and, subject to any regulations and directions of the Chief Commissioner, only one commissioner can act in the name of the Charity Commissioners.

The Charities Act sets out various ongoing regulatory requirements, although they are not very extensive. Statements of account giving prescribed information about the affairs of a charity must be sent to the Charity Commissioners on request, except for a charity with a permanent endowment.

In relation to a charity with a permanent endowment, a statement relating to the permanent endowment must be sent every year to the Charity Commissioners without request, unless the charity is exempted by order or regulation. A charity is deemed to have a permanent endowment unless all property held for the purposes of the charity can be expended for those purposes without distinction from capital and income.

Powers

The Charity Commissioners have various powers to investigate and seek the audit of charities in appropriate circumstances. They also have power to exchange information with other Gibraltar government departments, and to promote co-operation between charities.

The Charity Commissioners have a wide range of powers, including:

- Power to start enquiries.
- Power to call for documents and search records.
- Power to order an audit of the charity, in appropriate circumstances.
- Exchange of information within certain prescribed parameters.
- Co-operation between charities, with a view to promoting and making more effective charitable work.
- Making certain applications to court, in particular, to apply the cy-près arrangements in appropriate circumstances. As is the case in England and Wales, the cy-près doctrine allows the court to direct a gift to an organisation which comes closest to fulfilling the purpose of a gift, which otherwise cannot be completed. This may occur because the named recipient of the gift does not exist, is dissolved, or no one conducts the activity for which the gift was made.
- Power to make schemes or alter the application of charitable property, and to act to protect charities.

7. WHICH BODIES OR PERSONS MANAGE CHARITABLE ORGANISATIONS AND WHAT GENERAL REQUIREMENTS MUST THEY MEET?

Charitable organisations can be set up as trusts or corporate vehicles (usually limited by guarantee). A board of trustees or board of directors (each governed by the constitutional documents) have power to manage the charity. This is subject to the Charities Act and, as applicable, general trust and/or corporate law.

The main responsibilities and obligations of trustees or of a board of directors of a charity are to ensure effective donations are made in accordance with the constitutional documents of the charity. Any donations must, of course, be subject to all required governance procedures, including accounting and financial record keeping and reporting.

8. WHAT ARE THE ACCOUNTING/FINANCIAL REPORTING REQUIREMENTS?

There is a general duty for charities to provide statements of account. In the case of a charity with a permanent endowment the charity must send yearly statements to the Charity Commissioners, unless it is exempted by order or regulation (*see Question 6*). In the case of a charity without a permanent endowment, the statement of account is provided on request. These statements do not have to be independently audited, but the Charity Commissioners can require accounts for such period as they think fit to be investigated and audited independently.

TAX

Tax on income

Registered charities are exempt from tax on income, from whatever source in Gibraltar or internationally.

Tax on capital gains

There is no capital gains tax in Gibraltar.

Tax on property used by the organisation

There is no capital gains tax or other imputed tax for the use of property by charities in Gibraltar. Registered charities owning property are also usually exempt from rates generally applicable to properties, but they pay stamp duty on the acquisition of real estate.

Value added tax (VAT)

There is no VAT in Gibraltar.

10.   WHAT, IF ANY, ARE THE TAXATION BENEFITS FOR DONORS TO CHARITIES?

Individual donors are generally entitled to claim tax relief, in relation to payments of up to GB£5,000 made to registered charities in Gibraltar.

The Income Tax Act provides for payments to charities, of amounts equal to the tax paid (at the standard rate) by individuals on donations they make to charity (of up to GB£5,000 per year).

DISADVANTAGES

11.   WHAT ARE THE MAIN DISADVANTAGES OF CHARITABLE STATUS?

The main disadvantage of charitable status is that the organisation is limited to undertaking and discharging purely charitable purposes.

There are a number of organisations in Gibraltar undertaking broadly philanthropic purposes (extending beyond purely charitable work). These entities are not capable of being registered as charities under Gibraltar law (and may therefore be taxed differently). They are, however, able to operate on a wider basis in philanthropy than purely charitable purposes might allow.

OVERSEAS CHARITIES

12. IS IT POSSIBLE TO OPERATE AN OVERSEAS CHARITY IN YOUR JURISDICTION? WHAT ARE THE REGISTRATION FORMALITIES? HOW (IF AT ALL) ARE OVERSEAS CHARITIES TREATED DIFFERENTLY IN YOUR JURISDICTION FROM CHARITIES SET UP UNDER DOMESTIC LAW?

It is common for overseas charities (for example, large UK and other international charities) to seek local registration, by setting up a local association in Gibraltar. The registration processes are the same as those for a domestic based charity.

13. IS IT POSSIBLE TO REGISTER A DOMESTIC CHARITY ABROAD, AND HAS YOUR JURISDICTION ENTERED INTO ANY INTERNATIONAL AGREEMENTS OR TREATIES IN THIS AREA?

The authors are not aware of any international agreements between Gibraltar and other territories in relation to registration and reciprocal recognition of charity regulators.

Gibraltar is keen to develop the efficacy of cross-border giving. The facilitation of charitable donation payments is a matter of interest and debate among the local profession. There is also discussion of the possible extension of the definition of charitable purposes, and/or the creation of a separate category of philanthropy in certain limited circumstances.

REFORM

14. ARE THERE ANY PROPOSALS FOR REFORM IN THE AREA OF CHARITY LAW?

There are a number of local initiatives to modernise Gibraltar's charitable and philanthropic legislation and regulation procedures.

Both government and private sector organisations are looking at updating the Charities Act. Regard is being had to developments in other jurisdictions keen to broaden the registration and regulation of philanthropic work. Various initiatives (for example, the recently established Gibraltar Philanthropy Forum, consisting of private sector participants) aim to develop this area of work.

ONLINE RESOURCES

GIBRALTAR PHILANTHROPY FORUM

W http://gibraltarphilanthropyforum.com

Description. The Gibraltar Philanthropy Forum seeks to promote philanthropy and discussion of its key issues and challenges, gathering potential donors, philanthropy specialists, decision makers and opinion leaders in a philanthropy friendly jurisdiction.

REGULATORY AUTHORITY

CHARITIES COMMISSION

T +350 20070771

Address No 6 Covent Place, Gibraltar

W No website for the Gibraltar Charity Commission at present.

Description. The Charity Commission for Gibraltar regulates registered charities in Gibraltar.

IRELAND

John C O'Connor and Helen McGrath, O'CONNOR, SOLICITORS

OVERVIEW AND MAIN TRENDS

1.   WHAT IS THE HISTORICAL BACKGROUND TO CHARITY LAW AND CHARITABLE ORGANISATIONS IN YOUR JURISDICTION?

Legislative background

Charity law in Ireland has its origins in feudal laws designed to regulate the passing of land to corporations, including religious bodies (this practice had meant that feudal lords had been unable to receive their dues from the land). Despite attempts to impose restraints, the church gained significant wealth and land until its suppression in England and Ireland in the Reformation by King Henry VIII. The suppression of the churches created a vacuum where the charitable activities of the churches needed to be filled. In 1601 the Statute of Charitable Uses was passed by Queen Elizabeth I to fill this gap and this set out a number of "charitable purposes". In 1634 similar provisions were introduced in Ireland with the enactment of An Act for the Maintenance and Execution of Pious Uses, and these two Acts formed the basis of charity law in Ireland up to the 1800s. The Acts did not define charitable purposes, but the courts could view a purpose as charitable if it had both a public benefit element and came within the "spirit and intendment" of the Act.

There was a significant development in the law in 1891 with the seminal case of *Commissioners for Special Purposes of Income Tax v Pemsel [1891] AC 531*, which identified four categories of charitable trust:

• Trusts for the relief of poverty.

• Trusts for the advancement of education.

• Trusts for the advancement of religion.

• Trusts beneficial to the community.

This classification remains in place in Ireland today following the coming into force of the Charities Act 2009 with some minor adjustments (providing the words "or economic hardship" in the case of trusts for the relief of poverty) (*see Question 3*).

Regulatory background

In 1844 the Commissioners of Charitable Donations and Bequests were established to ensure charitable donations would not be misapplied. After the formation of the Irish State the Commissioners came under the authority of the Attorney General and provided for the management of charitable bodies. They continued in being until 2014, when their functions were transferred to the new Charities Regulatory Authority (called the Charities Regulator), which was established on the 16 October 2014 pursuant to the Charities Act 2009 and has been introduced on a phased basis.

The Charities Regulator not only provides for the registration of charities but will also regulate charitable bodies. While much of the Act has been commenced as at the law-stated date of this article, sections 91 to 98 of the Charities Act 2009, dealing with non-cash collections and various miscellaneous provisions, have yet to be implemented. Up to the introduction of the 2009 Act, the former Commissioners of Charitable Donations and bequests, under the old governing legislation, had no power to maintain a register of Charities so for the first time the Charities Regulator now requires all charitable organisations (as defined by the Act) to register with the Charities Regulator (*see Question 6, Charities Regulator*).

## 2.	ARE INDEPENDENT CHARITABLE ORGANISATIONS COMMON AND SIGNIFICANT IN YOUR JURISDICTION? WHAT IS THE CURRENT SIZE AND SCOPE OF THE SECTOR AND THE MAIN TRENDS?

The need for a new regulatory authority for the Irish charity sector is underlined by the significant growth of non-profit organisations in recent years which range in size and scope from very large organisations to small local voluntary groups. There are just over 18,600 non-profit organisations in Ireland according to Benefacts, a database of civil society organisations in Ireland. The majority of these have been established in the last 25 years, highlighting the sector's rapid growth. They have a combined income of EUR7.09 billion, total net assets of EUR5.75 billion and employ over 107,000 (*source: https://benefacts.ie*). 48.52% of the sector's income currently comes from state grants and contracts while over 50% comes from fundraising and donations. Following the global downturn the charities sector in Ireland experienced a decrease in income between 2009 and 2012, although the number of volunteers increased.

In Ireland all charities which carry out fundraising activities must register with the Charities Regulator but to obtain tax exemptions for charities, charitable organisations must also register with the Revenue Commissioners and obtain a CHY number (*see Question 6, Revenue Commissioners*). There are over 8,000 such charities registered with both the Revenue and the Charities Regulator to benefit from tax exemptions for charities under Irish law and this number is growing. Less than 20% of the Irish non-profit organisations operate nationally and 4.5% operate internationally, with some 43.1% having their main office in Dublin (*source: A Portrait of Ireland's Non-Profit Sector, published by the Wheel in 2014*).

LEGAL FRAMEWORK

## 3.	IS THERE A LEGAL DEFINITION OF A "CHARITY"? WHAT ARE THE PRINCIPAL SOURCES OF LAW AND REGULATIONS RELATING TO CHARITABLE ORGANISATIONS AND ACTIVITIES?

Definition of charity

Charitable organisations. Since the coming into force of the Charities Act 2009, charitable organisations are defined as either:

- The trustees of charitable trusts, which are trusts established:

- for charitable purposes only (*see below*);
- under a deed of trust that requires the trustees to apply all of the property of the trust in furtherance of its charitable purposes.
- Bodies (corporate or unincorporated) that promote a charitable purpose only.

A charitable organisation must apply all of its property in furtherance of that charitable purpose (other than monies spent in the operation and maintenance of the body, such as payment of wages of staff members or, in the case of a religious organisation, on accommodation and care of its members). Payments made to "members" or "trustees" of charitable organisations and trusts can only be made in accordance with the rules set out in the Act (*section 89, Charities Act 2009*).

Charitable purposes. To be a charity, an organisation must be restricted to engaging in solely charitable purposes that should be for the public benefit. The *Pemsel* categories have largely been adopted into statute by the 2009 Act (with the expansion of the prevention or relief of poverty to now include relief of economic hardship) (*see Question 1, Legislative background*). Purposes will not be held to be charitable unless they are for the public benefit, and gifts will not be viewed as being for the public benefit unless they are intended to benefit the public or a section of the public. If a gift confers a benefit on a person other than in his or her capacity as a member of the public any such benefit must be reasonable in all the circumstances and must be ancillary to and necessary for the public benefit.

The 2009 Act defines "purposes that are of benefit to the community" as including the:

- Advancement of community welfare, including the relief of those in need by reason of youth, age, ill-health, or disability.
- Advancement of community development, including rural or urban regeneration.
- Promotion of civic responsibility or voluntary work.
- Promotion of health, including the prevention or relief of sickness, disease or human suffering.
- Advancement of conflict resolution or reconciliation.
- Promotion of religious or racial harmony and harmonious community relations.
- Protection of the natural environment.
- Advancement of environmental sustainability.
- Advancement of the efficient and effective use of the property of charitable organisations.
- Prevention or relief of suffering of animals.
- Advancement of the arts, culture, heritage or sciences.
- Integration of those who are disadvantaged, and the promotion of their full participation, in society.

The following are not recognised as charitable purposes under the 2009 Act:

- Advancement of sport.
- Advancement of trade unions or chambers of commerce.
- Advancement of a political party or body promoting a political cause (unless relating to advancement of a charitable purpose).

Principal sources of law

Irish charities are governed by the following:

- The Charities Acts 1961 to 2009.

- Legislation relating to fundraising, such as the Street and House to House Collections Act 1962, the Gaming and Lotteries Act 1956 and the National Lotteries Act 1986.
- The Valuation Act 2001, which made material changes to charitable exemptions from rates and provides that charity related property is eligible for a rateable exemption if a charitable organisation uses the land or building part exclusively for charitable purposes and otherwise than for private profit (*Schedule 4, Valuation Act 2001*) (*see Question 9, Local taxes on property used by a charity*).

LEGAL BODIES

4. WHAT ARE THE FORMS OF ORGANISATIONS THAT ARE USED FOR CHARITABLE PURPOSES? WHAT ARE THEIR ADVANTAGES/DISADVANTAGES?

In May 2016 Benefacts published statistics on the Irish non-profit sector. This identified that of the 18,600 formally constituted non-profit organisations, over 8,800 are companies limited by guarantee. The balance was largely made up of unincorporated trusts or associations.

Company limited by guarantee

Companies limited by guarantee (CLGs) are the most popular form of organisation utilised for charitable purposes in Ireland (*see above*). Company legislation was consolidated in Ireland with the coming into force of the Companies Act 2014. A CLG is a form of public company with separate legal personality to its members, whose liability is limited to the amount they undertake to contribute to the assets of a company in the event of a wind-up, subject to a minimum of EUR1. If a guarantee company has no share capital the members will not be required to buy any shares in the company.

Under Irish company legislation a CLG must have at least two directors, however, if a company registers with the Revenue Commissioners for charitable tax exemption the Revenue will require those companies to have at least three directors. The governing instrument of the CLG is the constitution, which is comprised of the memorandum and articles of association of the company.

The directors and officers of incorporated charities (including CLGs) fall within the definition of a charity trustee under the Charities Act 2009 and are obliged to comply with all of a charity trustee's obligations under that Act, in addition to their duties as directors under the Companies Acts (*see Question 7*).

Advantages. There are the following benefits of operating as a CLG:

- It is a distinct legal entity from its members, and can enter into legal contracts and agreements in a relatively transparent manner.
- It can own property, and does not need to hold property in the name of its trustees.
- It can be wound up.
- Its members have limited liability.
- It will not cease on the death of all of the trustees/members and will continue in existence despite changes in membership and without the requirement of an application to court or the Charities Regulator, unlike a charitable trust (*see below, Charitable trust*).

Disadvantages. One of the downsides of operating the more complex structure of a CLG may be the costs associated with preparation and filing of annual accounts and returns with the Companies Registration Office which is not required of, for example, an unincorporated association, which only reports to the Charities Regulator. In addition, directors must comply with the obligations both of charity trustees under the Charities Act 2009, and of directors under the Companies Acts (*see above*).

Charitable trust

Although they have been overtaken in popularity by the CLG, historically the preferred structure for charitable organisations was the charitable trust, established by a deed of trust which places assets owned by trustees in trust for charitable purposes.

Unlike CLGs, these trusts do not have a separate and distinct legal personality from their trustees, and the duties and liabilities of charitable trustees were governed by common law and equitable principles which had evolved over several hundred years. In addition to the Charities Act 2009 Act, trustees must comply, in their role as trustee, with the provisions of the Trustee Act 1893.

The Charities Act 2009 now defines a charitable trust as a trust established:

- For a charitable purpose only.
- Under a deed of trust, which requires the trustees of the trust to apply all of the property in furtherance of the charitable purpose (except for monies expended in the management of the trust and as outlined by the Act).

The trustees of a charitable trust are identified in the deed of trust or a deed of appointment. Under the Charities Act 2009 charity trustees are however also defined as including:

- The trustees in whose name charitable property is vested.
- Any officer of the body or any person for the time being performing the function of an officer of the body (and therefore senior employees may in certain circumstances fall within the definition of a charity trustee).

Under the Land and Conveyancing Law Reform Act 2009, to protect a purchaser of land held in certain trusts, there must be a minimum of two trustees appointed to the trust although the Charities Regulator will seek the appointment of three. If a charitable tax exemption is being sought, the Revenue Commissioners will also require a minimum of three trustees (*see Question 5*). Charitable trusts established by deed need not comply with company law and the statutory duties for directors of a company will not apply to the directors or trustees of a charitable trust. They will, however, still be subject to the duties and obligations set out in the Charities Act 2009.

Advantages. Charitable trusts are a flexible and economic structure. Their flexibility may suit trusts managing significant assets with experienced trustees and without a large staff and with access to professional advisers.

Disadvantages. Charitable trusts cannot benefit from some of the benefits of a CLG, such as separate legal personality, limited liability, ease of succession of title and any change to the trustees may require a deed of appointment of new trustees and property will need to be vested in the new trustees (*see above, Company limited by guarantee: Advantages*).

Unincorporated association

Unincorporated associations have no separate legal identity from their members. They are usually established by rules or a constitution, and are no different from an unincorporated club in Irish law.

Such bodies do not have the benefit of limited liability and therefore the members are personally liable for their actions. The officers and directors may, however, still fall within the definition of a charity trustee for the purposes of the Charities Act 2009, with all the applicable statutory obligations. Under the Charities Act 2009 a charitable organisation may agree with a charity trustee to obtain indemnity insurance in respect of acts done by the charity trustee in good faith. Where an unincorporated association wishes to enter into contracts or operate as an employer or acquire an interest in land, it may be sensible to incorporate the structure, for example into a company limited by guarantee (*see above, Company limited by guarantee*). An unincorporated association may, however, suit a small organisation with limited assets, provided it takes out all necessary insurances to protect the individual members of the association.

Advantages. Unincorporated associations are the preferred type of arrangement for small voluntary organisations, as they are not required to comply with company law and the Companies Acts, unlike CLGs. The unincorporated associations may suit some smaller charities, particularly those that may be able to fall under the *de minimis* provisions for a requirement to file an annual statement of account with the Charities Regulator. The *de minimis* provisions relate to charitable organisations who either:

- Have gross income or total expenditure of less than EUR10,000 in a financial year, or such greater amount not exceeding EUR50,000 as may be prescribed.
- Are centres for education designated by the Minister for Education and Skills.

Disadvantages. Unincorporated associations do not benefit from limited liability and their members are personally liable for their actions.

Others

A small number of charities (less than 2%) are established as either benevolent societies under the Friendly Societies Acts or as industrial and provident societies under the Industrial and Provident Societies Acts. It is no longer possible to establish a benevolent society under the Friendly Societies Act following the implementation of the Friendly Societies and Industrial Provident Societies (Miscellaneous Provisions) Act 2014, however it is still possible to establish an industrial and provident society. Both bodies are regulated by the Registrar of Friendly Societies in addition to the Charities Regulator when acting as charities. Although industrial and provident societies enjoy the benefits of limited liability, they must either be a co-operative society, or there must be a reason why they are not registered as a company, and the society must have at least seven founder members.

5. WHAT ARE THE QUALIFICATION REQUIREMENTS/FORMALITIES TO SET UP THESE ORGANISATIONS?

For all organisations, charities wishing to obtain the charitable tax exemption from the Revenue Commissioners must register with the Revenue Commissioners and apply for relief from tax on their income and property by obtaining a CHY number. When applying to the Revenue Commissioners charities must submit:

- A copy of their governing instrument (which can be furnished in draft format for a charity that is newly formed).
- A statement of their activities to date.
- Plans for the next 12 months, including any trading activities being undertaken/proposed.

They must also provide the Revenue with:

- Their annual reports and other documentation, if applicable.
- The latest financial statements of projected income and expenditure of the organisation.
- A list of names, addresses, occupations and tax numbers of the officers, trustees or directors.

Company limited by guarantee

The Companies Act 2014 allows one or more persons to form a company by subscribing to a constitution. To establish a company the following must be sent to the Companies Registration Office:

- A registration fee.
- A constitution, which must include a memorandum of association, articles of association and an objects clause.
- Form A1, giving details of the company's:
  - name;
  - registered office;
  - e-mail address;
  - company secretary and directors, and confirmation of their consent to act as such;
  - subscribers and their shares (if any).
- The form must incorporate a declaration that the requirements of the Companies Acts have been complied with.

The old doctrine of ultra vires has been changed significantly in the 2014 Act. The 2014 Act provides that the validity of an act done by a company limited by guarantee (CLG) must not be called into question on the grounds of lack of capacity by virtue of any provision in the objects clause.

Although private companies can have a maximum of 149 members, there is no limit on the number of members for public companies, including CLGs. A CLG can be incorporated with as few as one member (whereas seven members was the minimum under prior legislation) and has no upper limit in relation to its number of members.

Charitable trust

To establish a charitable trust it is necessary to enter into a deed of trust, which:

- Identifies the charitable purposes for which the trust is established.
- Identifies the trustees.
- Sets out in detail the powers of the trustees.

Unincorporated association

There are no formalities to establish unincorporated associations, although they will frequently adopt rules and a constitution.

All charities must register with the Charities Regulator if they operate within the Republic of Ireland and demonstrate a clear public benefit and charitable purposes. Under Irish law certain bodies cannot apply to become charities, including:

- Approved bodies for the sole purpose of the promotion of sports.
- Organisations set up for private benefit.

- Trade unions.
- Chambers of commerce or political parties.
- Organisations promoting a political cause (unless such political activity relates solely to advancing their charitable purposes).

ONGOING REGULATORY REQUIREMENTS

6.   WHAT ARE THE MAIN REGULATORY AUTHORITIES FOR CHARITABLE ORGANISATIONS? WHAT ARE THEIR POWERS OF INVESTIGATION/AUDIT/SANCTIONS?

Charities Regulator

This is the primary regulator for all charitable organisations in the Republic of Ireland. Charities must register with the Charities Regulator to carry on activities. It is now an offence for any charitable organisation which is unregistered to:

- Advertise or invite members of the public to give money or property to the organisation.
- Accept or cause others to accept a gift, money or property on behalf of the organisation.

The Charities Act 2009 builds on pre-existing legislation and in particular the Charities Act 1961, as amended by the Charities Act 1973. The 1961 Act provided procedures for the operation of Charitable Commissioners and also set out their jurisdiction and powers. Those powers were extended in the 1973 Act before being transferred over the Charities Regulator in the 2009 Act.

Under the earlier legislation, the Charities Regulator now has the powers to:

- Appoint trustees of a charitable trust either to fill a vacancy or as additional trustees, for example, where a trustee has died.
- Authorise the sale of lands held on a charitable trust and to authorise the sale of charitable property and the surrender of a lease or mortgage or exchange of a charitable property. The Charities Regulator can authorise the sale of land, for example, where there is no express power of sale in a trust document. The Charities Regulator ensures that the sale is, with some allowed exceptions, at full market value and will further ensure the proceeds are applied in line with the charity's trust instrument.
- Frame schemes applying charitable property as near as possible to the intentions of the original donor where the existing scheme is no longer capable of being carried on according to its original terms (*cy-près* schemes).
- Advise trustees experiencing difficulty in administering a charitable trust. Where trustees follow such advice they will not then be held liable for the consequences of having followed such advice and by following the advice the trustees will be deemed to have acted in accordance with the terms of the trust (*section 21, 1961 Act*).
- Compromise claims by or against a charity.
- Make vesting orders, freeing charity property from the operation of onerous covenants in leases in certain circumstances.
- The power to frame schemes of incorporation.

Many of these powers are of a quasi-judicial nature.

The Charities Regulator has also taken over the operation of a common investment fund (CIF) from the Commissioners for Charitable Donations and Bequests in which it invests funds for charities. The CIF relates to funds which were deposited with the Commissioners prior to its dissolution, however, the CIF is not accepting new funds any longer, although new money will be accepted into existing funds.

It is important to note that despite the broad range of powers that have been given to the Charities Regulator its investigative powers are contained in Part 4 of the 2009 Act and commence on 5 September 2016. From that date the Charities Regulator will then have the power to appoint an inspector to investigate the affairs of a charitable organisation and prepare a report on the charitable organisation. The inspector may require the production of documents and either the inspector or officer or member of staff of the authority may apply to a judge for a search warrant to enter on to the charitable organisation's property and seize documents if satisfied that there has been a failure to comply with any request for the production of documents. Part 5 of the Act provides for the establishment of a Charity Appeals Tribunal to whom decisions of the Charities Regulator may be appealed.

In addition, the Charities Act 2009 includes 21 statutory offences for charity trustees, including for example, failing to comply with a direction from the Charities Regulator requiring the auditing of accounts (see Question 7, Charity trustees).

Registrar of Companies and Office of Director of Corporate Enforcement

These regulatory authorities apply to charitable organisations that are registered as companies with the Companies Registration Office. Common law fiduciary duties of directors have now been placed on a statutory footing under the Companies Act 2014, and the Act sets out a four tier categorisation of offences for breaches of the Act (see Question 7).

It was clarified, following the commencement of the Companies Act 2014, that the Companies Registration Office does not have an investigative function. Therefore, the Office cannot prosecute offences which require that evidence be adduced which can be obtained only following a more comprehensive investigation. Those offences are prosecutable by the Director of Corporate Enforcement. This means in effect that the Companies Registration Office will deal with only those matters which can be identified on the basis of evidence available from Companies Registration Office records or court orders. All other matters will fall to be dealt with by the Office of the Director of Corporate Enforcement.

The Companies Act 2014 creates a four tier categorisation of offences for breaches of the Companies Act, ranging from:

- Category 4 offences (the least serious), which attract a Class A fine (where the fine does not exceed EUR5,000).
- Category 1 offences, which can result in:
  - summary convictions leading to either or both of: a fine of up to EUR5,000; a term of imprisonment not exceeding 12 months;
  - convictions on indictment resulting in either or both of: a term of imprisonment of up to ten years; a fine of up to EUR500,000.

Revenue Commissioners

Charities that wish to take advantage of the charitable tax exemption must register with the Revenue Commissioners (see Question 5). Charities which have obtained a charitable tax exemption may be investigated and/or prosecuted by the Revenue Commissioners in the event of a tax fraud or avoidance. The Revenue Commissioners also have the power to withdraw a charitable organisation's charitable tax exemption as this falls under their sole remit.

See box, *Regulatory authorities*.

7. WHICH BODIES OR PERSONS MANAGE CHARITABLE ORGANISATIONS AND WHAT GENERAL REQUIREMENTS MUST THEY MEET?

Charity trustees

Charity trustees have a wide number of obligations under the Charities Act 2009. The Charities Act has also created 21 new statutory offences for charity trustees, including:

- Knowingly or recklessly providing information or particulars to the Charities Regulator that are false or misleading for the purposes of an application for registration.
- Advertising or inviting members of the public to give money to and accept money on behalf of charitable organisations which are not registered or deemed to be registered.
- Where the charitable organisation changes its name in contravention of the Act the charity trustees are each guilty of an offence.
- Holding out that a body which is not registered, is registered under the Act (including representing that a charitable organisation has a seat of management inside the state when in fact it is outside the state).
- Contravening the duty to keep proper books of account.
- Contravening the duty to furnish an annual statement of account.
- Contravening the audit requirements where those are applicable to the charitable organisation or obstructing or failing to co-operate with a qualified person appointed by the Charities Regulator to carry out an audit of the charitable organisation's accounts.
- Failing to comply with a direction from the Charities Regulator requiring the auditing of accounts.
- Failing to submit an annual report in accordance with the Act.
- Failing to comply with the direction of the Charities Regulator to afford an auditor or independent person appointed by the Charities Regulator with any facility to which they are entitled.
- Acting as a charity trustee while disqualified.

A trustee might face the following potential penalties for an offence under the Act (*section 10, Charities Act 2009*):

- On summary conviction to either or both of: a fine not exceeding EUR5,000; imprisonment for a term not exceeding 12 months.
- On conviction on indictment to either or both of: a fine not exceeding EUR300,000; imprisonment for a term not exceeding ten years.

If a person is convicted of an offence under the Act they may also be required to pay to the Charities Regulator the costs and expenses in relation to the investigation, detection and prosecution of the offence.

The Act also provides that in certain circumstances a person may be disqualified from acting as a charity trustee.

The obligations of charitable trustees apply equally to directors of charitable organisations established as companies, and to charity trustees of other charitable organisations established by deed or as friendly societies or unincorporated associations.

Directors

In addition to their obligations as charity trustees, directors of charitable companies must comply with fiduciary duties, which were set out under common law and have now been put on a statutory basis under the Companies Act 2014. These are the duties to:

- Act in good faith in what the director considers to be the interest of the company.
- Act in accordance with the company's constitution and exercise his or her powers only for the purposes allowed by law.
- Act honestly and responsibly in relation to the conduct of the affairs of the company.
- Have regard to the interest of the company's members.
- Exercise the care, skill and diligence which:
  - should be exercised by a reasonable person having both knowledge and experience; and
  - may reasonably be expected of a person in the same position as the director and the knowledge and experience which the director actually has.
- Avoid any conflict between the director's duties to the company and the director's other interests, including personal interests, unless the director has been specifically released from his or her duty to the company and the matter concerned by a resolution in a general meeting.
- Not to use the company's property information or opportunities for his or her own or anyone else's benefit unless it is expressly permitted by the company's constitution and the use has been approved by a resolution in a general meeting.
- Not to agree to restrict the director's power to exercise independent judgement except as expressly permitted by the company's constitution or if this has been approved by a resolution in a general meeting.

Breach of certain of these duties may render the director liable to account for any gain and to indemnify the company for any loss.

8.   WHAT ARE THE ACCOUNTING/FINANCIAL REPORTING REQUIREMENTS?

All charities

Charity trustees for all registered charities must prepare and submit to the Charities Regulator a report known as the annual report in respect of the charity's activities in a financial year.

For charities that are registered companies, if the company has attached its financial statement in the form required by the Companies Acts to its annual return to the Companies Registration Office, it must attach a copy to the annual report as the annual statement of accounts (see below, Companies).

Charities that are not registered companies must attach an annual statement of accounts in the form prescribed by ministerial regulation. If the gross income or expenditure of a charity does not exceed EUR100,000 the charity trustees can instead attach an income and expenditure account, together with a statement of assets and liabilities. In the case of centres of education designated by the Minister for Education and Skills and for education bodies and charities where the gross income or total expenditure of the charity is less than EUR10,000 per annum (or such higher amount as may be provided, up to a ceiling of EUR50,000) the charity may not be required to provide an annual statement of account, although the charity will still be required to file an annual report and the Charities Regulator may require further information.

Where applicable, the charity must attach to the annual report an auditor's report or independent persons report.

Companies

Charities that are registered as companies must file an annual return with the Companies Registration Office, including a Form B1 together with required documentation, which for most companies will include audited financial statements, which give a true and fair view of the assets, liabilities and financial position of the company at its financial year's end and of the profit or loss of the company for the financial year. There are exemptions for filing full audited financial statements for small companies (including companies limited by guarantee) that can satisfy two of the following three requirements:

- Their balance sheet total does not exceed EUR4.4 million.
- Their turnover does not exceed EUR8.8 million.
- The number of employees does not exceed 50.

However, it is necessary to check the charity's governance documents in case these require an audit in any event.

TAX

Irish tax law provides a number of significant tax exemptions for charities. Charities must apply separately to the Irish Revenue Commissioners for registration, and comply with their assessment procedure to obtain tax exemption status and a CHY number (*see Question 5*). The mandatory registration of a charity with the Charities Regulator does not constitute an automatic tax exemption status for the charity.

Tax on income

Charities are exempt from paying income tax from trading profits and from investment of funds held for charitable purposes, provided the profits are applied solely to or for charitable purposes (this will include the normal running expenses of a charity) (*sections 207 and 208, Taxes Consolidation Act 1997*).

Tax on capital gains

Charities are exempt from paying tax on capital gains that are applied for charitable purposes.

Tax on property used by the organisation

Normally if a company is registered as a charity with the Charities Regulator it will qualify for an exemption from corporation tax, although this exemption will not necessarily apply to trading companies established by charities, unless the trading companies' profits are either gifted or covenanted to the charity.

Value added tax (VAT)

There is no general exemption for charitable organisations from VAT, however in certain circumstances they may be entitled to refunds of VAT on purchased items.

Capital acquisitions tax (CAT) (gift and inheritance tax)

Charities are, unlike individual recipients of gifts and inheritances, able to take such donations entirely free of CAT (*section 76, Capital Acquisitions Tax Consolidation Act 2003*).

Stamp duty

Transfer or leases of land in Ireland attract stamp duty, which is payable by the purchaser or lessee. A transfer or lease of land to a charity will, however, be exempt from stamp duty.

Local taxes on property used by a charity

The occupiers of commercial premises in Ireland are liable to pay rates. A charity occupying commercial property will be exempt from paying rates provided it can establish that it falls within Schedule 4 of the Valuation Act 2001 (*see Question 3, Principal sources of law*).

Deposit interest retention tax (DIRT)

DIRT is deducted from interest earned on deposit accounts. It will not be applied to deposits of charities with a CHY number, however, charities will be required to make a declaration to the relevant financial institution in the prescribed form and must notify the financial institution if there is any change in their charity status.

Local property tax

In certain circumstances residential properties owned by a charity may be exempt from local property tax, where the property is used to provide special needs accommodation and support for those who have a particular need (in addition to a need for general housing) to enable them to live in the community. Charities may also benefit from a local property tax exemption where the residential property is used solely as residential accommodation in connection with facilitating recreational activities in the course of carrying on its charity's primary purpose.

10.   WHAT, IF ANY, ARE THE TAXATION BENEFITS FOR DONORS TO CHARITIES?

The Irish Revenue operates a donation scheme whereby tax relief will be applied to either corporate or personal donations above EUR250. The relief is given at the donor's marginal rate of income tax and this is grossed up for pay as you earn (PAYE) only taxpayers. In the case of self-assessed and corporate donors relief is claimed in their respective tax returns but without the benefit of grossing up.

DISADVANTAGES

11. WHAT ARE THE MAIN DISADVANTAGES OF CHARITABLE STATUS?

Since the commencement of the Charities Act 2009, charitable organisations that intend to operate or carry on activities in Ireland must register with the Charities Regulator and it is an offence to advertise or fundraise or accept money on behalf of a charity that is not registered (*see Question 6, Charities Regulator*). The issue of the disadvantages of registration of a charity, therefore, does not arise.

OVERSEAS CHARITIES

12. IS IT POSSIBLE TO OPERATE AN OVERSEAS CHARITY IN YOUR JURISDICTION? WHAT ARE THE REGISTRATION FORMALITIES? HOW (IF AT ALL) ARE OVERSEAS CHARITIES TREATED DIFFERENTLY IN YOUR JURISDICTION FROM CHARITIES SET UP UNDER DOMESTIC LAW?

A non-resident charity based in a European Economic Area/European Free Trade Association (EEA/EFTA) country can apply to the Revenue Commissioners for a determination that it would qualify for the tax exemptions available under the Taxes Consolidation Act (*see Question 9*). A determination under this section is known as a DCHY number and receipt of such a notice of determination will permit the charity after a period of two years to seek an authorisation to operate the charitable donations scheme.

Charities which are established in an EEA state and have a principal place of business in the Republic of Ireland can apply to be registered with the Charities Regulator (*see Question 6, Charities Regulator*).

13. IS IT POSSIBLE TO REGISTER A DOMESTIC CHARITY ABROAD, AND HAS YOUR JURISDICTION ENTERED INTO ANY INTERNATIONAL AGREEMENTS OR TREATIES IN THIS AREA?

The Charities Regulator is developing relations with regulators in other jurisdictions.

REFORM

14. ARE THERE ANY PROPOSALS FOR REFORM IN THE AREA OF CHARITY LAW?

There has been significant change and reform of the charitable sector in the last five years, with the implementation of the Charities Act 2009 and the Companies Act 2014, including a new statutory regulator for charities and consolidated company legislation for the near 70% of charitable organisations that are registered as companies (*see Question 3*).

Despite this legislation, which includes the introduction of a definition of a charity trustee, the law governing trustees is at this stage outdated (the Trustee Act 1893). It is anticipated that there will be further reform of the area when the Trustee Act is updated. Similarly Part IV of the Charities Act 2009, which has provisions covering investigations and formal powers to the Charities Regulator to carry out investigations and searches and appoint investigators, has yet to be implemented.

ONLINE RESOURCES

BENEFACTS.IE

W https://benefacts.ie

T +353 1 5367130

Description. Benefacts provides searchable access to regulatory, financial and governance data about the non-profit sector. The Benefacts database includes all registered charities and thousands of other non-governmental organisations (NGOs), including education institutions, social enterprises and sports and professional bodies.

REGULATORY AUTHORITIES

CHARITIES REGULATOR

W www.charitiesregulatoryauthority.ie

T +353 1 6331500

Description. The Charities Regulator is the regulator for charitable organisations in Ireland and operates a registration database for charities as well as having a statutory investigative and regulatory function. The website also contains links to the Charities Acts.

COMPANIES REGISTRATION OFFICE

W www.cro.ie

T +353 1 8045200

Description. The Companies Registration Office deals with the registration of companies and business names in Ireland.

OFFICE OF THE REVENUE COMMISSIONERS

W www.revenue.ie

T +353 1 6763377 (Charities Section)

Description. The Charities Section of the Revenue Commissioners deals with charitable tax exemptions.

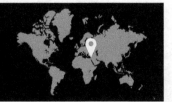

ISRAEL

Asher Dovev, HERZOG, FOX & NEEMAN

OVERVIEW AND MAIN TRENDS

Tzedakah is the Hebrew word for charity: giving aid, assistance and money to the poor and needy, or to other worthy causes. However, the nature of *tzedakah* is very different from the idea of charity. The word "charity" suggests benevolence and generosity, a magnanimous act by the wealthy and powerful for the benefit of the poor and needy. The word *tzedakah* is derived from the Hebrew meaning righteousness, justice or fairness. In Judaism, giving to the poor is not viewed as a generous, magnanimous act; it is simply an act of justice and righteousness, the performance of a duty, giving the poor their due.

During the Ottoman period, from 1517 to 1917, public endowments had to be established by the Muslim Tribunal in accordance with Sharia law. The public endowments were registered in the Endowments Books, some of which have survived to date. Under Sharia law, it is forbidden to revoke a public endowment once it has been established.

In 1909, the Ottoman Associations Law (number 121) (Associations Law) was enacted, which was intended to regulate the establishment of charities and their activities. The Associations Law continues to apply, in a limited manner, to associations that were established until 1980 under the Associations Law.

The King's Order In Council 1922 to 1947 (section 53) was enacted during the period of the British Mandate (1917 until 1948), which existed until the establishment of the State of Israel. Under this, each of the Jewish and Muslim faiths had autonomy regarding the establishment and management of religious endowments (that is, in the case of the Jewish faith, the tribunal had jurisdiction to give decisions in accordance with Jewish Law).

The Endowments for Charities Ordinance was enacted in 1924. Under this, the District Court registered non-religious endowments. In addition, the Endowments for Charities Ordinance (the Public Trustee) was enacted in 1947, together with the Charities regulations, under which the Public Trustee was vested with both:

- Broad authority regarding the registration of endowments.
- The right to participate in the management of endowments.

Under the British Mandate there were two parallel ways in which endowments could be established:

- Establishing an endowment under the applicable religious law as a religious endowment.
- Establishing an endowment in accordance with the Endowments for Charities Ordinance 1924 and its regulations.

Since the establishment of the State of Israel, a number of laws and regulations have been enacted to establish a substantive legal basis for charities, including their encouragement and regulation.

2. ARE INDEPENDENT CHARITABLE ORGANISATIONS COMMON AND SIGNIFICANT IN YOUR JURISDICTION? WHAT IS THE CURRENT SIZE AND SCOPE OF THE SECTOR AND THE MAIN TRENDS?

There are about 38,000 Amutot (*see Question 3, Principal sources of law*) and about 1,000 registered charitable companies.

According to the Central Bureau of Statistics, the total amount of donations (by individuals and corporations) made to non-profit organisations (NPOs) in Israel during 2014 was about NIS20 billion. For the same year, the NPOs expended about NIS132 billion for their respective activities.

The Israeli Center for Third Sector Research has categorised the main activities of NPOs into the following areas:

- Religion.
- Culture and recreation.
- Health and welfare.
- Education and research.
- Philanthropy.
- Community based organisations.
- Housing and development.
- Trade unions.
- Environment.
- Memorial.
- International organisations.

LEGAL FRAMEWORK

3. IS THERE A LEGAL DEFINITION OF A "CHARITY"? WHAT ARE THE PRINCIPAL SOURCES OF LAW AND REGULATIONS RELATING TO CHARITABLE ORGANISATIONS AND ACTIVITIES?

Definition of charity

The promotion of non-profit activities is effected through non-governmental/non-profit organisations (NPOs). Although charity has a long tradition in Jewish culture, the term "charity" has no clear definition under the legislation applicable to NPOs (*see Question 4*). NPOs' objectives are not defined under the applicable laws as "charity" but rather as "public benefit" objectives. However, Israeli tax legislation has recognised charity for tax purposes and offers certain tax benefits for NPOs that are classified as public institutions (*see Question 9*).

Principal sources of law

The principal sources of law depend on the type of NPO:

- **Amuta.** These are non-profit societies/organisations (which are called in Hebrew "Amutot", the plural of Amuta). They are incorporated as legal entities which have a legal personality and are governed by the Amutot Law 1980 (Amutot Law).

- **Charitable company (CC).** These companies are incorporated as legal entities and are governed by the Companies Law 1999 (Companies Law). They are also sometimes referred to as Public Benefit Companies.

- **Charitable fund (CF).** Similar to CCs, these companies are incorporated as legal entities and are governed by the Companies Law. A CF must first be registered as a CC and only if it meets certain additional criteria, can it be registered as a CF.

- **Public endowments.** These are regulated under the Trust Law.

This Q&A largely considers the Amuta and CC, as these are the most common forms.

LEGAL BODIES

4. WHAT ARE THE FORMS OF ORGANISATIONS THAT ARE USED FOR CHARITABLE PURPOSES? WHAT ARE THEIR ADVANTAGES/DISADVANTAGES?

Non-profit organisations (NPOs) are established and operated under the following statutory frameworks:

- **Amuta.** The Amutot Law established a relatively uncomplicated way to create a non-profit legal entity, so the vast majority of NPOs are incorporated as Amutot.

  An Amuta must register with the Registry of Amutot (which is an integral part of the Ministry of Justice). A requirement of incorporation is that the purposes of the Amuta must not be contrary to the interests of the State of Israel, and the main purpose of the Amuta must not be making profit.

  For its incorporation, an Amuta must submit to the Registrar of Amutot, among other things:

  – a list of its purposes;

  – its bye-laws, which could either be the standard bye-laws appearing in the Amutot Law or original bye-laws drafted by the founders.

  The Amuta must not distribute any profits, directly or indirectly, to its members, including its founders. In addition, an Amuta cannot be registered if any of its objects negates the existence or democratic nature of the State of Israel, or if there are reasonable grounds for concluding that the Amuta will be used as cover for illegal activities. The Amutot Law does not specify a list of purposes, so an Amuta's purposes can be any legal not-for-profit purposes that are not aimed for distribution of profits to its members.

- **Charitable company (CC).** A CC must be registered by both the Registrar of Companies and by the Registrar of Endowments (both integral parts of the Ministry of Justice).

  A CC's objectives must be set out in its bye-laws and state one of the following "public purposes", specified in the schedule to the Companies Law (*section 345A, Companies Law*):

  - quality of the environment, protection of the environment of knowledge of nature and of the environment;
  - health or lifesaving;
  - religion, tradition or commemoration;
  - protection of animals and concern for their welfare;
  - human rights;
  - education, vocational training, culture and art;
  - science, research or higher education;
  - sport;
  - immigration, immigrant absorption or settlement;
  - charity or welfare;
  - community welfare, or social or national activity;
  - the rule of law, government or public administration; and
  - the establishment of funds or organisations for the encouragement or support of bodies active for one or more of the purposes listed in the schedule to the Companies Law.

  For a company to be recognised as a CC, its bye-laws must prohibit any distribution of any dividend to the CC's shareholders.

- **Charitable fund.** The Companies Law defines a "Charitable Fund" as charitable company with bye-laws that include the purpose of funding one or more of the following:

  - charitable companies;
  - public endowments registered with the Registrar of Endowments;
  - non-profit associations operating for public purposes;
  - non-profit higher education institutions;
  - health organisations;
  - hospitals;
  - other entities whose purposes are aimed at promoting or funding public activities, and which were so approved by the Registrar of Endowments.

  In addition, the company must have a liquid capital of NIS5 million or more.

  The Companies Law provides for three kinds of CFs:

  - charitable family fund;
  - charitable private management fund;
  - charitable public management fund.

  The material differences between the CFs relate to the ability to control the CF, the number of donors to the CF and the reporting obligations to the Registrar of Endowments.

  The approval of a CC as a CF in accordance with the Companies Law is not automatic and is given only on a company's request to the Registrar of Endowments. Even if a CC fulfils the conditions for becoming a CF, it does not have to become a CF.

Advantages of a CC:

- The Companies Law, under which a CC is incorporated, is a relatively new and sophisticated law addressing all aspects of CCs.
- The possibility to allot shares to the shareholders in different holding rates.
- The possibility to appoint board and audit committee members who are not shareholders.
- The possibility to transfer shares of the CC to another shareholder.

Advantages of an Amuta:

- The possibility to incorporate an NPO for any legal non-profit making purpose.
- The possibility to include in the articles of association that only one member of the amuta can appoint all of its management committee's members.
- No need to file notices about changes in the members of the amuta and easier to manage NPOs with a large number of members.

5. WHAT ARE THE QUALIFICATION REQUIREMENTS/FORMALITIES TO SET UP THESE ORGANISATIONS?

Amuta

For an Amuta to be registered, certain mandatory provisions apply relating to the:

- Founders of the Amuta:
  - there must be at least two founders;
  - the founders must be at least 18 years old;
  - the membership in an Amuta is personal, not transferable and cannot be bequeathed. Additional members must be at least 17 years old.
- Purpose of the Amuta:
  - it must be legal;
  - it cannot be for the distribution of profits to its members;
  - the main purpose cannot be profit making;
  - it cannot be a purpose that denies the existence of Israel or its democratic nature.
- Name of the Amuta:
  - cannot be misleading or abusive;
  - cannot be identical or similar to a name of another corporation that is registered in Israel or which was registered in Israel in the two years that preceded the incorporation of the Amuta, or to the name of another Amuta that has already commenced its incorporation.

Charitable company (CC)

For a charitable company to be registered, the following rules apply:

- **Registering a new company as a CC.** For a new company to be registered as a CC, the company must file a request to the Registrar of Endowment. This request should include various documents, including:
  - general documents that are required to registrar a company under the Companies Law. These documents should include the company's bye-laws, which determine that the company is a CC;
  - a declaration signed by the first members of the company's audit committee, stating their willingness to be appointed as members of the audit committee;

- details regarding the company's founders, including their identification numbers and addresses;
- a breakdown of the assets that will be granted to the company; and
- signed affidavits of the company's shareholders, directors and members of the audit committee, stating that they are aware of the request to register the company as a CC.

- **Registering an existing registered company as a CC.** For a company acting for profitable purposes to be registered as a CC, the company should resolve (shareholder special resolution) to amend the company's bye-laws so that the company's purposes are replaced with at least one of the purposes appearing in the schedule to the Companies Law. In addition, a section prohibiting any distribution of dividends to the shareholders must be added.

The company's amended bye-laws must be approved and registered by the Registrar of Endowments before the company can be registered as a CC. In addition, a company requesting to be registered as a CC must submit the following documents to the Registrar of Endowments:

- an affidavit signed by the majority of the company's directors and its general manager stating the company's bye-laws were amended;
- the amended bye-laws and a copy of the shareholders' signed resolution to amend the bye-laws;
- a declaration signed by the first members of the company's audit committee stating their willingness to be appointed as members of the audit committee;
- signed affidavits by the company's shareholders, directors and members of the audit committee stating that they are aware of the request to register the company as a CC.

ONGOING REGULATORY REQUIREMENTS

6.   WHAT ARE THE MAIN REGULATORY AUTHORITIES FOR CHARITABLE ORGANISATIONS? WHAT ARE THEIR POWERS OF INVESTIGATION/AUDIT/SANCTIONS?

Regulatory authorities

Amutot. These are regulated by the Registrar of Amutot.

Charitable companies (CC). These are regulated by the Registrar of Endowments. Charitable companies must be registered with the Companies Registry (using a single application procedure for registry with both bodies).

Powers

Amuta. The Registrar of Amutot's powers of investigation and supervision includes:

- The authority to demand information from functionaries of the Amuta.
- Entry to various places where the Amuta allegedly operates from.
- Appointment of inspectors from the Ministry of Justice for the purpose of auditing and supervising the Amuta's actions.
- Appointment of external examiners to examine an Amuta's compliance with the provisions of applicable law and the provisions of its articles of association.

The following specific rules apply:

- **External examiners.** External examiners can conduct inspections in relation to a restricted list of matters published by the Registrar of Amutot on the Ministry of Justice's website, in the manner and frequency as directed by the Registrar of Amutot. The matters include:
  - inspection as to whether a certain Amuta is conducted in accordance with the Amutot Law and in accordance with its objectives and articles of association;
  - examination of the Amuta's financial reports and its financial viability.

  In addition, external examiners can demand information from the Amuta and its:
  - members;
  - functionaries except for its internal auditor;
  - employees;
  - other related persons to be determined by the Minister of Justice, regarding the Amuta.

  Further, the Registrar of Amutot can instruct the external inspectors to require information from anyone who had any of these roles during the four years preceding the date of the request. The Amutot Law also regulates the manner in which the external examiner must file a report.

- **Inspectors.** The Registrar of Amutot can conduct an investigation into the activity and conduct of Amutot, including with respect to each Amuta's management committee, office holders and different committees and, importantly, its financial operations. The investigation powers granted to an inspector appointed by the Registrar of Amutot are very wide. The appointed inspector must submit his conclusions to the Registrar of Amutot, which can include a recommendation for the Amuta to be wound up.

- **Documents.** The Registrar of Amutot can require the Amuta to submit various documents. The Amuta must provide a detailed list of reports to the Registrar of Amutot, such as notices of change of address, election or expiration of office of a management committee member, and any legal proceedings brought against the Amuta or against a member of the management committee (*section 38, Amutot Law*).

  The documents submitted to the Registrar of Amutot are available for public inspection on demand, as well as the:
  - findings of the Registrar of Amutot or an inspector appointed by it;
  - the final report of an independent auditor;
  - the final report of an investigation;
  - an application for a liquidation filed by the Registrar of Amutot;
  - any other document held by the Registrar of Amutot regarding the Amuta.

  This is as long as the Registrar of Amutot is not of the view that any document or part of it should be prevented from being accessed by the public.

  Documents relating to pending procedures regarding the investigation, audit or enforcement are only available for public scrutiny at the end of the procedure (*Amutot Law*). In addition, the Registrar of Amutot can limit access to only the conclusions arising from the procedure.

  The Registrar of Amutot can advertise online, itself or through others, the documents that are submitted by the Amuta, as long as the names of those who provided the documents are not published. The Registrar of Amutot can also determine rules regarding online publications. A list of the five highest salaries (without names) is posted on the Registrar of Amutot's website.

- **Guidance.** The Registrar of Amutot can publish information and guidance to an Amuta, including training to assist in managing their affairs in accordance with the provisions applicable to them. In this regard, the Registrar of Amutot published guidelines for proper management of Amutot (Guidelines for Amutot), which include explanations and examples. The Guidelines for Amutot also include instructions for Amutot that wish to obtain a certificate of proper management (*see Question 8*).

- **Name of the Amuta.** The Registrar of Amutot, with the consent of the legal adviser to the government, can unilaterally change the name of an Amuta if the Amuta did not change its name in the manner required by the Registrar of Amutot.

- **Imprisonment.** Members of an Amuta, its employees and the audit committee are subject to a term of three years' imprisonment if the information provided under the Amutot Law is false.

CCs. All reporting duties that apply to Amutot also apply to CCs. CC's are subject to the Guidelines of Amutot. However, a CC must also comply with the additional reporting duties to the Registrar of Endowments, including in relation to (*section 140, Companies Law*):

- Changes in bye-laws.
- Change of the registered office.
- Appointments to and resignations from the board of directors.
- Transfer of shares or the allotment of new shares.

The Companies Law expands and defines the regulatory authority of the Registrar of Endowments and particularly the powers to appoint inspectors. This includes the authority of the Registrar of Endowments to require information from the CC's functionaries or persons related to it, and enter locations where the company operates to get this information. Investigations and supervisions of CCs are conducted by the Registrar of Endowments itself or by inspectors who are nominated from the employees of the Ministry of Justice, to work under the auspices of the Registrar of Endowments.

The rules relating to external examiners, and the publishing of information online, are the same as those applying to Amutot (*see above, Amutot, External examiners*) (but the regulatory authority is the Registrar or Endowments).

The Registrar or Endowments can also (*Companies Law*):

- File a derivative action against the CC.
- Approve changes in the CCs purposes, or its specific position and role during any liquidation process of the CC.

Any amendment to a CC's purposes is subject to the Registrar of Endowments' prior written approval. However, where the proposed amendment gives rise to a significant change to the CC's original purposes, the amendment must also be approved by the District Court. The District Court has discretion in this regard. The District Court examines whether it is right and just to allow the amendments, taking into account the current purposes of the CC, its activities and the obligations assumed by the CC with respect to the proposed amendment. This procedure also applies where an Amuta wishes to change its purposes, except that the authorising body is the Registrar of Amutot.

7.   WHICH BODIES OR PERSONS MANAGE CHARITABLE ORGANISATIONS AND WHAT GENERAL REQUIREMENTS MUST THEY MEET?

Amuta

An Amuta must have the following bodies:

- General meeting of the members.
- Management committee.
- Audit committee (the general meeting can appoint an external auditor or another body approved for this matter by the Registrar, instead of the audit committee).

In addition, an Amuta must appoint an auditor if its yearly turnover exceeds the amount specified by the Amutot Law, after obtaining the audit committee's consent for the appointment. The Amuta's management committee is responsible for the approval of the internal auditor's annual work plan, after the audit committee's review.

General meeting of the members. The general meeting of the members sets the Amuta's policy and its implementation. It usually appoints the members of the management committee and audit committee, and supervises the conduct of these bodies.

Management committee. The management committee manages the Amuta's affairs. It also has residual authority with regard to any management authorities that are not granted, by the Amutot Law or the Amuta's bye-laws, to any other body.

The management committee must have at least two members, to be appointed out of the members of the Amuta. If one of the members is a corporation, it can appoint its representative as a member of the management committee.

The members must act in favour of the Amuta, within the framework of its objects and according to its bye-laws and to the general meeting's resolutions.

The Amutot Law itself does not place any duty of care, loyalty or fiduciary duty on the management committee's members, and there are no provisions regarding insurance or compensation. However, in a number of judicial decisions, the Israeli courts have stated that the members of an Amuta's management committee are subject to duties equivalent to those that exist with regard to the board of directors of regular companies. These include fiduciary duties, including:

- Refraining from any activity involving a conflict of interest between the member's position within the Amuta and another position held by the officer or their personal affairs.
- Disclosing to the company any information relating to the company's affairs that a member becomes aware of due to his position in the company.
- A duty of care.

The Amutot regulations (remuneration to a chairperson, to a member of the management committee and to a member of the audit committee), issued by the Minister of Justice, set out the fees that an Amuta can pay to the members of its management committee, which are determined according to the size and turnover of the Amuta. However, since these fees are relatively low, they cannot be considered as normal or proper payments.

Audit committee. The Amuta's audit body, which is a mandatory body elected by the general meeting of the members of the Amuta, is either an audit committee consisting of members of the Amuta or an external auditor.

The following rules apply:

- There must be at least two members.
- The members must also be members of the Amuta.
- A member of the Amuta cannot be a member of both the management committee and audit committee.
- A member can receive payment or remuneration according to the regulations set by the Minister of Justice.

The roles of the audit committee or the audit body are to:

- Examine the order of the Amuta's operations and the conduct of its bodies, including the suitability of the conduct in relation to the Amuta's objects.
- Examine whether the implementation of the Amuta's objects are performed in an effective and economical way.
- Monitor the execution of the general meeting's and management committee's resolutions.
- Recommend possible solutions to the management committee to correct defects in the Amuta's conduct.
- Examine the Amuta's financial affairs.
- Examine the Amuta's conduct in general.
- Examine the Amuta's internal audit system and the functioning of the internal auditor, and the internal auditor's work plan, before the management committee approves it. If required, the audit committee should propose changes to the work plan.
- Examine the scope of work of the Amuta's accountant, including their remuneration, and make recommendations to the body that determines their remuneration, in accordance with the Amutot Law.
- Determine the arrangements regarding the treatment of complaints raised by the Amuta's employees relating to:
  - defects in the management of the Amuta's affairs;
  - protective measures to be provided to employees who have raised complaints against the Amuta.
- Bring its conclusions to the general meeting and the management committee.

The audit committee can invite an employee of the Amuta to participate in the discussions. However, the employee cannot be present at the time of the decision making. The audit committee can invite the Amuta's secretary and/or its legal adviser to be present during deliberations and decision making. In addition, the Amuta's internal auditor is invited to attend meetings of the audit committee and can convene the audit committee if necessary. The Amuta's accountant will be invited to attend meetings of the audit committee to discuss issues regarding the Amuta's financial reports.

Charitable companies (CCs)

A CC's management is similar to the management of any company acting for profitable purposes. A CC has a:

- General meeting of the company's shareholders as the decision-making body.
- Board of directors.
- A general manager as its management body.

In addition, a CC's general meeting must appoint an audit committee, whose members cannot at the same time act as officers of the company.

The roles of the audit committee of a CC are identical to those of an Amuta (*see above, Amuta*), with certain additions such as the duty to determine whether to approve specific transactions with related and interested parties. Among other things, an agreement with an officer who is not a director or a member of the audit committee regarding their terms of service and employment requires the approval of both the audit committee and the board of directors. In addition, the audit committee can decide on whether these transactions are significant or in the ordinary course of business. In addition, the audit committee must report on its meetings to the internal auditor and its accountants.

A CC's board of directors must appoint an internal auditor if its yearly turnover exceeds NIS10 million.

CC's management bodies are subject to a number of other limitations and requirements:

- The shareholders and board members are subject to the duties that exist with regard to regular companies. For directors, this includes the duty of care and a fiduciary duty. This includes refraining from any activity involving a conflict of interest between the officer's position within the company and another position held by the officer or related to his personal affairs. The rights, obligations and liabilities of the members of the audit committee are the same as of the members of the board. For shareholders, these include the duty to act in good faith and in the customary manner, and to refrain from any abuse of power in the company.

- Any transaction of a CC is subject to the sections of the Companies Law (Chapter Five) which apply to public companies, if a conflict could arise and if the transaction is:

  - with a director or member of the audit committee, or with a corporation controlled by them;

  - an exceptional transaction with a director's relative, an audit committee member's relative, the shareholder of the company or their relative, and the CC's entrepreneur or their relative.

In this regard, the approval of the audit committee, the board of directors and the general meeting of shareholders is required. In addition, the court must approve the transaction, after it has given the registrar of endowments an opportunity to comment. The court can approve the transaction only after it is satisfied that, in the circumstances of the case, it is just and proper to do so (*section 354L(a), Companies Law*).

The application of these provisions of the Companies Law results in CCs being subject to a far higher level of control and supervision than private companies.

- Regulations published by the Ministry of Justice determine a maximum rate for the benefits that a director or a member of a CC is entitled to receive.

8. WHAT ARE THE ACCOUNTING/FINANCIAL REPORTING REQUIREMENTS?

Amuta

An Amuta must maintain books of account and an accounting system that includes, as a minimum:

- A receipts and expenditures book.
- An external documentation file.

In addition, once a year, the management committee must prepare a balance sheet and a report on income and expenses (financial reports), together with an annual narrative report specifying the conduct of the Amuta for the year of the report. The financial report must be provided to the Amuta's audit committee (or the external auditor or other body approved for this matter by the registrar) and subsequently approved by the general meeting of the members of the Amuta.

Where an Amuta's turnover exceeds NIS300,000, it must specify in its financial reports any donation exceeding NIS20,000 made to the Amuta by a foreign state or governmental body of a foreign state. Members of an Amuta, its employees and the audit body are subject to three years' imprisonment if the information provided is false.

Every Amuta that receives any funding from the State of Israel must obtain a certificate of proper management, which must be renewed on an annual basis. An Amuta that is applying for a certificate of proper management from the Registrar of Amutot, must also report in its financial reports the identity of any donor whose donations to the Amuta exceed NIS20,000 in a given year. The purpose of the certificate of proper management is to ensure that the public funds provided to Amutot, either through state grants or by donations from the public, both:

• Are applied in accordance with proper management procedures.

• Will be used to promote the purposes for which they were established.

To obtain such a certificate, the Amuta must establish that for a consecutive period of two years it has acted in accordance with applicable law, including complying with its reporting obligations to the registrar.

Further, the application by an Amuta to be granted a certificate of proper management should include the following:

• The most recent financial report.

• A description of the Amuta's activities, its income, its financial requirements, its use of money received by the Amuta, the number of employees and volunteers working for the Amuta, and so on.

• Minutes of the general meeting that approved the annual and the narrative reports.

• A recommendation issued by the audit committee regarding the financial report.

• A list of the five top salaries in the Amuta.

Charitable companies (CCs)

All accounting/financial reporting duties that apply to Amutot also apply to CCs (*see above, Amuta*). However, unlike an Amuta, a CC must submit its accounting reports to the Registrar of Endowments rather than the Registrar of Amutot.

The financial report and the narrative report must be approved by the general meeting of the CC's shareholders and be filed with the Registrar of Endowments no later than 30 June of the year after the year of the report.

As with an Amuta, a CC that receives any funding from the State of Israel must obtain a certificate of proper management. A CC that is applying for a certificate of proper management from the Registrar of Endowments must also report in its financial statements the identity of any donor whose donations to the CC exceeded NIS20,000 in a given year.

Disclosure duties

On 12 July 2016 the Disclosure Duty for Those Supported by a Foreign State Entity Law (Amendment) 2016 (Disclosure Law) was approved by the Israeli parliament. It will enter into force on 1 January 2017 and will apply to donations received as of that date.

The Disclosure Law (unofficially, the Transparency Law) includes amendments to three laws: the Amutot Law, the Companies Law and the Disclosure Duty regarding Those Supported by a Foreign State Entity Law 2011.

The Disclosure Law imposes increased reporting and disclosure duties on NPOs the main funding of which is derived from foreign state entities.

The Amutot Law defines the term "foreign state entity" in a relatively broad definition, to mean:

- A foreign country, including union, organisation or a group of foreign countries (foreign union).
- An organ, authority or an agency of a foreign country or a foreign union.
- A foreign local or district authority, governmental authority of a foreign country or of a country which is a member of an alliance of countries in a foreign country (foreign body).
- Union, organisation or a group of foreign bodies.
- The Palestinian Authority as defined under Israeli law.
- A statutory corporation incorporated under a law of a foreign country or where the body holds more than one-half of a certain means of control in a corporation, or in the event the body appointed a corporation to act on its behalf.
- Where a foreign company's annual turnover during the last fiscal year for which it had to file financial statements was mainly originated from any of the bodies listed above.

The Disclosure Law determines that an NPO that benefits from funding by foreign state entities must report that funding in their annual report.

The NPO must also mention in its annual report that the names of the foreign state entities from which they have received the donations are listed on the Registrar's website. In addition, NPO's must indicate this funding in:

- Publications aimed at and available to the public in billboards, television, press or the internet and which were intended for the promotion of their goals.
- Their applications by mail and e-mail to public workers and elected public officials.
- The reports they draft and distribute to the public.

The Disclosure Law also determines that if an NPO operates a website it must publish on that website the fact that its main funding derives from foreign state entities.

An NPO that does not comply with any reporting duty is subject to a financial penalty. A CC that does not comply with reporting duties may face additional financial sanctions.

Lastly, a representative of a NPO mainly funded by a foreign state entity, which actively participates in a meeting of a parliament committee, must disclose its funding to the committee's chairman.

TAX

HOW ARE CHARITIES TAXED, AND WHAT (IF ANY) ARE THE PRINCIPAL EXEMPTIONS AND/OR RELIEFS FROM TAXATION THAT THEY ENJOY?

Tax on income

Non-profit organisations' (NPOs') income is tax exempt if the NPO meets the definition of a "public institution" and unless the income is categorised as business income (*section 9(2), Income Tax Ordinance [New Version] 1961 (Income Tax Ordinance)*). For an NPO to be recognised as a public institution, it must have two characteristics:

- It must have at least seven shareholders or members, of whom a majority are not related to one another.
- It must act for a public purpose. A purpose concerning religion, culture, education, science, health, welfare or sport, and any other purpose approved by the Minister of Finance, is a public purpose (*Income Tax Ordinance*).

The exemption is not absolute and depends on the classification of the public institution's income. The following income does not qualify for this exemption:

- Income obtained from a business.
- Income obtained from a dividend or interest.
- Income obtained from a body of persons controlled by the public institution, which engages in a business.

The NPO claims the exemption in its tax returns and no pre-clearance is necessary from the government.

Tax on capital gains

A NPO which is a recognised public institution is tax exempt, including on its capital gains when selling its assets (other than real estate). An exemption in respect of capital gains from land appreciation requires an approval (*section 61(b), Land Appreciation Tax Law 5723-196*). In addition, various conditions apply. For example, the subject property must have been owned by the NPO for at least five years before the sale.

Tax on property used by the organisation

NPOs can obtain an exemption on local authority taxes, known as Arnona. However, this exemption is not automatic and requires an application by the NPO to the local municipality.

Value added tax (VAT)

NPOs are exempt from VAT. However, NPOs are generally not eligible to obtain any refund on VAT output tax. Where a NPO purchases goods or services, it cannot receive any refund on VAT paid.

Other

NPOs are subject to a special "wage tax" on the total gross amount paid to its employees, currently at a rate of 7.5%.

10.   WHAT, IF ANY, ARE THE TAXATION BENEFITS FOR DONORS TO CHARITIES?

A person who makes a donation to an NPO is eligible to receive a tax credit under section 46 of the Income Tax Ordinance, provided that the following conditions are complied with:

- The NPO is qualified as a "public institution", the purposes of which include the "public purposes" defined in section 9(2) of the Income Tax Ordinance.
- The Minister of Finance has approved the NPO as a public institution.
- The Finance Committee of The Knesset has confirmed the Minister of Finance's approval.

The tax credit is equal to 35% of the donation. However, in any tax year the credit granted must not exceed the lower of 30% of the assessee's chargeable income in that particular year or NIS9,212,000.

DISADVANTAGES

11.   WHAT ARE THE MAIN DISADVANTAGES OF CHARITABLE STATUS?

Non-profit organisations (NPOs) are strictly regulated under Israeli law, including in relation to filing, reporting and other obligations. In a number of cases, these obligations exceed the statutory obligations imposed on private companies. For example, where a charitable company (CC) or Amuta intends to change its purpose or articles, the approval of the regulatory body (that is, the Registrar of Endowments or Registrar of Amutot) and in certain circumstances the court is required. Further, with regard to transactions that require special approval, CCs are subject to the same somewhat onerous provisions that apply to public companies.

OVERSEAS CHARITIES

12.   IS IT POSSIBLE TO OPERATE AN OVERSEAS CHARITY IN YOUR JURISDICTION? WHAT ARE THE REGISTRATION FORMALITIES? HOW (IF AT ALL) ARE OVERSEAS CHARITIES TREATED DIFFERENTLY IN YOUR JURISDICTION FROM CHARITIES SET UP UNDER DOMESTIC LAW?

An overseas charitable entity can establish a non-profit making activity in Israel in one of two ways:

- Registering the overseas charitable entity as a foreign non-profit organisation in Israel. This enables the entity to operate directly in Israel.
- Incorporating a non-profit organisation in Israel as a related party, such that the overseas charitable entity is a shareholder (holding less than 50%), or member or board member of the Israeli entity (that is, as an Amuta or as a charitable company (CC)).

A foreign company operating in Israel, that complies with the provisions of section 345GG(a) of the Companies Law (public purposes and prohibition on distribution of dividends to the shareholders) must register as a CC (*section 345, Companies Law*).

The Minister of Justice can exempt foreign companies from the application of the relevant provisions of the Companies Law. In this regard, the Ministry of Justice has discretion and will consider, among other things, the:

- Specific circumstances of each case.
- Laws of the company's place of incorporation or the provisions of the foreign law that apply to its activity in Israel as a foreign CC.
- Application of other laws in Israel.
- Source of the company's assets.

Therefore, if a foreign charitable entity intends to operate directly in Israel, the entity must be registered in Israel as a CC. In this regard, the entity will be exempt from income tax in Israel solely on its Israel-sourced income, provided that the conditions set out in section 9(2) of the Income Tax Ordinance are complied with:

- The CC must have at least seven shareholders of whom a majority must not be related to one another.
- The entity must act for a public purpose according to the definition in the Income Tax Ordinance (see Question 9).

The United States-Israel Tax Treaty provides that contributions by a US citizen or resident to an Israeli public charity or private foundation are deductible under US law, if both the:

- Israeli charity would qualify as a public charity under US law.
- Contributions otherwise would be deductible under US law.

The treaty limits the deductions to:

- 25% of an individual US donor's Israel-source gross income.
- 25% of a corporate US donor's Israel-source taxable income.

A reciprocal rule applies to Israeli donors who contribute to US public charities or private foundations. However, the treaty does not provide that a charitable organisation that is tax exempt in one country is tax exempt in the other country.

13. IS IT POSSIBLE TO REGISTER A DOMESTIC CHARITY ABROAD, AND HAS YOUR JURISDICTION ENTERED INTO ANY INTERNATIONAL AGREEMENTS OR TREATIES IN THIS AREA?

Israel has not entered into any specific international agreements or treaties in this area. However, Israeli law does not prevent an Israeli charity from registering abroad if it operates abroad.

REFORM

14. ARE THERE ANY PROPOSALS FOR REFORM IN THE AREA OF CHARITY LAW?

During 2014 the Ministry of Justice published a document detailing the principles for enactment of a new Amutot Law (Memorandum of Law). The new Amutot Law will address certain gaps in the current Amutot Law, such as the principal-agent problem, classification of an Amutot according to their sources of financing, and the nature of an amutot's activities. However, as the Israeli legislator has recently comprehensively amended both the Amutot Law and the Companies Law (with respect to CC's), it is unclear if and when the Israeli legislator will publish an official bill further to the Memorandum of Law.

ONLINE RESOURCES

ISRAELI CORPORATIONS AUTHORITY

W www.justice.gov.il/Units/RasutHataagidim/units/RashamAmutot/Pages/Default.aspx

Description. This website is the official website of the Israeli Corporations Authority, which is the entity in charge of the registration, supervision, enforcement and control over all of the corporations in Israel, and encompasses the business sector as well as the non-profit sector, and maintained by it. The information is up-to-date and provided in Hebrew. The website includes mainly technical information about the various corporations regulated by the Registrar of Endowments and by the Registrar of Amutot. The information available about CCs is: the CC's name and registration number, shareholders, board members, share capital and registered office, and so on. The information available about Amtot is far less detailed and only includes the name and registration number, registered address and whether the Amuta was provided with a certificate of proper management.

GUIDESTAR ISRAEL

W www.guidestar.org.il/en/node/144114

Description. The GuideStar Israel website provides information available on existing NPOs operating in Israel. It features official information, as listed in the applicable Registrar in the Ministry of Justice's databases for all NPOs in Israel, and is supplemented by additional, more detailed and substantive information supplied by the NPOs themselves, such as financial statements and narrative reports. The website does not provide regulatory information.

ITALY

Francesco Facchini, Giacomo Ficai and Alessia Vignudelli,
FACCHINI ROSSI & SOCI

OVERVIEW AND MAIN TRENDS

1. WHAT IS THE HISTORICAL BACKGROUND TO CHARITY LAW AND CHARITABLE ORGANISATIONS IN YOUR JURISDICTION?

The Italian legal framework does not provide a clear definition of charity. In recent years the term "third sector" has been adopted to identify, among others, volunteering, social assistance and charitable purposes. Entities that actively carry on such charitable activities include non-governmental and non-profit-making organisations or associations and foundations.

Italian law allows anyone the opportunity to form an association or a foundation, and Article 18 of the Constitution protects this right. Associations and foundations are the most common legal form for charitable organisations and are regulated by the Civil Code.

In the 1990s, specific provisions were introduced to regulate and support fundraising activities for non-profit purposes, in particular through several tax reliefs. In this respect, one of the most important amendments was the introduction in 1997 of the status of ONLUS (*Organizzazione non lucrativa di utilità sociale*), which allows non-profit organisations pursuing social purposes to benefit from a variety of tax exemptions.

2. ARE INDEPENDENT CHARITABLE ORGANISATIONS COMMON AND SIGNIFICANT IN YOUR JURISDICTION? WHAT IS THE CURRENT SIZE AND SCOPE OF THE SECTOR AND THE MAIN TRENDS?

Official data on the size and scope of charitable organisations and trends in the third sector are in the national census of 2011.

From 2001 to 2011, the number of non-profit institutions increased by 30%, with related employment growth.

The third sector has more than 300,000 non-profit institutions, mainly incorporated as an association. Unrecognised associations are around 200,000, while recognised ones are about 68,000 (*see Question 4*). Even though other legal forms have become more common (especially foundations and social co-operatives), associations are still the main legal form adopted by charitable organisations, particularly non-profit institutions. Although associations are active in a number of fields, most workers are employed by entities carrying out activities related to social and healthcare assistance and civil protection.

The combined income of the Italian third sector exceeds EUR60 billion per year, of which around 65% is from private funding (33% of this is from voluntary donations and/or contributions by entities' members and by private individuals). In 2011, associations and foundations collected over 65% of the total income, confirming the key role played by such organisations in the third sector (source: *http://censimentoindustriaeservizi.istat.it*).

LEGAL FRAMEWORK

3.   IS THERE A LEGAL DEFINITION OF A "CHARITY"? WHAT ARE THE PRINCIPAL SOURCES OF LAW AND REGULATIONS RELATING TO CHARITABLE ORGANISATIONS AND ACTIVITIES?

Definition of charity

Italian law does not provide a legal definition of charity, except for the concept of ONLUS (*see Question 1*), which relates to a special tax regime.

Article 1 of Law No. 106 of 6 June 2016 (Third Sector Reform Law) defines the third sector as an ensemble of private non-profit entities pursuing civic, social or solidarity purposes.

Principal sources of law

The legal and regulatory framework for charitable organisations includes:

- Civil Code (*Book I, Title II, Chapter I and II*). Articles 12 to 38 cover associations and foundations.
- Presidential Decree no. 361 of 10 February 2000, which regulates procedures concerning recognition by the state of private legal entities.
- Presidential Decree no. 917 of 22 December 1986 (Tax Code), for income tax treatment.
- Article 6 of Decree no. 601 of 29 September 1973, which provides a specific corporate tax regime for non-profit entities with legal personality.
- Presidential Decree no. 633 of 26 October 1972, for VAT purposes (VAT Decree).
- Legislative Decree no. 460 of 4 December 1997, introducing a specific tax regime applicable to ONLUS (ONLUS Decree).
- Law no. 106 of 6 June 2016 (Third Sector Reform Law).

LEGAL BODIES

4.   WHAT ARE THE FORMS OF ORGANISATIONS THAT ARE USED FOR CHARITABLE PURPOSES? WHAT ARE THEIR ADVANTAGES/DISADVANTAGES?

Italian law provides many alternative legal forms that can be used for charitable aims. The ONLUS Decree includes most of these in the list of entities that can acquire ONLUS status and qualify for tax benefits.

The most common legal forms used for charitable purposes are associations and foundations (other common forms include committees, co-operatives and social enterprises).

Associations

An association is a collective entity formed by at least two associated persons with common defined non-profit purposes, usually altruistic and/or ideal. Associations are essentially person based non-profit organisations (a fundamental requirement is a plurality of members).

The Civil Code distinguishes the following two categories of associations (both can acquire ONLUS status).

Association with legal personality (recognised association (*associazione riconosciuta*)). This is an association recognised by a competent public authority, and registered as a legal entity in the legal persons register kept by the public authority (the local representative of the national government (*prefettura*) or the regional government). The main advantages are:

- As a legal entity, it is autonomous from its members, and its assets are separate from the personal assets of its members and directors. Members are only liable for the association's obligations up to their membership fee and any additional contributions.
- It can use special benefits provided by law, such as the ability to call up contributions from public institutions.
- It can be recorded in the cadastre (public real estate registry) as owner of real estate assets.
- It can receive inheritances and gifts.

The main disadvantages are:

- The incorporation of a recognised association requires a public notary deed and the procedure for legal recognition can be complex.
- It must comply with specific corporate governance requirements (*see Questions 5* and *7*), transformation and dissolution of the entity, and allocation of residual assets.
- Capital must be allocated to the association, to secure its solvency towards third parties. However, a minimum amount of capital is not specified.

Association without legal personality (unrecognised association (*associazione non riconosciuta*)). This is not recognised by a public authority, so it is not a legal entity. The main advantages are:

- Incorporation is not subject to specific formalities, although a specific form is required to receive particular types of property (for example, real estate) as a contribution.
- Corporate governance is freely agreed among the members, without specific requirements and limitations, except for those relating to specific assets or required for ONLUS status.

The main disadvantages are:

- Not being a legal entity, an unrecognised association and its members or directors do not have full separation of assets or limited liability. However, there is a partial financial separation (imperfect financial autonomy), according to which the members are only responsible if the association's assets cannot satisfy all its liabilities.
- Members cannot request division of the association's fund. In case of termination or exclusion of a member, it cannot claim repayment of membership fees and contributions.
- To acquire ONLUS status, its incorporation deed must be registered with the Tax Authority.

Foundations

A foundation is an entity established by one or more parties (individuals and/or entities) to allocate specific assets (for example, money or property) for a defined purpose, that is, generally altruistic and/or ideal. Foundations are essentially property based non-profit organisations (the fundamental requirement is represented by assets dedicated to specific purposes). The main advantages are:

- A foundation is a legal entity, benefiting from full financial autonomy.
- It can be set up by a will.
- A foundation can qualify as an ONLUS.

The main disadvantages are:

- A foundation must be incorporated by public deed and must apply for legal recognition.
- Once it obtains recognition or at least has started activity, it cannot be revoked by the founder or by the founder's heirs.
- It is generally under the control of a public authority.
- There are special requirements and limitations for administration and representation of the foundation.

Specific provisions regulate dissolution of the foundation, in particular liquidation of its assets.

Following the privatisation of state-owned banks (*Decree Law No. 153/1999*) in relation to foundations, participations in these banks were transferred to new institutions (banking foundations (*Fondazioni bancarie*)). They have the following characteristics:

- Private non-profit organisations to pursue social utility objectives and foster economic development.
- They must invest their profits in non-profit activities, such as scientific research, education, fine arts, conservation and promotion of cultural works and activities, and the environment, health and social care for needy members of society.
- They can only carry out entrepreneurial activities if these are directly ancillary to the foundation's social aims.

This reform has resulted in several grant-making foundations in Italy, with a corporate purpose to support and fund non-profit initiatives. Banking foundations cannot qualify as ONLUS.

Other forms

ONLUSis not a different legal form, but a status established by the ONLUS Decree available to different legal forms (*see Question 5*). It has fiscal benefits, subject to certain conditions.

Italian contractual law does not provide for a specific definition of a trust. However, since Italy has signed the Hague Convention on the Recognition of Trusts 1985 (Hague Trusts Convention), a trust constituted according to foreign law can be recognised in Italy if it meets the conditions in Article 2 of the Hague Trusts Convention. In particular:

- Assets secured in the trust are distinct and separate from the assets of the settlor, the trustee and the beneficiary.
- Assets secured in the trust are managed by the trustee.
- The trustee must manage and dispose of the trust's assets in accordance with the instructions provided by the trust deed, and in compliance with the law.
- The trustee is accountable for the management of the trust.

If the above conditions are satisfied, a trust can also be regarded as:

- An autonomous taxable person for corporate income tax purposes (*Article 73, Tax Code*).
- An ONLUS, provided that conditions set by the ONLUS Decree are met (*see Italian Tax Authority Circular Letter no. 38, 2011*).

5.   WHAT ARE THE QUALIFICATION REQUIREMENTS/FORMALITIES TO SET UP THESE ORGANISATIONS?

Recognised associations

Establishing a recognised association requires a formal procedure and specific documents, in particular:

- The incorporation deed must be a public deed, signed in the presence of a notary or a public official.
- The association's bye-laws, also prepared as a public deed, contain rules to regulate the association, and must be registered with the Tax Authority.

The notarial deed of incorporation must contain the following:

- Name of the entity and its address.
- Purpose of the entity.
- The entity's assets.
- Internal rules of organisation.
- Rights and obligations of the members and conditions for admittance (and minimum requirements to be a member of the association, even if provisions that prohibit new members are not allowed).

A request for recognition of the legal personality of the association, together with the required documentation, must be submitted to the competent public authority. This can be the local representative of the national government (*prefettura*) or the regional government, depending on the geographical scope of the activities.

Foundations

Establishing a foundation requires the following documents:

- The foundation deed, that is, a unilateral deed containing the will of the founder.
- The endowment act, which disposes assets for allocation to the foundation. This is also a unilateral deed.
- The foundation's bye-laws, which must be prepared as a public deed. It contains the rules that will regulate the foundation, and must be registered with the Tax Authority.

The notarial deed of foundation must include the same information as that for an association, except that it must include rules for payment of returns on the assets instead of minimum requirements to be a member. A request for recognition of the legal personality of the foundation is also required (*see above, Recognised associations*).

ONLUS

To qualify as an ONLUS, an entity must be registered and obtain official authorisation from the Ministry of Finance (*Article 11, ONLUS Decree*). Article 10 of the ONLUS Decree provides that the incorporation deed and bye-laws of the entity must be drawn up as a public deed or equivalent (private notarised or registered deed) and contain the following:

- Exclusive purpose of social solidarity.
- Prohibition on carrying out activities different from those in the bye-laws, except for activities directly linked to previous ones.

- Prohibition on distributing, even indirectly, to members and third parties any profit, management surplus, funds, reserves or capital.
- Requirement to use any profit or management surplus only for institutional or related activities.
- In case of dissolution, assignment of residual assets to another ONLUS.
- Obligation to draw up annual balance sheets or annual financial statements.
- Membership without time limits and with the right to vote.
- Obligation to insert the term non-profit organisation of social utility or ONLUS in the name and in any communication addressed to the public.

The requirement to pursue a non-profit purpose of social solidarity is met if the entity performs one or more of the following activities (presumed solidarity activity):

- Social assistance and social healthcare.
- Charity.
- Protection and promotion of historic and art property.
- Protection and promotion of nature and environment.
- Protection of culture and art (to the extent public funds are used).
- Scientific research of particular social interest conducted by foundations, universities or research centres.

An ONLUS cannot distribute, even indirectly, profits and surpluses, as well as funds or capital during its whole life. An exception is for indirect charity, when an ONLUS transfers money to another non-profit entity that operates in one of the above sectors, and the transferred funds are used solely for specific social utility projects (*Article 10(2-bis), ONLUS Decree*).

ONGOING REGULATORY REQUIREMENTS

6. WHAT ARE THE MAIN REGULATORY AUTHORITIES FOR CHARITABLE ORGANISATIONS? WHAT ARE THEIR POWERS OF INVESTIGATION/AUDIT/SANCTIONS?

Regulatory authorities and powers

Powers and duties of the now abolished Agency for the Third Sector are exercised by the Ministry of Welfare.

Under the Civil Code, the competent public authority (local representative of the national government (*prefettura*) or the regional government) manages recognition of associations and foundations (*see Question 5*) and monitors that, among others, decisions taken by:

- The association's assembly comply with public order or morality.
- Directors of foundations do not diverge from the foundation's purpose and comply with the law.

See box, *The regulatory authorities*.

7. WHICH BODIES OR PERSONS MANAGE CHARITABLE ORGANISATIONS AND WHAT GENERAL REQUIREMENTS MUST THEY MEET?

Associations

The organisational structure of an association can vary, depending on the scope, size and kind of activity, but there must be at least the following two corporate bodies:

- **Members' meeting.** All members are entitled to attend it and vote. The members' meeting is the deliberative body and fundamental to the life of a recognised association. Under the Civil Code, resolutions are adopted by a majority of the members (each member has one vote, irrespective of membership fees paid). Qualified majorities are required to adopt resolutions on specific subjects (for example, amendment of the incorporation deed or dissolution of the association).
- **Directors.** The directors are the executive body of the association (managing the association is exclusively the task of the directors). Only individuals can be appointed as directors. Non-member individuals can also be appointed as directors. The directors are responsible to the association for their actions.

The incorporation deed can set up additional bodies, for example a board of auditors, an executive committee or a board of arbitrators.

The corporate structure of unrecognised associations is not expressively regulated by the Civil Code, but the provisions for recognised associations usually apply. Directors and, in general, people acting on behalf of the association, are responsible for liabilities incurred by the association.

Foundations

The administrative body of a foundation can be a sole director or a group of directors, and it can be appointed in various ways. The appointment of the administrative body can be decided directly by the founder in the foundation deed, or delegated to third parties. The directors can be appointed for life or a fixed period. Directors are responsible for managing the foundation's assets and pursuing its purposes.

8. WHAT ARE THE ACCOUNTING/FINANCIAL REPORTING REQUIREMENTS?

The Civil Code requires recognised associations to prepare approved annual financial statements. Under the ONLUS Decree, an ONLUS must draw up annual financial statements.

In 2009 the ONLUS Agency issued specific guidelines for annual reporting by non-profit organisations, under which non-profit organisations must provide the following:

- A balance sheet with assets, liabilities and equity.
- A statement on income and expenses for the period, divided by function (*Rendiconto di gestione*).
- Explanatory notes with clarification of specific items.
- Mission report, describing objectives and projects necessary for the pursuit of institutional objectives, and the degree of achievement.

In 2011, the Italian Accounting Board (OIC), together with the now abolished Agency for the Third Sector, issued Accounting Standard no. 1 for non-profit entities. This outlines a set of general rules and evaluation criteria for the preparation of non-profit entity financial statements.

Tax accounting obligations are imposed by the Income Tax Law regulations and VAT Decree for non-commercial entities (*see Question 9*) that also carry on business activities. Such entities must keep, among others:

- Journal book.
- Inventory book.
- VAT registers.

Non-profit organisations that carry out the public collection of funds must also draw up within four months of the end of the financial year a separate report, which clearly shows, possibly through an explanatory report, revenue and expenditure relating to each celebration, anniversary or campaign performed.

TAX

9.   HOW ARE CHARITIES TAXED, AND WHAT (IF ANY) ARE THE PRINCIPAL EXEMPTIONS AND/OR RELIEFS FROM TAXATION THAT THEY ENJOY?

Income tax

A charitable entity is subject, in principle, to corporate income tax (IRES) at a rate of 27.5% on its income. Determination of the tax base depends on the entity and whether it is commercial or non-commercial.

Commercial entities are subject to the same regime for corporations. All income from activities performed by the entity is business income, regardless of the source.

Non-commercial entities follow the same principles applicable to individuals. Their income falls into the following categories (each with specific rules to calculate the tax base):

- Property income (for example, rent from immovable properties).
- Capital income (for example, interest and dividends).
- Business income.
- Miscellaneous income (for example, capital gains on the disposal of shares or real estate).

Non-commercial entities can also carry out commercial activity that receives business income (usually connected to its institutional purposes, and sometimes necessary to obtain financial resources to carry out its statutory aim). Non-commercial entities must keep separate accounts for its commercial activities.

Costs related to goods and services used for non-commercial activities can be tax deductible (for an amount based on the ratio between the amount of revenue from the commercial activity and the total amount of revenue it receives).

Proceeds from core activities carried out in accordance with the official purpose of the entity (for example, membership fees, donations received, fundraising from occasional public collections and public contributions) are not subject to corporate income tax (*Article 148, Tax Code*).

In general, financial income (for example, interest and capital gains) is subject to final withholding tax. Starting from fiscal year 2015, dividends received by non-commercial entities are exempt, for a portion equal to 22.26% of the amount received.

Under Article 6 of Presidential Decree no. 601/1973, entities involved in specific activities (for example, social assistance, charity, instruction, and cultural) benefit from a reduction by half of corporate income tax due.

Under Article 73 of the Tax Code, despite the legal form of incorporation:

- A commercial entity is an entity whose sole or main purpose is to perform commercial activity (the activities in Article 2195 of the Civil Code, that is, industrial production of goods and services, intermediary activities in the movement of goods, transport activity, banking or insurance and activities auxiliary to them).
- A non-commercial entity is an entity, either public or private, whose sole or main purpose is not a commercial activity.

To classify an entity as commercial or non-commercial, reference should be made to the sole or main purpose in the incorporation deed or bye-laws of the entity (if a public deed or private deed notarised or registered) or, in the absence of such documents, to the activities essential for realising the main scope of the entity and which are effectively performed.

An entity can lose the status of non-commercial entity if it effectively carries out mainly commercial activity for an entire tax period, regardless of any incorporation deed/bye-laws provisions.

Both commercial and non-profit entities can be subject to IRAP (regional tax), at a rate generally equal to 3.9% (but only on realised business income).

ONLUS

A special tax system is provided for an ONLUS. An ONLUS can only carry out institutional activities, except for those directly related to statutory purposes (collateral activities) (*see Question 5*).

Article 150 of the Tax Code provides that revenue from collateral activities by an ONLUS is not taxed. An ONLUS is only taxed on property income, capital income and miscellaneous income (*see above, Income tax*).

To benefit from the above exemption:

- The institutional activities of the ONLUS must prevail over its collateral activities.
- Income from collateral activities must be less than two-thirds of the total amount of the costs incurred in the relevant period.

An ONLUS is subject in principle to regional tax, though some regions have exemptions.

Tax on capital gains

Capital gains from the disposal of assets are subject, in principle, to corporate income tax (*see above, Income tax*).

Tax on property used by the organisation

Income from immovable property is generally subject to income tax, on its cadastral value, by applying specific provisions under the cadastral law.

Immovable properties are also in principle subject to municipal tax (*Imposta Municipale Propria (IMU)*). However, immovable properties owned by non-profit entities which are used exclusively for the entity's institutional activities are exempt from IMU.

Value added tax (VAT)

In principle, institutional activities by non-commercial entities (including charities and non-profit organisations) are outside the scope of VAT, provided that the entities do not carry on business activity as their main or exclusive object. However, any business activity exercised secondarily by non-commercial entities is subject to VAT.

There is a specific anti-avoidance rule for the internal activity of a non-commercial entity towards its members/associates. Sales of goods or provision of services to members/associates are deemed to be commercial (and therefore subject to VAT) if the activities are paid for through specific proceeds or an incremental contribution (in addition to the ordinary membership fee).

Input VAT incurred by non-commercial entities can be deducted if a business activity is performed, and the input VAT relates to purchases directly attributable to the business activity. The activities must also be separately accounted for from the institutional activity. If a particular good or service is used for both commercial and institutional activity, input VAT is deductible for the part attributable to the commercial activity.

The VAT Decree provides for special relief for an ONLUS.

Also, advertising services rendered to all non-profit organisations is not subject to VAT.

Other

In principle, transfers of assets due to death or donation (or other transfers for no consideration) are subject to inheritance or gift tax, paid by the beneficiary or recipient.

Transfers by death or donation in favour of recognised foundations or associations, with an exclusive purpose of assistance, study, scientific research, education or other public benefit purpose, and to ONLUS entities, are exempt from inheritance and gift tax (*Article 3, Presidential Decree no. 346 1990 on inheritance and gift tax*).

Exemption from indirect taxes (registration tax, mortgage and cadastral tax, donations tax and so on) has been recently introduced, with reference to binding assets to the assistance of disabled persons, for example through trusts, associations or destinated assets (*patrimoni destinati*).

10.   WHAT, IF ANY, ARE THE TAXATION BENEFITS FOR DONORS TO CHARITIES?

Donations by private individuals

Individuals (and non-profit bodies) can deduct from their gross tax amount payable an amount equal to up to 26% of cash donations they make to an ONLUS (up to EUR30,000), provided that the cash donation is made available to the ONLUS through a bank transfer or other traceable payment system (for example, postal payment) (*Article 15, Tax Code*).

Donations by business income taxpayers

Under Article 100 of the Tax Code, entities and individuals that generate business income (as companies, commercial and non-commercial entities, and individuals performing business activity) can deduct from their total business income donations in money or in kind made to the following:

• ONLUS (up to 2% of total net income, up to a maximum of EUR30,000). The same benefit is granted for donations to non-governmental organisations (NGOs) that co-operate with developing countries, since they are in the same category as an ONLUS. The list of NGOs recognised by the Foreign Ministry is available on the Foreign Ministry's website, at *www. cooperazioneallosviluppo.esteri.it*.

- Social development associations registered in the appropriate national register (up to 2% of total net income).
- Recognised foundations and associations whose statute includes the protection, promotion and development of properties of artistic, historic or landscape value.

Alternatively, donations to an ONLUS by individuals and any kind of entity can be deducted from taxable income, up to the higher of 10% of total net income and EUR70,000.

Public contribution

A specific public contribution can be granted to non-profit entities and charities that meet specific requirements (in principle, entities that qualify as ONLUS). Individuals, in their annual income tax return, can choose a beneficiary to which the state will assign an amount equal to five per thousand of their income tax payable (IRPEF).

DISADVANTAGES

11.   WHAT ARE THE MAIN DISADVANTAGES OF CHARITABLE STATUS?

Since charitable organisations mainly perform non-commercial activities, input VAT cannot generally be deducted (*see Question 9*).

OVERSEAS CHARITIES

12.   IS IT POSSIBLE TO OPERATE AN OVERSEAS CHARITY IN YOUR JURISDICTION? WHAT ARE THE REGISTRATION FORMALITIES? HOW (IF AT ALL) ARE OVERSEAS CHARITIES TREATED DIFFERENTLY IN YOUR JURISDICTION FROM CHARITIES SET UP UNDER DOMESTIC LAW?

If associations and foundations established abroad have their seat of administration or main purpose in Italy, they must register in the Register of legal entities (*Article 25, Law no. 218 of 31 May 1995*).

Non-resident or international non-profit entities are governed by Articles 153 and 154 of the Tax Code, according to which only incomes earned in Italy are subject to Italian Income Tax, except those exempt from tax and those subject to withholding tax (*Article 153, Tax Code*).

Article 154 of the Tax Code provides that the income of non-resident non-profit entities is determined in the same way as non-resident individuals (*Article 23, Tax Code*).

The Tax Authority has clarified that non-resident non-profit organisations can qualify for ONLUS status, and be subject to the same tax treatment as resident organisations (*Circular no. 24/E, 2006*). In practice, there is nothing to prevent the recognition of ONLUS status in favour of non-resident entities.

13.   IS IT POSSIBLE TO REGISTER A DOMESTIC CHARITY ABROAD, AND HAS YOUR JURISDICTION ENTERED INTO ANY INTERNATIONAL AGREEMENTS OR TREATIES IN THIS AREA?

Non-profit organisations incorporated under Italian law are not prevented by Italian law from registering and operating abroad. Further, the Italian Ministry of Foreign Affairs and International Cooperation oversees and supports activities of non-profit Italian organisations in the field of social solidarity and development co-operation (for example, granting a qualification to non-governmental organisations (NGOs) to implement development co-operation projects).

REFORM

14.   ARE THERE ANY PROPOSALS FOR REFORM IN THE AREA OF CHARITY LAW?

Laws and regulations regarding non-profit organisations are fragmented. On 6 June 2016, the Third Sector Reform Law was published in the Official Journal (*Gazzetta Ufficiale*). This provides general principles for reform and harmonisation of the third sector. It delegates powers to the government to implement such principles, through one or more decrees until 12 months from publication of the Reform Law.

The reform includes:

- A review of the Civil Code regarding associations and foundations.
- Reorganisation and harmonisation of tax reliefs and regulations applicable to third sector entities (for example, review of the definition of non-commercial entity for tax purposes, rationalisation of tax benefits, new measures for raising venture capital and, more generally, for funding the third sector).

ONLINE RESOURCES

OFFICIAL GAZETTE

W www.gazzettaufficiale.it

Description. Official website containing Italian legislation, in Italian.

MINISTRY OF FINANCE

W http://def.finanze.it

Description. The official website of the Ministry of Finance, containing Italian legislation and circulars issued by the Tax Authority, in Italian.

REGULATORY AUTHORITIES

ITALIAN TAX AUTHORITY

W www.agenziaentrate.gov.it

Description. Official website of the Italian Tax Authority, available also in English.

ITALIAN PREFECTURES

W www.prefettura.it

Description. The official website of the Italian prefectures, in Italian.

ITALIAN REGIONAL GOVERNMENTS

W www.regione.lombardia.it

Description. Each Italian region has its own website. For example, the website of Milan's region (Regione Lombardia).

Eric Fort and Guy Harles, ARENDT & MEDERNACH SA

OVERVIEW AND MAIN TRENDS

1. WHAT IS THE HISTORICAL BACKGROUND TO CHARITY LAW AND CHARITABLE ORGANISATIONS IN YOUR JURISDICTION?

The Grand Duchy of Luxembourg (Luxembourg) has always been a country of private initiatives, originally to contribute to the general interest, particularly in religious, professional and labour union matters. Later on, the focus shifted and the goal of private initiative was directed towards new forms of mutual aid such as cultural, sporting and social activities, in keeping with the evolution of society.

Economic evolution in the country was triggered by living standards, which led people to consider philanthropy as a major point of interest. These changes in social behaviour induced an exponential increase in the number of charitable institutions, which took the form of non-profit organisations and public utility foundations. These organisations are characterised by the economic selflessness of their actions and the improved social climate they bring about.

2. ARE INDEPENDENT CHARITABLE ORGANISATIONS COMMON AND SIGNIFICANT IN YOUR JURISDICTION? WHAT IS THE CURRENT SIZE AND SCOPE OF THE SECTOR AND THE MAIN TRENDS?

Private charitable institutions such as non-profit organisations and public utility foundations exist in parallel to state or governmental non-profit organisations.

The state or governmental non-profit organisations are incorporated under specific legislation, which differs from the legislation applicable to non-profit organisations and foundations.

An example of a successful entity is the *Fondation de Luxembourg*, a private and independent charitable organisation with public utility status, incorporated in 2008 with an initial capital of EUR5 million (*source: Ministry of Culture, www.culture.lu*). Its mission is to promote private philanthropic activity to Luxembourg or foreign donors, by providing information and advice encouraging them to make a long-term commitment to the development of significant philanthropic projects. The *Fondation de Luxembourg* also offers the possibility of operating under its umbrella to foundations established by philanthropists.

This article focuses on private bodies. The total number of such entities, irrespective of whether they are independent, is remarkable in relation to the relatively low population of 580,000. In fact, Luxembourg has many charitable structures: the number of non-profit organisations and public utility foundations registered in the Memorial C (the official gazette of legal notices concerning companies and non-profitable organisations) was about 8,500 in

April 2009 (*source: page 7, Report for Œuvre Nationale de Secours Grande-Duchesse Charlotte, 31 March 2010*).

Further, the average monthly increase for the first half of 2016 is at least 40 associations, according to the Luxembourg Trade and Companies Register. The total number of organisations with public utility status is 260, according to the Luxembourg direct tax administration. These figures point to significant vitality in the non-profit sector.

LEGAL FRAMEWORK

3. IS THERE A LEGAL DEFINITION OF A "CHARITY"? WHAT ARE THE PRINCIPAL SOURCES OF LAW AND REGULATIONS RELATING TO CHARITABLE ORGANISATIONS AND ACTIVITIES?

Definition of charity

The basis for Luxembourg's legal charity regime was implemented by the law of 21 April 1928.

This legislation provides for the creation of the non-profit organisation, as well as the foundation.

A non-profit organisation is defined as an institution which has no industrial or commercial activities and which does not seek to make profits for its members. Concerning the foundation, the absence of a profit-seeking motive is also essential in defining its charitable aim. The legislator has provided greater precision by restricting permitted activities, such as achieving philanthropic aims in relation to social, scientific, artistic, educational, sporting or touristic aims.

As a result, constituting such an organisation shows the real commitment of founders and volunteers for the sole benefit of the general interest.

Principal sources of law

As Luxembourg is at the heart of Europe, legislation is often inspired by neighbouring countries such as France, Belgium and Germany.

In this case, the law of 21 April 1928 finds its roots in the Belgium law of 27 June 1921. It has been regularly amended, notably on 4 March 1994 introducing the recognition of foreign charitable entities, and the possibility for a Luxembourg charitable entity to transfer its registered office to another country without losing its legal personality.

LEGAL BODIES

4. WHAT ARE THE FORMS OF ORGANISATIONS THAT ARE USED FOR CHARITABLE PURPOSES? WHAT ARE THEIR ADVANTAGES/DISADVANTAGES?

Two types of Luxembourg entities can qualify as charitable organisations:

- The non-profit organisation (*association sans but lucratif*) (*ASBL*).
- The public utility foundation (*fondation d' utilité publique*).

Further, Luxembourg law has introduced an umbrella foundation, by launching the *Fondation de Luxembourg* in December 2008 (*see Question 2*).

Non-profit organisation

A non-profit organisation is a group of individuals or entities who work towards a public-interest goal. A member of a non-profit organisation cannot receive earnings from the non-profit organisation.

Contrary to companies, activities of non-profit organisations are not profitable but selfless.

Advantages. The articles of association of a non-profit organisation determine all provisions for the nomination and powers of the directors. As a result, the governance rules are not imposed by law and can be freely organised.

A non-profit organisation can be incorporated by a notarial deed or a deed signed under private seal. Costs and expenses of a notarial deed can therefore be avoided.

A non-profit organisation can have any non-profitable purpose, without legal limitation or prohibition.

A non-profit organisation can own any movable assets, and can receive donations from living persons or by will.

Further main advantages of a non-profit organisation result from its tax regime (*see Questions 9 and 10*).

Disadvantages. The incorporation of a non-profit organisation requires the commitment of at least three founders. In contrast to certain companies or foundations which can be incorporated by a single person, a person wishing to create a non-profit organisation will have to find at least two other partners.

A donation to a non-profit organisation which exceeds EUR30,000 in value is subject to the approval of the Minister of Justice, unless the donation has been made by bank transfer from a bank in the EU or the European Economic Area. This prior approval can negatively impact the non-profit organisation, as it may discourage donors from donating considerable amounts, and/or delay the receiving of funds.

Unlike companies, a non-profit organisation only acquires its legal personality after performance of filing and registration with the Trade and Companies' Register requirements (*see Question 5*). As a result, once incorporated, a non-profit organisation cannot be immediately operative.

A non-profit organisation does not necessarily address the needs of private families in relation to a charitable programme.

A significant amount of information regarding a non-profit organisation must be published and kept up to date on an annual basis, especially information about the identity and address of each of its members entitled to vote (*see Question 5*). As a result, no confidentiality is possible with respect to the members' identities.

A non-profit organisation can only hold real estate for the achievement of its purpose. This prohibition can limit the real estate that can be contributed to or acquired by a non-profit organisation.

Public utility foundation (*fondation d'utilité publique*)

A public utility foundation (foundation) is an independent, separately constituted non-profit entity, with its own established and reliable source of income and its own governing board.

A foundation is a legal person which has no members. Its purpose must be stated in its articles of association.

While a non-profit organisation can have any non-profitable purpose, the foundation must have one of the purposes listed by Luxembourg law, for example a philanthropic, social, religious, scientific, artistic, educational, sports related or touristic aim.

The foundation cannot carry out any industrial or commercial operations. However, the foundation can pursue an accessory profitable aim, provided this is dependent on the main non-profitable activity.

To have legal personality, the foundation must not pursue a profitable aim.

Advantages. The foundation only requires the presence and activity of directors.

The articles of association of a foundation determine all provisions for the nomination and powers of the directors. The governance rules of a foundation are not imposed by law, and can be freely organised.

The law provides that donations to a foundation cannot cause prejudice to the rights of the donor's heirs, who are by law entitled on the death of the donor to part of the donor's net wealth (*héritiers réservataires*).

Further main advantages of the foundation result from its tax regime (*see Questions 9 and 10*).

Disadvantages. Luxembourg law only recognises a foundation that fulfils a public philanthropic purpose. It cannot be used to manage assets for the benefit of private families only.

A foundation only acquires legal personality on its approval by Grand Ducal decree. As a result, the process of incorporation of a foundation can take time.

Like a donation made to an non-profit organisation, a donation to a foundation which exceeds EUR30,000 is subject to the approval of the Minister of Justice, unless the donation has been made by bank transfer from a bank in the EU or European Economic Area. This prior approval can negatively impact a foundation, as it can discourage donors to donate considerable amounts and delay the receipt of funds.

A foundation does not necessarily address the needs of private families in relation to a charitable programme.

In the same way as for a non-profit organisation, a foundation can only hold real estate for the achievement of its purpose. This prohibition can limit the real estate that can be contributed to or acquired by a foundation.

Trusts

Trusts do not exist under Luxembourg law. However, Luxembourg has ratified the Hague Convention on the law applicable to trusts and on their recognition 1985 (Hague Trusts Convention). Luxembourg therefore recognises trusts created in accordance with a law specified by the Hague Trusts Convention, provided the trust is not manifestly incompatible with public policy (*Article 18, Hague Trusts Convention*).

Luxembourg law will not recognise a trust which deprives an heir of his or her share of the deceased person's net wealth to which the heir is entitled under Luxembourg law on succession. In other words, the settlement of assets into a trust cannot be used to circumvent compulsory Luxembourg heirship rules.

5. WHAT ARE THE QUALIFICATION REQUIREMENTS/FORMALITIES TO SET UP THESE ORGANISATIONS?

Non-profit organisation

The main requirements for the incorporation of a non-profit organisation are:

- A selfless activity.
- A minimum of three members at the moment of incorporation and throughout its lifetime.
- A registered office located in Luxembourg.
- Articles of association containing the information required by law.

The information to be contained in the articles of association of a non-profit organisation is quite substantial, and consists of the following:

- The name of the non-profit organisation.
- The location of its registered office.
- The purpose of the non-profit organisation.
- The minimum number of members (which cannot be less than three), and the name, first name, profession, address and nationality of each voting member.
- Powers of management structures and mode of appointment of the directors.
- Powers of deliberative structures, method to convene the general meeting of members, and formalities to notify resolutions of the general meeting of members to third parties.
- Conditions to become a member, and for termination of membership.
- Maximum amount of subscription paid by the members.
- Conditions to amend the articles of association of the association.
- Approval of the annual accounts, and allocation of capital of the association in case of dissolution.

The formalities of incorporation are, however, quite simple, as the set-up of a non-profit organisation mainly requires the drawing up of articles of association containing the above information. Incorporation can be performed by private deed or before a notary.

A non-profit organisation can request public utility status through an application addressed to the Minister of Justice, provided that it has a philanthropic, social, religious, scientific, artistic, educational, sports related or touristic aim.

There is no specific application form, but a letter of motivation and various documents, including articles of association, annual accounts and/or business plans (projects) must be submitted.

This public utility status allows the donors of the non-profit organisation to benefit from a tax deduction, provided that certain conditions are fulfilled.

The application is considered by the Minister of Justice, who will seek the opinion of the Minister of Finance and the Council of State. Following the issuance of these opinions, a Grand Ducal decree is passed to grant the public interest status. The opinion of the Minister of Finance concerns in particular the capacity of the association to finance its purpose.

With respect to registration requirements, the articles of association of a non-profit organisation must be published in the Luxembourg *Recueil électronique des sociétés et associations*.

One month after publication of the articles of association, a list indicating the name, first name, address and nationality of each member of the non-profit organisation must be filed with the Luxembourg Trade and Companies' Register. Each year, any modification of the list of voting members must also be filed.

Public utility foundation

A foundation can be created by any person who decides to assign, by notarial deed in his/her lifetime or by will after his/her death, all or part of his/her assets to the creation of a foundation. The notarial deed or the will must contain the articles of association of the foundation.

The notarial deed or will of the founder must then be submitted to the Minister of Justice. After approval by the Minister of Justice, the articles of association of the foundation must be approved by Grand Ducal decree.

The positive opinion of the Minister of Finance will essentially depend on the amount allocated to the foundation. It is generally considered that this amount is sufficient if it allows the foundation to carry out its purpose without any further revenue for several years.

The articles of association of a foundation must contain certain information specified by law, namely:

- The purpose of the foundation.
- Its name and registered office (which must be in Luxembourg).
- Certain information relating to the directors.
- The intended purpose of the assets in case of dissolution of the foundation.

In principle, the fact that the articles of association reflect the will of its founder(s) means that it should not be possible to amend them. However, it seems impossible, in practice, to prohibit any changes. As a result, changes are authorised if the articles of association provide the conditions for the changes (subject to the approval of the Minister of Justice). If nothing is provided for in the articles of association, changes can only take place with the approval of the Minister of Justice and the majority of the directors.

With respect to registration requirements, once approved by the Minister of Justice and by Grand Ducal decree, the articles of association must then be published in the Luxembourg *Recueil électronique des sociétés et associations*. The foundation must also be registered with the Trade and Companies' Register.

To receive tax-favoured donations, an application must be filed with the Minister of Finance.

ONGOING REGULATORY REQUIREMENTS

Non-profit organisation

In principle a non-profit organisation is not subject to a specific regulatory authority, except
for non-profit organisations requesting public utility status which are subject to the control of
the Minister of Justice and the advice of the Minister of Finance (*see Question 5*).

As a result, certain public regulatory authorities have general powers over a non-profit
organisation (for example, the tax administration for donations received by the non-profit
organisation, the Minister of Justice for donations exceeding EUR30,000, and the courts for
its dissolution in some cases).

A non-profit organisation can be dissolved by the general meeting and by a court decision, if
one of the following events occurs:

- Its term expires.
- Its purpose ceases to exist.
- The non-profit organisation has only one member left.

After payment of all liabilities, the liquidators will allocate the assets of the association to the
purpose foreseen in the articles of association.

Public utility foundation

The control of a foundation is exercised:

- At the moment of its creation (approval of the incorporation and granting of legal
  personality).
- In the event of changes to the articles of association.
- Indirectly, upon judicial dissolution, dismissal of negligent or incompetent administrators,
  and on the acceptance of donations.

In addition, the Minister of Justice verifies that the assets of the foundation are or have been
allocated in accordance with the purpose of the foundation.

The District Court can dismiss a director who has proven to be negligent or ineffective,
who does not fulfil the obligations foreseen by the law or the articles of association, or who
disposes of the foundation assets for a purpose other than its statutory purpose.

The foundation is in principle dissolved by the expiry of its term.

It can further be dissolved by a court decision, if it is not able to provide the services for which
it has been constituted.

In such circumstances, the court will appoint one or several liquidators, who will distribute
the assets in accordance with the statutory provisions. If the allocation foreseen in the articles
of association cannot be realised, the liquidators will transfer the assets to the Minister of
Justice, who will decide on their allocation in keeping with the purpose of the foundation.

7.   WHICH BODIES OR PERSONS MANAGE CHARITABLE ORGANISATIONS AND WHAT GENERAL REQUIREMENTS MUST THEY MEET?

Non-profit organisation

Management. A non-profit organisation is managed by a board of directors appointed by the general meeting of members, which acts in the name and on behalf of the non-profit organisation.

The board of directors manages the business of the association and represents it in all judicial and extra-judicial matters.

Because of its collegiate form, the board of directors can delegate its powers to a member or to a third person. Such a delegation can only concern the daily management of the non-profit organisation.

The board of directors can decide alone on the delegation of powers to a member of the non-profit organisation. When powers are delegated to a third person, the consent of the general meeting of voting members is required if this delegation is not provided for in the articles of association.

Director's liability. Directors can incur civil liability resulting from a breach of their duties, or an individual contract between them and the non-profit organisation that pursues personal objectives.

This could be, for example, a violation of Luxembourg law or the articles of association of the non-profit organisation.

As directors act in the name and on behalf of the non-profit organisation, only the non-profit organisation can take action against directors for their liability to the non-profit organisation. Members cannot do this individually.

Third parties can bring legal proceedings against directors under Article 1382 of the Civil Code, which provides general civil liability for directors committing a fault that is not a management fault.

Control by the members. The control of the directors by the members is as follows:

- A simple majority of members can dismiss directors, unless otherwise provided by the articles of association.
- The board of directors must annually present to the general meeting of members simplified accounts, showing the profits and losses for the financial year and a budget setting out the foreseeable profits and losses for the next financial year.

Non-profit organisation liability. A non-profit organisation is linked to its members by agreement. Its liability to third parties is based on this agreement, and can for example result from a violation of its statutory duties. In particular, a non-profit organisation can be liable for:

- Faults caused by its directors or its employees.
- Violation or non-performance of an agreement with a third party.
- Another fault which caused an injury to a third party (based on Article 1382 of the Civil Code, which provides for general civil liability).

Public utility foundation

Management. A foundation is managed by a board of directors.

The articles of association must specify the identity of the first directors, the method of appointing subsequent directors, and their powers.

The directors of a foundation represent the foundation in judicial and extra-judicial proceedings.

A court can, on request of a third party or of a prosecutor, dismiss the directors in case of negligence or incompetence. New directors are then appointed in accordance with the articles of association or, if the court decides, the Minister of Justice.

Director's liability. Directors cannot incur civil liability for a breach of their liabilities if the foundation incurs liability on their behalf to third parties, for all actions taken in exercising their duties.

However, based on general rules of civil law, third parties can bring legal proceedings against directors based on Article 1382 of the Civil Code, which provides for general civil liability if directors commit a fault that is not a management fault.

Further, the District Court can dismiss a director who has proven to be negligent or ineffective, who does not fulfil the obligations foreseen by law or the articles of association, or who disposes of foundation assets for a purpose other than the foundation's statutory purpose (*see Question 6*).

Control by the members. The foundation does not have members. It is the result of a unilateral act (of one or more persons) and allocation of assets to a specified non-profit purpose. There is therefore no general meeting of members and no control from any members.

Foundation's liability. As the foundation has no members it cannot be liable to members. The founder cannot incur the foundation's liability, since he or she has renounced the assets which he or she contributed to the foundation.

However, the foundation remains liable to third parties, and its assets can be used to pay or indemnify the foundation's creditors.

The foundation can also be liable for faults caused by its directors, other bodies or its employees, based on Article 1382 of the Civil Code which provides for general civil liability.

8. WHAT ARE THE ACCOUNTING/FINANCIAL REPORTING REQUIREMENTS?

Non-profit organisation

A non-profit organisation must prepare annual accounts (at least in a simplified form) since the board of directors must present a simplified form of the accounts to the general meeting of members each year.

Regarding filing and publishing requirements, in principle the annual accounts of a non-profit organisation do not have to be registered with the Trade and Companies Register, except that:

- A non-profit organisation that has requested and received public utility status must register its annual accounts with the Trade and Companies' Register. However, they will not be published in the *Recueil électronique des sociétés et associations*.
- A donation to a non-profit organisation which exceeds EUR30,000 is subject to the approval of the Minister of Justice (with certain exceptions) (*see Question 4*). A non-profit organisation wishing to request such approval must register its annual accounts with the Trade and Companies Register (but they will not be published in the *Recueil électronique des sociétés et associations*).

A non-profit organisation can have its accounts audited but is not obliged to do so.

Public utility foundation

A foundation has accounting and financial reporting requirements. The directors must provide the Minister of Justice with the foundation's annual accounts and budget, within two months following the end of the financial year. These documents are then published in the *Recueil électronique des sociétés et associations*. These annual accounts do not have to be independently audited.

TAX

9.   HOW ARE CHARITIES TAXED, AND WHAT (IF ANY) ARE THE PRINCIPAL EXEMPTIONS AND/OR RELIEFS FROM TAXATION THAT THEY ENJOY?

Taxes on income and tax on capital gains

A Luxembourg corporate entity is generally subject to corporate income tax (*impôt sur le revenu des collectivités, CIT*) and municipal business tax (*impôt commercial communal, MBT*) on any income received, including distributions and capital gains.

Corporate income tax is levied at an effective maximum rate of 21% in 2016 (increased to 22.47%, including a solidarity surcharge of 7% for the employment fund). Lower rates apply if the taxable profits do not exceed EUR15,000.

Municipal business tax is levied at a variable rate, according to the municipality in which the company is located (6.75% for Luxembourg-city).

A Luxembourg transparent entity is not itself subject to corporate income tax but is subject to municipal business tax. Any income realised by the entity is directly attributed to and taxed at the level of its partners.

According to Article 159 of the Income Tax Law, as amended, Luxembourg charities are considered corporate entities, and so are subject to corporate income tax and municipal business tax. Article 159 of the Income Tax Law refers to non-profit organisations (*associations sans but lucratif*), public interest establishments (*établissements d'utilité publique*) and other foundations (*autres fondations*), without differentiating between those with legal personality and those with no legal personality.

Consequently, a Luxembourg charity is considered an autonomous corporate entity, separate from its partners, irrespective of whether it has legal personality. Any income realised by a Luxembourg charity is taxed at the level of the charity, and is not immediately attributed to its partners.

However, due to the benefits it provides to society, a charity as a fully taxable subject (subjective tax liability) can benefit from a tax exemption on its activities (objective tax exemption) (*Article 161, Income Tax Law and Article 3, municipal business tax law of 1 December 1936 (Gewerbesteuergesetz) as amended*) provided that, based on its charter/by law and activity, it directly and solely pursues cultual, charitable or general interest purposes.

In particular, the activity(ies) carried-out by the charity must pursue any of the following:

- Aims in the general or public interest.
- Charitable aims.
- Cultual aims, as further defined in Articles 17 to 19 of the Tax adaptation law (as amended) (Luxembourg tax law provides for specific definitions which only apply for tax purposes).

Aims pursued in the general or public interest refer to activities serving the general good of society, on a material, intellectual or moral basis, for example:

- Improving public health, through physical training (for example, sports).
- Assisting youth.
- Supporting science, the arts, or maintaining historical buildings.

Activities or a purpose serving the general good of a limited group of people identified according to specific criteria do not fall within the definition of serving the general good of society.

Charitable aims refer to assisting people in need due to their economic situation only. Assistance to people in need due to their physical/body, mental or psychiatric condition is excluded.

Cultual aims refer to the promotion of public religious entities, while other religious entities (private entities) should be considered to be pursuing an aim in the general or public interest.

The articles of incorporation or statutes of charities must be drafted in a clear and concise manner, so that the charity meets at least one of the above criteria.

Further, this purpose must be the exclusive purpose of the charity, so that the charity cannot:

- Pursue any purposes other than those in the general or public interest, charitable purposes, or cultual purposes.
- Pursue lucrative purposes.
- On exit of a member, repay to that member an amount higher than the member's initial contribution.
- Grant advantages to certain persons, through paying excessive compensation or reimbursement of administrative fees that goes beyond the charity's purposes.
- Use, on liquidation of the charity, liquidation proceeds for purposes other than those in the general or public interest, whether charitable or cultual.

A charity cannot carry out the above aim(s) through another entity, but must carry them out directly. However there are some exceptions. A charity can, for example, limit its activities to the co-ordination of other charities under its control which are pursuing cultual, charitable or general interest purposes. Other exceptions can be granted by the tax administration, on a case-by-case basis.

Once all the above conditions are met, a charity can benefit from a total tax exemption from corporate income tax and municipal business tax, under Article 161 of the Income Tax Law and Article 3 of the Municipal Business Tax Law. Subscription fees that a charity can ask from its members are in any case excluded from the charity's taxable base, irrespective of whether the charity meets the above criteria.

The tax exemption does not apply to Luxembourg withholding tax. A Luxembourg charity is subject to a non-recoverable withholding tax of 15% on distributions (and certain specific interest income).

Tax on property used by the organisation

Luxembourg tax is not levied on property used by the charity.

Value added tax (VAT)

Under the Law of 12 February 1979 on value added tax (VAT Law), a charity can qualify as a taxable person for value added tax (VAT) purposes if it performs economic activities independently and on a continuing basis, irrespective of whether these activities are profitable or not. An economic activity can be any activity related to the production, trade or supply of services. A charity can carry out economic activities as its main activity or as an ancillary activity.

A charity can carry out taxable activities or VAT exempt activities. If the charity performs VAT taxable activities, it benefits in principle from a right to recover input VAT on costs incurred in the context of such activities, and must register for VAT under the regular regime.

If it performs VAT exempt activities, it cannot recover any input VAT on costs incurred in relation to the exempt activities. In this case, it is only required to register for VAT under a simplified regime, if it receives taxable supplies of services or goods (to some extent) from abroad, for which the charity is liable to self-assess Luxembourg VAT due.

Article 44 paragraphs (1), (t), (u) and (v) of the VAT Law contains three specific VAT exemptions concerning the activities of a charity:

- The supply of services closely linked to sport or physical education by a charity, to persons taking part in sport or physical education.
- The supply of services, and the supply of goods closely linked to them, to their members in their common interest, in return for a subscription fixed according to their rules by charities, with aims of a political, trade union, religious, patriotic, philosophical, philanthropic or civic nature.
- The supply of services and goods in connection with occasional fundraising events organised exclusively by a charity for its own benefit, provided that the charity pursues an aim of common or general interest, and is not a taxable person due to its main activity.

Other

Net wealth tax. Luxembourg entities are generally subject to net wealth tax on their net assets. Net wealth tax is levied at 0.5% on net assets not exceeding EUR500 million, and at 0.05% on the portion of the net assets exceeding EUR500 million. Net worth is referred to as the unitary value (*valeur unitaire*), as determined at 1 January of each year. The unitary value is in principle calculated as the difference between assets estimated at their fair market value (*valeur estimée de réalisation*), and liabilities to third parties.

Charities which, based on their charter/by law and activity, directly and solely pursue cultual, charitable or general interest purposes, are exempt from net wealth tax on all movable and immovable property (*Article 3, Net Wealth Tax Law*). In this regard, a charity can only own immovable property if it is necessary for the realisation of its purpose.

10.   WHAT, IF ANY, ARE THE TAXATION BENEFITS FOR DONORS TO CHARITIES?

Individual as well as corporate donors can deduct donations made to charities from their taxable base, under Article 112 of the Income Tax Law. The following conditions must be fulfilled:

- The donor must be a tax resident of Luxembourg, or a non-resident taxpayer who submits its tax return to the Luxembourg tax administration and opts to be considered a tax resident.
- The donation must generally be made in cash directly to the charity (except for donations to national cultural funds and to cultural institutions or organisations, where a donation in kind is possible).
- The charity must be a Luxembourg organisation recognised as of public interest, a Luxembourg non-profit association recognised as of public interest, a Luxembourg foundation recognised as of public interest, or a non-governmental organisation on the list of the Luxembourg tax administration.
- These conditions also apply to donations to similar non-governmental entities and organisations in another EU member state, or in a member state of the European Free Trade Association.
- The total amount of donations made by the donor must be at least EUR120, and must not exceed 20% of the donor's total net income or EUR1 million. Amounts in excess of these limits can be carried forward for the next two years, subject to the same conditions and limits.
- The donor must provide a receipt indicating the donor's name, the date of the donation, and the voluntary basis of the donation.

Article 112 of the Income Tax Law explicitly refers to donations. Contributions made to charities entitled to receive such contributions according to their bye-laws (for example, membership or subscription fees) are excluded and cannot be deducted for tax purposes.

DISADVANTAGES

11.   WHAT ARE THE MAIN DISADVANTAGES OF CHARITABLE STATUS?

There is no specific disadvantage of charitable status, except for non-recoverable withholding tax on distributions (and on certain interest payments) (*see Question 9*).

OVERSEAS CHARITIES

12.   IS IT POSSIBLE TO OPERATE AN OVERSEAS CHARITY IN YOUR JURISDICTION? WHAT ARE THE REGISTRATION FORMALITIES? HOW (IF AT ALL) ARE OVERSEAS CHARITIES TREATED DIFFERENTLY IN YOUR JURISDICTION FROM CHARITIES SET UP UNDER DOMESTIC LAW?

According to the Law of 21 April 1928 concerning non-profit organisations and foundations, organisations validly incorporated abroad in accordance with the law of the country of their registered office or of their registration are recognised automatically, except if their goal or activities breach public order. These organisations have the same capacity as that granted in their country of origin.

A transfer of their registered office to Luxembourg can be performed without losing legal personality. The charity will then be subject to Luxembourg law.

A Luxembourg donor can deduct a donation from its taxable income if the beneficiary is a public utility organisation domiciled in an EU member state, or a member state of the European Free Trade Association. A certificate must be given to the tax authority, to allow it to verify that the conditions for deductibility are met.

A non-resident donor can request tax deduction of a donation to a Luxembourg organisation, on condition that it submits an income tax return and chooses to be regarded as a Luxembourg tax resident.

13. IS IT POSSIBLE TO REGISTER A DOMESTIC CHARITY ABROAD, AND HAS YOUR JURISDICTION ENTERED INTO ANY INTERNATIONAL AGREEMENTS OR TREATIES IN THIS AREA?

Domestic charity organisations can be registered abroad if the Luxembourg legal requirements are respected, but the registered office must be located in Luxembourg (*Article 2(1), Charity Law*).

Further, Luxembourg is not party to any international agreements or treaties regarding charity law, so the law of the relevant foreign jurisdiction must be checked.

REFORM

14. ARE THERE ANY PROPOSALS FOR REFORM IN THE AREA OF CHARITY LAW?

A reform is pending to simplify the operation of charitable organisations and reduce administrative burdens. It will also introduce full regulation of public utility organisations, to supplement the existing law and determine the regime, obligations and control of such entities. The legislative agenda has not yet been defined.

Further, the legislator intends to introduce the private foundation into Luxembourg law. The purpose of a private foundation is the management of assets for the benefit of one or more beneficiaries or one or more primary objectives, which must be different to those objectives reserved exclusively to public foundations governed by the Law of 21 April 1928. Further, the new entity will be precluded from pursuing any liberal, commercial, industrial or agricultural activity. There is currently no clear agenda for its implementation.

ONLINE RESOURCES

LEGILUX

W www.legilux.public.lu

Description. The Legilux website provides access to the applicable legal provisions, laws and codes.

REGISTRE DE COMMERCE ET DE SOCIÉTÉS

W www.rcsl.lu

Description. This website provides in particular access to published information about all registered companies and non-profit organisations.

REGULATORY AUTHORITY

MINISTRY OF JUSTICE

W www.mj.public.lu

T +352 247 84537

Description. The Ministry of Justice is headed by the Minister, Félix Braz, and consists of four different entities that manage civil, criminal, and commercial, matters, as well as judicial organisation and prisons.

MEXICO

Daniel Del Río, Julio J Copo Terrés, Mariana Arrieta
and Eduardo Ramos Parra, BASHAM, RINGE & CORREA S.C

OVERVIEW AND MAIN TRENDS

1. WHAT IS THE HISTORICAL BACKGROUND TO CHARITY LAW AND CHARITABLE ORGANISATIONS IN YOUR JURISDICTION?

Charitable organisations are usually incorporated as a civil association (*Asociación Civil*) (AC) in accordance with local and federal civil codes. An AC is generally understood to be an association of individuals with common objectives not forbidden by law, who do not have a preponderant economic interest. This is in contrast to corporations (*Sociedades*), whose main objective is to be profitable.

The AC was included in the Federal Civil Code of 1928, but there were very few charitable organisations at that time. Under Mexico's presidential system at the time, that monopolised all social and welfare activities as duties of the state, most of the charitable activities were related predominantly to the Catholic Church or were created to support political interests.

Following an economic crisis in 1982, Mexico adopted a series of neoliberal policies that decreased the state's obligations and allowed for broader social participation in all aspects of national life. In addition, a highly destructive earthquake in 1985, as well as the controversial results of the 1988 presidential elections, led civil society to look for alternatives to better organise itself and participate more actively in charitable organisations.

The 1990's saw a steady increase in the number of charitable organisations, which continued during the next decade. In 2010, the National Institute for Social Development (INDESOL) estimated that there were more than 40,000 charitable organisations.

2. ARE INDEPENDENT CHARITABLE ORGANISATIONS COMMON AND SIGNIFICANT IN YOUR JURISDICTION? WHAT IS THE CURRENT SIZE AND SCOPE OF THE SECTOR AND THE MAIN TRENDS?

Although incorporation and operation of charitable organisations has been steadily increasing, the number is still low in comparison with other countries of the region, taking into account the number of charitable organisations per capita. With a population in Mexico of close to 120 million, there are only 0.000333 organisations per individual.

The Mexican National Institute for Social Development estimated that there were about 40,000 charitable organisations in Mexico in 2010. However, in 2012, only 7,320 charitable organisations were registered as tax-deductible organisations with the Mexican Tax Administration Service (SAT).

Charitable organisations mainly operate in relation to the following:

- Education.
- Development.
- Women.
- Immigration.
- Health.
- Environment.
- Welfare.
- Science and technology.
- Human rights.
- Arts and culture.

LEGAL FRAMEWORK

3. IS THERE A LEGAL DEFINITION OF A "CHARITY"? WHAT ARE THE PRINCIPAL SOURCES OF LAW AND REGULATIONS RELATING TO CHARITABLE ORGANISATIONS AND ACTIVITIES?

Definition of charity

There is no legal definition of "charity" as such. According to the National Institute for Statistics and Geography (INEGI), non-for-profit organisations are defined as social organisations both:

- Not seeking or distributing profit.
- Whose decisions and operation are institutionally autonomous and separated from the government.

Principal sources of law

The principal sources of law are the:

- Federal and local civil codes.
- Federal and local Laws for the Promotion of Activities carried out by Organisations of the Civil Society (*Ley de Fomento de las Organizaciones de la Sociedad Civil*).
- Local laws for the Private Assistance Institutions Law (*Ley de Instituciones de Asistencia Privada*) (institutions for private assistance are non-profit organisations with legal personality and their own assets, that execute undesignated welfare acts).
- Federal Income Tax Law (*Ley del Impuesto sobre la Renta*).

LEGAL BODIES

Civil association (*Asociación Civil*) (AC)

The AC is the most common form for an organisation with charitable purposes. It is regulated in accordance with each state's civil code.

Advantages. Incorporation as a civil association is relatively simple and charitable organisations can start their operations fairly quickly. If certain conditions are met, they can choose to apply for a tax-deduction status and for federal funds to be used in their activities. It is advisable to do so, as this translates into transparency and accountability for possible donors, along with the possibility for donors to deduct the contributions made for Income Tax purposes (subject to certain thresholds).

Disadvantages. Obtaining tax-deduction status (*see Question 9*) can take between four to six months, and may require amendment of the articles of incorporation and ancillary documentation proving the AC's charitable activities.

ACs may lack local regulation or scrutiny from local authorities, and therefore could be used for illicit purposes (for example, this allows for people to use this type of organisation to implement, for example, aggressive tax planning strategies). From a federal standpoint, this has resulted in the strengthening of tax controls including:

- Further scrutiny relating to receiving the ruling authorising tax-deduction status.
- Informative returns.
- Limiting activities outside of the AC's scope.
- Digital tax invoices.
- Requiring ACs to periodically submit their electronic accounting records.

Institutions for private assistance (*Institución de Asistencia Privada*) (IAP)

Institutions for private assistance are incorporated under the private assistance laws of each state. They can be charitable organisations or trusts that use private means for social assistance.

Advantages. IAPs are highly regulated institutions and regarded as credible. They have preferential access to information and support through the Private Assistance Board (*Junta de Asistencia Privada*) (*see Question 6*). They also can apply for the tax-deduction status.

Disadvantages. IAPs are bureaucratic and political, as the Private Assistance Board usually includes governmental officials (*see Question 6*). Incorporation of an IAP can be complicated, supervision is constant, and solid organisations with previous experience as charitable organisations may find that the Private Assistance Board is more a burden than a support.

5. WHAT ARE THE QUALIFICATION REQUIREMENTS/FORMALITIES TO SET UP THESE ORGANISATIONS?

Civil association (*Asociación Civil*) (AC)

An AC is incorporated before a notary public and must be registered with the Public Real Estate Property Office (*Registro Público de la Propiedad y del Comercio*) (*http://data.consejeria. cdmx.gob.mx/index.php/dgrppyc*) once incorporated. The following must be in place:

- At least two legal or moral persons for incorporation.
- Authorisation for the use of the association's name by the Ministry of Economy.
- A draft of the articles of incorporation, including details of powers of attorney and the board of directors.

Once incorporated, the AC must obtain the Taxpayer Id Number before the Tax Service Administration (*Servicio de Administración Tributaria*) (SAT), along with the tax electronic signature and the electronic password for entering the tax authority's digital services.

Certain ACs can apply for the tax-deduction status before the SAT (*see Question 9*) and for CLUNI (*Clave Única de Inscripción al Registro Federal de las Organizaciones de la Sociedad Civil*) registration before the National Institute for Social Development (INDESOL) to apply for federal funds.

Institutions for private assistance (*Institución de Asistencia Privada*) (IAP)

An IAP is incorporated before the Private Assistance Board (*Junta de Asistencia Privada*). The following must be in place:

- At least two legal or moral persons for incorporation.
- Application before the Private Assistance Board (*Junta de Asistencia Privada*).
- CVs of all members of the board of directors.
- A work programme.
- A budget for the first year of operations.
- Authorisation for the use of the IAP's name by the Ministry of Economy.
- A draft of the articles of incorporation, including details of powers of attorney and the board of directors.
- Registration before the Public Real Estate Property Office (*Registro Público de la Propiedad y del Comercio*).

Once incorporated, the IAP must obtain the Taxpayer Id Number, the tax electronic signature and the electronic password.

Certain IAPs can apply for the tax-deduction status before SAT (*see Question 9*).

ONGOING REGULATORY REQUIREMENTS

6. WHAT ARE THE MAIN REGULATORY AUTHORITIES FOR CHARITABLE ORGANISATIONS? WHAT ARE THEIR POWERS OF INVESTIGATION/AUDIT/SANCTIONS?

Regulatory authorities

The main federal regulatory authorities for charity organisations (both civil associations (*Asociación Civil*) (ACs) and institutions for private assistance (*Institución de Asistencia Privada*) (IAPs)) are the:

- Department of Economy.
- Public Real Estate Property Office.
- SAT.
- Commission for the Promotion of Activities of Civil Society Organisations.
- Federal or local authority that certifies its charitable activities for tax purposes.

IAPs are regulated and supervised by the Local Private Assistance Board (*Junta de Asistencia Privada*) (Board) of each state, which are made up of both public and private parties. For example, in Mexico City, the Board is composed of:

- A president designated by the mayor of Mexico City.
- The Secretary of Public Affairs for Mexico City.
- The Secretary of Finance for Mexico City.
- The Secretary of Social Development for Mexico City.
- The Secretary of Health for Mexico City.
- The head of the National System for the Integral Development of Families in Mexico City.
- Five representatives from the organisations supervised by the Board.

Powers

The powers of investigation/audit/sanctions depend on the authority:

- **Tax Administration Service.** This can investigate, audit and penalise charity organisations if they breach their fiscal obligations, including possibly revoking their tax-deduction status. Due to charitable organisations' tax-exempt status and the fact that they are allowed to issue invoices deductible for donors, they are subject to additional administrative controls. This includes informative returns that they must comply with (to avoid abuse or aggressive tax planning).
- **Public Real Estate Property Office.** This has no powers of investigation, sanction or audit over charitable organisations. Its function is to record the creation of entities and the movements made concerning property (transfer of property), and to give publicity to acts performed by these entities (to make them executable and valid in relation to third parties).
- **Ministry of Economy.** This can authorise the corporate name of the charitable organisation, but has no powers of verification or audit, and cannot impose sanctions.
- **The National Institute for Social Development (INDESOL).** This is in charge of promoting the activities carried out by civil society organisations, and nourishing and efficiently managing the federal economic resources that these organisations are entitled to access to carry out their activities and fulfil their purpose. In this regard, INDESOL has powers of

verification and audit, and can impose sanctions on civil society organisations misusing the resources provided by the federal government or carrying out activities different than those of their purpose, among others.

- **Board.** Locally, there are certain regulatory authorities that have powers of verification and audit, and can impose sanctions, in relation to IAPs. For example, the Board can verify and audit IAPs' compliance with the law and their obligations under the private assistance laws of each state. The Board regularly supervises the IAP, which must provide access to their accounting books regularly. In addition, the Board can carry out inspection visits to ensure that the IAP is operating in accordance with their articles of incorporation. IAPs must also pay the Board 0.006 times their gross income (which goes towards maintenance of the Board).

7.   WHICH BODIES OR PERSONS MANAGE CHARITABLE ORGANISATIONS AND WHAT GENERAL REQUIREMENTS MUST THEY MEET?

Civil association (*Asociación Civil*) (AC)

The civil association is governed by a board of directors in accordance with its articles of incorporation. Each associate (that is, the individuals constituting the association) constitutes a vote in the general assembly.

The Federal Civil Code does not establish limitations on who can act as a director of an AC. Therefore, every capable person of legal age can act as a director. However, the bye-laws of the AC can establish certain restrictions on who can act as a director.

The board of directors is constituted of more than one director.

The general assembly is empowered to resolve any of the following matters concerning the association:

- Admission and exclusion of associates.
- The anticipated dissolution of the association or its extension to a longer period than that initially contemplated.
- Appointment of the director or directors when they were not appointed through the bye-laws.
- Reversal of any appointment.
- Any other matter expressly referred to in the bye-laws.

Institutions for private assistance (*Institución de Asistencia Privada*) (IAP)

The founders of IAPs decide on the type of services to be rendered by the IAP, but the supreme administrative body of an IAP is the board of trustees (patronage). The patronage's obligations and tasks are to:

- Fulfil and comply with the will of the founder or founders.
- Represent the IAP and administer its assets in accordance with the bye-laws and the Private Assistance Law.
- Comply with the purpose of the IAP.
- Comply with and observe the agreements and other dispositions set by the Private Assistance Board (*Junta de Asistencia Privada*). For example, IAPs must present certain general information, and report annually on the activities it carries out before the Private Assistance Board (and cover the fees provided by the Private Assistance Law (six per thousand of its gross income annually)).

- Use the IAP's funds exclusively for its purpose.
- Address any other matter expressly referred to in the bye-laws.

IAPs can only be liquidated by approval of the Executive Council of the Private Assistance Board. This process can be initiated through a petition of the founders of the institution, through the patronage or as a consequence of an investigation of the Private Assistance Board.

8. WHAT ARE THE ACCOUNTING/FINANCIAL REPORTING REQUIREMENTS?

Civil association (*Asociación Civil*) (AC)

All charitable associations must keep accounting books. However, unlike business companies, these do not need to be approved in the civil association's meetings. The associates can review the accounting books at any time, but it is not mandatory. Charitable associations' financial statements do not need to be audited, but they do need to be kept and in order. If desired, charitable associations can issue financial statements for non-profitable organisations using the Mexican Financial Reporting Standards (*Normas de Información Financiera*).

In addition, ACs must have electronic accounting records, periodically submit their financial information before the SAT, file informative returns for certain activities and have their financials available to the general public.

Institutions for private assistance (*Institución de Asistencia Privada*) (IAP)

All IAPs must keep their financial statements and accounting reports in books or information systems that comply with the provisions of the tax regulations (that is, the Tax Code, Income Tax Act, and so on) (*section 54, Chapter VIII, Private Assistance Institutions Law for Mexico City*). The books must be submitted to the Private Assistance Board (*Junta de Asistencia Privada*) within 15 days following either the:

- Last operation registered (for existing IAPs).
- Incorporation of the IAP (for new IAPs).

Only if the IAP is required to have their financials subject to external tax report are they required to file the results of the report before the Private Assistance Board.

TAX

9. HOW ARE CHARITIES TAXED, AND WHAT (IF ANY) ARE THE PRINCIPAL EXEMPTIONS AND/OR RELIEFS FROM TAXATION THAT THEY ENJOY?

Tax on income

Charitable organisations' income is exempt from income tax if the organisation has been authorised as a tax-deduction organisation (*donataria autorizada*) by the SAT. This only applies for ACs. This is because ACs can carry out a wide range of activities that may or may not be authorised under law as tax exempt. IAPs are recognised as exempt from incorporation, as they are dedicated to executing undesignated welfare acts and subject to clearance before incorporation.

In addition, if a tax-deduction organisation receives revenue from activities different from those authorised by the SAT, they must consider these items as "distributable balance" and pay the relevant income tax at the corresponding rate (with applicable deductions). However, under a tax holiday, they are released from payment at least until 17 December 2016.

To be recognised as a tax-deduction organisation, the articles of incorporation must include certain specific sections. For example, in the case of dissolution, all of the organisation's equity must be transferred to another tax-deduction organisation. In addition, charitable organisations must evidence their non-profitable activities through documentation issued by an authorised governmental body and that they have fulfilled their tax obligations.

The tax regime can be summarised as follows:

- Charitable organisations are exempt from income tax and donors can deduct their contributions up to a certain threshold.
- Donations are exempt from VAT and, under certain local tax laws, they could access additional tax incentives.

Section 82 of the Mexican Income Tax Law lists the "authorised" activities:

- Welfare. To aid people in regions with scarce resources, indigenous communities or sectors of the population regarded as vulnerable due to age, sex, disability or any other vulnerable groups (for example, relating to sexual orientation, and rehabilitation of alcohol or substance abusers) by performing activities to achieve better living conditions for them, among other specific targets. This can also include the promotion of actions that improve the livelihood and conditions of the population, defence of human rights, participation in matters of public interest, civil protection actions, promotion and defence of consumer rights, and other related activities.
- Educational. Public or private entities with official recognition by the state. In addition, charitable entities dedicated to the granting of scholarships.
- Investigation. Scientific or technological research.
- Cultural. Promotion, diffusion, creation, education and investigation of music, plastic arts, dramatic arts, dance, literature, architecture and cinematography and other artistic activities; protection, conservation, restoration and recovery of the nation's cultural heritage including the art of indigenous communities; libraries and museums.
- Ecological. Investigation and preservation of wild flora, fauna and natural habitats; preservation, maintenance and restoration of the ecological balance; prevention and control of water, soil or air pollution.
- Economic aid. Charitable entities dedicated to giving support and financial aid to other charitable organisations.

Given the fact that the tax-exempt status is a benefit regime, there are a number of rules and procedures aimed at supervising and monitoring charitable organisations' activities. (As previously stated, certain controls apply, such as electronic accounting records, periodically submitting financial information before the SAT, filing informative returns for certain activities and making financials available to the general public. In addition, their equity should be destined exclusively for their charitable purpose; they should keep record of the donations received; in the case of liquidation, equity should be transferred to other authorised charitable organisations; they cannot receive/grant onerous donations; and they must file their annual returns.)

Value added tax (VAT)

Donations received are exempt from VAT.

Tax on capital gains

It is considered as an "unlawful tax practice" for tax-deductible organisations to participate directly or indirectly as owners of shares, equity quotas, settlors or trustees, or other types of arrangements dedicated to business activities.

The only exceptions are shares, equity interests or securities traded over recognised stock markets. In these cases, it is considered that the investment and gains obtained by the tax-deductible organisation fall under the scope of its authorised activities, so no taxation is levied for these gains.

In addition, as of April 2016, the General Tax Rules for 2016 allow new activities, allowing tax-deductible organisations to participate in the equity of certain financial institutions.

Tax on property used by the organisation

This depends on the local laws.

For example, in Mexico City, tax-deductible organisations can apply for a 100% tax credit for the relevant property tax if their activities fall under the scope of section 283 of the Federal Fiscal Code for Mexico City (that is, promotion of human rights, attention to vulnerable groups, research and scientific activities, urban development, and so on).

Other

Under certain local tax laws, there could be additional tax incentives. For example, a tax holiday for payroll tax, property tax and acquisition real estate tax. However, these tax incentives strictly depend on the location of the tax-deductible organisation.

10.   WHAT, IF ANY, ARE THE TAXATION BENEFITS FOR DONORS TO CHARITIES?

Donors (individuals or entities) can deduct for income tax purposes all their contributions to charitable organisations, capped at 7% of their gross income filed in the previous fiscal year.

DISADVANTAGES

11.   WHAT ARE THE MAIN DISADVANTAGES OF CHARITABLE STATUS?

Charitable entities must comply with several burdensome administrative management/expenses controls. In addition, there are restrictions on the use of their equity. In some cases, this could compromise the development of their own charitable activities (for example, they cannot give cash incentives to the population they are trying to help and the beneficial activities or goods must be granted in kind).

The law has a grey area in relation to tax treatment where a charitable organisation does additional activities (for example, certain commercial or other ancillary activities) to obtain additional funds to be applied to their non-profitable activities. Generally, revenue from executing activities other than those allowed should be considered as a distributable balance and subject to income tax. However, there are certain activities that are very closely related to the non-profitable activities. For example, tax-deductible organisations cannot collect "recovering fees" from their donors (that is, any amounts received for the services rendered to the end-users, such as museum admittance fees).

In addition, "donations under condition" are not deductible for the donors. For example, a tax-deductible organisation sets up a public event for raising funds, at which a certain performer (artist) will appear. The law is not clear whether this is a tax-deductible activity (even if the money raised will be 100% dedicated to an authorised activity) as both:

• The tax-deductible organisation will receive a donation.

• The donor will receive a tax deductible invoice plus the possibility to enjoy a specific event.

A similar consideration applies when a certain business company donates the foods and beverages that are to be served at this same event, but has the right to do marketing activities before and after the performance.

OVERSEAS CHARITIES

12. IS IT POSSIBLE TO OPERATE AN OVERSEAS CHARITY IN YOUR JURISDICTION? WHAT ARE THE REGISTRATION FORMALITIES? HOW (IF AT ALL) ARE OVERSEAS CHARITIES TREATED DIFFERENTLY IN YOUR JURISDICTION FROM CHARITIES SET UP UNDER DOMESTIC LAW?

If the foreign charitable entity falls under the authorised categories of exempt activities in the Mexican Income Tax Law (*see Question 9*), it should be allowed to open an office and conduct activities in Mexico (although this is very uncommon). This is under the premise that the Federal Civil Code recognises the existence, legal capacity, corporate controls, amendments and dissolution of foreign entities, and given the fact that the Income Tax Law does not require a tax-deductible entity to be incorporated under Mexican legislation.

To achieve tax-deductible status, the foreign charitable organisation must fulfil all the standard tax requirements (that is, its bye-laws must include the same restrictions as under Mexican Law) and it must evidence the performance of its non-profitable activities in Mexico. In addition, the Mexican tax authorities would request that any funds raised and received from Mexico remain within Mexico in the case of dissolution or closing of the Mexican branch.

This is different if the foreign charitable organisation is considered as a foreign tax resident, where the provisions of the income tax law that would be in force are not those of tax-exempt entities but rather the provisions for foreign tax residents.

13. IS IT POSSIBLE TO REGISTER A DOMESTIC CHARITY ABROAD, AND HAS YOUR JURISDICTION ENTERED INTO ANY INTERNATIONAL AGREEMENTS OR TREATIES IN THIS AREA?

It should be possible to register a domestic charity abroad, but we have never seen this in practice. The registration of a domestic charity entity abroad would pose certain administrative and tax issues. For example, donations received from Mexican donors should only be used for Mexican charitable activities (which are the ones allowed by the local law), the accounting records should be separated (domestic/foreign), and so on.

However, if a tax-deductible organisation changes its corporate domicile abroad (outside of Mexico), there is a pending reform to provide that all of its equity should be transferred to another Mexican tax-deductible organisation before migrating abroad.

On the other hand, Mexico has signed double tax treaties with France and the US that include certain provisions regarding the tax-exempt organisations and the possibility to have cross-border donations.

REFORM

14.   ARE THERE ANY PROPOSALS FOR REFORM IN THE AREA OF CHARITY LAW?

On 8 September 2016, the Executive Office presented before the Mexican Congress certain amendments to the Mexican Income Tax Law related to the tax-deductible organisations. The amendments still need to be passed by the Chamber of Deputies and Mexican Senate to have full force as of 2017. The proposals are aimed at the following:

- New "authorised" activity (economic aid for productive projects performed by small-scale agriculture or artisans located in undeveloped areas within Mexico).
- Including "recovering fees" as an authorised income for tax-deductible organisations.
- Tax-deductible organisations migrating abroad or losing clearance from the SAT will be obliged to transfer all of their equity to another Mexican tax-deductible organisation, and file an informative return in connection with that.
- Introducing a new certification for the different types of Mexican tax-deductible organisation, to be more efficient for the entities involved in the sector, and to monitor their non-profitable activities ("A", "AA" or "AAA" certification with evidence of the legal fulfilment of their obligations).

ONLINE RESOURCES

CIVIL CODE FOR MEXICO CITY (*CODIGO CIVIL PARA EL DISTRITO FEDERAL*)

W www.aldf.gob.mx/archivo-c9dc6843e50163a0d2628615e069b140.pdf

Description. Official website for the Civil Code for Mexico City, maintained by the Parliament of Mexico City. No translation into English is available.

INCOME TAX LAW (*LEY DEL IMPUESTO SOBRE LA RENTA*)

W www.diputados.gob.mx/LeyesBiblio/pdf/LISR_181115.pdf

Description. Official website for the Federal Income Tax Law, maintained by the Federal Parliament. No translation into English is available.

PRIVATE ASSISTANCE INSTITUTIONS LAW FOR MEXICO CITY (*LEY DEL INSTITUCIONES DE ASISTENCIA PRIVADA PARA EL DISTRITO FEDERAL*)

W www2.df.gob.mx/virtual/tlahuac/transparencia/fraccion1/LEYES/LEY%20DE%20 INSTITUCIONES%20DE%20ASISTENCIA%20PRIVADA%20PARA%20EL%20DF.pdf

Description. Official website for the Private Assistance Institutions Law for Mexico City, maintained by the Government of Mexico City. No translation into English is available.

REGULATORY AUTHORITIES

TAX SERVICE ADMINISTRATION (*SERVICIO DE ADMINISTRACIÓN TRIBUTARIA*) (SAT)

W www.sat.gob.mx/Paginas/Inicio.aspxT

T +52 55 6272 2728

Description. Decentralised organ of the Ministry of Finance, in charge of the application of tax and customs law.

SECRETARY OF ECONOMY

W www.gob.mx/se

T +52 55 5729 9100

Description. Website for the Ministry of Economy, in charge of authorising names for incorporation of entities.

PUBLIC REAL ESTATE PROPERTY OFFICE IN MEXICO CITY

W www.tramites.cdmx.gob.mx/temas/muestraTS/15

T +52 55 5140 1700

Description. Website for the Public Real Estate Property Office in Mexico City.

BOARD OF PRIVATE ASSISTANCE FOR THE FEDERAL DISTRICT (*JUNTA DE ASISTENCIA PRIVADA DEL DISTRITO FEDERAL*)

W www.jap.org.mx

T +52 55 5279 7270

Description. This Board is in charge of the supervision of institutions for private assistance (*Institución de Asistencia Privada*) (IAPs).

Reinier W L Russell, RUSSELL ADVOCATEN

OVERVIEW AND MAIN TRENDS

1. WHAT IS THE HISTORICAL BACKGROUND TO CHARITY LAW AND CHARITABLE ORGANISATIONS IN YOUR JURISDICTION?

The Netherlands has a long and rich philanthropic tradition that is still prominent in the many almshouses, orphanages and hospitals adorning the townscape of the old cities. In the Middle Ages care for the poor and other weak members of society was funded by donations of private individuals, either to the church, the town or to their own foundations. They did so for the glory of God and the well-being of the neighbour, even if the prestige of the city and the reputation of the family also played a role. As early as in the Middle Ages the city authorities took over such tasks, but they were primarily funded by the income from donated land and gifts. Moreover, this was merely a supplement; the prime responsibility rested with the churches and the citizens.

In the 19th century the role of the authorities remained limited. At that time the state was considered as a night guard, whose responsibilities were limited to police, justice and militia, although the government provided education as well. The care for the poor and sick, and the cultural life, were left to private initiative. Many of these private organisations were founded based on religious beliefs.

Over time, the government took over more tasks and from the 1950s the welfare state took shape by the introduction of a system of benefits and subsidies. Funding of social objectives was almost entirely taken over by the government. This was only possible because the government could benefit from natural gas revenues, low wages (and thus also low benefits) and the introduction of a state loan as a financing tool in the 1970s. Due to state aid the Dutch non-profit sector became the biggest in the world, which employs 14% of the working population. Now that the government cuts down on these tasks, philanthropic organisations are gaining more importance.

Legislation

As early as in the Middle Ages, foundations and brotherhoods were established that supported the poor locally and maintained almshouses. The most important types of charity organisations, foundations and associations, therefore have a long tradition. The most important difference between these two organisations is that, unlike an association, a foundation does not have members. Historically, the most frequently used type of charitable organisation was the foundation as this was in line with traditional charity based on funds that were formed by bequests. Associations were better suited for the introduction of new activities for which the support of society was necessary.

Even though foundations fulfilled a very important social function, for instance regarding care for the poor, statutory regulations for foundations were lacking. This was introduced in 1956 and substituted in 1976 by a new regulation in the overall review of the Dutch Civil Code.

The law of associations had been introduced a century earlier, mainly because this type of organisations was also used for political activities. An association was therefore only granted legal personality when it was acknowledged by the government. This acknowledgement depended on the assessment of the objectives of the associations. In 1976, when the law of associations was included in Book 2 of the Dutch Civil Code, this prior assessment was abolished.

2.   ARE INDEPENDENT CHARITABLE ORGANISATIONS COMMON AND SIGNIFICANT IN YOUR JURISDICTION? WHAT IS THE CURRENT SIZE AND SCOPE OF THE SECTOR AND THE MAIN TRENDS?

Size and scope

In The Netherlands there are many charitable organisations that are prominent in society, for instance by collections, lotteries and other public campaigns. In 2013, about 65,000 good causes were active in The Netherlands that received over EUR4 billion in donations, which equals an average amount of more than EUR250 per citizen. About 70% of the Dutch people donate money to good causes each year. This places the country in the top ten donors in the world. The non-profit sector, also including education and healthcare, is mostly funded by government subsidies (however, that is taxpayers' money). Charitable organisations mostly fund special projects falling outside the scope of general funds or for which no subsidies are available. The government tries to cut down more and more in these areas. Therefore, charitable organisations are gaining importance and also the requirements placed on these organisations.

Trends

The most important developments within the philanthropic sector in The Netherlands are the increased transparency and professionalism. Both, the government and the donors make greater demands regarding the registration of donations and subsidies, partly as a result of reports on misuse of donations for other objectives than what they were donated for and on abuse of tax benefits by businesses. Therefore, since 2014, charitable organisations must disclose information on themselves on their website (*see Question 5*). The government offers organisations fulfilling these increased demands extended tax benefits.

Directors of charitable organisations have a key role in this. Over the past few years, the Dutch legislator has taken initiatives to ensure that the requirements for directors of charitable organisations are better in line with those for directors of other types of companies, even when they work on an honorary basis (*see Question 14*).

To promote the further professionalism of the charity sector, different types of training have been developed. For directors of charitable organisations, a co-organised post-graduate training programme of the Free University Amsterdam and the Erasmus University Rotterdam on Governing Charitable Funds offers young professionals the necessary training to act as a professional director of a charitable organisation. This programme further aims to promote continuity, diversity and expertise within charitable organisations.

Young professional directors, who successfully completed the course on Managing Philanthropic Funds, can join the Network Young Philanthropic Professionals (NYPP) (*www.nypp.nl*). The NYPP facilitates continuing training, seeks to bring together young professionals and is a platform for young philanthropic professionals to exchange experiences.

LEGAL FRAMEWORK

Definition of charity

The Dutch legislator has developed a specific vocabulary to distinguish between different
types of charity and to tailor the rules to different types of charitable organisations. There are
three types of charitable organisations, each with a specific aim:

- Public Benefit Organisation (PBO) (*Algemeen Nut Beogende Instelling (ANBI)*).
- Organisation Representing Social Interests (ORSI) (*Sociaal Belang Behartigende Instelling (SBBI)*).
- Foundation Supporting an ORSI (*Steunstichting (SBBI)*).

Public Benefit Organisation. A PBO must be almost entirely dedicated to the "general good",
which the legislator has divided into the following 13 separate aims:

- Welfare.
- Culture.
- Education, science and research.
- Protection of nature and environment, including promoting sustainability.
- Healthcare.
- Care for the young and the elderly.
- Development co-operation.
- Animal welfare.
- Religion, ideology and spirituality.
- Promoting the democratic legal order.
- Social housing.
- A combination of the above aims.
- Supporting a PBO by financial or other means.

Particular types of PBOs are almost entirely dedicated to cultural aims. These organisations
are referred to as Cultural PBOs (*Culturele ANBI*), and additional tax benefits are available to
them (*see Questions 5 and 10*).

Organisation Representing Social Interests. Whereas PBOs are focused on the general
good, ORSIs are focused on the social interests of a selected group, usually its members. At
the same time, an ORSI must contribute to society by engaging in activities promoting:

- The individual development of its members.
- The social cohesion of society.
- A healthier society.

ORSIs include, for example, youth associations, choirs, sports associations, music groups, and so on.

Foundation Supporting an ORSI. The sole purpose of a Foundation Supporting an ORSI
is to provide temporary financial support for an ORSI for the occasion of a jubilee. These
foundations are recognised for a maximum of one year in order to support a particular jubilee.
A Foundation Supporting an ORSI must be active in the field of sports or music.

In practice, the terms "charity" or "philanthropy" are used regularly. Therefore, where in the remainder of this chapter any reference is made to charity or philanthropy, this will mean the general good and/or social interests, unless stated otherwise.

Principal sources of law

Charity law in The Netherlands relates in particular to the conditions under which a charity is recognised and the specific tax (deduction) rules that become available and/or are applicable. In this regard, the following laws are of particular importance:

- **State Taxes Act (*Algemene wet inzake rijksbelastingen*).** This act provides the main legal framework for the recognition of charitable organisations. It distinguishes the three types of charitable organisations, and their primary characteristics (*Articles 5b, 5c, and 5d, General Tax Act*).

- **Implementing Regulations to the State Taxes Act 1994 (*Uitvoeringsregeling Algemene wet inzake rijksbelastingen 1994*).** These implementing regulations provide further rules on the implementation of the General Tax Act. In particular, it includes the basic rules for recognition of PBOs, ORSIs and foundations supporting an ORSI (*Articles 1a-1f, Implementing Regulations to the State Taxes Act 1994*).

- **Income Tax Act 2001 (*Wet inkomstenbelasting 2001*).** For charitable organisations, this Act defines which types of donations are recognised, and in which cases and to what extent they are deductible regarding (corporate) income tax (*Articles 6.32-6.40, Income Tax Act 2001*).

- **Income Tax, Donations and Public Benefit Organisations Decree (*Besluit inkomstenbelasting, giften en algemeen nut beogende instellingen*).** This decree provides further details on the state policy with regard to donations and the recognition of Public Benefit Organisations (PBOs).

- **Dutch Civil Code (*Burgerlijk Wetboek*).** Book 2 of the Dutch Civil Code provides the legal framework for different legal forms, including the foundation and the association, which are most commonly used for charitable organisations.

As the Dutch charity sector is characterised by a high degree of self-regulation, the legal framework is limited and the sector itself has developed various soft law instruments to provide guidance for directing charitable organisations. This includes for example the SBF Code for Good Governance 2015 (*SBF-code Goed Bestuur*).

LEGAL BODIES

4. WHAT ARE THE FORMS OF ORGANISATIONS THAT ARE USED FOR CHARITABLE PURPOSES? WHAT ARE THEIR ADVANTAGES/DISADVANTAGES?

In principle, there are two legal forms that are most suitable for a charitable organisation: the foundation (*stichting*) and the association (*vereniging*).

Foundation

Foundations by law must have a board of directors. Therefore, only directors take the decisions, although in practice often in co-operation with a supervisory board, which is optional. The foundation does not have members. The focus is on its objective, and the assets of the foundation are used to achieve this objective. Any profits made must be used for the objective of the foundation.

There are the following advantages to foundations:

- Low formation standards.
- No start-up capital required.
- Foundations have no members with an official role in the decision-making process (unlike an association).
- Because of a limited legal framework there is a lot of freedom to shape a foundation.
- A foundation is a legal person, so the directors' liability is limited.
- Potential tax exemption if the foundation is not operating a business.

There are the following disadvantages to foundations:

- In principle, directors are not employed and therefore do not fall under the employee insurance schemes.
- Foundations have no shareholders who can provide venture capital.

Association

In addition to foundations, associations are also frequently used legal forms for charitable organisations. Besides members, an association has directors and often a supervisory board (optional). They co-operate to achieve the association's objective without the intention to make profit. Any profit made must be used to achieve the objective of the association.

There are two types of associations:

- Associations with full legal capacity.
- Associations with limited legal capacity.

Associations with full legal capacity are, just like foundations, incorporated. This also means that in principle, directors cannot be held directly liable. However, this requires that the association is established by notarial deed.

This is different for associations with limited legal capacity. Such an association is not incorporated and therefore the directors are personally liable for all obligations of the association. For the establishment of such an association no notarial deed is necessary.

It is recommended and also quite common to establish a charitable association by notarial deed. Therefore, subsequent references to associations in this article will relate to associations with full legal capacity (unless stated otherwise).

Advantages of associations include:

- Low formation standards.
- No start-up capital required.
- The members exercise supervision of the directors (in the general meeting).
- Because of a limited legal framework there is a lot of freedom to shape an association.
- If the association is established by notarial deed, it is incorporated and the directors' liability is limited.
- Potential tax exemption if the association is not operating a business.

Disadvantages of associations include:

- Members are involved in the decision-making process (in the general meeting), which can, for example, slow down the decision-making process.
- In principle, directors are not employed and therefore do not fall under the employee insurance schemes.
- Associations have no shareholders who can provide venture capital.

There are also other types of legal entities in The Netherlands, such as partnerships, private limited companies and public limited companies. These are meant for profit-making entities and therefore less suited for good causes, and they are not permitted if an entity wants to be acknowledged as a charitable organisation.

Other legal forms

Besides foundations and associations, churches usually employ charitable activities as well. Although a different legal regime applies to the legal form and organisation of churches, they can be recognised by the Dutch Tax Authority as charitable organisations (usually as a PBO) if they pursue charitable purposes. In The Netherlands many churches are recognised as charitable organisations.

Trusts

Under Dutch law it is possible to set up a separated private fund (*Afgezonderd Particulier Vermogen (APV)*), which could encompass also the Anglo-American trusts. The capital of APVs is used for private purposes and therefore, in principle, they cannot be registered as a PBO or ORSI.

5.   WHAT ARE THE QUALIFICATION REQUIREMENTS/FORMALITIES TO SET UP THESE ORGANISATIONS?

Requirements for incorporation of a foundation or association

Foundation. A foundation (*Articles 2:285 et seq., Dutch Civil Code*) is established by notarial deed, by one or multiple persons (either natural or legal persons). This deed must be in Dutch and filed with the Chamber of Commerce. The deed of incorporation contains the articles of association which must include the following:

- The name of the foundation.
- The aim of the foundation.
- Information on how directors are appointed and dismissed.
- The municipality (in The Netherlands) where the foundation has its registered office.
- The intended use of the remaining assets in the case of termination. When a foundation wishes to qualify as a PBO, the articles of association must provide that in the case of termination all remaining assets will be intended for the purpose of another PBO with a similar objective.

In addition, the foundation may not aim at making profit.

Association. Associations (*Articles 2:26 et seq., Dutch Civil Code*) with full legal capacity are established, just like foundations, by notarial deed, by at least two or more persons (either natural or legal persons). This deed, in Dutch, must be filed with the Chamber of Commerce. The articles of association included in the deed must contain the following:

- The name of the association.
- The aim of the association.
- The obligations of the members towards the association.
- Information on how the general meeting shall be convened.
- Information on how directors shall be appointed and dismissed.
- The municipality (in The Netherlands) where the foundation has its registered office.
- The intended use of the remaining assets in case of termination.
- To qualify as a PBO, the articles of association must provide that in the case of termination the remaining assets will be intended for the purpose of another PBO with a similar objective.

In addition, the association cannot have the purpose to distribute potential profit among its members.

Requirements for recognition as a charitable organisation

For a foundation or association to be recognised as a charitable organisation, an application for the PBO status, ORSI status, or Foundation Supporting an ORSI status can be made with the Dutch Tax Authorities.

PBO status. To obtain and maintain the PBO status, the following requirements must be met:

- The organisation is not a company with capital divided into shares, a co-operative, a mutual insurance society or another body that can issue participation certificates. A foundation or an association is therefore a suitable legal form.
- At least 90% of the organisation's efforts must be focused on the general good.
- Integrity requirements apply for the organisation and those persons that are directly involved in the organisation (such as directors).
- A director or person determining the PBO's policy cannot treat the organisation's assets as personal assets. The organisation must ensure that the assets are segregated.
- A PBO cannot retain more assets than reasonably required for the organisation's work. For this reason the organisation's assets must remain limited.
- The directors' remuneration must be restricted to an expense allowance or a minimum attendance fee.
- A PBO must possess an up-to-date policy plan.
- The PBO's costs must be in reasonable proportion to its expenditure.
- Funds remaining after the dissolution of the organisation must be allocated to a general good objective identical to the organisation's objective (this must be included in the articles of association).
- A PBO is governed by specific administrative obligations. The administration must show:
  - what amounts have been paid per director for reimbursement of expenses and attendance fees;
  - the expenses of the PBO; and
  - the income and the assets of the PBO.
- The PBO must have its registered office in The Netherlands or in an EU member state, or in Aruba, Curaçao, Saint Martin, Bonaire, Saint Eustatius or Saba. Under certain conditions, a PBO can be registered in another designated state (*see Questions 12 and 13*).

Further, a PBO must disclose specific information on a website, including:

- The organisation's name.
- The Legal Entities & Partnerships Identification Number (*Rechtspersonen Samenwerkingsverbanden Informatie Nummer (RSIN)*) or tax number. The RSIN will be provided on registration of the foundation or association at the Dutch Chamber of Commerce.
- The contact details of the PBO.
- The PBO's object.
- The policy plan.
- The position of the directors.
- The names of the directors.
- The payment policy for directors and other staff.
- A report of the activities that have already been carried out.
- A financial statement.

To obtain the Cultural PBO status, the charitable organisation must fulfil the requirements for PBO status and be almost entirely dedicated to cultural objectives. These could be in the fields of visual arts, architecture, heritage, dance, film, music, theatre, and so on.

ORSI status. To obtain and maintain the ORSI status, the following requirements must be met:

- The charitable organisation must pursue social interests (this should be reflected in its articles of association or the organisation's regulations).
- The charitable organisation's activities should reflect the organisation's objective.
- The charitable organisation is not obliged to pay tax on profits, or has been exempted to do so.
- The directors' remuneration must be restricted to an expense allowance or a minimum attendance fee.
- The ORSI must have its registered office in The Netherlands or in an EU member state, or in Aruba, Curaçao, Saint Martin, Bonaire, Saint Eustatius or Saba. Under certain conditions, an ORSI can be registered in another designated state (*see Questions 12 and 13*).
- The charitable organisation will use donations or inheritances for its objective.

Foundation Supporting an ORSI status. These charitable organisations can only be a foundation. Further, to maintain the Foundation Supporting an ORSI status, the following requirements must be met:

- The ORSI, supported by a Foundation Supporting an ORSI, must be active in the field of sports or music.
- The Foundation Supporting an ORSI must be established for a one-off expenditure or investment for a special anniversary held every five years of the supported ORSI.
- One Foundation Supporting an ORSI can be registered per jubilee of an ORSI.
- When fundraising, a Foundation Supporting an ORSI must clearly indicate the purpose of the fundraising.
- The Foundation Supporting an ORSI indicates the calendar year of its fundraising as supporting foundation. When fundraising, the calendar year must be clearly indicated.
- The Foundation Supporting an ORSI must spend the money raised in the calendar year of the jubilee, or in the calendar year before or after.
- The foundation meets the administrative obligations.

- The articles of associations contain the following information:
  - the calendar year during which the foundation intends to be registered as a Foundation Supporting an ORSI;
  - the name, address and Legal Entities & Partnerships Identification Number (*Rechtspersonen Samenwerkingsverbanden Informatie* Nummer *(RSIN)*) or tax number of the ORSI in the field of sports or music. The RSIN will be provided on registration of the foundation with the Dutch Chamber of Commerce;
  - the purpose for the establishment, that is, exclusive fundraising for the support of an ORSI in the field of sports or music;
  - the purpose of the money raised, that is, an incidental investment or a unique expenditure for a special anniversary held every five years;
  - a definition of the investment or expenditure;
  - the commitment that any remaining money will be paid to a PBO, after the termination of the Foundation Supporting an ORSI.

ONGOING REGULATORY REQUIREMENTS

6.   WHAT ARE THE MAIN REGULATORY AUTHORITIES FOR CHARITABLE ORGANISATIONS? WHAT ARE THEIR POWERS OF INVESTIGATION/AUDIT/SANCTIONS?

Regulatory authorities and their powers

The legislative framework for charitable organisations is characterised by self-regulation. Therefore, the national legislator only provides a basic legal framework. In this regard, to obtain a PBO status, ORSI status or Foundation Supporting an ORSI status, an application must be made with the Dutch Tax Authorities.

In addition, sector organisations have developed various codes of conduct on good governance for charitable organisations. The most prominent sector organisations are:

- Cooperating Sector Organisation on Philanthropy (*Samenwerkende Brancheorganisaties Filantropie (SBF)*). This organisation is a co-operation of:
  - Charitable Organisations The Netherlands (*Goede Doelen Nederland*), the association for fundraising organisations in the charity sector;
  - Association of Foundations in The Netherlands (*Vereniging Fondsen in Nederland (FIN)*), the association for private charitable capital funds in the charity sector;
  - Institute for Fundraising (*Instituut Fondsenwerving (IF)*), an association of locally operating fundraising organisations;
  - Contact in Government Affairs (*Contact in Overheidszaken (CIO)*), a co-operation of all major Dutch churches to facilitate the dialogue with the government.
- Central Bureau on Fundraising (*Centraal Bureau Fondsenwerving (CBF)*). The CBF provides accreditation of charitable organisations.

Powers

The national legislator provides a limited framework for the:

- Legal form of the charitable organisation (*see Questions 4 and 5*).
- Requirements to obtain specific tax benefits (*see Questions 3 and 5*).

The Dutch Tax Authorities not only decide on approval or rejection of applications for a PBO status, ORSI status and/or Foundation Supporting an ORSI status, but also execute continuous supervision on recognised charitable organisations with regard to the applicable criteria. If a charitable organisation fails to meet these criteria, the Dutch Tax Authority can decide to withdraw a previously provided status.

Sector organisations have developed codes of conduct which are applicable to its members. Certain organisations in the sector provide accreditation of charitable organisations, such as the CBF. As of 1 January 2016, a new system for accreditation of charitable organisations (*validatiestelsel*) has been adopted by the sector. The applicability of these codes of conducts by sector organisations is optional.

7. WHICH BODIES OR PERSONS MANAGE CHARITABLE ORGANISATIONS AND WHAT GENERAL REQUIREMENTS MUST THEY MEET?

Governance of a charitable organisation

In governing a charitable organisation, a distinction is made between three different roles in the Dutch charity sector:

- Supervising.
- Managing.
- Day-to-day managing/execution.

There are different ways in which these roles can be designated to certain bodies/persons within the organisation. This depends also on whether the charitable organisation is a foundation or an association. These bodies/persons can include:

- Supervisory board.
- General meeting (associations only).
- Management board (under the articles of association).
- Titular management.
- Management/personnel.

A board of directors is the only mandatory body of a foundation (*Article 2:291, Dutch Civil Code*). Regarding an association, a board of directors and a general meeting of the members are mandatory (*Articles 2:40 and 2:44, Dutch Civil Code*). Though recommended, a separate supervisory board is not obligatory for a charitable organisation. In a foundation, the different roles could therefore be allocated to the board of directors alone. In associations, the general meeting will usually supervise the board. The bodies of the organisation and their roles are usually defined in the articles of association.

Requirements for directors

The Dutch Civil Code provides that the board's task is to manage (*Articles 2:44 and 2:291, Dutch Civil Code*) but the articles of association may contain limitations to this task. Directors must manage a charitable organisation in a proper way to discharge their duties. This general requirement has been further developed by jurisprudence (*see below*).

In particular, the board must keep financial records and prepare the balance and state of assets and expenditures after the end of each financial year (*Article 2:10, Dutch Civil Code*).

In addition, directors must comply with the articles of association. If they do not do so, they run the risk of dismissal (*Article 2:298, Dutch Civil Code*).

The regulations on PBOs identify in particular certain additional requirements for the directors of charitable organisations:

- Directors must comply with integrity requirements.
- A director or person determining the policy cannot treat the institutions assets as personal assets. The assets must be segregated.
- The directors' remuneration must be restricted to an expense allowance or a minimum attendance fee (this requirement is also stated for ORSIs).

For other requirements applicable to PBOs, ORSIs and Foundations Supporting an ORSI, see *Question 5*.

Further requirements for directors depend to a large extent on the codes of conduct that the charitable organisation imposes on itself. This will usually relate to issues such as:

- The objective of the charitable organisation.
- Usage of the organisation's funds.
- Fundraising.
- Structure of the organisation.
- Risk management.
- Composition of the board.
- Division of tasks (management and supervision).
- Allowances, reimbursement of expenses.
- Conflict of interest.
- Internal evaluation of directors and members of the supervisory board.
- Financial reporting.
- Communication policy.
- Volunteers' policy.

Director's liability

Dutch law requires directors to carry out their management duties in a proper way. If one or more directors fail to so, they can be held jointly and severally liable by the charitable organisation for the damage it suffers as a result (*Article 2:9, Dutch Civil Code*). This type of liability is known as "internal director's liability", because only the charitable organisation itself (the other directors of the foundation or association, and for the association also the general meeting) can file a claim against the inadequately performing director(s). An example of improper behaviour by a director is a situation in which he or she represents the charitable organisation and enters into a transaction where he or she has a conflict of interest. Consequently, this director can be held jointly and severally liable by the charitable organisation for any damage it suffers.

Although the associations and foundations are incorporated, one or more of its directors can be held jointly and severally liable towards creditors of the charitable organisation. This type of liability is called "external director's liability" (*Article 6:162, Dutch Civil Code*). The special conditions necessary to establish external director's liability are as follows:

- The director, at the moment the debt was incurred, knew or should have known, that the company would not be able to repay the debt and that the creditor would suffer damage as a result.
- The director has allowed or permitted the company not to perform its obligations.

The burden of proof rests with the creditor(s).

Not only directors, but also persons who are not officially registered as a director can risk director's liability when they act as a de facto director.

8.   WHAT ARE THE ACCOUNTING/FINANCIAL REPORTING REQUIREMENTS?

Directors must ensure that there is an accurate administration of the charitable organisation. To maintain the PBO, ORSI, or Foundation Supporting an ORSI status, an entity must have an administration which clearly provides:

- What amounts have been paid by the charitable organisation, per director, to reimburse their expenses and attendance fees.
- The expenses made by the charitable organisation.
- The income and the assets of the charitable organisation.

Although recommended from a governance perspective, in principle there is no obligation for charitable organisations to prepare annual financial reports. This would be different when the charitable organisation is operating a commercial business.

To assist charitable organisations, the Dutch Accounting Standards Board (DASB) (*Raad voor de Jaarverslaggeving (RJ)*) has developed guidelines for preparing financial reports. In particular, the Guidelines RJ640 for non-profit organisations and RJ650 for fundraising organisations are relevant. These guidelines consider, among others, the preparation of the annual report, the balance sheet and the statement of income and expenditures.

TAX

9.   HOW ARE CHARITIES TAXED, AND WHAT (IF ANY) ARE THE PRINCIPAL EXEMPTIONS AND/OR RELIEFS FROM TAXATION THAT THEY ENJOY?

Tax on income

Foundations and associations can, in principle, be exempted from paying tax on income, as long as they do not manage a business.

Tax on capital gains

Not applicable.

Tax on property used by the organisation

The common rules for tax on capital gains also apply to charitable organisations. A 30% tax rate is levied on a fixed rate of 4% of annual capital gains. A small amount of the organisation's capital is exempted from tax on capital gains.

Value added tax (VAT)

Foundations and associations can, in principle, be exempted from a VAT return, as long as they do not manage a business. This means they cannot request to receive (or be requested to pay) the outstanding balance that results from deducting the VAT received from the VAT that was paid in the VAT return.

Furthermore, the sales of products/services by a charitable organisation can in certain cases be exempted from VAT.

Other

When a charitable organisation is recognised by the Dutch Tax Authority, several tax exemptions can be applied. The main tax exemptions are as follows:

- **PBO.** The following tax benefits apply to PBOs:
  - the PBO does not pay inheritance tax on the inheritances and gift tax on the gifts it receives, when they are allocated to the general good;
  - under certain conditions, the PBO is eligible for a return of 50% of the tax on energy.
- **ORSI.** The following tax benefits apply to ORSIs:
  - the ORSI does not pay inheritance tax on the inheritances and gift tax on the gifts it receives, when they are allocated to the object of the ORSI;
  - under certain conditions, the ORSI is eligible for a return of 50% of the tax on energy.
- **Foundation Supporting an ORSI.** There are no specific tax benefits for Foundations Supporting an ORSI, however, donors' gifts to a Foundation Supporting an ORSI are deductible from the taxable (corporate) income (*see Question 10*).

10.   WHAT, IF ANY, ARE THE TAXATION BENEFITS FOR DONORS TO CHARITIES?

Tax benefits are available for gifts both by companies and individuals to charitable organisations that have been recognised by the Dutch Tax Authority. The benefits available to a donor depend on the type of:

- Gift.
- Charitable organisation.

Type of gift

The Dutch legislator has restricted the tax benefits for donors to two specific types of gifts:

- Periodic gifts
- Ordinary gifts.

Periodic gifts, among others where a fixed donation is made for at least five years, are fully deductible from the taxable income tax. In other cases, the gift is regarded as an ordinary gift. These gifts are deductible from income tax, but a minimum and maximum threshold is applicable.

Type of charitable organisation

PBO. The following rules apply to PBOs:

- For donors of a PBO, their gifts are deductible from the taxable (corporate) income.
- For donors of a Cultural PBO, specific rules apply for deducting gifts. Under certain conditions 150% of the gift is deductible from the taxable income for a natural person. For legal persons, a gift to a cultural PBO is 125% deductible from the taxable (corporate) income.

ORSI. The gifts of donors of an ORSI are deductible from the taxable (corporate) income.

Foundation Supporting an ORSI. The gifts of donors of a Foundation Supporting an ORSI are deductible from the taxable (corporate) income. As a Foundation Supporting an ORSI is recognised for a maximum of one year, donors can only deduct gifts under the rules for ordinary gifts.

DISADVANTAGES

11. WHAT ARE THE MAIN DISADVANTAGES OF CHARITABLE STATUS?

In the charity sector, some of the main disadvantages of being recognised by the Dutch Tax Authority as a charitable organisations are as follows:

PBOs. The main disadvantages of PBOs are:

- Inclusion in the publicly accessible PBO register of the Dutch Tax Authority.
- Obligation to host a website disclosing the following information:
  - the organisation's name;
  - the Legal Entities & Partnerships Identification Number (*Rechtspersonen Samenwerkingsverbanden Informatie Nummer (RSIN)*) or tax number (the RSIN will be provided on registration of the foundation or association at the Dutch Chamber of Commerce);
  - the contact details of the PBO;
  - the PBO's object;
  - the policy plan;
  - the position of the directors;
  - the names of the directors;
  - the payment policy for directors and other staff;
  - a report of the activities that have already been carried out;
  - a financial statement.
- Requirement to prepare an up-to-date policy plan.
- Directors' remuneration must be restricted to an expense allowance or a minimum attendance fee.

ORSIs. The remuneration for directors of an ORSI must be restricted to an expense allowance or a minimum attendance fee.

The above disadvantages, in particular regarding the publication requirements, are the main reason why only a limited amount of private capital funds in the charity sector have applied to have their status recognised with the Dutch Tax Authorities.

OVERSEAS CHARITIES

Charitable organisations that are registered in another jurisdiction can, under certain conditions, be recognised by the Dutch Tax Authority and receive the same tax benefits as domestic charitable organisations. Charitable organisations can be recognised by the Dutch Tax Authority if they are domiciled in:

- The Kingdom of The Netherlands (including The Netherlands, Aruba, Curaçao, Saint Martin, Bonaire, Saint Eustatius and Saba).
- An EU member state.
- Other (designated) states in specific cases. Other designated states include jurisdictions that the Dutch government has agreed treaties with, regarding the relevant taxation rules.

Also, on an ad-hoc basis, individual foreign charitable organisations are granted the PBO or ORSI status. In these cases, to obtain the PBO status, the Dutch Tax Authority will assess whether they meet certain additional requirements. In principle, these charitable organisations must provide, on an annual basis, information to the Dutch Tax Authority to verify whether the organisation still meets the requirements for recognition as a PBO. The charitable organisation must ensure that this information is credible, for example, by providing an audit report from a registered accountant.

13.   IS IT POSSIBLE TO REGISTER A DOMESTIC CHARITY ABROAD, AND HAS YOUR JURISDICTION ENTERED INTO ANY INTERNATIONAL AGREEMENTS OR TREATIES IN THIS AREA?

It is possible to register a charity in another jurisdiction. The Dutch government has also agreed certain tax-related treaties relevant to charitable organisations (*see Question 12*).

REFORM

14.   ARE THERE ANY PROPOSALS FOR REFORM IN THE AREA OF CHARITY LAW?

A legislative proposal is pending (Management and Supervision of Legal Persons Bill (*Wetsvoorstel bestuur en toezicht rechtspersonen*)) to further align the rules on management and supervision of, among others, foundations and associations with those rules that already apply to limited liability companies. This reform is particularly relevant as requirements and the liability regime currently applying to directors and members of the supervisory board of companies will become applicable also to directors and members of the supervisory board of foundations and associations. In addition, the law will provide more extensive rules on possibilities for dismissal and suspension.

Besides, the Dutch Accounting Standards Board (DASB) (*Raad voor de Jaarverslaggeving*) is working on a revision of financial reporting guideline RJ650 for fundraising organisations.

ONLINE RESOURCES

OVERHEID.NL

W www.wetten.overheid.nl

W www.treatydatabase.overheid.nl/en/

Description. Official website of the Dutch government including the legislative text of all acts and regulations referred to in this article. International treaties are also available in English via the Treaty Database.

REGULATORY AUTHORITY

BELASTINGDIENST.NL

W www.belastingdienst.nl

T +31 55 538 53 85

Description. Dutch Tax and Customs Administration. The website is available mainly in Dutch and partly in English.

SINGAPORE

Elaine Seow E-Lin, BRADDELL BROTHERS LLP

OVERVIEW AND MAIN TRENDS

1. WHAT IS THE HISTORICAL BACKGROUND TO CHARITY LAW AND CHARITABLE ORGANISATIONS IN YOUR JURISDICTION?

After Singapore gained political independence in 1965, charity law was one of the areas of Singapore law which was regularised by the Singapore Parliament. On 1 January 1983, the Charities Act (*Cap. 37*) came into force. It was based on the UK Charities Act 1960, with modifications considered appropriate for Singapore. The Act provided for, among other things, the registration and administration of charities and their affairs. It established the office of Commissioner of Charities, a position which held (and still holds) a wide range of supervisory powers over charities. The Act has subsequently been amended and continues to apply (*see Question 3, Principal sources of law*).

Charitable organisations were required to be registered under a register of charities. Corporate governance procedures were implemented, such as requiring statements of account on the affairs of a charity to be submitted annually to the Commissioner.

The information in this article is stated as at the law-stated date, and subject to changes in the legislation, rules and practices by the relevant authorities. For more information, please contact the author at the contact details provided.

2. ARE INDEPENDENT CHARITABLE ORGANISATIONS COMMON AND SIGNIFICANT IN YOUR JURISDICTION? WHAT IS THE CURRENT SIZE AND SCOPE OF THE SECTOR AND THE MAIN TRENDS?

Size and scope of sector

In Singapore most charitable organisations (except for public schools) are established independently as private organisations and form a significant part of the not-for-profit sector in Singapore. There are however, one-time government grants available to charities to assist them in their operations, including subsidies for:

- The charities' leadership or staff to attending training courses.
- Providing consultancy services from external consultants to improve their corporate governance.
- Their info-communications technology infrastructure and accounting functions, to comply with legislative and regulatory requirements.

Charities do not otherwise receive funding from the government, except in relation to tax benefits (*see Question 9*).

The latest available data shows the current number of registered charities as 2,227. This does not include charities which are exempt from registration: universities, educational institutions (schools), hospitals or religious bodies which have been established by an Act of Parliament and any other institution which the Minister by order declares to be an exempt charity. These stand at 133 at the law-stated date of this article. The total receipts of the charity sector came in at SG$13.9 billion (as at available data in 2013). The statistics in this article are gathered from a search on the charities portal at the time of writing.

Main trends

The main trends have been the continued growth of charitable operations in the two sectors of religious organisations and social and welfare organisations, which together form the majority (at least three-quarters) of all charities.

LEGAL FRAMEWORK

3. IS THERE A LEGAL DEFINITION OF A "CHARITY"? WHAT ARE THE PRINCIPAL SOURCES OF LAW AND REGULATIONS RELATING TO CHARITABLE ORGANISATIONS AND ACTIVITIES?

Definition of charity

A charity is defined as "any institution, corporate or not, which is established for charitable purposes and is subject to the control of the High Court in exercise of the Court's jurisdiction with respect to charities" (*section 2(1), Charities Act (Cap 37)*).

Principal sources of law

The main legislation regulating charities in Singapore is the Charities Act (*Cap. 37*) (*see Question 1*). The subsidiary legislation under the Act is the:

- Charities (Large Charities) Regulations (*Cap. 37, RG 9*).
- Charities (Registration of Charities) Regulations (*Cap. 37, RG 10*).
- Charities (Exempt Charities) Order (*Cap. 37, OR 2*).
- Charities (Prohibition of Fund-Raising Appeal) Order (*Cap. 37, OR 4*).
- Charities (Prohibition of Fund-Raising Appeal) Order (*Cap. 37, OR 5*).
- Charities (Registration) (Commencement) Notification (*Cap. 37, N 1*).
- Charities (Exempt Charities) Order 2011 (*Cap. 37, S 91/2011*).
- Charities (Accounts and Annual Report) Regulations 2011 (*Cap. 37, S 352/2011*).
- Charities (Exemption from section 39A) Regulations 2011 (*Cap. 37, S 487/2011*).
- Charities (Designation of Sectors) Notification 2012 (*Cap. 37, S 498/2012*).
- Charities (Fund-raising Appeals for Local and Foreign Charitable Purposes) Regulations 2012 (*Cap. 37, S 530/2012*).
- Charities (Restriction of Fund-raising Appeal) Order 2013 (*Cap. 37, S 689/2013*).
- Charities (Prohibition of Fund-raising Appeal) Order 2013 (*Cap. 37, S 695/2013*).

The text of this legislation is available at Singapore Statutes Online (*see below, Online resources: Singapore Statutes Online*).

LEGAL BODIES

4. WHAT ARE THE FORMS OF ORGANISATIONS THAT ARE USED FOR CHARITABLE PURPOSES? WHAT ARE THEIR ADVANTAGES/DISADVANTAGES?

There are three main forms of organisations used for charitable purposes, the company limited by guarantee, the society and the trust. All of these organisations can potentially qualify as a particular type of charity, the institution of a public character (IPC) as long as they meet certain requirements (*see below, Institution of a public character (IPC)*).

Company limited by guarantee

No shares are issued for a company limited by guarantee. The company is composed of members, who undertake to contribute (up to a financial limit) to the payment of the company's debts and liabilities, in the event of the company being wound up. If the member ceases to be a member before the company is wound up, that member will continue to be liable for one year afterwards, for debts and liabilities of the company contracted before their membership ceased.

Advantages. There are two main advantages in maintaining a company limited by guarantee.

- The company is a separate legal entity from the members, and can:
  - sue and be sued in its own name;
  - enter into contracts in its own right;
  - own property in its own name.

  From an operations perspective, this is convenient when the charity enters into contracts with other parties, such as service providers or fund-raisers, or continues as a going concern, with perpetual succession. Even if the company has to replace directors or members, there need not be a direct connection for any individual to set up as an office-bearer.

- Members have the option of limiting the amount they guarantee to a nominal amount, which would not deter a member from taking up the role.

Disadvantages. One disadvantage is that the financial costs of maintaining a company limited by guarantee can be significant, in particular in relation to:

- Complying with annual corporate governance procedures required by the Accounting and Corporate Regulatory Authority of Singapore (ACRA). It is mandatory to:
  - hold an AGM of the members;
  - lodge its AGM resolutions and annual return;
  - keep minutes of the AGM;
  - lodge resolutions; and
  - lodge any change in officers and company particulars with ACRA within stipulated statutory deadlines.

- Preparing and lodging charity-compliance submissions with the Commissioner or sector administrators.

The other disadvantage is that the promoters or directors of the company may view maintaining a formal corporate vehicle as too rigid.

Society

A society is established by ten or more members registering with the Registrar of Societies under the Societies Act (*Cap 311*).

Advantages. A society is viewed as more flexible, being self-regulating and more informal than a company, as it can decide, among other things, on:

• Its own constitution and rules.

• The rates and methods of payment for entrance fees, subscriptions and other dues.

Disadvantages. There is no separate legal personality and all members of the society may be personally liable for any liability incurred by the society.

Trust

A trust is recognised under Singapore law. A charitable trust is a form of organisation established as a trust deed. The settlor's trust property is administered by a group of persons (in their role as trustees) for a charitable intention set out in the trust deed. A charitable trust promotes a charitable purpose and does not benefit any specific persons.

Advantages. A trust is more straightforward than a company or society as there are fewer formal restrictions. It is chosen for specific scenarios, such as where the settlor:

• Specifies that the trust assets are to be held, invested and disbursed for a specified charitable cause(s).

• Documents those wishes for the assets to be used in a structured manner (primarily popular in the causes of disbursing funds for scholarships or medical expenses for the needy).

Disadvantages. There is no separate legal personality and trustees bear all legal liability incurred, which may be onerous for the trustees if there are ongoing activities and transactions where the trustees are expected to be directly and constantly involved. As at the law-stated date of this article, there are 92 registered trusts in the public database, which arguably evidences that this vehicle is not popular.

Institution of a public character (IPC)

The IPC is a "superior" category of registered charity which is able to issue to donors tax deductible receipts for qualifying donations. This enables donors to claim tax relief (from their assessable income) on the amount donated, at the stipulated prevailing deduction rate. For the requirements to achieve IPC status, see *Question 5, Institution of a public character (IPC)*.

5.   WHAT ARE THE QUALIFICATION REQUIREMENTS/FORMALITIES TO SET UP THESE ORGANISATIONS?

To be registered as a charity, all charities must comply with the following:

• Exclusively charitable purposes, with objects wholly or substantially beneficial to Singapore.

• At least three governing board members with two Singapore citizens or permanent residents (*see Question 7*).

Company limited by guarantee

A company must first be incorporated with the Accounting and Corporate Regulatory Authority of Singapore (ACRA). It must at the time of incorporation meet the following requirements:

- Have at least one individual who is ordinarily resident in Singapore acting as a director.
- Have at least one company secretary residing locally who is qualified to be a company secretary under the Companies Act.
- Have a minimum of two members, although they need not be locally resident.

To qualify for charitable status (*see Question 7*), the requirement of three governing board members can be satisfied by the directors and/or members assuming that responsibility alongside their existing duties. To constitute the three governing board members, these can be either of the directors, or members, or a combination. After incorporation, the company must:

- Appoint an auditor.
- Apply for charity registration within three months of incorporation.

The company's constitution must feature the number of members and the amount guaranteed and the object of exclusively charitable purposes (*see above*).

Society

There must be a minimum of ten persons to form a society, which must be registered with the Registry of Societies. The three key office holders (President, Secretary and Treasurer) and their deputies must be either:

- Singapore citizens, for a society whose object, purpose or activity is to represent persons who advocate, promote or discuss any issue relating to any civil or political right, including human rights, environmental rights and animal rights.
- Singapore permanent residents, in the case of:
  - religious societies;
  - societies which identify themselves publicly as, or whose membership is confined exclusively to, members of a single race;
  - any society whose object, purpose or activity is to represent, promote any cause or interest of, or discuss any issue relating to, a class of persons defined by reference to their gender or sexual orientation;
  - any society whose object, purpose or activity is to promote or discuss the use or status of any language;
  - any arts groups, except those promoting classical music/works.

In addition, the majority of the committee members must be Singapore citizens.

The Constitution and rules which govern the society must be submitted to the Registry of Societies on registration and must contain the object of charitable intentions (*see above*).

Trust

For any body or association of persons established for religious, educational, literary, scientific, social or charitable purposes, such bodies can establish a charitable trust and be registered as one. To do so, a trust deed must be drawn up which contains details of the:

- Trustees.

- Charitable intentions of the trust, the benefit(s) of which must be wholly or substantially to the community in Singapore.
- Objects, rules and regulations of the trust.

Charitable trusts are regulated under the Trustees Act (*Cap. 337*) under the supervision of the Ministry of Law and each relevant Sector Administrator (*see Question 6*). A charitable trust must have a board of trustees consisting of at least three persons (*see Question 7*).

Institution of a public character (IPC)

This is available for all registered charities (*see Question 4, Institution of a public character (IPC)*). To qualify for IPC status, the activities of an IPC as stated in its governing constitutions must:

- Be beneficial to the community in Singapore as a whole.
- Not be confined to sectional interests or groups of persons based on race, creed, belief or religion.
- Meet the objectives of its Sector Administrator (*see Question 6, Regulatory authorities*).

ONGOING REGULATORY REQUIREMENTS

6.   WHAT ARE THE MAIN REGULATORY AUTHORITIES FOR CHARITABLE ORGANISATIONS? WHAT ARE THEIR POWERS OF INVESTIGATION/AUDIT/SANCTIONS?

Regulatory authorities

There are six regulatory bodies which oversee charities, the office of the Commissioner of Charities and the five Sector Administrators that assist the Commissioner's office in overseeing charities in their relevant sectors.

The Commissioner's office, which is also referred to as the Charities Unit, and forms part of the Ministry of Culture, Community and Youth (MCCY) is the main regulatory authority. It oversees charities whose charitable objectives relate to the sectors of:

- Religion.
- Arts and heritage.
- Environmental protection or improvement.
- Animal welfare.
- Any other sector or activities which do not fall under the five Sector Administrators (*see below*).

The five Sector Administrators are the:

- Ministry of Education, which oversees charities whose objects relate to the advancement of education.
- Ministry of Health, which oversees charities whose objects relate to the promotion of health.
- Ministry of Social and Family Development, which oversees charities whose objects relate to the relief of poverty or those in need by reason of youth, age, ill-health, disability, financial hardship or other disadvantages.
- People's Association, which oversees charities whose objects relate to the advancement of citizenship or community development.

- Sport Singapore (previously known as Singapore Sports Council), which oversees charities whose objects relate to the advancement of sport.

See box, *Regulatory authorities*.

Powers

The Commissioner of Charities has powers to:

- Identify and investigate alleged misconduct or mismanagement in the administration of charities.
- Conduct inquiries.
- Take remedial or protective action in connection with misconduct or mismanagement.
- Issue sanctions, which may include removal of individuals responsible for such breaches from their positions.

Other powers include powers to:

- Obtain documents.
- Search records of charities for inspection.
- Appoint auditors to investigate the charities.
- Restrict transactions which may be entered into, or the nature or amount of the payments which may be made, by the charities under investigation.
- Issue prohibition orders on charities from conducting fund-raising.

The Sector Administrators are also empowered to:

- Obtain documents.
- Search records of charities for inspection.
- Appoint auditors to investigate the charities under their supervision.

The Sector Administrators also assist the Commissioner to conduct field visits to charities to better understand the charity sector and to promote good governance and best practices.

7.   WHICH BODIES OR PERSONS MANAGE CHARITABLE ORGANISATIONS AND WHAT GENERAL REQUIREMENTS MUST THEY MEET?

The organisation must have at least three governing board members (who are entrusted with the general control and management of the administration of the charity), of whom at least two must be Singapore citizens or permanent residents. The board member must also:

- Be qualified to act as a director under the Singapore Companies Act (*Cap. 50*) if acting within a company, meet the criteria as a member according to the society's constitution (and this is also reviewed by the Registrar of Societies upon its registration as a society) if acting within a society, and qualified to act as a trustee if under a trust.
- Be at least 18 years old.
- Not have been convicted, whether in Singapore or elsewhere, of an offence involving dishonesty, fraud or moral turpitude.
- Not be a bankrupt or have made a composition or arrangement with, or granted a trust deed for, his or her creditors and not been discharged in respect of it.
- Not lack capacity (within the meaning of the Mental Capacity Act (*Cap. 177A*)) to exercise his or her functions as governing board member or key officer.
- Not have declared his or her unwillingness to act.

- Not, due to any absence or failure to act, be impeding the proper administration of the charity.
- Not have been removed from the office of governing board member or key officer or trustee for a charity by an order made by the Commissioner or by the High Court of Singapore on the ground of any misconduct or mismanagement in the administration of the charity for which he or she:
  - was responsible or to which he was privy; or
  - by his or her conduct contributed to or facilitated.
- Not be disqualified from being a board member under any other criteria from time to time stipulated under the Charities Act.
- Not be subject to a disqualification order under the Companies Act (*Cap. 50*).
- Not be convicted for an offence involving unlawful expenditure of the society's funds or unfit to act as an officer of a society under the Societies Act (*Cap 311*).

In addition to the above requirements, for IPCs at least half of the governing board members must comprise of Singapore citizens and be independent of one another.

8. WHAT ARE THE ACCOUNTING/FINANCIAL REPORTING REQUIREMENTS?

All registered charities:

- Must file their annual statement of accounts within six months of the end of the financial year to the Commissioner of Charities or Sector Administrator (where applicable) (*see Question 6*). The governance evaluation checklist, which is a standard set of questions to charities in the form of a self-evaluation checklist on its internal corporate governance compliance issued each year to each registered charity, must be submitted at the same time.
- With an annual income or expenditure exceeding SG$500,000 must be independently audited.

All institutions of a public character (IPCs) must be independently audited.

Company limited by guarantee

Annual accounts must be prepared and:

- Audited by an independent auditor.
- Approved by the directors.
- Presented before the members in the mandatory yearly annual general meeting (AGM).
- Subsequently lodged with the Accounting and Corporate Regulatory Authority of Singapore (ACRA) within 30 days of the AGM, together with details of the AGM.

Society

Annual accounts must be prepared and for societies whose gross income or expenditure exceeds SG$500,000 in the financial year in question, audited by a qualified company auditor.

If the society holds an AGM, it must submit the annual return and audited accounts within one month of the holding of the AGM to the Registrar of Societies.

If no AGM is held, it must submit the accounts once in every calendar year within one month after the close of its financial year.

Trust

Trustees must keep accounts for charitable trusts registered as a body corporate under the Trustees Act and the accounts must be audited annually. These accounts must subsequently be filed with the Public Trustee in Singapore, and every copy is open to inspection by the public on payment of a prescribed fee.

TAX

9. HOW ARE CHARITIES TAXED, AND WHAT (IF ANY) ARE THE PRINCIPAL EXEMPTIONS AND/OR RELIEFS FROM TAXATION THAT THEY ENJOY?

Tax on income

Registered charities are granted automatic income tax exemption under the Singapore Income Tax Act. They are not required to file income tax returns.

Tax on capital gains

Capital gains are not taxable in Singapore.

Tax on property used by the organisation

A registered charity may be granted property tax exemption for property that it uses, provided the property is used exclusively for:

- A place for public religious worship.
- A public school receiving grant in aid from the government.
- Charitable purposes.
- Purposes conducive to social development in Singapore.

Partial exemption may be granted if only parts of the building qualify for exemption.

Goods and Services Tax (GST)

GST is the equivalent of VAT in Singapore.

Registered charities are treated the same as other businesses, which is to register for GST if their annual taxable supplies exceed SG$1 million. This rule applies even if these are non-business activities. GST-registered charities must charge and account for GST on taxable supplies including grants, donations and sponsorships.

10. WHAT, IF ANY, ARE THE TAXATION BENEFITS FOR DONORS TO CHARITIES?

Donors are granted a tax deduction at stipulated prevailing rates for qualifying donations to institutions of a public character (IPCs) (not simply registered charities). The current rate is 250% of the amount of donation made to local causes.

DISADVANTAGES

The following are the main disadvantages of charitable status:

- Mandatory yearly compliance requirements to submit business plans, and disclose activities and financial information to the Commissioner of Charities, with all details made available to the public for inspection.
- Requirement to make particulars of the charities and their key officers available on a register maintained by the Commissioner, and open to the public for inspection.
- Requirements to comply with strict fund-raising rules and spending ratios for fund-raising activities.
- Requirements that the charitable purposes must substantially (if not wholly) benefit Singapore for the charity or institution of a public character (IPC) and its donors to enjoy certain tax benefits. This arguably restricts the extent of local charities to appeal to donors.
- The operational costs to maintain audit requirements and engage in general ongoing compliance.

OVERSEAS CHARITIES

It is not possible to operate an overseas charity in Singapore as a charity per se. To be considered a charity, the overseas charity must follow the same registration and qualifying criteria as a local charity:

- Exclusively charitable purposes, with objects wholly or substantially beneficial to Singapore.
- At least three governing board members with two Singapore citizens or permanent residents.

See *Questions 5* and *7*.

The overseas charity can set up a Singapore chapter to do so and register the Singapore chapter with the Commissioner of Charities.

Alternatively, an overseas charity can operate in Singapore either as an:

- International non-profit organisation (INPO) under the International Organisations Programme Office (IOPO) of the Singapore Economic Development Board (EDB).
- International charitable organisation (ICO) under the EDB.

Donations to foreign charities and to local charities for foreign charitable purposes are not tax deductible.

13. IS IT POSSIBLE TO REGISTER A DOMESTIC CHARITY ABROAD, AND HAS YOUR JURISDICTION ENTERED INTO ANY INTERNATIONAL AGREEMENTS OR TREATIES IN THIS AREA?

Registering charities abroad will depend on the various jurisdictions' laws. There are no known international treaties or agreements in this area as at the law-stated date of this article.

REFORM

14. ARE THERE ANY PROPOSALS FOR REFORM IN THE AREA OF CHARITY LAW?

There is intended to be an implementation of a public rating of charities. There will also be a review of the current legislation (as the last review was in 2010).

ONLINE RESOURCES

SINGAPORE STATUTES ONLINE

W http://statutes.agc.gov.sg

The following are available on the site:

- Charities Act.
- Charities (Accounts and Annual Report) Regulations.
- Charities (Registration of Charities) Regulations.

Description. Official Singapore website for online publication of legislation.

REGULATORY AUTHORITIES

CHARITY PORTAL

W www.charities.gov.sg

T +65 6337 6597

Description. The office of the Commissioner of Charities (also known as Charities Unit) operates an online web portal called the Charity Portal. This online portal contains basic information for the registering of charities, compliance requirements, details of registered charities and institutions of a public character (IPCs), and online submission of annual compliance documents.

MINISTRY OF EDUCATION (FINANCIAL MANAGEMENT BRANCH, FINANCE AND DEVELOPMENT)

W www.moe.gov.sg

T +65 6879 6743

Description. For charities and IPCs with charitable objectives related to education.

MINISTRY OF HEALTH (IPC SECTION, AGEING PLANNING OFFICE)

W www.moh.gov.sg

T +65 6325 9220

Description. For charities and IPCs with charitable objectives related to health.

MINISTRY OF SOCIAL AND FAMILY DEVELOPMENT (SECTOR LICENSING AND REGULATION DIVISION)

W www.msf.gov.sg

T +65 6354 8659

Description. For charities and IPCs with charitable objectives related to social welfare.

PEOPLE'S ASSOCIATION (FINANCE DIVISION)

W www.pa.gov.sg

T +65 6340 5030

Description. For charities and IPCs with charitable objectives related to community.

SPORTS SINGAPORE (COMPLIANCE & APPS ADMIN DEPARTMENT)

W www.sportsingapore.gov.sg

T +65 6500 5099/+65 6500 5480

Description. For charities and IPCs with charitable objectives related to sports.

SOUTH AFRICA

Shirley Fodor and Tatyana Radebe, WERKSMANS ATTORNEYS

OVERVIEW AND MAIN TRENDS

South Africa's legal system is affected by the Roman Dutch and English legislative regimes' historic impact on its development. However, the spirit of *Ubuntu* (a Zulu word that denotes the essential human virtues including compassion and humanity) with which the South African Constitution is infused is pervasive in post-Apartheid legislation.

Charity law in South Africa is broadly classed under the heading of "welfare". As such, the Constitution places welfare within the ambit of co-operative government (*part 2, Volume 31, LAWSA*), with national and provincial government enjoying concurrent jurisdiction. Each province can promulgate its own welfare statutes in addition to the nationally applicable statutes like the Non-Profit Organisations Act 1997 and the Companies Act 2008. The Non-Profit Organisations Act 1997 represents the culmination of the efforts of the Directorate for Non-Governmental Organisations, under the auspices of the Department of Welfare. It takes a holistic approach to the welfare sector, creating an enabling environment to address the needs of the greater South African society.

The vast majority of non-profit organisations are independent non-governmental organisations.

Given the wide disparity in socio-economic status, charitable organisations take many forms. There are about 100,000 registered non-profit organisations and at least 50,000 unregistered non-profit organisations in South Africa (*www.ngopulse.co.za*). These are comprised of:

- Non-profit companies, registered under the Companies Act.
- Trusts, registered in accordance with the Trust Property Control Act 1988.
- Various community-based voluntary associations (which can be registered under the Non-Profit Organisations Act, but this is not obligatory).

LEGAL FRAMEWORK

3.   IS THERE A LEGAL DEFINITION OF A "CHARITY"? WHAT ARE THE PRINCIPAL SOURCES OF LAW AND REGULATIONS RELATING TO CHARITABLE ORGANISATIONS AND ACTIVITIES?

Definition of charity

There is no formal, legal definition of "charity". Under the normal rules of interpretation, words are accorded their ordinary, grammatical meaning. The guiding principle is that of *Ubuntu (see Question 1)*.

Principal sources of law

The principal sources of law are the:

- Constitution of South Africa.
- Non-Profit Organisations Act.
- Companies Act.
- Trust Property Control Act.
- Income Tax Act.

LEGAL BODIES

4.   WHAT ARE THE FORMS OF ORGANISATIONS THAT ARE USED FOR CHARITABLE PURPOSES? WHAT ARE THEIR ADVANTAGES/DISADVANTAGES?

Non-profit companies established under Schedule 1 of the Companies Act

Advantages. The main advantages of this type of company are:

- A non-profit company enjoys all of the benefits of juristic personality, including the protection of directors and members from personal liability. The primary difference is that there is an absolute prohibition on the declaration of dividends.
- The founders can elect to have members or not to have members. This allows for greater flexibility in oversight.
- This form of business entity is widely understood internationally, and facilitates the obtaining of donations from larger donors who are more comfortable dealing with a formal structure.
- The normal rules of accountability, governance and transparency apply, and may result in personal liability of the directors if they are proven to have acted contrary to their fiduciary duties.
- This form may be registered as a public benefit organisation under the Income Tax Act.

Disadvantges. The main disadvantages of this type of company are:

- This form is administratively intensive with higher costs.
- In the event that the non-profit company is wound up for any reason, any assets remaining following the payment of all obligations must be donated to a charitable organisation of a similar kind. There is an absolute prohibition on the remaining assets being returned to the founders/members.

External non-profit companies

Advantages. The main advantages of this type of company are:

- A non-profit company that is duly incorporated outside of South Africa can be incorporated as an external non-profit company in South Africa. A mirror image of the foreign company is created in South Africa.
- The process of seconding employees from the home office is relatively easy to achieve.
- This form can be registered as a public benefit organisation under the Income Tax Act, provided that the non-profit company qualifies for tax benefits of a similar kind in its home jurisdiction.

Disadvantages. The main disadvantages of this type of company are:

- A South African representative must be appointed who is permanently resident in South Africa.
- An office must be maintained in South Africa, with a potential cost implication.
- If the constitutional documents of the home entity are not in English, a sworn translation must be obtained for registration purposes in South Africa, again with a cost implication. Any changes to the constitutional documents that may occur after registration of the external non-profit company must likewise be provided and registered in the form of a sworn translation in English.
- Any changes that occur at the home company level must be made in South Africa. This places a high administrative burden on those in South Africa to ensure they continually update the status of the company and its directors with the Companies and Intellectual Property Commission.
- There is a possibility that any litigious claims made against the South African-registered company can be made against the non-South African assets and vice versa. The company is viewed as a single unit.

Non-profit trusts registered in accordance with the Trust Property Control Act

Advantages. The main advantages of this type of non-profit trust are:

- Trusts are generally flexible legal structures that can be used for a variety of purposes. The trust deed must be registered with the Master of the High Court in the jurisdiction where the primary assets of the trust will exist. While the Trust Property Control Act caters for all forms of trusts, non-profit trusts can only apply for tax benefits if they comply with the requirements of the Income Tax Act.
- The formation requirements and ongoing obligations of trusts are less complex than those of a non-profit company, and less costly.
- Unlike companies, the requirements for public disclosure for trusts is limited, unless it is registered as a public benefit organisation under the Income Tax Act, in which case the disclosure requirements are the same.

Disadvantages. The main disadvantages of this type of company are:

- It does not have a separate legal personality or limited liability. While the trustees can to a limited extent be protected from personal liability, this does not apply where they have acted improperly.
- Trusts are taxed in the same manner as individuals. If the trust follows an altruistic pursuit that is not recognised by the Income Tax Act or does not receive a special dispensation from Treasury, the potential tax liability may be higher than anticipated.
- Donors tend to prefer a company structure. They derive a sense of security from the enhanced disclosure requirements.

Voluntary associations registered in accordance with the Non-Profit Organisations Act

Advantages. The main advantages of this type of association are:

- Voluntary associations are the easiest to establish and maintain, and are more suitable for small non-profit organisations with a limited budget and few personnel.
- It acquires separate legal personality once registered, but registration is not obligatory.
- Given the simplicity of establishment and operation, voluntary associations tend to be favoured by the less sophisticated community based non-profit organisations, where income and activities are limited.

Disadvantages. The main disadvantages of this type of association are:

- This structure is not well known outside of South Africa and is viewed with scepticism, in particular by prospective donors.
- This structure is only suitable for small non-profits. The structures are not sufficiently developed for large organisations in which accountability and transparency are paramount.

Unregistered voluntary associations

The advantages and disadvantages are the same as for Voluntary associations registered in accordance with the Non-Profit Organisations Act (*see above*). However, it is highly unlikely that this type of association will receive substantial donations. It is usually a "by the community, for the community" arrangement.

5. WHAT ARE THE QUALIFICATION REQUIREMENTS/FORMALITIES TO SET UP THESE ORGANISATIONS?

All non-profit entities, irrespective of the form they take, must pursue either:

- Some form of public benefit activity.
- An object relating to one or more cultural or social activities, or communal or group interests.

The nature of the activities undertaken determines whether or not the entity qualifies for public benefit organisation status. This status confers tax benefits. There is a list in the Income Tax Act of activities that are currently considered suitable for this status. However, if the activity contemplated does not fall within one of the recognised categories of public benefit activity, the persons associated with the activity can approach the South African Treasury Department and obtain a dispensation. For example, a new category was recently created relating to the provision of infrastructure to public hospitals on a pro bono basis that would ensure adequate electricity supply (despite the current pressures on the national power grid).

Non-profit company

A non-profit company is registered under Schedule 1 of the Companies Act. At least one object of the company must be a public benefit object. All of the assets and income, however derived, must be used to advance its stated objects. There is an absolute prohibition on the declaration and/or payment of dividends.

A non-profit company is not obliged to have members (*Companies Act*). However, if the incorporators require it, the Memorandum of Incorporation (one of the constitutional documents) of the non-profit company must set out the rights and obligations of the members, including how membership is obtained and terminated. The Memorandum of Incorporation also contains the members' voting rights and entitlements.

A non-profit company must have a minimum of three directors serving as its board of directors. These directors need not be South African citizens or residents. In addition to the directors, the non-profit company must appoint a public officer to interact with the Receiver of Revenue. The public officer must be permanently resident in South Africa.

External non-profit company

An external company is effectively the mirror image of a foreign registered non-profit company in South Africa. The incorporation processes are identical to those for a South African non-profit company. However, in lieu of filing a South African Memorandum of Incorporation, the constitutional documents of the home country (with sworn, notarised English translation) must be filed. In addition to the director and public officer requirements, the external non-profit company must appoint a South African resident representative.

Charitable trusts

The trust is one of the most common legal forms for non-profit organisations in South Africa. Trusts in South Africa are governed by the Trust Property Control Act and, in certain respects, the common law. Save for tax purposes, a trust has no legal personality under South African law. It is an accumulation of assets and liabilities which vest in the trustees for the benefit of the beneficiaries. The assets and liabilities do not form part of the personal estate of a trustee but only vest in him in his capacity as trustee. The trustee sits in a fiduciary position vis-à-vis the beneficiaries. The trust deed must include the manner in which the trustees are identified as being eligible for appointment, their number, how they are appointed and their powers.

To form a trust, the founder must prepare a trust deed which identifies and appoints the initial trustees. The founder both:

• Pays the prescribed fee (at the Magistrate's court).
• Submits proof of payment together with the registration forms and relevant information relating to the trustees with the Master of the High Court (Master), having jurisdiction over the area in which the primary assets are situated (this frequently links to the location of the trust bank account) (*section 4, Trust Property Control Act*).

A person who is appointed as a trustee can only act as such if authorised in writing by the Master (*section 6, Trust Property Control Act*). The Master gives this authority by issuing letters of authority to the trustees once the trust deed is lodged and registered. The Master does not issue letters of authority to a trustee unless the trustee either:

• Has provided security to the satisfaction of the Master for the due and faithful performance of his duties as trustee.
• Has been exempted by the trust deed, the Master or by court order from providing security.

The Master usually exempts trustees who are South African residents, but it can be difficult to persuade him to exempt a non-resident trustee. Security is in the form of a bond issued by a registered insurance company to the value of the anticipated assets of the trust, and the trust usually bears the cost of the issue of the bond.

Voluntary associations

Under the common law, there are certain associations which can be corporate bodies that enjoy separate legal personality (known as a universitas) but which are unincorporated under any other legislation or as a result of registration. When deciding whether the association is a universitas or an unincorporated association, a court has regard to the association's constitution, as well as its nature, objectives and activities. An association must generally meet all of the following requirements to be a universitas:

- It must continue as an entity regardless of any change in membership.
- It must be able to hold property distinct from its members.
- No member can have any rights, based on membership, to the association's property.

It is also more likely that a court will treat a voluntary association as a universitas if it is registered under the Non-Profit Organisations Act.

The association's constitution governs matters relating to, among other things, the membership, management, powers and dissolution of the association.

The formation of a voluntary association requires an agreement by three or more persons to achieve a common objective, other than the making of profits. This agreement is commonly in the form of a written constitution that sets out the objects of the association and the rights and obligations of its members and governing body.

ONGOING REGULATORY REQUIREMENTS

6.   WHAT ARE THE MAIN REGULATORY AUTHORITIES FOR CHARITABLE ORGANISATIONS? WHAT ARE THEIR POWERS OF INVESTIGATION/AUDIT/SANCTIONS?

Regulatory authorities

Companies. The Companies and Intellectual Properties Commission, under the auspices of the Department of Trade and Industry, regulate companies. The Commission's powers are set out in the Companies Act and include the creation of a:

- Panel that has the ability to investigate complaints lodged.
- Tribunal that has the ability to adjudicate on any matter relating to the Companies Act.

Depending on the seriousness of the violation, the sanctions can include (*Chapters 7 and 8, Companies Act*):

- A fine.
- The director's exclusion from office.
- A prison sentence.

Trusts. Trusts must be registered with the Master of the High Court that has jurisdiction in the area in which either the:

- Majority of the trust assets are situated.
- Testator has passed away.

Trustees can only act if they possess Letters of Authority. The Master oversees the process. Any party who is aggrieved by the acts taken by the Trustees or Master can apply to a court of appropriate jurisdiction to obtain redress. The nature of the sanction imposed depends on the nature of the complaint. The Trust Property Control Act does not specify offences that carry a sanction, but the act complained of may be sanctioned under the common law or other legislation.

Voluntary associations

There is no designated regulatory body.

Non-profit companies, trusts and voluntary associations can choose to register as non-profit organisations under the Non-Profit Organisations Act. According to the Department of Social Development (which is the primary regulator for the sector) there are many benefits of a system of registering non-profit organisations. The system (*www.dsd.gov.za/npo/index. php?option=com_content&task=view&id=66&Itemid=114*):

- Improves the credibility of the non-profit sector because non-profit organisations account to a public office.
- Brings organisations into a formal system.
- Helps to organise the non-profit sector.
- Helps in obtaining benefits like tax incentives and funding opportunities.

The Minister of Social Development can prescribe benefits or allowances applicable to registered non-profit organisations (*section 11, Non-Profit Organisations Act*).

If a non-profit company, trust or voluntary association registers as a non-profit organisation under the Non-Profit Organisations Act, the sanctions for failure to comply with its provisions are fines and/or imprisonment.

7. WHICH BODIES OR PERSONS MANAGE CHARITABLE ORGANISATIONS AND WHAT GENERAL REQUIREMENTS MUST THEY MEET?

Non-profit company

A non-profit company must have a minimum of three directors serving as its board of directors. These directors need not be South African citizens or residents. In addition to the directors, the non-profit company must appoint a public officer to interact with the Receiver of Revenue. The public officer must be permanently resident in South Africa.

External non-profit company

An external company is effectively the mirror image of a foreign registered non-profit company in South Africa. In addition to the director and public officer requirements, the external non-profit company must appoint a South African resident representative.

Charitable trusts

The trust deed must include the manner in which the trustees are identified as being eligible for appointment, their number, how they are appointed and their powers. For more information, see *Question 5, Charitable trusts*.

Voluntary associations

The association's constitution governs matters relating to the management of the association.

8. WHAT ARE THE ACCOUNTING/FINANCIAL REPORTING REQUIREMENTS?

Companies

All companies must file an annual return with the Companies and Intellectual Property Commission. Depending on whether the founders have elected to comply with the higher transparency and accountability provisions of Chapter 3 (which is recommended in the non-profit setting), a company secretary and auditor must be appointed, and annual financial statements audited. If the company is registered as a public benefit organisation for income tax purposes, both of the following must be done:

- Annual financial statements must be provided to the Receiver, together with a register of all donations given.
- 18A tax exemption certificates must be issued for qualifying donations and a register of this must be kept.

Trusts

The reporting requirements of a charitable trust depend largely on the contents of the relevant trust deed. There is no reporting requirement to the Master. As a minimum, annual financial statements must be prepared. If the trust is registered as a public benefit organisation, the same provisions apply as to companies.

Voluntary associations

There are no accounting or financial requirements to the extent that the voluntary association is unregistered.

If any of the above entities are registered as non-profit organisations under the Non-Profit Organisations Act, they must both:

- Complete financial statements annually (in accordance with generally accepted accounting principles).
- Report to the directorate for non-profit organisations.

TAX

Tax benefits do not automatically accrue to a non-profit entity/organisation. An application must be made to the South African Revenue Service for tax exemption status. Once the Receiver approves the application, the non-profit entity is known as a Public Benefit Organisation. The Receiver only approves public benefit organisation status if the entity's sole or principal object is to carry on one or more of the approved public benefit activities listed in Part 1, Ninth Schedule of the Income Tax Act. These public benefit activities include welfare and humanitarian, healthcare, education, religion, and conservation activities.

Provided that a foreign charitable entity that intends to register in South Africa is tax exempt in the home country, it is likely to qualify for tax exempt status in South Africa.

Tax on income

If public benefit organisation status is obtained, the entity is not taxed on receipts and accruals that fall within and are directly related to the public benefit activity. All other income and receipts are taxed in the normal way. Companies enjoy a more favourable tax regime to trusts and voluntary associations, as these are taxed based on income received, as an individual would be.

Tax on capital gains

Public benefit organisations do not qualify for full exemption from capital gains tax. Any capital gain or capital loss made by a public benefit organisation on the disposal of an asset that has been used for a business undertaking or trading activity (or substantially the whole of which has been used in such an undertaking) is taken into account for the purposes of capital gains tax. Any capital gain or capital loss made by a public benefit organisation on the disposal of an asset which has been used as a non-trading asset, minimal trading asset or permissible trading asset is disregarded for the purposes of capital gains tax.

Value added tax (VAT)

VAT is regulated by the Value-Added Tax Act 1991 (VAT Act). The VAT Act is different from the Income Tax Act in that it refers to an "association not for gain" and a "welfare organisation" as opposed to a registered public benefit organisation or public benefit activity. This considerably widens the scope of its applicability. Any person or association must register for VAT if an enterprise is carried on with taxable supplies in excess of ZAR1 million (*section 23, VAT Act*). An entity can also voluntarily register for VAT even if it does not meet the threshold, if certain conditions are met. Voluntary registration applies if either:

- The value of taxable supplies has already exceeded the minimum threshold of ZAR50,000 within the preceding 12 months.
- There is a written contractual commitment to make taxable supplies exceeding ZAR50,000 within the next 12 month period.

For the purposes of the VAT Act, an "association not for gain" is a religious institution or other society, association or organisation which both:

- Is not carried on for profit.
- Is required to use any property or income solely to further its aims and objectives.

Where an association not for gain has met the requirements for compulsory or voluntary VAT registration, it is treated like any other business that makes taxable supplies, with the following exceptions:

- No output tax is payable on donations.
- The association can apply to account for VAT on the cash (payments) basis instead of the accrual (invoice) basis, which enables associations which rely extensively on cash flow to fund their day to day operations.
- Certain goods donated to the association are exempt from VAT on import.

For the purposes of the VAT Act, a welfare organisation is one that carries on or intends to carry on any welfare activity relating to:

- Welfare and humanitarian.
- Healthcare.
- Land and housing.
- Education and development.
- Conservation, environment and animal welfare (*Government Notice no. 112 in Government Gazette no. 27235, published 11 February 2005*).

The tax benefits of a welfare organisation are that:

- It can register for VAT even if it makes no taxable supplies.
- Where no charge is made for supplies, the organisation can still register for VAT and obtain input tax relief on its purchases relating to its welfare activities.

In addition, when a welfare organisation receives a grant that will be used for carrying on the organisation's welfare activities, the grant is subject to VAT at the zero rate.

10. WHAT, IF ANY, ARE THE TAXATION BENEFITS FOR DONORS TO CHARITIES?

Section 18A of the Income Tax Act allows taxpayers to make a deduction from their taxable income when they make donations to certain organisations. A donation only qualifies for a deduction if it complies with the following requirements:

- The donation must be made to an approved public benefit organisation that has status under section 18A to issue receipts.
- The public benefit organisation must use the donation to carry out a public benefit activity under the Income Tax Act. Alternatively, the public benefit organisation must provide funds to another public benefit organisation carrying on that activity.
- The donation must have been made bona fide and should not be a payment for services which the organisation has provided to the taxpayer.
- The donation can either be in the form of cash or property in kind, but not in the form of a service.
- The donation cannot exceed 10% of the taxpayer's taxable income, as the excess amount will not qualify for a tax deduction (*Tax Exemption Guide for Public Benefit Organisations in South Africa (Issue 4), published by the South African Revenue Service on 12 December 2014*).

The public benefit organisation that received the donation must issue a receipt to the donor. The donor can claim a tax deduction from the Receiver when submitting their annual tax returns by attaching the 18A receipt received from the public benefit organisation. The Income Tax Act requires the public benefit organisation to certify that both the:

- Receipt is issued for the purposes of section 18A of the Income Tax Act.
- Donation has been or will be used exclusively for the object of the public benefit organisation in carrying out the relevant public benefit activity.

If the non-profit organisation/entity has not obtained public benefit status, there is no tangible benefit to the donor.

DISADVANTAGES

11. WHAT ARE THE MAIN DISADVANTAGES OF CHARITABLE STATUS?

The main disadvantages of charitable status are the:

- Inability to declare and pay dividends or distributions to the founders or members.
- Obligation to donate any assets remaining on wind-up to a charitable entity of a similar kind.

OVERSEAS CHARITIES

12. IS IT POSSIBLE TO OPERATE AN OVERSEAS CHARITY IN YOUR JURISDICTION? WHAT ARE THE REGISTRATION FORMALITIES? HOW (IF AT ALL) ARE OVERSEAS CHARITIES TREATED DIFFERENTLY IN YOUR JURISDICTION FROM CHARITIES SET UP UNDER DOMESTIC LAW?

See *Question 5*.

Overseas charities are not generally treated differently in South Africa to charities set up under domestic law, once the overseas charity has been properly set up in South Africa. However, South Africa falls within a common monetary area that is subject to Exchange Control Regulations, with limitations being imposed on the level of annual foreign expenditure. Depending on the donation's size, an application may have to be made to the Exchange Control Department of the South African Reserve Bank before the payment is made.

13. IS IT POSSIBLE TO REGISTER A DOMESTIC CHARITY ABROAD, AND HAS YOUR JURISDICTION ENTERED INTO ANY INTERNATIONAL AGREEMENTS OR TREATIES IN THIS AREA?

It is possible to register a South African charity abroad. There are no international agreements in this regard.

REFORM

14. ARE THERE ANY PROPOSALS FOR REFORM IN THE AREA OF CHARITY LAW?

There are currently no proposals for reform.

ONLINE RESOURCES

THE DEPARTMENT OF SOCIAL DEVELOPMENT

W www.dsd.gov.za/npo/index

Description. The Department of Social Development has oversight of the sector. The information is in English and up to date.

NGO PULSE

W www.ngopulse.org

Description. NGO Pulse is a resource for non-governmental organisations in South Africa. It provides details of current events and concerns as well as service providers to the sector and employment opportunities. Information is in English and up to date.

REGULATORY AUTHORITIES

THE DEPARTMENT OF SOCIAL DEVELOPMENT

W www.dsd.gov.za

T +27 12 312 7500

Description. Committed to the agenda of social transformation that is embodied in the principle of social justice and the Bill of Rights contained in the South African Constitution. Endeavouring to create a better life for the poor, vulnerable and excluded. It is constituted by the Minister Bathabile Olive Dlamini and Deputy Minister Hendrietta Bogopane Zulu, who can appoint task teams and committees to address the concerns of the sector.

THE SOUTH AFRICAN REVENUE SERVICE

W www.sars.gov.za

T +27 12 483 1700

Description. The South African Revenue Service is the tax collecting authority established under the South African Revenue Service Act 34 of 1997 as an autonomous agency, responsible for administering the South African tax system and customs service. Information is in English and up to date.

SWEDEN

Michael Karlsson and Gustav Engvall,
MANNHEIMER SWARTLING ADVOKATBYRÅ

OVERVIEW AND MAIN TRENDS

Charitable work and the idea of helping less privileged people have a long history in Sweden. The church fostered the idea of helping people in need as early as the Middle Ages. This type of work intensified during the 18th century, as associations were created to help provide for people in certain guilds. This included financial support to families that lost a family member. As the number of poor people increased in Sweden during the early 19th century many organisations were established to focus on private charitable work.

The view on charitable work changed in the early 20th century. One reason for that was that it was seen as degrading to receive aid in the general view of the public, as it entailed an obligation for the receiver to be grateful. The view of charities changed further as social-political issues appeared on the political agenda. One idea was that social policy ought to be publicly funded, as well as rights-based and equal to everyone, so that the need for charity would be limited. After the Second World War the debate between two sides, about whether social works should be provided by private parties or the public, grew stronger.

This debate and the level of charitable work in Sweden have been affected by the dominance of the social democratic party over the last century. According to the social democratic philosophy, everyone is to be treated equally. Everyone should have access to publicly available healthcare, schools and, if needed, social allowance. The long period of social democratic governance in Sweden has resulted in vast welfare reforms. The need for charity has been somewhat limited compared to other countries. This could explain why there are fewer organisations in Sweden focusing exclusively on charitable work than elsewhere.

In recent years private charity initiatives have become more important, due to an increased focus on the need for aid in Sweden and abroad as a result of the current global situation. Recent developments indicate that the importance of activities by Swedish charity organisations in Sweden and abroad may increase.

2.   ARE INDEPENDENT CHARITABLE ORGANISATIONS COMMON AND SIGNIFICANT IN YOUR JURISDICTION? WHAT IS THE CURRENT SIZE AND SCOPE OF THE SECTOR AND THE MAIN TRENDS?

It is difficult to estimate the number of organisations performing charitable work in Sweden. This work is typically, but not exclusively, performed by non-profit organisations that are not necessarily registered, hence the uncertainty in numbers. The number of non-profit organisations has been estimated at 200,000. In April 2016, roughly 416 non-profit associations, foundations and religious communities have fulfilled the requirements for and received 90-accounts from the Swedish Fundraising Control (*Svensk Insamlingskontroll, SFI*). Out of these, 145 have qualified to and are members of the Swedish Fundraising Council (*Frivilligorganisationernas Insamlingsråd, SFC*) (*see Question 6*).

The total amount donated to charitable organisations has steadily increased over the years. In 2014, the total revenue of all non-profit organisations with 90-accounts was roughly SEK17,778 million, an increase of 6% compared to 2013. Out of the total revenue, 35% were donations by the general public. Donations from the general public increased by 6% compared to 2013. To qualify as one of the ten most successful non-profit organisations as to donations from the general public, an organisation would have to raise at least SEK163 million.

Overall, by the 2000s, turnover in the non-profit sector has reached about SEK140 billion. The non-profit sector also employs roughly 150,000 people.

It is difficult to make an exhaustive list of the activities carried out by charitable organisations in Sweden, as they vary widely. However, the Income Tax Act (*Inkomstskattelag SFS: 1999:1229*) can be used for guidance. Under the Income Tax Act, foundations, non-profit associations and religious communities can receive favourable treatment if they work to pursue certain public utility purposes. Foundations, non-profit associations and religious communities promoting one or more of the following philanthropic purposes, but not excluding others, can qualify:

- Culture.
- Environmental care.
- Care of children.
- Political activities.
- Religious activities.
- Healthcare.
- Charitable work to those in need.
- To strengthen Swedish defence in connection with military or other authorities.
- Education.
- Scientific research.
- Other equivalent activities.

A non-profit association can carry out these types of activities in a variety of ways. Further, the above list is not exhaustive for non-profit associations. Such associations can carry out another type of work, but can then be subject to less favourable treatment under the Income Tax Act.

LEGAL FRAMEWORK

3.   IS THERE A LEGAL DEFINITION OF A "CHARITY"? WHAT ARE THE PRINCIPAL SOURCES OF LAW AND REGULATIONS RELATING TO CHARITABLE ORGANISATIONS AND ACTIVITIES?

Definition of charity

There is no legal definition of a charity and no specific body of law governing charity work in Sweden. Charitable work has evolved over time and different types of legal entities have provided charitable work. The most common legal entities for charitable work are non-profit associations (*Ideella föreningar*) and foundations (*Stiftelser*) (*see Questions 4 and 5*).

Principal sources of law

Sweden has no charity act and no specific legal body monitoring charitable activities, so a number of laws and regulations apply. To a large extent, the legal structure of the organisation or legal entity decides which law applies. The most common form of association for charities and other non-profit organisations in Sweden are non-profit associations.

Under Swedish law there is no separate act or statute for non-profit associations. This type of organisation is to a large extent governed by principles in case law and the analogous use of legal rules covering other forms of associations. The Economic Associations Act (*Lag om ekonomiska föreningar SFS 1987:667*) is of special interest. It directly applies to economic associations (*ekonomiska föreningar*), that is, associations with an intention to make profit, and is often analogously applied to various types of associations that are not formally regulated.

Another form for conducting a charity is a foundation. A foundation is not a form of association, but is constituted by the separation of property. The Foundation Act (*Stiftelselag SFS: 1994:1220*) introduced basic legal rules for foundations.

Different rules apply to a charitable organisation, depending on its activities. For example, if a non-profit association or foundation engages in commercial activity, has large assets or is the parent to a subsidiary body, it must keep books in accordance with the Accounting Act (*Bokföringslag SFS: 1999:1078*).

Charitable work is also subject to control under general laws, for example tax regulations, and by certain regulatory organisations (*see Question 6*).

LEGAL BODIES

4. WHAT ARE THE FORMS OF ORGANISATIONS THAT ARE USED FOR CHARITABLE PURPOSES? WHAT ARE THEIR ADVANTAGES/DISADVANTAGES?

Non-profit associations

Non-profit associations in Sweden can generally be categorised into three different types of associations:

- Those who do not engage in commercial activity but by other means aim to promote a non-profit objective.
- Those who have a clear intent to generate funds for its members, but do not engage in commercial activity to do this (for example, trade unions).
- Those who despite conducting commercial activity, have a non-profit objective, that is, funds received are not distributed to its members, but are used for other means.

A non-profit association has legal personality and can acquire rights and assume liability. It can also be a party in judicial proceedings. A non-profit association is often organised in a similar way to economic associations. There is usually a members' meeting and an administrative body, usually a board, to make decisions.

Advantages. The lack of a separate statute for non-profit associations provides a lot of freedom for such associations to organise themselves to suit their purpose and activities.

Disadvantages. There are no obvious disadvantages of being a non-profit association, given the freedom it has in the absence of specific legislation.

Foundations

Foundations are not associations and consequently have no members. The Foundation Act sets out four different categories of foundations:

- General foundations.
- Fundraising foundations.
- Collective agreement (*kollektivavtals*) foundations.
- Pension or personnel foundations.

The aim of a foundation is to promote the objective and/or persons chosen by the founder, on a long-term basis. For example, to support education or scientific research, or to provide financial aid to certain groups.

A foundation is founded when its property has been separated from the founder and transferred to an administrator obliged to administer the property, in accordance with the foundation's objective. A foundation can meet its objective by using the yield of the separated property to give cash donations to certain individuals or groups, or by becoming involved in business activity, for instance in the healthcare, educational or housing sectors.

An important feature of the foundation as a legal structure is its duration. The separated property must, at the outset, be valuable enough to keep the foundation functioning for at least five to six years. An undertaking to inject funds into a foundation is not taken into account when calculating the value of the separated property.

Similarly to non-profit associations, foundations are legal persons and can sign agreements and have rights and obligations in their own right. The Foundation Act stipulates that the liability of a foundation is limited to its assets. The representatives of the foundation are generally not personally liable for the actions of the foundation. However, board members, appointed auditors and other representatives can be liable to pay damages to the foundation itself, if economic loss has been caused due to the representatives' negligence.

A foundation is not dissolved until it has no assets left after paying its debts (which are limited to its assets). If a foundation is completely financed with the yield of its separated property, that is, the property itself is not used and does not decrease in value, the foundation is of a permanent nature. A business conducting foundation, on the other hand, can be subject to voluntary or compulsory wind-up, much like a non-profit association.

Advantages. The aim of a foundation is to promote the objective and/or persons chosen by the founder on a long-term basis. This is an advantage for a founder wishing to establish a long-term charity for a specific purpose.

Disadvantages. The statutory registration and supervision by the authorities can be a disadvantage to foundations in comparison with non-profit associations. However compared with other legal persons, foundations have a high degree of self-governance.

5. WHAT ARE THE QUALIFICATION REQUIREMENTS/FORMALITIES TO SET UP THESE ORGANISATIONS?

Non-profit associations

The steps to form a non-profit association have been identified in Swedish case law:

- An agreement of co-operation must be made by two or more legal or natural persons.
- The agreement must be formalised by adoption of a charter, which must include information on the name and objective of the association.
- A board must be appointed.

Once these steps have been taken, the non-profit association is considered to exist with legal personality.

Generally, there is no requirement to register a non-profit association with the authorities. However, the association can be registered with the Companies Registration Office (*Bolagsverket*) if it will conduct commercial business and wishes to protect its trade name. It can also apply to the Tax Agency (*Skatteverket*) for an organisation number. Large non-profit associations (defined as associations exceeding certain thresholds in terms of number of employees, balance sheet total and net turnover) that operate commercial business must register with the Companies Registration Office.

Foundations

A foundation is formed when the founder signs a formation document, specifying the intent to create a foundation and to separate certain property which must be used for a specified purpose. The specification of intent must include the foundation's aim and intended activities, and the group of potential beneficiaries.

The separation of property is finalised when the property has been separated from the founder's other assets, by way of transfer to a party other than the founder, who is obliged to administer the property (which is then out of reach from the founder's creditors).

Although not a requirement for the formation, a foundation must be registered within six months from formation with one of the county administration boards (*Länsstyrelser*) appointed by the government, in or near the county where the foundation has its seat of administration.

ONGOING REGULATORY REQUIREMENTS

6. WHAT ARE THE MAIN REGULATORY AUTHORITIES FOR CHARITABLE ORGANISATIONS? WHAT ARE THEIR POWERS OF INVESTIGATION/AUDIT/SANCTIONS?

Regulatory authorities

Charity organisations are not subject to public regulation in Sweden as such, given the lack of charity legislation. There is no governmental body that regulates non-profit associations or inspects their activities. Foundations are registered and supervised by county administration boards (*see box, The regulatory authorities*).

Powers

If the relevant county administration board suspects that the foundation is not administered in accordance with the Foundation Act or its charter, for example it has not filed an annual report, lacks an appointed auditor or is reported by the public, it has a right and duty to intervene. For this purpose, the foundation must let the county administration board inspect its cash and bank balances, and its accounting documents and protocols.

If faults are revealed, the county administration board has power to order board members or external administrators to take certain measures, or even to dismiss them. It can also bring an action for damages on the foundation's behalf against board members, administrators, and auditors, if they wilfully or negligently cause financial damage to the foundation, for example by deviating from the foundation document.

Supervision by private organisations

Due to the lack of public regulatory control, private initiatives also monitor and inspect non-profit organisations. The most important is the Swedish Fundraising Control (*Svensk Insamlingskontroll, or SFI*).

A non-profit association, foundation or religious community that wants to receive acknowledgment for its charitable work can apply for a "90-account" from the SFI. A 90-account is a seven-figure bank account starting with the number 90. It is an accreditation of the work carried out by the account holder. The general view among the public is that organisations approved by SFI are sincere and worth donating money to.

The basic aim is to control how fundraising organisations use donations from the public. This includes the methods and costs of fundraising procedures, promoting proper advertising and ensuring that donations reach their destination.

If approved by SFI, the organisation can use a 90-account for donors to deposit their donations. This is a confirmation for potential donors that donations are managed responsibly, and that the money is used for the specified purpose without unnecessary costs.

To be approved by SFI and get a 90-account, a charity organisation must comply with the SFI regulations. In particular:

- The organisation must raise funds for humanitarian, charitable, cultural or other public utility purposes, and the objective of the fundraising must be specific enough to enable SFI to regulate its fulfilment. A 90-account is not assigned to an organisation with political objectives, nor if the objective of the organisation does not comply with law, regulations and good practice.
- The organisation must be a legal person with its headquarters in Sweden. An approved organisation is usually a non-profit association, foundation, or religious community.
- The persons in charge must be suitable for the assignment and appropriately experienced.
- The organisation must be governed by a board of directors with at least three board members and three deputy board members. At least half of the board members and deputy board members must reside in the European Economic Area (EEA). All members must be solvent and of full age and legal capacity.
- The board must regularly review the finances of the organisation and ensure that raised funds are used for the stated purpose, without unnecessary costs. The bookkeeping must be controlled by an authorised auditor.
- All fundraising activities must be supervised by persons with the appropriate knowledge and experience. Advertising must be ethical and not unnecessarily expensive. The raised funds must be used for the stated purpose.

global.practicallaw.com/**charity-guide**

- SFI can examine the finances and administration of the organisation at any time. The organisation must provide SFI with all relevant information and documentation to enable this. The organisation must keep books in accordance with the Accounting Act, and prepare annual financial statements in accordance with the Annual Statements of Accounts Act.

If the costs of the fundraising activities and administration of the organisation exceed 25% of the organisation's total income three years in a row, the organisation will be disqualified as a 90-account user. Failure to comply with the SFI regulations will also lead to disqualification.

A 90-account holder can also apply for membership of the Swedish Fundraising Council (*Frivilligorganisationernas Insamlingsråd, SFC*). The SFC is a joint industry body for charity organisations, which promotes ethical and professional fundraising. It has developed a code of standards applicable to its members. Besides the reputational benefit, members are also invited to events where they share experiences and are trained by the SFC. The SFC also influences public opinion on ethical and professional fundraising. The key words for the SFC's ethical fundraising are respect, openness, trust and quality.

Another organisation that monitors charity work in Sweden is Charity Rating, which is a non-profit association focusing on the interests of donors. Charity Rating analyses how non-profit organisations use donations and carry out their work. Charity Rating collects information about a large number of non-profit organisations and rates them. Among other things, Charity Rating provides information about an organisation's transparency, management and ability to deliver. Rated and analysed organisations are selected by Charity Rating through dialogue with industry bodies, such as the SFC, and other non-profit organisations. Rated and analysed organisations only include non-profit organisations and foundations performing charity at a regional level, excluding local charity work.

In addition, the donor might also take a monitoring role. For example, the donor might stipulate certain requirements for the recipient to fulfil, in order to receive and use the donation.

7. WHICH BODIES OR PERSONS MANAGE CHARITABLE ORGANISATIONS AND WHAT GENERAL REQUIREMENTS MUST THEY MEET?

Non-profit associations

A non-profit association is often organised in a similar way to an economic association. A non-profit association usually has a members' meeting and an administrative body, usually a board, to make decisions.

Due to the significant organisational freedom, the tasks of the different bodies in non-profit associations vary. The basic tasks of the members' meeting are to decide on amendments to the charter of the association and to appoint the board. The normal function of the board is to manage the association's activities in an acceptable way, and represent the association in its external relations. Legal capacity, being solvent and of full age (that is, 18 years old) are not prerequisites for being appointed as a board member. Nor is there a required number of board members, which means that the board can consist of only one person.

Foundations

A foundation can have its own internal administration, where its activities are managed by a board consisting of one or several natural persons.

Alternatively, a foundation can be managed by an external legal person, for example a bank, government agency or association, with the executive body of this legal person responsible for the foundation's affairs.

There are no differences in terms of duties, powers or liabilities between these two ways of administrating a foundation. An internal administration is solely appointed to administer the foundation and can be organised in a variety of ways. A related administration means lower costs relating to the board, and the possibility to co-ordinate the administrative functions of the foundation with those of the external legal person.

There are a number of administrative provisions in the Foundation Act. For example in a foundation with its own administration:

• The board represents the foundation and has authority to sign for it.
• The board cannot consist solely of the founder or founders.
• All board members must be solvent and of full age and capacity.

For foundations with external administrations, the legal person acting as administrator represents the foundation and has signing authority. The external administrator must be solvent and cannot be the same as the founder.

8.   WHAT ARE THE ACCOUNTING/FINANCIAL REPORTING REQUIREMENTS?

Non-profit associations

A non-profit association must keep books if the value of its assets exceeds SEK1.5 million, or if the association operates a commercial business or is the parent entity of a group of entities.

Non-profit associations that are required to keep books must prepare an annual report or annual accounts. An annual report is required if the association for the last two financial years has exceeded at least two of the following thresholds:

• More than 50 employees.
• Balance sheet total exceeding SEK40 million.
• Net turnover exceeding SEK80 million.

The same applies if the association is the parent entity in a group of entities and the group exceeds the above thresholds.

Non-profit associations that are required to keep books but do not exceed the thresholds above must prepare annual accounts instead of an annual report.

Non-profit associations that are not required to keep books have no legal obligation to prepare an income statement or balance sheet, but such requirements or similar can be set out in the association's statues.

Non-profit associations that are required to prepare an annual report are generally also required to have an auditor.

Foundations

The main rule is that a foundation must keep books if the value of its assets exceeds SEK1.5 million. However, certain foundations, such as fundraising foundations, collective agreement foundations and foundations that operate commercial business, must keep books even if the value of its assets does not exceed SEK1.5 million. Foundations that are required to keep books are generally required to submit an annual report to the relevant county administration board.

All foundations must have an auditor. Foundations that are required to submit an annual report must have an authorised or approved public accountant, while other foundations can have a general auditor.

TAX

Tax on income and capital gains

The tax rules applicable to legal persons in the Income Tax Act generally apply to both non-profit associations and foundations, so they are subject to tax on income and capital gains in the same way as other legal entities. However, if the association or foundation has a public utility purpose, it can qualify for a partial tax exemption and only pay tax on income derived from real property or commercial business.

Although the assessment by the Tax Agency is made on a case-by-case basis, according to case law it is possible to sell merchandise to raise money without the operations being defined as commercial business. Circumstances implying that operations are not commercial businesses include:

- An obvious discrepancy between the price and the market value for the merchandise (preferably, that the merchandise lacks value for the recipients).
- The sale is not made in a competing market.
- The clear objective for the sale is charity.

Purposes considered to be of public utility (*see Question 2*) include supporting education, scientific research or providing help for people in need. In respect to non-profit associations, promotion of, for example, culture, religion or politics, are also considered as activities conducted for a public utility purpose.

In addition, to qualify for the partial tax exemption:

- The organisation's activities must exclusively or nearly exclusively be attributable to the qualifying purpose, and the organisation must spend a substantial part of its annual revenue on the qualifying activities (about at least 90% to 95%).
- A non-profit association must also be open to the public, that is, nobody can be refused membership unless there is a specific reason relating to the nature of the association, for example that members must be of a certain age, live in a certain area, or practise a certain sport or activity. This requirement does not affect foundations, as they do not have any members.

Tax on property used by the organisation

If the organisation owns real property, the organisation is subject to property tax, just as with other legal entities. The tax exemption on income (*see above, Tax on income and capital gains*) does not affect the taxation of property held by the organisation.

Value added tax (VAT)

Only non-profit associations that operate commercial business can be subject to VAT and have the right to deduct incoming VAT. If the non-profit association is only partially subject to income tax (*see above, Tax on income and capital gains*), its operations are generally not considered as commercial business.

10. WHAT, IF ANY, ARE THE TAXATION BENEFITS FOR DONORS TO CHARITIES?

A tax deduction implemented in 2012 was abolished as of 1 January 2016, so there is no longer a possibility to receive tax benefits for donations to charity organisations.

DISADVANTAGES

11. WHAT ARE THE MAIN DISADVANTAGES OF CHARITABLE STATUS?

Since there is no specific legal regime applicable to organisations conducting charity nor any legal definition of charitable status, there are no real general disadvantages of being a charitable organisation. The supervision that comes with being exempted from certain taxes and qualifying for a 90-account (*see Question 6*) is a possible disadvantage. However, it is not mandatory for a charity organisation to apply for a tax exemption or a 90-account.

OVERSEAS CHARITIES

12. IS IT POSSIBLE TO OPERATE AN OVERSEAS CHARITY IN YOUR JURISDICTION? WHAT ARE THE REGISTRATION FORMALITIES? HOW (IF AT ALL) ARE OVERSEAS CHARITIES TREATED DIFFERENTLY IN YOUR JURISDICTION FROM CHARITIES SET UP UNDER DOMESTIC LAW?

There is no separate regulation for overseas charities. Only organisations seated in Sweden can apply for a 90-account (*see Question 6*). However, this is not usually a problem, since many international charity organisations operate in Sweden through local branches with Swedish headquarters. The branch is set up as a local office with an independent management. The person appointed as manager must register the branch with the Companies Registration Office (*Bolagsverket*). Branch letters, invoices, order forms and websites must contain information about the foreign charity's:

- Legal form and registered office.
- Foreign registration.
- Company number in the register.
- Branch name and registration.

13. IS IT POSSIBLE TO REGISTER A DOMESTIC CHARITY ABROAD, AND HAS YOUR JURISDICTION ENTERED INTO ANY INTERNATIONAL AGREEMENTS OR TREATIES IN THIS AREA?

This issue is a question for the authorities in the relevant jurisdiction. Sweden has not entered any international agreements or treaties in this area.

REFORM

14. ARE THERE ANY PROPOSALS FOR REFORM IN THE AREA OF CHARITY LAW?

To the best of the authors' knowledge there are no proposals for reform in the area of charity law. However, changes to other legislation, for example tax legislation, can affect charitable organisations.

ONLINE RESOURCES

SWEDISH PARLIAMENT

W www.riksdagen.se/sv/dokument-lagar

Description. Official website of the Swedish Parliament. All legislation referred to in in the article is available in Swedish on this website.

REGULATORY AUTHORITIES

SWEDISH TAX AGENCY

W www.skatteverket.se

T +46 8 564 851 60

Description. The Swedish Tax Agency is the governmental authority responsible for taxation of charitable organisations.

SWEDISH COUNTY ADMINISTRATION BOARDS

W www.lansstyrelserna.se

T +46 10 22 30 303

Description. The county administration boards are the representative authorities of the government in the 21 counties of Sweden, responsible for among other things the supervision of foundations.

SWITZERLAND

Benoît Merkt, LENZ & STAEHELIN

OVERVIEW AND MAIN TRENDS

1. WHAT IS THE HISTORICAL BACKGROUND TO CHARITY LAW AND CHARITABLE ORGANISATIONS IN YOUR JURISDICTION?

In Switzerland, charitable organisations appeared in the Middle Ages. They were essentially rooted in the concept of Christian charity and enabled notably the construction and/or support of hospitals, alms houses and orphanages.

Those organisations form the basis of some charitable organisations that still exist today in Switzerland. For example, one of the oldest Swiss foundations, the Inselspital in Bern, was founded in 1354 and is still operating today, more than 650 years later.

During the 18th century, non-profit organisations fulfilled an important relief function as a consequence of the general scarcity following wars in Europe which also had consequences on the Swiss territory.

One century later, under the influence of the liberal policy which dominated Switzerland following the adoption of the federal Constitution in 1848, several civil society organisations emerged. The most flourishing non-profit organisations in the 19th century were associations which still play today a major role in various fields such as the regulation of economic activities, civil rights, education, social causes and sport. Later in the 19th century, during the industrialisation period, political and social organisations were founded to support the rural population, urban workers and orphans suffering from social deprivation. From 1804 to 1824, the Swiss Johann Heinrich Pestalozzi, father of modern pedagogic, founded several orphanages and schools to support children in need and provide them with education.

Following the aftermath of the wars devastating Europe during the century, in 1863 a Swiss citizen, Henry Dunant, founded the International Committee for Relief of the Wounded in Geneva which intended notably to guarantee the neutrality, protection and relief of wounded soldiers. This organisation later evolved into the International Committee of the Red Cross (ICRC) (*Comité international de la Croix-Rouge (CICR)*) which has its seat in Switzerland.

In the 20th century, Switzerland's policy of external neutrality and its strong domestic federalism regime resulted in non-profit organisations becoming important vehicles of social dialogue and communication between regions of Switzerland. In addition, the adoption of the Swiss Civil Code in 1907 marks the birth of modern foundation and association law by harmonising at the federal level the legal regimes of foundations and associations.

The expansion of the International Committee of the Red Cross (ICRC) and the formation of the League of Nations in Geneva in 1925 bolstered the development of Switzerland, and Geneva in particular, as a hub for the incorporation of charitable foundations of international scope.

More recently, in the mid-1990s and following the adoption by the United Nations of the Millennium Development Goals in 2002, the Swiss charitable sector experienced an increased trend in addressing issues of disparity and gap between the richest and the poorest countries. This marks the starting point of a succession of major new foundations and associations of international scope which pursue their charitable objectives abroad. Key actors in the field of charity worldwide have their seat in Switzerland and play an important role in the main charity fields, such as the defence of human rights, the relief of the poor, education, health, environment, disaster relief, science and research as well as art.

2. ARE INDEPENDENT CHARITABLE ORGANISATIONS COMMON AND SIGNIFICANT IN YOUR JURISDICTION? WHAT IS THE CURRENT SIZE AND SCOPE OF THE SECTOR AND THE MAIN TRENDS?

The charitable sector plays a significant role in Switzerland. Both foundations (*Stiftung/fondation*) and associations (*Verein/association*) are commonly used vehicles of philanthropy. Other Swiss legal forms are not excluded from pursuing public utility purposes and benefit from a tax exemption. However, these legal entities will not be discussed in this article.

Associations

The registration in the Register of commerce is not mandatory for associations having a non-profit purpose. Therefore, there is no reliable data available on the number of associations established in Switzerland. Consequently, a central picture of the entire Swiss non-profit sector is currently not available. Associations are a common legal form used in particular by international sports federations.

Foundations

In 2016, there were 13,075 charitable foundations registered in Switzerland, over half of which have been established in the past 20 years. 300 new foundations were created in 2015 alone. The number of foundations deleted from the Register of commerce has also increased over the past years with more than a thousand estimated removals since 2009. According to the statistics of the Swiss Supervisory Authority of Foundations, in 2015 4,079 foundations were supervised at the federal level. This represents the number of Swiss foundations which are active in Switzerland and abroad and not just locally. Thus, approximately one-third of Swiss foundations have an international scope of activity which outlines the trend emphasised above towards global philanthropy that has been in constant progression in Switzerland, especially since the mid-1990s (*see Question 1*).

The total amount of assets held by foundations in Switzerland has been estimated to exceed CHF70 billion, of which between CHF1.5 to CHF2 billion is distributed each year for their charitable purposes. However, foundations are often small. A study of 2003 conducted by the Swiss Supervisory Authority of Foundation has shown that a quarter of foundations under its supervision had less than CHF500 million in assets and 85% had assets under CHF5 million.

LEGAL FRAMEWORK

Definition of charity

As such, there is no legal concept of "charity" under Swiss law. The concept corresponding to
the notion of charity is the tax law concept of "public utility" which is discussed in *Question 9*.

Principal sources of law

The principal sources of Swiss law relating to foundations and associations are included in the
Civil Code (CC), in particular:

- Article 80 to 89bis of the CC concerning foundations.
- Article 60 to 79 of the CC regarding associations.

As far as tax law is concerned, the Federal Direct Tax Act (FDTA) is applicable. Article 56g of
the FDTA defines the requirements for public interest organisations to be tax exempt, which
are laid out in greater detail in the Federal Tax Administration's Circular No.12 of 8 July 1994
and guidelines of 18 January 2008 established by the Swiss Tax Conference for the cantonal
tax authorities.

LEGAL BODIES

In Switzerland, the two forms of legal entities that are commonly used for charitable purposes
are foundations (*see below, Foundation*) and associations (*see below, Association*).

Foundation

A foundation is an autonomous legal entity consisting of a pool of assets irrevocably
committed to one or more defined purpose(s) (*Article 80, Civil Code (CC)*). As an autonomous
and separate legal entity, it benefits from full legal personality.

A foundation is established by one or several founder(s), who can be Swiss or foreign
individuals or a legal entity. International organisations and/or governmental entities can also
be founders of a Swiss foundation. In practice, a minimum initial capital of CHF50,000 must
be contributed by the founder.

A foundation can have any kind of clearly defined purpose(s) provided that it is lawful, not
impossible nor immoral. The foundations are not required to pursue charitable purposes, that
is, activities that are in the interests of the public or that can be considered as altruistic.

The founders' control over a foundation is essentially exercised at the time of the constitution of the foundation (for example, the founders typically select and appoint the members of the initial board of the foundation). Once constituted and enrolled in the Register of commerce, the foundation becomes an autonomous legal entity thus falling outside of the direct control of the founder. The founder, however, can retain the right to amend the purpose clause of the foundation provided that:

- Ten years have elapsed since the foundation's constitution or the last amendment.
- Such amendment is expressly provided by the statutes.

The supreme body of a foundation is the board of the foundation, which is vested with executive functions and in particular with the administration and the representation of the foundation (*see Question 7*).

Under Article 84 of the CC, Swiss foundations are subject to the supervision of a governmental authority (*see Question 6*). Foundations with international scope are subject to federal supervision of the Swiss Supervisory Authority of Foundations based in Bern (Supervisory Authority). In case a foundation has a local scope of activity, it can be subject to the cantonal supervisory authority of its canton of seat.

Association

An association is an autonomous separate legal entity formed by individuals or corporate members. An association acquires legal personality as soon as its intent to exist as an independent corporation is made apparent from its statutes (*Article 60, Civil Code*). Therefore, associations acquire their legal personality independently from their enrolment in the Register of commerce (*see Question 5*).

Contrary to foundations, associations are composed of members. In practice, there must be a minimum of two members to constitute an association.

Under Article 64 of the CC, the supreme body of an association is the general assembly which is also the general meeting of the members of the association (*see Question 7*). A membership fee can be imposed by the statutes (*Article 71, CC*). Since the members of an association exercise supervision of the association, an association is not subject to an external supervisory authority.

The main purpose of an association cannot be economical, which means that it cannot procure to its members an advantage directly linked to its commercial or industrial activities. In other words, associations with an ideal purpose can carry out commercial activities to achieve their purpose(s) while associations with an economic purpose cannot carry out commercial activities to achieve their purpose(s), except if the economic purposes are secondary and ancillary to the association's ideal purpose(s).

Comparison between association and foundation

The two vehicles do not have the same features as such; both types have advantages and disadvantages. For example, the supreme governing body of an association is the general assembly of its members, whereas that of the foundation is its board. In addition, the members of a foundation's board have a fiduciary duty to act in the best interest of the foundation. There is no such duty for members of an association. Consequently, members of an association can vote decisions and influence its activities based on their own interests, which may in some cases depart from those of the association and potentially also its donors.

Furthermore, the purpose of an association can be changed by the general assembly of members, however, in principle, the purpose of a foundation cannot be changed except in extraordinary circumstances. As a consequence, a foundation is in general preferred by donors as it offers an increased stability and security over time as regards the exclusive use of its assets in strict compliance with the purpose it is incorporated for.

Moreover, unlike associations, Swiss foundations are subject to State supervision. The supervision provides an additional protection towards ensuring that the funds cannot be diverted from the purpose of the foundation.

5.   WHAT ARE THE QUALIFICATION REQUIREMENTS/FORMALITIES TO SET UP THESE ORGANISATIONS?

Foundation

The first step in the constitution of a foundation is the drafting of its statutes: the foundation's purpose and its resources, its general organisation, bodies and their respective powers are set out in the foundation's statutes.

Once the statutes are approved by the founder, they must be cleared by the competent supervisory authority, cantonal or federal, depending on the scope of the foundation's activity.

After the preliminary clearance of the statutes by the supervisory authority, it is advisable to file a request for preliminary tax exemption with the tax authorities. Following the supervisory authority's preapproval and the granting of the preliminary tax exempt ruling by the tax authorities, the foundation is formally constituted by public notary deed.

The foundation will acquire legal personality on registration in the Register of commerce (*see Question 4, Foundation*). A bank account will then be opened in the name of the foundation and the founder will pay the initial capital to the foundation, following which the Supervisory Authority will issue a decision assuming supervision.

Association

An association acquires its legal personality as soon as its members adopt written statutes laying down the members' intent to be organised as a corporate body. The statutes need to include provisions regarding the purpose(s), the resources and the organisation of the association (*Article 60 paragraph 2, CC*).

Thus, contrary to foundations, an association is easier to set up as its legal personality is not subject to the enrolment in the Register of commerce. However, under Article 61 paragraph 2 of the CC, associations must be enrolled in the Register of commerce if:

• It conducts a commercial operation in the pursuit of its purpose.
• It is subject to an audit requirement.

Similarly to the foundation, the tax exempt status can also be granted to an association, provided that the entity fulfills the conditions listed in *Question 9*.

ONGOING REGULATORY REQUIREMENTS

6. WHAT ARE THE MAIN REGULATORY AUTHORITIES FOR CHARITABLE ORGANISATIONS? WHAT ARE THEIR POWERS OF INVESTIGATION/AUDIT/SANCTIONS?

Regulatory authorities

Associations are not subject to any governmental supervision whereas foundations are subject to the supervision of the federal or cantonal Supervisory Authority of Foundations, depending on whether it will be active on a local, national, or international level (*Article 84 d, Civil Code(CC)*).

In addition, if an association or a foundation benefit from a tax exemption for public interest, they must comply with the requirements for such exemption, not only at the time of the request but also on an ongoing basis. The tax authorities are thus entitled to regularly check whether this is effectively the case. This verification typically occurs when the entity files its annual tax return. In this context, the charity sends its audited accounts to the tax administration. Therefore the tax authorities also exercise some kind of supervision on charities in this respect.

Powers of the Supervisory Authority of Foundations

The Supervisory Authority of Foundations has the following prerogatives on foundations:

* It ensures that the foundation's assets are allocated according to the foundation's purpose(s). To warrant such compliance, each foundation must provide the Supervisory Authority with an annual report including:
  – an annual activity report,
  – an audit report; and
  – the accounts of the foundation.
  In addition, each document must be approved by the board.
* It can intervene when needed in the organisation of the foundation (*Articles 81 paragraph 2 and 83d, CC*).
* Some activities of a foundation require preapproval from the Supervisory Authority, for example for:
  – any modification of the statutes;
  – the adoption and/or modification of bye-laws;
  – the merger of a foundation; and
  – its dissolution.
* The Supervisory Authority must be regularly informed about any modifications in the composition of the board.

The supervisory power of the Supervisory Authority is broad and covers all the activities of the foundation. If a foundation does not comply with its statutes or Swiss law, the Supervisory Authority can intervene and render binding decisions. In serious cases, the Supervisory Authority has the power to revoke board members.

However, according to the Swiss Supreme Court, the Supervisory Authority should refrain from intervening and acting instead of the board of the foundation. The Swiss Supreme Court held that the Supervisory Authority could not exercise an opportunity control over the decisions of the board (for example in relation to the choices made by the board to attain the purpose of the foundation) (*Swiss Federal Court Ruling, 5A_232/2010 of 16 September 2010, para. 3.2.*).

7. WHICH BODIES OR PERSONS MANAGE CHARITABLE ORGANISATIONS AND WHAT GENERAL REQUIREMENTS MUST THEY MEET?

Foundation

The board is the supreme governing body of the foundation and is vested with management duties. The governance structure of a foundation is very flexible. Therefore, the statutes of a foundation can provide for an unlimited number of other corporate bodies. For instance, the statutes can provide for an executive committee and/or a managing director to whom powers can be delegated by the foundation board, a secretariat, permanent or ad hoc committees or other bodies such as advisory boards. Those bodies can also be delegated managing powers by the foundation board.

Minimal number of board members. Swiss law does not impose a minimal number of board members. However, according to the practice of the Federal Supervisory Authority of Foundations, the board should be composed of a minimum of three board members. The Swiss Foundation Code further recommends that the board should be composed of between five and seven members (*Swiss Foundation Code 2015, Recommendation 6*). The foundation board must be composed of individuals. Legal entities cannot be foundation board members (*Article 120, Federal Ordinance on the Register of commerce*).

According to the practice of the Federal Supervisory Authority of Foundations, at least one foundation board member with signatory power must be:

- A Swiss citizen.
- A citizen of a member state of the EU or of the European Free Trade Association (EFTA) with his/her domicile in Switzerland.

Qualifications of board members. Swiss law does not provide for a specific threshold of knowledge or qualifications to be met. Therefore, each board member must have the knowledge and qualifications enabling him/her to carry the foundation's aim in its best capacity. In particular, a prospective board member should accept this mandate solely if he/she is able to execute it correctly. In this respect, the Swiss Foundation Code foresees that the prospective board members must have the abilities and the time enabling and allowing for the good fulfillment of their mandate (*Swiss Foundation Code 2015, Recommendation 6*).

Appointment procedure. The procedure is generally set out in the statutes. The initial board members are appointed by the founder in the foundation deed and the foundation board in practice renews itself by co-optation. The appointment must be done either through:

- A circular resolution.
- Minutes of meeting.

After the appointment of the new board member, the member must be enrolled in the Register of commerce and the Supervisory Authority must be informed about the appointment (*Article 95 letter i and j, ORC*).

Association

The managing committee and the general assembly are the two bodies of an association (*Articles 64 to 69, the Civil Code (CC)*). The general assembly is the association's supreme governing body whereas the managing committee is the executive body of the organisation.

All members of the association collectively form the general assembly. However, an association's general assembly can also be composed of delegates to whom the members' voting rights are delegated from.

The general assembly holds the following inalienable powers (that is, powers it cannot delegate):

- The power to adopt and amend the statutes.
- The control over the association.
- The power to discharge and dismiss members of the managing committee.
- The power to dissolve the association.

Furthermore, the general assembly holds all powers that are not vested in other corporate bodies of the association (*Article 65 para. 1, CC*). In this context, unless provided otherwise in the statutes of the association, all members have equal voting rights in the general assembly.

Under Article 69 of the CC, the managing committee is the managing body of an association. It can be composed of members of the association or of third parties. The managing committee is responsible for the daily management of the affairs of the association, such as delegated to by the general assembly and all other powers that have been delegated by the general assembly (*Article 69, CC*). Any legal entity must present consolidated accounts if it controls other legal entities (*Article 963, Swiss Code of Obligations*).

8.   WHAT ARE THE ACCOUNTING/FINANCIAL REPORTING REQUIREMENTS?

Foundation

Under Article 83b of the Civil Code (CC), a foundation must appoint an external and independent auditor in Switzerland, which is in charge of the audit of the annual financial statements of the foundation and its financial situation. The establishment and presentation of these accounts must comply with generally approved accounting principles, such as the Swiss GAAP RPC 21 or the International Financial Reporting Standards (IFRS).

The auditor must submit its annual report to the foundation board, which in turn will notify it to the competent Supervisory Authority. This annual report constitutes an important aspect of the supervision conducted by the Supervisory Authority. In addition, the auditor is also responsible for verifying that the foundation's activity is in compliance notably with its statutes and bye-laws, if any.

Depending on the size of the foundation, this review can either be an ordinary audit carried out by an expert auditor or a limited audit carried out by an approved auditor. A foundation may exceptionally be exempted from its obligation to appoint an external auditor when:

- The foundation's balance sheet total is below CHF200,000 for two consecutive terms.
- The foundation does not undertake any public fundraising (*Article 1, Federal Ordinance on Auditors*).

Under Article 84a of the CC, in case the board of foundation suspects that the foundation is in long-term insolvency or in an overindebtedness situation, the foundation board must do an intermediary balance sheet and notify it to the auditor. If the auditor finds that the foundation is insolvent or in an overindebtedness situation, the auditor must transmit the report to the Supervisory Authority.

Association

A Swiss association is in principle not required to have external auditors, unless:

- It is considered a large entity.
- A member of the association so requires.

An association is considered a large entity if two of the following figures are exceeded in two successive business years:

- Total assets of CHF10 million.
- Turnover of CHF20 million.
- Average annual total of 50 full-time staff.

In this context, the association will be subject to the ordinary audit.

The establishment and presentation of these accounts must comply with generally approved accounting principles, such as the Swiss GAAP RPC 21 or the International Financial Reporting Standards (IFRS).

TAX

9.   HOW ARE CHARITIES TAXED, AND WHAT (IF ANY) ARE THE PRINCIPAL EXEMPTIONS AND/OR RELIEFS FROM TAXATION THAT THEY ENJOY?

Tax on income, capital gains and property used by the organisation

If an association or foundation operates exclusively to serve a public utility purpose, it can be exempt from all direct taxes in Switzerland, including income and wealth taxes, if it meets the various other conditions for tax exemption discussed below.

The criteria to determine whether a legal entity qualifies for tax exemption are:

- Set out in Article 56g of the Federal Direct Tax Act (LIFD) and Article 23 paragraph 1f of the Federal Law on Harmonisation of Direct Taxes of Cantons and Communes (LHID).
- Laid down in greater detail in the Federal Tax Administration's Circular No 12 of 8 July 1994 (Circular 12/1994) and in Guidelines of 18 January 2008 established by the Swiss Tax Conference for the cantonal tax authorities (Guidelines 2008).

The following cumulative conditions must be fulfilled:

Swiss based entity. Firstly, the legal entity must be subject to Swiss tax law, which means that it must be incorporated under Swiss law.

In theory, but this is quite rare in practice, a for-profit legal entity, such as a company limited by shares or a co-operative company that pursues a public utility purpose, can also be totally or partially tax exempt if the statutes expressly exclude any distribution to its shareholders and directors. A non-profit organisation is in essence barred from distributing its net earnings, if any, to individuals who exercise control over it, such as members, officers, directors, or trustees.

Pursuit of a public utility purpose. The legal entity must pursue a public utility purpose. Public utility is not defined in generic and abstract terms in the Circular 12/1994, which merely provides examples of such activities, which include activities of a charitable, humanitarian, health, ecological, educational, scientific or cultural nature.

For a purpose to be considered of general interest, the activity must be aimed at an unrestricted circle of beneficiaries. General interest is not recognised if the circle of beneficiaries is too narrowly limited.

Public utility within the meaning of the LIFD is not limited to activities carried out in Switzerland. It is thus possible to exempt the worldwide activities of a Swiss based entity if these activities pursue public utility purposes and the entity meets the other conditions of tax exemption.

Lack of self-interest. The notion of public utility includes a subjective element, that is, the lack of self-interest. An activity only meets this condition if it serves the public interest and is based on altruism in the sense of devotion to the community. The absence of self-interest requires on the part of the members of the foundation board/or executive committee of an association a sacrifice in favour of the general interest which overrides their own interest.

Practical consequences of this requirement are as follows:

- Board members of a foundation or members of the executive committee will in principle not be remunerated.
- In certain cantons, such as Geneva, the practice of the tax administration allows a remuneration for time spent. However, the remuneration cannot exceed the one paid for attendance of official commissions in Geneva.
- The remunerated employees and the chief executive officer of a non-profit entity cannot serve on the foundation board of a Swiss foundation (except without voting rights).
- For activities exceeding the usual scope of duties of a board member, such as, for instance, a board member providing services at arm's length in his field of expertise (services that would in any case have to be obtained from third parties), an appropriate compensation can be paid.

Exclusion or limited profit making activity. The tax exempted activity must be exercised exclusively for the benefit of public utility. The condition of the exclusivity of the use of the funds for the benefit of public utility or common good does not prevent the legal entity from carrying out income generating activities, if the income resulting from such activities is used exclusively for the public utility purpose and that the commercial activity remains secondary. A legal entity that combines commercial purposes with its purposes of public utility can benefit from a partial exemption.

Effective activity. The public utility purpose must be effectively pursued. In other words, the mere fact that a legal entity claims that it exercises an activity which is tax exempt is not sufficient. Entities whose principal purpose is to constitute capital or accumulate the proceeds of their investments without specific goals to carry out future tasks are not entitled to tax exemption. The fulfilment of this requirement is monitored regularly both by the Supervisory Authority (for foundations only) in the context of the annual filing of the foundation's activity report and by the tax authorities to which the audited annual accounts are filed on a yearly basis. It is also verified in the context of the renewal of an organisation's tax exempt status (usually granted at the cantonal/municipal level for a ten-year period).

Irrevocable use of funds. The funds used in furtherance of the purposes which justify the tax exemption must be irrevocably (that is, forever) committed to these purposes. In the event of liquidation of the legal entity, its remaining assets must be entirely assignable to one or several public utility and tax exempt entities pursuing similar objectives to those of the entity. In no case must the entity's assets be returned to the founder or board members or to any of their successors or assignees, or be used in any way for their profit, in whole or part.

These conditions must be expressly stated in a provision of the foundation's statutes which cannot be modified.

The exemption can only be granted on request, with the applicant having to prove that it meets the above legal conditions. Such request must be addressed to the cantonal tax authorities since the cantons are competent to rule on tax exemption requests.

Despite the fact that under Article 129(2) of the Swiss Constitution, the harmonisation of direct taxes imposed by the Confederation, the cantons and the communes applies to tax liability, the object of the tax and the tax period, procedural law and the law relating to tax offences, and that the principle of tax exemption at the cantonal level of public utility entities is anchored in Article 23 paragraph 1f of the LHID, differences may appear in cantonal laws and practices with respect to the conditions of tax exempt status. The differences in interpretation of the exemption conditions relate mainly to the remuneration of the board, the exemptions of activities carried out only outside Switzerland and profit-making activity of the tax-exempt entity. For instance, canton Thurgau has adopted a very restrictive approach regarding the exemption of activities carried out abroad, considering that only entities pursuing a "Swiss" public interest can be exempted. In other cantons, the conditions of tax exemption are applied with a certain degree of protectionism.

Content of the tax exemption. If the above requirements are met, a Swiss based legal entity can benefit from a full exemption of all direct taxes, including:

- Federal and cantonal profit taxes.
- Wealth taxes levied at cantonal level on the net wealth.
- Gift tax on the initial capital.
- Gift tax and inheritance tax on gifts/bequests made by Swiss residents.
- Gift tax and inheritance tax on gifts/bequests made by foreign resident.

Value added tax (VAT)

Following a partial revision of the VAT Act which entered into force on 1 January 2010, the situation of charities regarding VAT has been improved in several aspects. Charities that generate less than CHF150,000 of taxable turnover in Switzerland within a year are exempt from the obligation to register themselves as VAT taxpayers. However, each potential taxpayer has a general option right, which allows any entity to voluntary register as VAT taxpayer. As a consequence, any charity which carries on a business activity can register itself as a VAT taxpayer, irrespective of the amount of its taxable turnover or of its net profits.

Furthermore, the input tax deduction is no longer reduced if gifts (donations), dividends, and any other non-VATable revenues are made by the VAT taxpayer. This last rule, combined with an easier access to VAT registration, should significantly improve the input VAT recovery rate of Swiss charities.

Finally, the new VAT Act states that advertising services provided by charities for the benefit of third parties or provided by third parties for the benefit of charities must be considered as non-VATable activities with no right to claim back the VAT input tax (that is, VAT exempt transactions).

However, in such case it is possible for the charity to opt for the voluntary taxation of these activities. Therefore, VAT must be openly disclosed on the invoice and the advertising services are considered as ordinary VATable transactions. The option mechanism transforms an out-of-scope transaction into a VATable transaction. As a consequence, the input VAT deduction has no longer to be reduced proportionally.

The various rules summarised above, if correctly implemented by Swiss charities, can result in significant tax savings. This, however, requires that those organisations perform at least business/commercial activities, irrespective of whether the latter are profitable or not.

The VAT exemption can be granted through a formal request made according to the provisions set out in the Federal Act on Privileges, Immunities and Facilities (LHE). The LHE provides certain types of privileges to international organisations headquartered in Switzerland. Privileges can be granted in the fields of tax (exemption of VAT) and immigration (possibility to hire foreign workers without having to comply with ordinary proceedings and conditions of Swiss immigration law).

10. WHAT, IF ANY, ARE THE TAXATION BENEFITS FOR DONORS TO CHARITIES?

Advantages for individual donors

At the federal level, donations by Swiss residents over the annual amount of CHF100 made to legal entities pursuing objects of pure utility are fully deductible up to an aggregate cap of 20% of the donor's annual net taxable income, provided the donations are made to entities located in Switzerland.

At the cantonal level, the deductibility of donations made to charitable foundations for individuals depends on cantonal legislation and can go up to the same cap of 20% of the annual net taxable income. In Geneva, permitted deductions have increased up to 20% of the donor's annual income under the legislation which entered into force in 2009.

Advantages for corporate donors

Under federal law, payments made to charitable foundations can be deducted from the profits of a company up to a maximum of 20% after tax and deduction of the donation, provided that the foundation:

• Has its registered offices in Switzerland.
• Is exempt from taxes because its purpose and activity are for the benefit of the public and common good.

Payments made to charitable foundations and other entities can be deducted up to a maximum of 20% of profits, depending on cantonal legislation. In Geneva, deductions are allowed up to an amount of 20% of taxable profits, provided that the above conditions are fulfilled.

Foundation as donors

In case of a donation made by a charitable foundation, the charitable foundation might be subject to taxes on donations it makes. According to a long standing practice of the tax authorities, gifts made by a non-profit foundation are not subject to gift tax. However, if a foundation makes a gift which is not considered to be in furtherance of its philanthropic purpose, it could be subject to gift tax.

DISADVANTAGES

The disadvantages, if any, result from the restrictive conditions imposed to receive and keep a charitable status that limits the activities the entity can carry out and the way it does so.

For example, a charity can hold participations in commercial companies but cannot be actively engaged in the direction/management of such companies. In addition, the dividend received by the charity must be irrevocably allocated to its charitable purpose/activity.

Another example is the current restrictive practice regarding remuneration of foundations' board members. In most cantons (and notably in Geneva), the tax authorities are very reluctant to allow any remuneration for directors, arguing that this would violate the condition of altruistic use of funds.

OVERSEAS CHARITIES

In principle, only foundations incorporated in Switzerland are subject to Swiss law and to the supervision of a Swiss Supervisory Authority. Under Swiss international private law, with the exception of rare cases, a foundation or association is subject to the legal order of the state where it was incorporated, in particular to the extent that it had to comply with certain publicity or registration requirements.

In the case of charities incorporated abroad and carrying out certain activities in Switzerland, legal presence can be established through:

- A branch.
- A representative office.

Branch office

According to Swiss private international law, branch offices in Switzerland of companies with headquarters abroad are governed by Swiss law. Therefore, branch offices of companies with headquarters abroad can merely be established in Switzerland if they meet regular requirements of Swiss law on the establishment of branch offices. Branch offices must be entities with business operations. Therefore, entities which do not effectively conduct operations cannot be established as branch offices in Switzerland.

The Swiss branch of an entity with headquarters abroad is independent from an economic point of view of the parent entity but is not legally separate from the latter and therefore does not enjoy legal personality. The Swiss branch has no separate legal personality and therefore cannot enter into agreements in its own name but only on behalf of its foreign parent entity. There are no mandatory corporate bodies in a Swiss branch.

Under Article 935 of the Swiss Code of Obligations, a representative having its domicile in Switzerland must be appointed and registered with the competent trade registry. The powers of representation of the Swiss branch are decided by the parent entity.

Only a local office that conducts effective business activities with its own personnel and in its own premises independently from the parent entity qualifies as a branch. In other words, a certain degree of autonomy from the parent entity is necessary for the local office to qualify as a branch.

Regarding taxation, a Swiss branch will most likely qualify as a permanent establishment of the parent entity from a Swiss tax law perspective and could consequently be subject to taxation in Switzerland. It could benefit from tax exemption if the parent entity meets the Swiss conditions for tax exemption. The statutes of the foreign parent entity will be examined in light of Swiss tax law. A particular difficulty lies in the fact that a specific clause of non-return of the funds must appear in the statutes of the parent entity for its Swiss branch to benefit from tax exemptions.

Representative office

The Swiss representative office of an entity abroad conducts mere preparatory work for the parent company and is not independent from the latter, neither from an economic nor from a legal point of view.

As a consequence, if the representative office in Switzerland does not qualify as a branch within the meaning of Swiss private international law, establishing the representative office in Switzerland does not grant Swiss courts general jurisdiction over the parent charity, even for claims or disputes relating to the activities of such representative office.

The Swiss representative office does not have separate legal personality and cannot enter into any agreements. Therefore, it conducts mere representative functions and/or preparatory work. There are no mandatory corporate bodies in a Swiss representative office or any requirement to register a representative in the Register of Commerce (as the Swiss representative office cannot enter into contracts).

A representative office does not usually qualify as a permanent establishment from a Swiss tax law perspective and is not subject to taxation in Switzerland, considering that its scope of activities should be limited to mere preparatory work. It is, however, advisable to seek a ruling from the tax authorities in order to confirm that the Swiss representative office does not have a permanent establishment in Switzerland and is not subject to taxation in Switzerland.

Giving to overseas charities

In most cantons, such as Geneva, gifts and bequests by Swiss residents in favour of foreign resident charities are subject to gift and inheritance taxes, unless a reciprocity agreement is concluded with the country where the foreign charity is registered. In Geneva, it is possible to apply for a partial exemption which may amount to at least 25%, however, the relevant rate is determined on a case-by-case basis. The Geneva Government is also authorised to conclude reciprocity agreements with foreign countries.

Gifts and bequests by non-Geneva residents to Geneva resident charities have always been exempted from Geneva gift and inheritance taxes.

The deductibility of donations made to charitable entities under Swiss legislation is subject to the conditions that:

- The beneficiary is registered in Switzerland.
- It pursues objects of public utility.

Therefore, if a Swiss tax resident, individual or corporate, wishes to make a donation to a charity registered abroad, there will be no deduction allowed in Switzerland. The *Persche* case (*ECJ C-318/2007, 27 January 2009*) does not extend its effects to donations made by Swiss nationals to EU-based charities. However, for a beneficiary of charitable contributions registered in Switzerland, the domicile of the donor is of no relevance: the tax exemption still applies. Whether donors domiciled abroad are entitled to a deduction in their home state ordinarily depends on their home state laws.

13. IS IT POSSIBLE TO REGISTER A DOMESTIC CHARITY ABROAD, AND HAS YOUR JURISDICTION ENTERED INTO ANY INTERNATIONAL AGREEMENTS OR TREATIES IN THIS AREA?

Currently, Switzerland has not entered into any international agreements or treaties regarding the possibility to register a domestic charity abroad.

REFORM

14. ARE THERE ANY PROPOSALS FOR REFORM IN THE AREA OF CHARITY LAW?

The following proposals for reforms regarding foundations are currently being considered:

- The federal initiative "Making Switzerland more attractive to Foundations" has so far been approved by the Legal affairs Commission (motion Werner Luginbühl of 9 December 2014). Among other things, it aims at:
  - improving the availability of information;
  - clarifying the rules applicable to complaint procedures at the Supervisory Authority; and
  - limiting the liability of benevolent board members by excluding liability for "light" negligence.

  In addition, the federal initiative also proposes to reform tax laws applicable to public utility entities, notably regarding the possibility to provide compensations to board members.

- Another partial revision of the Swiss Value Taxation Act was adopted unanimously by the National Council in September 2015. The project proposes that public utility organisations will have to inform donors that they are not to receive any counterpart to their gift (in order to be exempt from tax). The project is now moving before the Council of States.

- On 2 March 2016, a federal legislative project dealing with the Supervisory Authority of Foundation was initiated. The project sets out the plan to separate the federal Supervisory Authority from the central administrative body of the federal government, and create a new legal body, with its own standing and legal personality. This would give more autonomy to the surveillance apparatus designed for foundations. Indeed, this new separate authority would exclusively be financed by fees levied for the supervision of foundations, contrary to the current authority which is part of the Federal Department of Interior.

ONLINE RESOURCES

FEDERAL CLASSIFIED COMPILATION (*RECEUIL SYSTÉMATIQUE/SYSTEMATISCHE SAMMLUNG DES BUNDESRECHTS*)

W www.admin.ch/gov/en/start/federal-law/classified-compilation.html

Description. This website provides a compilation of all the legislation relevant at a federal level. The English translation is provided for guidance only.

SWISS SUPREME COURT

W www.bger.ch/fr/index.htm

Description. This website publishes all the decisions of the Swiss Supreme Court. There is no English translation available.

REGULATORY AUTHORITY

FEDERAL SUPERVISORY AUTHORITY OF FOUNDATIONS

W www.edi.admin.ch/edi/fr/home/das-edi/organisation/services-specialises/autorite-federale-de-surveillance-des-fondations.html

Description. The Federal Supervisory Authority of Foundations supervises foundations with an international scope of activity.

UK (ENGLAND & WALES)

Anne-Marie Piper and Philip Reed, FARRER & CO

OVERVIEW AND MAIN TRENDS

1. WHAT IS THE HISTORICAL BACKGROUND TO CHARITY LAW AND CHARITABLE ORGANISATIONS IN YOUR JURISDICTION?

History of charitable activity

Charitable trusts emerged during the medieval period, as the wealthy were encouraged to leave legacies to the Church on death. Numerous schools and universities were also created during this period and were often endowed generously by their founders. This process intensified after the Reformation, as the wealthy were no longer able to make gifts to monasteries and so sought secular outlets for their legacies. At the same time, interest in preventing and alleviating poverty grew as a means to avoid social disorder, while monarchs realised that building roads and bridges to benefit the public was also a useful way to maintain communication and extend their control.

However, monies that were given for charitable purposes were often misapplied or mismanaged. The Statute of Elizabeth of 1601 established a commission to hear complaints about charities and, in its Preamble, set out what purposes were considered to be charitable. During and following the civil war, the commission became less effective and was eventually replaced by a system whereby a complainant could seek redress through the Attorney General.

During the 17th and 18th centuries, charity was increasingly pursued through groups of people getting together to subscribe to charitable associations and voluntary societies. Many charitable schools and hospitals were formed during this time. This trend increased throughout the 19th century, as industrialisation encouraged both the formation of charities and philanthropy. By this time, regulation of charities through the Attorney General had become unworkable and the Charitable Trusts Act of 1853 established the Charity Commissioners for England and Wales, with investigatory powers.

Charity law

Charity law continued to evolve during the 20th century through both legislation and case law. The powers of the Charity Commissioners grew under the Charities Act 1960, which established a public register of charities.

The Charities Act 1992 was the result of both growth in the voluntary sector during the 1980s and concerns of malpractice. It introduced new powers for the Charity Commissioners and a new regime for fundraising. The 1960 Act and most of the 1992 Act were consolidated by the Charities Act 1993 which, with further expansion of the voluntary sector during the 1990s, led to more widespread recognition of charity law in England and Wales as a distinct field requiring specialist advisers.

The Charities Acts 1992 and 1993 were amended by the Charities Act 2006 which, among other things, codified 300 years of case law on charitable purposes. It also established the Charity Commission as a body corporate in its own right and a new Charity Tribunal (the First-tier Tribunal (Charity), which provides a new appeal from some decisions of the Charity Commission. The Charity Commission and the Attorney General can also make references to the Charity Tribunal). Almost all the provisions of these Acts have now been consolidated in the Charities Act 2011. The most recent piece of legislation is the Charities (Protection and Social Investment) Act 2016, which further expands the powers of the Charity Commission.

2. ARE INDEPENDENT CHARITABLE ORGANISATIONS COMMON AND SIGNIFICANT IN YOUR JURISDICTION? WHAT IS THE CURRENT SIZE AND SCOPE OF THE SECTOR AND THE MAIN TRENDS?

There are currently over 165,000 registered charities in England and Wales. However, the real size of the sector is substantially larger. In addition to registered charities, there are thousands of charities that are exempt or excepted from registration and/or have income under the registration threshold. There are also an estimated 600,000 to 900,000 informal community groups that have no distinct legal form (which may or may not have charitable aims) and an unknown number of not-for-profit organisations that are not charities, including over 10,000 community interest companies (CICs).

The combined income of registered charities in England and Wales was over GB£71 billion in 2015/16, of which a reported GB£21.66 billion was made through voluntary donations. However, income varies widely in the sector.

LEGAL FRAMEWORK

3. IS THERE A LEGAL DEFINITION OF A "CHARITY"? WHAT ARE THE PRINCIPAL SOURCES OF LAW AND REGULATIONS RELATING TO CHARITABLE ORGANISATIONS AND ACTIVITIES?

Definition of charity

Charities in England and Wales are principally governed by the Charities Act 2011. Section 1 of the Charities Act provides that a charity is an institution which both:

- Is established for charitable purposes only.
- Falls under the control of the High Court in the exercise of its jurisdiction with respect to charities.

A charitable purpose is one of the following purposes which is for the public benefit:

- The prevention or relief of poverty.
- The advancement of education.
- The advancement of religion.
- The advancement of health or the saving of lives.
- The advancement of citizenship or community development.
- The advancement of the arts, culture, heritage or science.

- The advancement of amateur sport.
- The advancement of human rights, conflict resolution or reconciliation, or the promotion of religious or racial harmony or equality and diversity.
- The advancement of environmental protection or improvement.
- The relief of those in need by reason of youth, age, ill-health, disability, financial hardship or other disadvantage.
- The advancement of animal welfare.
- The promotion of the efficiency of the armed forces of the Crown or the efficiency of the police, fire and rescue services or ambulance services.
- Certain further purposes, including any that may reasonably be regarded as analogous to or within the spirit of those listed above.

Such purposes are charitable regardless of whether activities to fulfil them are carried out in the UK or overseas.

The public benefit test is not defined in statute and has been the source of much debate in recent years, including two significant cases in the Charity Tribunal which have helped shape the Charity Commission's current guidance (to which charity trustees must have regard) (*Independent Schools Council v Charity Commission for England & Wales and others [2011] UKUT 421 (TCC); Charity Commission for England & Wales and Others v Her Majesty's Attorney General (FTC/84/2011)*).

This guidance provides that a charity's purpose must be beneficial in a way that is identifiable and capable of being proved by evidence where necessary. Any detriment resulting from the purpose must not outweigh the benefit. A charity's purpose must benefit the public in general, or a sufficient section of the public, and must not give rise to more than incidental private benefit (unless that benefit is charitable in nature).

Sources of law

Charities in England and Wales are principally governed by the Charities Act 2011 (*see Question 1, Charity law*). Charities are also subject to laws applicable to their particular structures (for example, company or trust law) and to the law on matters such as tax, employment, contract, tort, intellectual property, data protection and competition.

There are certain non-profit organisations that are not charities (*see Question 4, Non-profit organisations that are not charities*). They cannot claim the beneficial tax treatment associated with charitable status, but have greater freedom and flexibility in not having to comply with charity law. Such bodies are subject to general legal restrictions that apply to their legal structure, that are in their governing documents, and that apply to their activities.

LEGAL BODIES

Charitable company limited by guarantee

Increasingly in England and Wales, charities are set up as charitable companies limited by guarantee (CCLGs). The structure is similar to a company limited by shares, but instead of shareholders the company has members, who guarantee to contribute a nominal amount if the company is wound up.

The members of a CCLG have no right to a share of profits, which must be applied for the CCLG's charitable purposes. If the company is wound up, its assets must be applied for similar charitable purposes, often by transfer to another charity.

CCLGs must comply with company law, in particular the Companies Acts (principally the Companies Act 2006 and those parts of the Companies Acts 1985 and 1989 that are still in force). In addition to being regulated by the Charity Commission, they are regulated by the Registrar of Companies, known as Companies House (*www.companieshouse.gov.uk*).

The directors are directors for company law purposes and trustees for charity law purposes, with legal obligations in each capacity, so that a CCLG is highly regulated.

Advantages. The liabilities of the members are limited to their guarantee and the structure has its own legal personality, so the trustees have some protection from liability. The company can hold assets, incur liabilities, enter into contracts, sue and be sued in its own name. It is therefore particularly suitable for a charity with complex activities. However, there are some circumstances (for example, breach of trust or fraudulent trading) in which trustees can be personally liable for losses to the charity.

Disadvantages. A charitable company must make filings with:

• The Charity Commission (annual return and set of accounts, and certain event-driven filings).

• Companies House (confirmation statement and set of accounts and similar event-driven filings).

It is answerable to both bodies within their remits.

Charitable trust

Historically, this was the legal structure of choice for charities. This has changed in recent years, mainly because of the advantages of the charitable company.

A charitable trust is formed by the trustees agreeing to hold assets on trust to be applied for charitable purposes. It has no legal identity separate from its trustees. It cannot for example own land or sign documents in its own name and, broadly, the charity's assets must be held and its activities conducted in the names of the individual trustees.

The trust deed usually sets out the procedure by which the trust can be dissolved. In any event a charitable trust will dissolve if and when all of its assets have been expended. Once all the liabilities of the trust have been settled and its assets spent, the trustees can apply to have the trust removed from the Register of Charities.

Advantages. A charitable trust does not need to comply with company law and can therefore be more flexible than a charitable company, although it is governed by trust law which is a complex area often requiring specialist advice. It need not report on its affairs to Companies House but it must report to the Charity Commission.

Disadvantages. The main disadvantage of a charitable trust is the absence of separate legal personality. The trustees are usually jointly and severally liable for the charity's liabilities. Many potential trustees are uncomfortable with this, although provided liabilities do not result from a breach of trust or other wrongdoing, the trustees are usually entitled to an indemnity from the charity's available assets.

In some instances (usually if the charity is only a grant-making body and its assets are cash and/or investments) it is still relatively common for a charitable trust to be used.

Charitable incorporated organisation (CIO)

The CIO is a corporate structure designed specifically for charities. It gives a charity and its trustees the benefit of limited liability protection and a separate legal personality, but is not subject to company law. The legal framework for CIOs is set out in the Charities Act 2011 and subordinate legislation (*Charitable Incorporated Organisations (General) Regulations 2012 (General Regulations); Charitable Incorporated Organisations (Insolvency and Dissolution) Regulations 2012 (Dissolution Regulations) and The Charity Tribunal (Amendment) Order 2012*).

Some charitable companies limited by guarantee may wish to re-register as CIOs and the legislation contains a mechanism for this. The government is currently carrying out a consultation on conversion, with an anticipated rollout in October 2016 (*www. gov.uk/government/uploads/system/uploads/attachment_data/file/512916/20160322_ CIOConversionConsultationDocumentFINAL.pdf*).

A CIO can be dissolved on a solvent or insolvent basis, and residual assets must be applied in accordance with the charity's constitution. There is a set of regulations on the dissolution of CIOs, which create a somewhat simplified version of the regime for companies under the Insolvency Act 1986 (*Charitable Incorporated Organisations (Insolvency and Dissolution) Regulations 2012*).

Advantages. The main advantage of a CIO over a company limited by guarantee is that CIOs need only file with the Charity Commission (and not with Companies House).

Disadvantages. The CIO is still a relatively new structure and is not as well understood as the charitable company.

It is possible that institutional lenders may be less willing to lend to a CIO than to a charitable company, due to the lack of a public register of charges (which exists at Companies House).

Unincorporated association

Unincorporated associations are usually used for simple charities that are membership based and do not have any significant activities or liabilities. They are governed by a constitution or rules.

The members usually elect an executive committee (or equivalent) to oversee administration. The members of the executive committee are the unincorporated association's trustees for charity law purposes.

Unincorporated associations can be dissolved subject to any procedure or restrictions set out in their governing documents.

Advantages. The advantage of an unincorporated association is that it is particularly simple to create and run. Unincorporated associations only have to make annual filings with the Charity Commission.

Disadvantages. As with a charitable trust, the association has no separate legal personality. The members hold assets and incur liabilities on the association's behalf.

The law relating to unincorporated associations is relatively underdeveloped.

Unincorporated associations are generally only suitable for small, membership-based charities that hold few or no assets and employ few or no staff.

Other types of charitable structure

99% of all charities in England and Wales are charitable companies limited by guarantee, charitable trusts, CIOs or unincorporated associations.

However, there are other legal forms that charities can take, for example:

- Royal Charter bodies (incorporated through a charter from the monarch).
- Community benefit societies (bodies with separate legal personality run for the benefit of the community).

Non-profit organisations that are not charities

A non-profit organisation that is not a charity cannot claim the beneficial tax treatment associated with charitable status, but has greater freedom and flexibility in not having to comply with charity law. Such organisations include:

- Non-charitable social enterprises (businesses with social as well as commercial objectives).
- Community interest companies (CICs) which benefit a particular community and whose profits are reinvested in the CIC for this purpose.
- Non-governmental organisations which campaign for specific changes in UK law.
- Community benefit societies.
- Non-charitable housing associations.

Such bodies are subject to general legal restrictions that apply to their legal structure, that are in their governing documents, and that apply to their activities.

Company limited by guarantee. Most non-charitable non-profit organisations are incorporated as companies limited by guarantee, with restrictions on how the members can share in any profits of the company. They are subject to company law but need not comply with charity law.

Community interest company (CIC). The CIC is a form of limited company established for the benefit of the community (*www.gov.uk/government/organisations/office-of-the-regulator-of-community-interest-companies*). It is not a charity and can be used for non-charitable activities, for example to run village shops or tourist sites. CICs can be companies limited by guarantee or by shares.

A CIC can distribute a percentage of its profits to its members/shareholders, meaning potentially both financial and social returns on investment. They are a popular vehicle for non-charitable social enterprises.

However, CICs are subject to an asset lock, so that a proportion of their profits cannot be distributed to members but must be reinvested in the company to continue to carry out activities for the benefit of the community.

CICs are regulated by the CIC Regulator and subject to company law and the specific CIC regulations. The powers of the CIC Regulator are set out in The Companies (Audit, Investigations and Community Enterprise) Act 2004 and the Community Interest Company Regulations 2005 (as amended).They must file a confirmation statement, annual community interest report and annual accounts with the CIC Regulator.

CICs can be wound up or dissolved in a similar manner to other companies but residual assets must be applied to another asset-locked body (if one is specified in the CIC's governing document) or under the directions of the CIC Regulator.

Other non-profit structures. As with charities, non-profit organisations can also take other forms, such as Royal Charter bodies and co-operative and community benefit societies (regulated by the Financial Conduct Authority. Under the Co-operative and Community Benefit Societies Act 2014, from 1 August 2014 existing benevolent societies and industrial and provident societies are referred to as registered societies).

5.   WHAT ARE THE QUALIFICATION REQUIREMENTS/FORMALITIES TO SET UP THESE ORGANISATIONS?

Charitable companies limited by guarantee

The first task when setting up a charitable company is to prepare the company's memorandum and articles of association. The memorandum of association is a formal document used to incorporate the company. The articles of association:

- Contain the charity's objects.
- List the powers that the charity's trustees can exercise in pursuit of those objects.
- Set out what happens to any surplus assets if the charity is dissolved.
- Contain procedural rules governing matters such as membership, appointment and retirement of trustees and meetings.

The charity's founders largely decide what to put in the articles, but there are some provisions that must be included, such as restrictions on trustee benefits and members receiving any share of profits. The Charity Commission produces a model memorandum and articles of association (*see www.gov.uk/topic/running-charity/setting-up*). If a charity uses these as its governing document, it usually makes registration with the Charity Commission more straightforward.

The first members and trustees then file an application for incorporation at Companies House. The new entity exists as a charitable company from the date of incorporation, although it cannot describe itself as a registered charity until it is registered with the Charity Commission. Registration with the Charity Commission is mandatory, provided the charity has income over the relevant threshold and is not exempt or excepted (*see Question 6*). The trustees must sign a declaration of their willingness to act as charity trustees and the charity's application for registration must explain to the Charity Commission how the charity will operate for the public benefit. Registration is more complex than incorporation and can take some time.

The charitable company must register with HM Revenue & Customs (HMRC) for tax purposes.

Charitable trusts

A charitable trust is typically created on execution of a trust deed for charitable purposes in relation to specified assets. The trust deed governs how the trust is run, often including similar provisions (and restrictions) to those for a charitable company's articles of association (*see above, Charitable companies limited by guarantee*).

Applications must then be made to the Charity Commission (provided the trust has sufficient income and is not exempt or excepted) and HMRC for registration as a charity (*see above, Charitable companies limited by guarantee*).

Charitable incorporated organisation (CIOs)

A new CIO requires a constitution broadly based on one of the models provided by the Charity Commission (*www.gov.uk/government/publications/setting-up-a-charity-model-governing-documents*). A foundation model is appropriate if the only members are to be the CIO's trustees. An association model is used if the CIO will have voting members other than or in addition to its trustees. Any significant deviations from either model must be cleared with the Charity Commission.

Registration with the Charity Commission follows broadly the same process as for other structures but a CIO only comes into legal existence on registration with the Charity Commission. Unlike other types of charity, there is no financial threshold for registration and CIOs cannot be exempt or excepted from registration.

The CIO must also register with HMRC for tax purposes.

Unincorporated associations

An unincorporated association's governing document is usually known as its constitution or rules. There is no prescribed format, but it will usually specify:

- The objects of the association.
- How the members and trustees of the association are appointed.
- How the association will be run.
- Restrictions on the distribution of the association's assets.

The association will be established when the members adopt the constitution and appoint an executive committee/trustees.

The association must apply to the Charity Commission (provided it has sufficient income and is not exempt or excepted) and to HMRC for registration as a charity (*see above, Charitable companies limited by guarantee*).

Non-profit organisations that are not charities

Company limited by guarantee. The incorporation procedure is identical to that for a charitable company (*see above, Charitable companies limited by guarantee*), except that there is more flexibility in the terms of the articles of association.

No registration with the Charity Commission is required.

Non-charitable companies limited by guarantee must also register with HMRC.

CIC. The procedure for setting up a CIC is broadly the same as establishing a charitable company (*see above, Charitable companies limited by guarantee*), except that the articles of association contain some different provisions including, for example:

- An object for the community benefit.
- The CIC's asset lock, restricting distribution of the CIC's assets to the shareholders/ members beyond a certain level (*see Question 4, Non-profit organisations that are not charities*).

The application for incorporation is submitted to the CIC Regulator and includes a community interest statement, describing the CIC's intended activities and the community it will serve.

CICs cannot register with the Charity Commission. They must register with HMRC in the same way as non-charitable companies.

ONGOING REGULATORY REQUIREMENTS

6.   WHAT ARE THE MAIN REGULATORY AUTHORITIES FOR CHARITABLE ORGANISATIONS? WHAT ARE THEIR POWERS OF INVESTIGATION/AUDIT/SANCTIONS?

Regulatory authorities and powers

Charity Commission. Charities in England and Wales are regulated by the Charity Commission, which is a non-ministerial government department (essentially, it has a governmental role, but it is not part of any government department and operates at arms' length from government).

The role of the Charity Commission includes:

- Ensuring that charities comply with their legal obligations (a quasi-judicial role under which it exercises some of the powers of the High Court).
- Ensuring the accountability of charities.
- Encouraging effectiveness and impact.
- Promoting public trust and confidence in charities.

Most charities in England and Wales that have an annual income of more than GB£5,000 must by law register with the Charity Commission. In considering an application for registration, the Charity Commission will, among other things, decide whether a charity's proposed purposes are in fact charitable.

A relatively small number of charities known as exempt charities are not required to register with the Charity Commission. Such charities are regulated by other bodies such as the:

- Department for Culture, Media and Sport (museums).
- Department for Education (academy trusts).
- Higher Education Funding Council for England (English universities).

They are not included in the Register of Charities or generally subject to regulation by the Charity Commission. Certain other charities (such as some military and religious charities) are excepted from registration under the Charities Act 2011 and similarly do not appear on the Register of Charities. Generally, this chapter considers registered, rather than exempt or excepted, charities.

Registered charities are required under the Charities Act 2011 and subordinate legislation to file an annual return and their accounts with the Charity Commission each year. Certain event-driven filings are also required, such as on any amendment to a registered charity's constitutional documents.

The Charity Commission has wide-ranging powers with regard to registered charities, and in some circumstances its consent is needed before a charity can act.

In the event of an alleged serious or repeated breach of charity law, it can:

- Open a statutory investigation into a charity.
- Freeze a charity's assets.
- Appoint an interim manager.
- Remove a charity's trustees and management.
- Appoint new trustees or direct the trustees to apply the charity's assets in a particular way.

The Charity Commission will generally only take such action where it considers there is a serious risk to the beneficiaries or the charity's assets, or where the charity's activities risk undermining public confidence in the charity sector.

In the context of growing public concern that some charities were mismanaging funds (*www. publications.parliament.uk/pa/cm201516/cmselect/cmpubadm/433/433.pdf*) or engaged in unethical fundraising practices (*www.telegraph.co.uk/news/politics/12111229/Poppy-seller-Olive-Cooke-faced-uncontrollable-deluge-of-charity-letters.html*) the Commission's regulatory powers have been extended under the Charities (Protections and Social Investment) Act 2016 (not yet fully in force at the time of writing). This Act introduces powers to:

- Issue official warnings to trustees or charities if it considers there has been a breach of trust, misconduct or other mismanagement (and controversially, charities are unable to appeal such a warning to the Charity Tribunal).
- Suspend and disqualify a trustee if his/her behaviour could damage public trust in the charity.
- Direct that specified action should not be taken by a charity or its trustees.

The Act also extends the range of circumstances that lead to automatic disqualification for trustees and management to include terrorism, sexual and money laundering offences.

HMRC. HMRC (*www.gov.uk/government/organisations/hm-revenue-customs/services-information*) is primarily responsible for the collection and administration of taxes in the UK.

One of the advantages of charitable status in the UK is the availability of tax exemptions and reliefs on income, gains, premises and transactions. A charity cannot benefit from such treatment without first applying to HMRC. To be recognised as a charity for UK tax purposes (*Schedule 6, Finance Act 2010*) an organisation must satisfy a number of conditions, including the management condition. HMRC will assess whether the management condition has been satisfied using the fit and proper persons test.

This test applies to those persons who have general control and management of the charity, and so will apply to the trustees of charities, directors of corporate charities, and any other officials with general control and management over the charity or its assets. HMRC's guidance suggests that factors that may lead it to decide that a manager fails this test include, for example, where an individual has a history of tax fraud or other fraudulent behaviour, or where an individual has previously been barred from acting as a charity trustee or disqualified from acting as a company director.

The Court of Justice of the European Union (CJEU) has made clear (*Hein Persche v Finanzamt Lüdenscheid, Case C-318/07, 27 January 2009*) that restricting cross-border charitable activity (by confining charitable tax relief only to organisations established in a member state, or by not permitting tax relief on a donation made to a charity in another member state) breaches the EU Treaty, in particular the principles of free movement of capital and freedom of establishment across member states. The UK government therefore amended UK legislation to allow EU, Norwegian and Icelandic (and since July 2014, Liechtensteiner) charities to claim tax reliefs in the UK and to allow donors resident in the UK to claim UK tax relief on donations made to charities in those states. However, it is not always straightforward to register such charities with HMRC, and it remains to be seen how this will be affected by the UK leaving the EU.

HMRC is unable to investigate every claim for charitable tax relief before it is paid. It therefore generally makes repayments claimed but carries out claims audits on charities, to check the validity and accuracy of claims. In cases where HMRC suspects tax avoidance or fraud, it has powers to undertake civil (or in severe cases criminal) investigations into charities.

Other regulatory and investigatory bodies. Numerous other bodies have investigatory powers into charities or their trustees, including the police, the Health and Safety Executive (for breaches of health and safety legislation) and the Information Commissioner (for breaches of data protection legislation).

Disqualification of directors. Where a charitable company has become insolvent, the insolvency professional dealing with the administration or liquidation must report to the relevant government department on the conduct of the directors in the three years of trading before the insolvency. The Secretary of State can, in certain circumstances, seek a disqualification order against one or more of the directors. It is up to the courts to decide how long a director is to be disqualified.

Non-profit organisations that are not charities

Company limited by guarantee. Non-charitable companies limited by guarantee are not subject to regulation by the Charity Commission and do not need to comply with the fit and proper persons test. However, they are subject to regulation by HMRC to ensure they comply with tax law, and by other statutory authorities. Their directors may also be subject to disqualification proceedings.

CICs. CICs are not subject to regulation by the Charity Commission and do not need to comply with the fit and proper persons test. However, they are subject to regulation by HMRC to ensure they comply with tax law, and by other statutory authorities. Their directors may also be subject to disqualification proceedings.

In addition, CICs are regulated by the CIC Regulator. The CIC Regulator does not engage in proactive scrutiny of CICs, but it has a duty to protect the reputation of CICs and must investigate complaints. The CIC Regulator has powers to intervene in cases of misconduct, if a CIC is not satisfying the community interest test, or if it considers that the CIC's assets are at risk.

The CIC Regulator's powers of intervention include:

- Appointing a manager.
- Appointing or removing directors.
- Transferring the CIC's property.
- Taking action in the name of the CIC.

7. WHICH BODIES OR PERSONS MANAGE CHARITABLE ORGANISATIONS AND WHAT GENERAL REQUIREMENTS MUST THEY MEET?

Charity trustees are the individuals with general control and management of the administration of a charity (*section 177, Charities Act 2011*). Most trustees are not paid for their role, but they can typically (within certain parameters) claim expenses, be paid for property let and services provided to the charity, and be paid interest on money lent to it.

To be eligible as a trustee of a charitable company or charitable incorporated organisation a person must be at least 16 years of age (the minimum age is 18 years for other types of charity). A trustee must be properly appointed under the charity's governing document and must not be disqualified from acting.

There are some duties to which all trustees are subject and some that apply slightly differently, depending on the type of legal entity. Generally, the duties can be summarised to:

- Act at all times in the best interests of the charity.
- Advance the objects of the charity.
- Act within their powers.
- Act personally (including by participating actively in the charity's management).
- Exercise proper stewardship over the charity and its assets.
- Act impartially.
- Avoid conflicts of interest and not profit from the charity.
- Comply with the statutory requirements of charities (including filing obligations).

Trustees must exercise such care and skill as is reasonable in the circumstances, having regard to any special knowledge or experience they have (or hold themselves out as having) and, if a trustee acts as trustee in the course of a business or profession, having regard to any special knowledge or experience that it is reasonable to expect of a person acting in the course of that kind of business or profession.

If a trustee acts in breach of his or her duties, for example by applying the charity's assets otherwise than in accordance with its objects, he/she can face personal liability. If, however, they have acted honestly and reasonably at all relevant times, the court may relieve them of such liability. In some circumstances, trustee indemnity insurance may also cover liabilities that have arisen due to a breach of trust. To the extent that any personal liability arises for a trustee in properly carrying out his or her duties, s/he is usually entitled to an indemnity from the charity's assets.

There are distinct requirements about individuals judged to be fit and proper to manage a charity for tax purposes (*see Question 6*).

8.   WHAT ARE THE ACCOUNTING/FINANCIAL REPORTING REQUIREMENTS?

All charities must maintain accounts. For registered unincorporated charities this obligation arises from the Charities Act 2011. There are further obligations on charitable companies (as for other types of company) in the Companies Act 2006.

Charities' accounts must be prepared in accordance with the appropriate Statement of Recommended Practice (SORP). For smaller charities, the SORP based on the Financial Reporting Standard for Smaller Entities is used and other charities should follow the SORP based on Financial Reporting Standard 102.

The size of the charity also affects whether the accounts must be audited or independently examined. Currently, charities with gross income over GB£500,000 a year, or gross income over GB£250,000 a year and assets over GB£3.26 million, must have their accounts audited. Below those thresholds, an independent examination is sufficient.

Various other annual reporting requirements apply to charities, depending on their legal character. For example, a charitable company must annually file a confirmation statement and its accounts with Companies House and file an annual return and its accounts with the Charity Commission (as well as making certain non-financial event-driven filings throughout the year). Other types of charity have different obligations (*see Question 4*).

TAX

A significant advantage for bodies registered as charities for UK tax purposes (*see Question 6*) is the ability to benefit from certain reliefs and exemptions. The tax treatment of charities in England and Wales is complex, and this section only covers the more significant tax benefits available.

Tax on income

The main exemptions from tax relating to the income of a charity are:

* An exemption from corporation tax for charitable companies.
* An exemption from income tax for the trustees of charitable trusts. This relates to income from land, bank interest, certain trading and other types of income.

This treatment is subject to the condition that the charity's income is applied for charitable purposes. Tax reliefs are lost (and can be lost with retroactive effect) if a charity makes non-qualifying expenditure, that is, expenditure otherwise than in pursuit of its charitable purposes.

Tax on capital gains

Exemption from tax on capital gains is generally available, whether otherwise payable as corporation tax (for charitable companies) or capital gains tax (for the trustees of unincorporated charities). The relevant funds must be applied for charitable purposes, or tax will be payable.

Tax on property used by the organisation

Charities are eligible for a mandatory 80% reduction in business rates (a local tax that is payable by commercial businesses to the local authority) on premises used for charitable purposes. A further reduction of up to 20% is available at the discretion of the relevant local authority.

In some circumstances an exemption from stamp duty land tax (otherwise payable on the purchase of land or property) is available.

Value added tax (VAT)

Charities are generally subject to the same VAT rules as other organisations, although there are some particular VAT reliefs and exemptions for charities. For example, subject to certain conditions, there is a VAT exemption for charity fundraising events, and charities pay no VAT on certain goods made available to disabled people.

10. WHAT, IF ANY, ARE THE TAXATION BENEFITS FOR DONORS TO CHARITIES?

Advantages for donors

Gift Aid. Personal income is taxed at different rates in England and Wales, depending on how much an individual earns. The basic rate is 20%. Those with income over GB£32,000 a year pay income tax at a higher rate on their earnings over this level, and are known as "higher rate" taxpayers. Income over GB£150,000 a year is taxed at the "additional rate".

The relief means that a donation of, for example, GB£1,000 is worth GB£1,200 to the recipient charity, because the charity can reclaim the basic rate tax paid by the donor. Higher and additional rate taxpayers can claim back the difference between the higher/additional rate of tax (currently 40% / 45%) and the basic rate on the total gross value of any relevant donations they make. This can be a significant sum on large donations. The donor must have paid sufficient UK income and/or capital gains tax in the relevant period to cover the amount of the reclaim.

The Gift Aid Small Donation Scheme (GASDS) allows charities to claim payments on small donations (up to GB£20) in circumstances where a Gift Aid declaration (that a sufficient amount of tax has been paid by the donor during the period, to cover the amount reclaimed) is not practical, such as street collections. The cap on claims was increased in April 2016 from GB£5,000 income a year to GB£8,000.

Payroll Giving. This scheme provides tax relief at source for individuals who give money to a charity by direct deduction from their pay. Once an employee has signed up the employer simply deducts the amount to be donated from the employee's pay before making the relevant tax deductions, allowing the donor to make a tax free donation to his or her chosen charity. However, unlike Gift Aid, the charity is not able to reclaim any tax on the donation.

Inheritance tax. Gifts to charities on death are exempt from inheritance tax.

Separately, where a testator leaves 10% or more of his/her net estate to charity a reduced inheritance tax rate of 36% (rather than 40%) is applied to the estate (where the deceased passes away after 6 April 2012).

Social Investment Tax Relief (SITR). Introduced by the Finance Act 2014, SITR is intended to encourage individuals to invest in social enterprises. Individuals making debt or equity investments in eligible organisations for at least three years up to a maximum of GB £1 million a year can claim back 30% of the cost of their investment from their income tax liability, in the year of the investment or the year before. A gain realised on the disposal of a qualifying investment may be exempt from capital gains tax.

Disadvantages for donors

The Tainted Charity Donations rules are anti-avoidance provisions, to prevent donors claiming tax relief on donations to charity where the donor's purpose is to obtain some benefit from the transaction (known as tainted donations).

Where a donation is deemed to be tainted, tax relief is denied and HMRC will require the donor to repay the tax relief claimed. In exceptional circumstances, where the charity knew that the donor was only making the gift because of the advantage he received, the charity may also be liable to a penalty.

DISADVANTAGES

11. WHAT ARE THE MAIN DISADVANTAGES OF CHARITABLE STATUS?

The principal disadvantage for charities is the regulation and public scrutiny that they attract in return for the tax advantages they receive.

Charities are, in addition, bound by complex legal requirements in many circumstances, for example when disposing of property, engaging with commercial partners and managing their investments. An organisation should therefore consider these factors carefully before deciding to set up and operate as a charity.

Charity trustees generally cannot be paid for their services as trustees under English law and there are strict restrictions on how they can benefit from their position as charity trustees, which includes entering into contracts with the charity. Trustees generally cannot be employed by the charity. Charities in England and Wales are therefore generally required to find people willing to assume the relevant legal responsibilities in a voluntary capacity, which can be challenging.

The Charity Commission requires a charity to have a registered office in England and Wales, and will usually require at least some of the charity's funds to be kept in an English or Welsh bank account. It will also sometimes require at least one trustee to be resident in England or Wales. Although this is usually not difficult to achieve, overseas charities looking to register a charitable presence in England and Wales should be aware of these requirements.

OVERSEAS CHARITIES

12. IS IT POSSIBLE TO OPERATE AN OVERSEAS CHARITY IN YOUR JURISDICTION? WHAT ARE THE REGISTRATION FORMALITIES? HOW (IF AT ALL) ARE OVERSEAS CHARITIES TREATED DIFFERENTLY IN YOUR JURISDICTION FROM CHARITIES SET UP UNDER DOMESTIC LAW?

Overseas charities in England and Wales

The Charity Commission only regulates charities that are governed by the laws of England and Wales. It is therefore possible for a charity based in another jurisdiction to operate in England and Wales without needing to register with the Charity Commission. However, in some cases the English courts have considered that they have jurisdiction over charities governed by foreign laws, where the trustees of the charity are based in England.

Generally, overseas charities cannot claim tax reliefs in the UK. However, bodies with purposes that are charitable under English law and have suitable restrictions in their governing documents, and which are based in the EU, Norway, Iceland or Liechtenstein, are theoretically able to register with HMRC to take advantage of UK tax reliefs (*Finance Act, 2010*) (*see Question 6*). At present, there is no possibility for overseas charities not based in the EU, Norway, Iceland or Liechtenstein to register with HMRC, so there is no possibility for them to claim tax reliefs in the UK.

Public visibility of charities in England and Wales is high. An overseas charity that is not registered with the Charity Commission may therefore struggle to be seen as credible, unless it is well-known internationally.

An overseas charity that does not have some form of legal operating structure in the UK may struggle to win contracts, secure leases or employ staff. An overseas charity that is planning to undertake significant operations in the UK or that wishes to be able to raise funds from UK donors (or both) should therefore consider whether to set up a separate English charity.

Giving to overseas charities

Generally, gifts to overseas charities are not eligible for tax relief in the UK, even if they are established for purposes that are charitable under English law.

However, the Finance Act 2010 was designed to permit European charities to benefit from tax relief in the UK, and to allow UK donors to make tax effective donations to European charities. Gifts from UK donors to charities in another EU member state, Norway, Iceland or Liechtenstein are eligible for Gift Aid, provided that the charity satisfies the conditions in the Finance Act 2010 and is registered with HMRC (*see Question 6*). Whether (and to what extent) these rules will continue to apply when the UK leaves the EU remains to be decided.

13. IS IT POSSIBLE TO REGISTER A DOMESTIC CHARITY ABROAD, AND HAS YOUR JURISDICTION ENTERED INTO ANY INTERNATIONAL AGREEMENTS OR TREATIES IN THIS AREA?

International treaties

The UK has a wide range of double tax treaties with other jurisdictions. Although charities are not always expressly referred to in these treaties they, as UK residents, are entitled to the same foreign reliefs as individuals. For example, the double tax treaty between the UK and Ireland provides a mutual charity exemption, allowing UK charities with an Irish source of income the same exemptions they would receive if the income were from a UK source (and vice versa).

Some treaties require an organisation to be subject to tax in order to claim tax exemptions. Charities are not strictly subject to tax where a statutory exemption applies to them, and in this situation a charity may not be able to claim relief (*HMRC International Tax Manual, INTM332210*).

Charities registered in more than one UK jurisdiction

Charitable purposes recognised by the law in the three jurisdictions of the UK (England, Wales and Scotland) are very similar, but not identical. An organisation wishing to operate as a charity throughout the UK must have objects that are charitable in all jurisdictions.

Dual-registered charities

To allow donors to benefit from tax relief in both the UK and the US, some charities set up a "dual-registered" structure. This involves setting up a section 501(c)(3) corporation (*section 501(c)(3), US Internal Revenue Code*) in the US and a charitable company limited by shares in England and Wales, of which the US entity is the sole shareholder. The US entity registers with the US tax authorities, electing for the English charity to be treated as a "disregarded entity", effectively a branch of the US entity for tax purposes.

Following this election, US taxpayers based in the UK can make donations to the English charity and benefit from US tax deductions. These donations can also be made under the Gift Aid scheme, allowing the English charity to reclaim tax on the gift (and donors who are higher and additional rate taxpayers to reclaim tax from HMRC).

REFORM

14.   ARE THERE ANY PROPOSALS FOR REFORM IN THE AREA OF CHARITY LAW?

Topics currently being reviewed by the Law Commission include:

- The powers of the Charity Tribunal.
- Regulation of the acquisition and disposal of land by charities.
- Remuneration of trustees supplying goods to a charity.
- Transfers of assets and liabilities on incorporation and merger.

Recommendations on these topics as well as a draft bill are expected to be published at the end of 2016.

ONLINE RESOURCES

LEGISLATION.GOV.UK

W www.legislation.gov.uk

Description. This website is managed by The National Archives on behalf of the government and it contains all UK legislation.

REGULATORY AUTHORITIES

THE CHARITY COMMISSION

W www.gov.uk/government/organisations/charity-commission

T +44 300 066 9197

Description. The Charity Commission is a non-ministerial government department and the official regulator of charities in England and Wales. This website contains links to the register of charities and the Charity Commission's guidance.

HM REVENUE & CUSTOMS (HMRC)

W www.gov.uk/government/organisations/hm-revenue-customs

T +44 300 123 1073

Description. HMRC is the UK tax authority, with which charities must be registered to gain beneficial tax treatment.

OFFICE OF THE REGULATOR OF COMMUNITY INTEREST COMPANIES

W www.gov.uk/government/organisations/office-of-the-regulator-of-community-interest-companies

T +44 29 2034 6228

Description. Known as the CIC Regulator, this office regulates community interest companies. The website provides official guidance.

REGISTRAR OF COMPANIES

W www.gov.uk/government/organisations/companies-house

T +44 303 1234 500

Description. Known as Companies House, this body regulates registered companies (including charitable companies) and maintains the register. Users can search for company information through the website.

OVERVIEW AND MAIN TRENDS

1. WHAT IS THE HISTORICAL BACKGROUND TO CHARITY LAW AND CHARITABLE ORGANISATIONS IN YOUR JURISDICTION?

This answer to *Question 1* is drawn from the detailed history of charity law in Northern Ireland as set out in the leading text by Kerry O'Halloran and Ronan Cormacain, *Charity Law in Northern Ireland*, Round Hall Sweet & Maxwell (2001).

Historical overview

Charity law in Northern Ireland was influenced by English feudalism, which determined the ownership of land and the structure of society, and the Norman French law of *mortmain* under which donors gifted lands to the Church to avoid feudal dues and to obtain prayers or masses for their souls. Gifts of property subject to the condition that they be used only by specific persons (*frankalmoigne*) assisted the Church and religious orders in growing their power and political influence.

After the Reformation many Irish abbeys and monasteries were dissolved and their lands taken by the Crown, which removed the main source of accommodation, care and education for the poor. Grants of property to the Church in exchange for spiritual benefits ended. The Court of Chancery developed the law of equity and exercised the jurisdiction of the King as *parens patriae* regarding minors and lunatics, and recognised charitable trusts.

The end of the 16th century saw the removal of the influence of the Catholic Church and the Elizabethans attempted to impose the new Protestant religion. In England this led to the Statute of Charitable Uses 1601 (or Statute of Elizabeth) and in Ireland the Statute of Pious Uses 1634, also known as the Statute of Charles, which is the legislative foundation for charity law in Ireland. It set out a list of objects including the establishment of schools, relief or maintenance of the poor and distressed, maintaining and repairing churches, schools, colleges or hospitals and the erection, building, maintenance or repair of bridges, paces and highways or any other lawful and charitable use and uses warranted by the law of the realm. This was never regarded as a definitive list and a public element was vital. As in modern charity law a gift could be judged charitable if it fell within the "spirit or intendment" of the Statute. The Statute was repealed by the Statute Law Revision Act (Ireland) 1878.

The judiciary reaffirmed that charitable purposes corresponding to the statutory definition were recognised in law. Judicial classification of charity developed through case law, in particular the *Pemsel* Case in which Lord Macnaghten accepted Sir Samuel Romilly's classification of charitable purposes from the case of *Morice v The Bishop of Durham (1804) 9 Ves. 399* and classified all recognised charitable purposes under the following four heads, adding that to be charitable a gift must also be beneficial to the community (*Commissioners for Special Purposes of Income Tax v Pemsel [1891] A.C. 531*):

- Trusts for the relief of poverty.
- Trusts for the advancement of education.
- Trusts for the advancement of religion.
- Trusts beneficial to the community not falling within the above.

This list has now been overtaken by the list of charitable purposes contained in the Charities Act (Northern Ireland) 2008 (2008 Act) (*see below, Legislative background* and *Question 3, Definition of charity*).

Legislative background

Northern Ireland is a part of the UK but is a separate legal jurisdiction with its own courts and body of law emanating from statute and common law. Charity law has been derived from a unified legislative framework. Ireland was partitioned into two separate jurisdictions in 1920, however, the laws emanating from 19th century legislation provided a common governing framework until the 1960s.

After 1800 until 1920, legislation affecting charities was passed by the British Parliament in Westminster such as, for example, the Educational Endowments (Ireland) Act 1885.

After partition and until the Stormont Assembly was prorogued in 1972 both Westminster and Stormont developed the statutory framework in Northern Ireland, such as the Charities Act (NI) 1964.

In 1972 after Stormont was prorogued, all legislative power reverted to Westminster and some legislation was made by Order in Council for Northern Ireland such as the Charities (Northern Ireland) Order 1987.

The Charities Act (NI) 1964 Act and the 1987 Order put Northern Ireland on a different statutory platform from England. This included statutory powers relating to trustees and particular powers which are currently vested in the Charities Branch of the Department for Communities in Northern Ireland. The 1964 Act and the 1987 Order are gradually being repealed. The Department for Communities is charged with responsibility for the legal framework for charities in Northern Ireland and oversees the work of the Charity Commission for Northern Ireland which is a non-departmental public body of the Department.

A fundamental change arose with the 2008 Act, a measure of the Northern Ireland Assembly which set out a new regulatory framework for the regulation of charities in Northern Ireland, setting up the:

- Charity Commission for Northern Ireland.
- Charities Tribunal for Northern Ireland.

Not all of this Act is currently in force (*see Question 3, Principal sources of law*).

2. ARE INDEPENDENT CHARITABLE ORGANISATIONS COMMON AND SIGNIFICANT IN YOUR JURISDICTION? WHAT IS THE CURRENT SIZE AND SCOPE OF THE SECTOR AND THE MAIN TRENDS?

Size and scope of sector

In Northern Ireland independent charitable organisations are common and significant. The sector is estimated at between 7,000 and 12,000 organisations. The Charities Commission for Northern Ireland commenced the registration of charities in December 2013. Over 5,000 have registered as at August 2016. In Northern Ireland registration is compulsory and there are no exceptions or exemptions from registration (*see Question 5*).

Information provided from HM Revenue & Customs (HMRC) in 2009 showed that over 6,500 organisations were recognised as charities for tax relief purposes. The most reliable survey of the sector, "State of the Sector" (which also includes voluntary and community organisations) was completed in 2016 by The Northern Ireland Council for Voluntary Action (NICVA) (*www.nicva.org*). The research provides information on the size, scope and finances of the Northern Ireland voluntary, community and social enterprise sector and is presented as an online resource.

The report revealed that there were approximately 6,127 organisations generating an income of GB£589 million including grants and contracts. 33% of the organisations had an income of less than GB£10,000. The organisations employed an estimated 44,703 individuals, with an estimated 75% of the paid workforce being female. There is an estimated 241,264 volunteers linked to organisations. The top five areas of work identified by organisations in the survey included: community development; education/training; health and wellbeing; and children.

Main trends

Registration has led to an increasing awareness and need for governance and support for governance arrangements for boards. Welfare reform is having a significant impact with an increasing reliance on charity services, including a prevalence of foodbanks. Charities carry out many activities and enter into contracts delivering services to public bodies such as health trusts and statutory agencies. Grant making is significant and there is significant trading in furtherance of charitable purposes, advice and support, work, research and campaigning to raise awareness. There has been an increase in trading subsidiaries and commercial arms and more complexity within group structures.

There are a considerable number of voluntary and community groups, many of which were established due to the "peace dividend" (that is, the improved economy in Northern Ireland after the signing of the Good Friday Agreement in 1998) and there is no method of definitively identifying these groups. There are also a number of not-for-profit organisations that are not charities, including a number of community interest companies and an increasing number of social enterprises.

Many of the charities active in Northern Ireland are local, being set up and run entirely within Northern Ireland, but many also have strong links and operate on an all-island basis throughout Ireland or are branches or committees of charities registered in England and Wales or Scotland.

A number of notable mergers have taken place in the sector.

LEGAL FRAMEWORK

Definition of charity

A "charity" is defined in section 1(1) of the Charities Act (Northern Ireland) 2008 (2008 Act), and means an institution which:

- Is established for charitable purposes only.
- Is subject to the control of the [High] Court in the exercise of its jurisdiction with respect to charities.

A "charitable purpose" in Northern Ireland is similar to but not identical to the provisions in the English and Welsh legislation. Charitable purposes are defined as the "purposes which are exclusively charitable purposes defined by section 2". Section 2 makes reference to two aspects:

- A charitable purpose is within the list of charitable purposes in section 2(2)
- Is for the public benefit (see section 3).

List of charitable purposes. The following charitable purposes are included in the list (*section 2(2), 2008 Act*):

- The prevention or relief of poverty.
- The advancement of education.
- The advancement of religion, which includes a belief in one god or more than one god, and any analogous philosophical belief (whether or not involving a belief in a god).
- The advancement of health or the saving of lives, which includes the prevention or relief of sickness, disease or human suffering.
- The advancement of citizenship or community development, which includes rural or urban regeneration and the promotion of civic responsibility, volunteering, the voluntary sector or the effectiveness or efficiency of charities.
- The advancement of the arts, culture, heritage or science.
- The advancement of amateur sport, which means sports or games which promote health by involving physical or mental skill or exertion.
- The advancement of human rights, conflict resolution or reconciliation or the promotion of religious or racial harmony or equality or diversity, which includes the advancement of peace and good community relations.
- The advancement of environmental protection or improvement.
- The relief of those in need by reason of youth, age, ill-health, disability, financial hardship or other disadvantage, which includes relief given by the provision of accommodation or care to the persons mentioned.
- The advancement of animal welfare.
- Any other purposes that are recognised as charitable purposes under existing charity law or under the Recreational Charities Act (Northern Ireland) 1958.
- Any other purpose that may reasonably be regarded as analogous to or within the spirit of the above.

These charitable purposes are similar to those in the legislation in England and Wales under the Charities Act 2006 and in Scotland under the Charities and Trustee Investment (Scotland) Act 2005. However, there are three notable differences:

- The 2008 Act does not have express charitable purposes for the promotion of efficiency of the armed forces or the Crown, police, fire rescue services or ambulance services (nor does the Scots law statute).

- Paragraph (h) relating to human rights and resolution of conflict also includes the advancement of peace and community relations under the Northern Ireland version in the 2008 Act only and no equivalent is found in the English and Welsh or Scots law versions.

- The advancement of religion in Northern Ireland includes any analogous philosophical belief whether or not involving a belief in God, but this is not included in the English and Welsh provisions, however, it is in the Scots law version.

Public benefit. The "public benefit test" is not defined in statute. The Charity Commission for Northern Ireland must provide guidance on the public benefit test and charity trustees must have regard to the Commission's guidance. A charity must provide a demonstrable benefit and this benefit must be provided to the public or to a section of it.

Principal sources of law

Charities in Northern Ireland are principally governed by the 2008 Act, which is partly in force, as amended by the Charities Act (Northern Ireland) 2013. The entire 2008 Act has not yet been brought into operation; in Northern Ireland this will occur through a series of commencement orders. As at May 2016 there have been seven commencement orders and a number of other Northern Ireland statutory rules affecting charities. The 2008 Act applies to charities, and some provisions such as fundraising also apply to other institutions. Notable areas which are yet to come into force include the new structure of the charitable incorporated organisation, funding of charitable institutions, and revised rules relating to the incorporation of charity trustees (which is currently regulated by the Charities Act (Northern Ireland) 1964) (*see Question 4, Charitable incorporated organisation (CIO)*).

The Charities Act (Northern Ireland) 1964 and the Charities (Northern Ireland) Order 1987 are partly in force and gradually being repealed. The 1964 Act is relevant to:

- Certain powers of the Department for Communities concerning:
  - publications of charitable gifts in wills and administrative actions and giving of receipts;
  - sending a certificate to the Attorney General for Northern Ireland where it considers that legal proceedings should be instituted in relation to any charity;
  - misdescribed beneficiaries in wills;
  - charity property, such as sale exchange or mortgage of charity lands, leases and proceedings to recover charity property and redemptions of rent charges;
  - miscellaneous provisions regarding charity trustees, such as the power of two-thirds to act for certain purposes and their duty to keep accounts.
- Facilitating the administration of charities, by providing for incorporation of charity trustees and appointment of new charity trustees (*see Question 4*).

The 1987 Order remains relevant in relation to its provisions regarding the value of land amendments to the 1964 Act.

LEGAL BODIES

Unincorporated associations

An unincorporated association comprises a group of people with a mutual interest who wish to carry out a common not-for-profit object. It is, therefore, a membership-led body. The association is governed by a constitution, which is a contract between the members setting out the rights, obligations and duties that each has to the other. The constitution sets out the:

- Objectives of the association.
- Membership criteria and structure.
- Procedures for elections of committee.
- An annual members' meeting (usually).

Unincorporated associations are popular for smaller organisations. The management committee is accountable to the members and carries out the activities of the association on their behalf. The management committee is likely to be regarded as the charity trustees. In addition, some individuals are appointed as trustees to hold the assets of the association and would be known as property trustees and their responsibilities and legal obligations would be set out in a declaration of trust. Often such property trustees are incorporated under a scheme of incorporation of trustees to hold the title on trust for the charitable purposes of the unincorporated association.

Section 10 of the Charities Act (NI) 1964 provides for incorporation of the charity trustees (to be revised under the 2008 Act when the relevant provisions come into force (*see Question 3*)). This allows trusts and unincorporated associations which hold property or enter into contracts to incorporate their charity trustees, meaning that property title can be held in the name of the incorporated body of charity trustees rather than in the individual names of trustees. It is not, therefore, necessary to enter into the administrative costs associated with updating title to the property, such as changing registered names. This does not, however, protect the individual trustees from personal liability.

Advantages. Unincorporated associations:

- Are low cost, easy to establish, and are free of regulation and control, other than control and regulation by the Charity Commission for Northern Ireland (*see Question 5*).
- Have few formal requirements.

Disadvantages. Unincorporated associations:

- Are not legal entities so they cannot enter into contracts or obligations, and individuals enter into contracts in their own names.
- Do not protect members from personal liability. The unincorporated association has no legal personality, therefore the members of the association and the management committee may incur personal liability.

Trusts

Trusts are recognised in Northern Ireland as vehicles for charitable organisations, and many older charities are established as trusts. Trusts are usually governed by a charitable trust deed:

- Setting out the objects of the trust.
- Identifying the trustees.
- Providing for the administration of the trust.

Trusts have a flat structure and have no membership requirement. They are commonly used for grant-making trusts or where property is settled. Trustees' statutory powers and duties are set out in the Trustee Act (NI) 2001.

It is possible to incorporate the charity trustees (*see above, Unincorporated associations*).

Advantages. Trusts:

- Are easily established and operated. A trust is not subject to annual fees that would be payable by a company.
- Can have continuity in governance. The trustees are not usually subject to election and can remain in office for a lifetime, however, some trusts provide for a fixed period of service. The terms of the trust deed will normally provide for new trustees to be appointed by existing trustees.
- Have accountability and control. Trustees are not held to account in the same way as a membership organisation structure.
- Allow for privacy. Trustees can exercise discretion and do not need to be accountable or give reasons for the way they have exercised their discretion. Their decisions cannot be questioned, except by the Commission or the court. If the trustees act outside the terms of the trust they can be taken to court for breach of trust.

Disadvantages. The disadvantages are that:

- Limited liability does not apply to trustees. The trustees are responsible for contracts they enter into on behalf of the trust or for actions taken against the trust. They are entitled to be indemnified by the trust but only to the extent of the size of the trust fund and they could incur personal liability for liabilities exceeding this amount. They do not have the same protection as directors of a charitable company with regard to actions taken against them by third parties, such as employee claims or breach of contract actions. They are particularly exposed to uninsurable risks.
- Trust structures can be inflexible. In particular, older trusts do not contain powers to vary the administrative powers of the trust and the objects for which the trust was set up in the first place may be outdated. To make an amendment to the trust deed a cy-près scheme under which the Commission or the court can amend the terms of the trust to accord with the intentions of the original settlor may be required.
- There are administrative hurdles to appointing new trustees, such as transferring the property of the trust into new names unless the charity trustees have been incorporated (*see above*).
- There is a lack of oversight/accountability. Trustees are not accountable to any members for their decisions and are answerable only to the Commission and the courts.

Companies limited by guarantee

A company limited by guarantee is the most commonly used type of incorporated body used by charities in Northern Ireland. It is established under the Companies Act 2006 or former Companies Acts. A memorandum and articles of association comprise the governing documents.

Advantages. The advantages are that the company:

- Has legal personality. The company is recognised in law as the legal person in Northern Ireland capable of owning property, entering into contracts or taking or defending court proceedings. It can employ staff and hold property in its own name, and trustees are not required to hold its property.
- Benefits from limited liability. As a legal person the debts and obligations and contracts belong to the company itself and not to the members. Members of the company have protection of limited liability guaranteed under the articles, which is usually GB£1. Directors or officers can incur personal liability, however, and limited liability will not always provide absolute protection.
- Democracy. The directors are answerable to the members and accountable to the members for the operations of the company and can be removed from office by the company members.
- Perpetual succession. The company continues to exist even if the members and directors change.

Disadvantages. The disadvantages to the company concern:

- Cost. There is a higher cost in establishing a company rather than an unincorporated association or trust, and annual fees are payable at Companies House. Company accounts may also be more expensive to produce. There are ongoing administration fees, such as for annual return/confirmation statements.
- Public access. Companies House has information about companies which can be accessed online by any member of the public, such as the company's governing document, and to find out who the directors are and to obtain a copy of the company's accounts. This can also be seen as an advantage in providing public openness and accountability.
- Statutory regulation. Compliance with the Companies Act 2006 provides detailed statutory obligations in relation to the administration of the company with strict time limits. A director of a company which is also a charity must comply with the duties and responsibilities and is also subject to the liabilities of company directors.

Societies

Certain forms of society can be set up to carry on business industry trade for the benefit of the community, including:

- Industrial and provident societies (IPSs), which are commonly used for housing associations and are governed by a set of rules, usually based on a model.
- Community benefits societies.
- Co-operative societies.
- Friendly societies.

The Registry of Credit Unions and Industrial and Provident Societies is responsible for registering the societies and for maintaining public records.

Advantages. The advantages of societies are that they have:

- A corporate identity.
- Limited liability.
- Perpetual succession (they continue despite change in membership).

- A body of members, which hold the management committee to account.

Disadvantages. The disadvantages for a society are that:

- The rules are less flexible than the articles of a limited company.
- Significant fees are payable, for example on changes and alterations of rules.
- The society must submit annual returns to the Registrar
- Annual returns and rules are in the public domain. This can also be seen as an advantage in providing public openness and accountability.
- Charitable status may be difficult to achieve. Not every society will meet the requirements for charity registration, but housing associations are usually accepted as charitable.

Charitable incorporated organisation (CIO)

The CIO is a new legal structure specifically for charities, which is not yet available as the relevant part of the Charities Act (Northern Ireland) 2008 has not been commenced (*see Question 3, Principal sources of law*). The CIO will be similar to a limited company but will not require dual registration under company and charity law. A CIO will be regulated by the Commission. It will be possible for charities incorporated as companies limited by a guarantee to convert to a CIO when it is available.

The CIO, when it is available, will have the advantages of the limited company but will be easier to set up as it will not require dual registration under company and charity law (*see Question 5*).

Other forms

There are other legal forms for charities in Northern Ireland, including Royal Charter bodies.

5. WHAT ARE THE QUALIFICATION REQUIREMENTS/FORMALITIES TO SET UP THESE ORGANISATIONS?

All charities in Northern Ireland regardless of legal form or structure must be registered with the Charity Commission for Northern Ireland, without exception. Charity trustees are responsible for registration. A failure to do so can constitute a breach of their statutory duty and the Commission may take legal action against them. An organisation must apply for registration as a charity in Northern Ireland if it:

- Has exclusively charitable purposes.
- Is governed by the law of Northern Ireland.
- Has control and direction over its governance and resources.

The Commission calls forward organisations to register on an incremental basis from two sources: a list published on its website known as the "Registration List" and from those organisations that have submitted an "expression of intent" (*see below*). Once called forward to register there is three months to complete the online registration application form. Registration is conducted online. There is a toolkit and registration support and guidance available on the Commission's website. Charities should prepare by checking the registration list. If the charity does not appear, the charity trustees should submit an "expression of intent" form to make the Commission aware of its existence. The charity trustees must collate the information required to complete the form, which includes:

- The charitable purposes/objects from the organisation's governing document.
- A public benefit statement.

There is a document and information checklist on the website.

The governing document, a bank statement and accounts of the charity must be uploaded at registration. All charity trustees must sign and upload a trustee declaration of compliance and eligibility to be a trustee.

Once registered, the charity appears on the register of charities for Northern Ireland on the Commission's website and is issued with an NIC Number.

Apart from registration, the various charity bodies have a number of requirements.

Unincorporated associations

A constitution is required (*see Question 4, Unincorporated associations*). There are no other formalities to set up this organisation.

Trusts

A trust deed is required (*see Question 4, Trusts*). There are no other formalities to set up this organisation.

Companies limited by guarantee

A form of memorandum signed by the subscribers and articles of association is required and must be submitted with an incorporation form with a fee to Companies House, which issues a certificate of incorporation (*see Question 4, Companies limited by guarantee*).

Societies

The following must be submitted to the Registrar:

- A set of rules, usually based on a model.
- An application for registration of a society.
- A fee.

See *Question 4, Societies.*

ONGOING REGULATORY REQUIREMENTS

6. WHAT ARE THE MAIN REGULATORY AUTHORITIES FOR CHARITABLE ORGANISATIONS? WHAT ARE THEIR POWERS OF INVESTIGATION/AUDIT/SANCTIONS?

Regulatory authorities

All charities in Northern Ireland must be registered with the Charity Commission for Northern Ireland (*see Question 5*).

Powers

The Commission has a number of wide-ranging powers affecting charities in Northern Ireland, including the power to do anything which is calculated to facilitate or is conducive or incidental to the performance of any of its functions or general duties. The Commission is not authorised to exercise functions which correspond to those of the charity trustee in relation to a charity, or otherwise to be directly involved in the administration of the charity.

Any member of the public or a charity trustee can raise a concern about a charity with the Commission, at which point the Commission will investigate the concerns and take one of the following decisions:

- To take no action, or refer the concern to another authority or regulator party.
- To provide self-regulatory guidance to the charity and its charity trustees. The Commission is likely to monitor the charity and ensure that follow up action is taken to resolve the concern.
- To provide regulatory guidance (*see below*). This occurs when clear issues arise within a charity, but the charity trustees are willing to co-operate with the Commission, which determines that the risk to the charity does not merit the opening of a more serious statutory inquiry. Regulatory guidance includes an action plan and timeline for the charity trustees to implement.
- To conduct a non-compliance visit.
- To notify the public through the register of charities
- To undertake a statutory inquiry. The Commission opens a formal statutory inquiry under section 22 of the Charities Act (Northern Ireland) 2008 (2008 Act) where there is a most serious risk to a charity, its assets or beneficiaries. A statutory inquiry is required to enable the Commission to utilise some of its formal and investigatory and protective powers. Results of statutory inquiries are generally published on the Commission's website. A review to the Commission's decision to open a statutory inquiry can be sought from the Charity Tribunal for Northern Ireland.

Generally, the Commission has a number of powers under the 2008 Act to make orders or directions in relation to charities in Northern Ireland, including the following.

To change charities' names. The Commission can do this if the name is the same as or too like the name of another charity or likely to mislead the public. This might be the case if the name:

- Gives the impression that the charity is connected to a government department of other district council.
- Is, in the opinion of the Commission, offensive.

To suspend or remove charity trustees. The Commission can make an order for the removal of a charity trustee, officer, agent or employee, in connection with a statutory inquiry. It has utilised this power on several occasions. The Commission can also appoint additional trustees or an interim manager.

To restrict transactions entered into by the charity, give specific directions for protection of the charity and direct the application of charity property. This can include instructing a person not to part with property without the Commission's consent.

Investigatory powers. This can include securing a warrant to obtain documents by entering and searching premises and directing individuals to attend to give evidence and produce documents.

Schemes to change, replace or extend the trusts of a charity. Under the 2008 Act the Commission has the power to make a scheme (cy-près) to change the purposes of a charity. This can arise where the current purposes can no longer be carried out or not in the way laid out in the governing documents such as the trust deed.

Consents for charitable companies. Where the legal structure is a company limited by guarantee, certain changes to be made to its articles of association must be approved by the Commission before they can take effect. These are "regulated alterations", including a change:

- To the statement of charitable purposes (objects) of the charity.
- A change to what happens to the company's property on winding up (dissolution clause).
- A change which authorises the charity's funds or property to be used to benefit the charity trustees (directors) or members or organisations connected with them.

The consent of the Commission is required before the special resolution making the alteration is passed by the charity. There are other transactions which require the specific consent of the Commission and these transactions cannot legally take place if the prior written consent of the Commission has not been obtained. These include transactions with directors or directors of subsidiary companies.

Powers for unincorporated charities. Certain statutory powers apply to unincorporated charities (that is, organisations which are not companies or other corporate bodies). If these bodies do not have the power within their constitution or governing document to make these changes, they can rely on these statutory powers to transfer all property to another charity or replace the purposes of the charity or modify administrative powers or procedures. There are also special arrangements for spending permanent endowment funds in certain circumstances. In some instances the Commission may request further information and direct the charity to give public notice of a proposed alteration, or can make an objection on procedural grounds or object on merit grounds. There are strict time periods for these outcomes.

Power to authorise transactions. The Commission can authorise transactions which are not otherwise legally possible for the charity trustees to make themselves. A charity may wish to apply for an authorisation where the charity trustees wish to make a transaction or payment which is in the best interests of the charity but they do not have the power to do so. The charity trustees may wish to make a transaction or payment which is not in the best interests of the charity but which they think they have a moral obligation to make.

Power to relieve charity trustees from liability for breach of trust or duty. Where the Commission considers that a person such as the charity trustee is or may be personally liable for a breach of trust or breach of duty but that the person has acted honestly and reasonably and ought fairly to be excused for the breach of trust or duty, the Commission may make an order relieving that person wholly or partly for any such liability.

Power to give advice and guidance. On the application of any charity trustee or trustee for a charity the Commission may give that person its opinion or advice in relation to any matter relating to the performance of that person's duties as a trustee in relation to the charity concerned, or otherwise relating to the proper administration of the charity. If the person then acts in accordance with this opinion or advice the trustee is considered to have acted in accordance with his or her trust.

Power to determine the membership of a charity. The Commission can determine who the members of the charity are.

Legal proceedings relating to charities. The Commission has the same powers as the Attorney General for Northern Ireland to bring legal proceedings concerning charities or the property or affairs of charities, or to compromise claims, except for the Attorney General's power to petition for the winding up of a charity (for the Commission's power to petition for a winding up *see below*).

Charity proceedings to be taken by the charity itself, by one of the trustees, or by an interested person, must be authorised by an order of the Commission.

Scheme for the administration of a charity. The Commission has the power to enter into a scheme of administration in relation to a charity. The Commission also has the power to present a petition to the High Court to wind up a charity company for example, after it has instituted a statutory inquiry and is satisfied that there has been misconduct or mismanagement in the administration of the charity, or that winding up is necessary to protect the charity property or to ensure that the property is properly applied but this provision is not in force yet.

7. WHICH BODIES OR PERSONS MANAGE CHARITABLE ORGANISATIONS AND WHAT GENERAL REQUIREMENTS MUST THEY MEET?

In the governing document of the charity, the people responsible for management may be variously described as trustees, directors, board members, governors, committee members, management committee, council of management or charity trustees. Unless specified otherwise, they are referred to in this article as charity trustees, and are the people legally responsible for the control, management and administration of a charity.

Formal requirements for charity trustees

Companies limited by guarantee are managed by the board of directors, who are legally both company directors and also charity trustees under trust and charity law. They must comply with their legal duties and responsibilities as company directors, in addition to those of charity trustees.

Charity trustees/directors of companies must be 16 years or over. In contrast, trustees of unincorporated charitable organisations must be 18 years old or over.

The following are disqualified from acting as charity trustees of a charity:

- A person convicted of an offence involving deception or dishonesty (unless it is a spent conviction).
- An undischarged bankrupt or a person who has made a composition or an arrangement with creditors.
- A person previously removed as a charity trustee or trustee for a charity.
- And in the case of a company charity a person subject to disqualification under company legislation.

Charity trustees must sign a declaration to confirm they are not disqualified. A waiver from disqualification can be sought from the Commission in some circumstances.

Duties

Charity trustees must ensure the charity:

- Complies with charity law and the requirements of the Charity Commission for Northern Ireland.
- Acts in accordance with the requirements of company law, trust law, health and safety law, employment law, bribery legislation and data protection law and many others, as appropriate.
- Does not breach any of the requirements or rules set out in its governing document.
- Acts only to further its charitable purposes.
- Remains solvent.

Charity trustees must:

- Ensure the charity is registered with the Commission.
- Prepare and submit annual returns, reports and accounts, as required by law.
- Act with integrity and avoid misusing charity funds or assets.
- Avoid potential conflicts of interest and manage any conflicts to ensure they are promoting accountability and transparency.
- Act with care and diligence to ensure they understand the charity's governing document and that it remains effective and up-to-date.
- Use the charity's funds and assets properly and only to further the charity's charitable purposes.
- Avoid undertaking activities that may place the charity's funds, assets or reputation at undue risk.
- Use reasonable care and skill in their work as charity trustees to ensure the charity is well run and efficient.
- Take special care when investing the funds of the charity or borrowing funds for it to use. They must consider taking external professional advice where there may be a risk to the charity or where they may be in breach of their duties.
- Always act in the best interests of the charity and only within the purposes of the charity.
- Demonstrate how they have carried out their charity's purposes for the public benefit.
- Have regard to the Commission's public benefit requirement statutory guidance at all times.

8.   WHAT ARE THE ACCOUNTING/FINANCIAL REPORTING REQUIREMENTS?

New regulations, The Charities (Accounts and Reports) Regulations (Northern Ireland) 2015, have been introduced in relation to charity accounting and reporting, with effect from 1 January 2016. Registered charities must report annually to the Charity Commission for Northern Ireland. All registered charities must complete and submit an online annual monitoring return form and their accounts and reports. For charities reporting on a full financial year that begins on or after 1 January 2016, or those registered with the Commission on or after 1 January 2016, the full reporting and accounting and regulations apply. Interim arrangements are in place where charities registered before 1 January 2016. The Statement of Recommended Practice: Accounting and reporting by Charities (The Charities SORP) will apply to charities preparing accruals accounts. Charities should read the Commission's guidance carefully.

A charity that is a company must comply with the Companies Acts and prepare and submit to the Commission on an annual basis:

- Its accounts.
- A trustees' annual report.
- An annual monitoring return.
- An independent examiners or auditors report for the charity.

For other charities, the reporting obligations depend on the charity's income:

- Less than GB£250,000 per year. The charity must prepare accounts and can choose to prepare them on a receipts and payments basis rather than an accruals basis. The accounts must be scrutinised by an independent examiner, that is, someone who the charity trustees assess as being capable of independently examining the accounts. The person must be independent of the trustees but there are no other specific qualification criteria. The trustees must prepare a trustees' annual report that also reports on how the charity has met the public benefit requirement, and complete an annual monitoring return. For these charities the return is more limited in scope than that for charities with larger income.
- More than GB£250,000 but less than GB£500,000. The charity must prepare accrual accounts and have them independently examined by a member of specific bodies provided for in the regulations and legislation. The trustees must complete a trustees' annual report that also includes how the charity has met the public benefit requirements and complete a full annual monitoring return.
- More than GB£500,000. The charity must prepare accruals accounts and have them audited. The trustees must complete an annual report that also reports on how the charity has met the public benefit requirement, and a full annual monitoring return.

If, however, a charity's governing document or other legislation requires it to prepare accruals accounts it must prepare such accrual accounts regardless of the income of the charity.

TAX

9.   HOW ARE CHARITIES TAXED, AND WHAT (IF ANY) ARE THE PRINCIPAL EXEMPTIONS AND/OR RELIEFS FROM TAXATION THAT THEY ENJOY?

Northern Ireland is part of the UK, and Northern Ireland charities can apply for recognition as a charity for UK tax purposes with Her Majesty's Revenue & Customs (HMRC). There is a significant advantage in being an organisation which is recognised as a charity for UK tax purposes as this entitles the organisation to benefit from particular tax reliefs and exemptions. For tax purposes, HMRC uses the meaning in the legislation applying to England and Wales when making a determination of eligibility for tax reliefs for Northern Ireland charities and there are some minor differences between that determination and the Charities Act (Northern Ireland) 2008.

Tax on income

There is an exemption from corporation tax for charitable companies and an exemption from income tax for charitable trusts, which applies to income arising from land, bank interest, gift aid payments and, in particular, trading income.

Tax on capital gains

A charity is exempt from tax on most capital gains it makes.

Tax on property used by the organisation

Charities are generally able to claim exemption from stamp duty land tax, which is the tax payable on purchase of land or property. It is also possible in Northern Ireland for charities to apply for relief from a local rate levied in non-domestic business premises. Charitable occupation comes with full rates exemption compared to the 80% mandatory relief that applies in the rest of the UK, however, this is currently subject to a review and may change, affecting in particular charity shops.

Value added tax (VAT)

Charities are generally subject to the same VAT rules as any other organisation. There are some particular VAT reliefs and exemptions available for charities. VAT implications of charity transactions, in particular new buildings of property, require specialist advice.

Other

Charities are exempt from inheritance tax, which is generally payable on gifts to charities on death.

10. WHAT, IF ANY, ARE THE TAXATION BENEFITS FOR DONORS TO CHARITIES?

Donors who are UK taxpayers can elect to add gift aid to their donations to charity, which allows charities to claim back the basic rate tax that the donor will have already paid on the donation. This can have a huge benefit to charities in Northern Ireland.

In Northern Ireland the payroll giving scheme provides tax relief at source for individuals who give money to a charity by direct deduction from their pay. Where an employee signs up to the scheme, the employer deducts the amount to be donated from the employee's pay before making the relevant tax deductions. This allows the employee to make a tax free donation to his or her chosen charity.

DISADVANTAGES

11. WHAT ARE THE MAIN DISADVANTAGES OF CHARITABLE STATUS?

The main disadvantage for charities concern the stringent regulation and also the public scrutiny and accountability that they attract in return for the tax advantages that they receive, in particular:

- The requirements that apply when charities dispose of property or manage their investments. Charity trustees must ensure that they have power to dispose of property and, if not, seek Commission permission. Charity Trustees of unincorporated charities must ensure that they meet the statutory duty of care in the Trustee Act (Northern Ireland) 2001 when exercising the power of investment and can demonstrate compliance.
- The new accountability and reporting requirements.

Charities rely on volunteers, as charity trustees cannot be paid for their services as trustees under the laws of Northern Ireland. The restrictions on how trustees can benefit in relation to transactions with the charity, and finding and retaining competent volunteer charity trustees, can be difficult.

OVERSEAS CHARITIES

12. IS IT POSSIBLE TO OPERATE AN OVERSEAS CHARITY IN YOUR JURISDICTION? WHAT ARE THE REGISTRATION FORMALITIES? HOW (IF AT ALL) ARE OVERSEAS CHARITIES TREATED DIFFERENTLY IN YOUR JURISDICTION FROM CHARITIES SET UP UNDER DOMESTIC LAW?

Many overseas charities operate in Northern Ireland. One of the most distinctive elements of the Charities Act (Northern Ireland) 2008 (2008 Act) is the unique arrangements it makes (which are not yet in force) for institutions that are recognised elsewhere that are present in Northern Ireland.

Section 167 of the 2008 Act will apply to any institution which is not a charity under the law of Northern Ireland, but which "operates for charitable purposes" in or from Northern Ireland. Organisations which meet these criteria are currently encouraged to submit an "expression of intent" online form to make the Commission aware of their existence (*see Question 5*).

These institutions will be required to prepare a financial statement and a statement of activities relating to their "operations for charitable purposes" in or from Northern Ireland in respect of each financial year.

The 2008 Act is silent on the meaning of "operates'", which may mean:

- Has a physical presence in Northern Ireland, such as a shop or office.
- Engages a fundraiser in Northern Ireland.
- Has a branch or Northern Ireland Committee in Northern Ireland.
- Provides services whether in the physical sense or online in the form of advice or assistance.

It is not yet known when section 167 will come into force, but it does not seem as if it will happen in the near future. It is not known how the overseas charity will be treated in relation to taxation or other issues. Currently, an overseas charity in Northern Ireland must comply with local law, for example, in relation to employment of staff in Northern Ireland.

13. IS IT POSSIBLE TO REGISTER A DOMESTIC CHARITY ABROAD, AND HAS YOUR JURISDICTION ENTERED INTO ANY INTERNATIONAL AGREEMENTS OR TREATIES IN THIS AREA?

Whether it is possible to register a domestic charity abroad will depend on the requirements of the other legal jurisdiction.

For example, Northern Ireland's adjoining jurisdiction the Republic of Ireland has its own charities regulator, the Charities Regulatory Authority. It can be a requirement under Irish law for a Northern Irish charity which is undertaking certain activities in the Republic of Ireland to register with the Irish Charities Regulatory Authority. In Scotland, a Northern Ireland charity may have to register with the Office of the Scottish Charity Regulator.

The authors are not aware of any specific international agreements or treaties at this time.

REFORM

14. ARE THERE ANY PROPOSALS FOR REFORM IN THE AREA OF CHARITY LAW?

There are no proposals for reform in the area of charity law in Northern Ireland.

ONLINE RESOURCES

LEGISLATION UK

W www.legislation.gov.uk

Description. This official website is delivered by The National Archives and provides a link to Northern Ireland legislation made either by the Northern Ireland Assembly or Westminster, that is, the UK government. Most of the information is annotated as to whether it is up-to-date or potentially out of date.

CHARITY TRIBUNAL FOR NORTHERN IRELAND DECISIONS

W www.courtsni.gov.uk

Description. This is the official online resource for decisions of the Charity Tribunal for Northern Ireland, which hears appeals from decisions of the Charity Commission for Northern Ireland.

REGULATORY AUTHORITIES

CHARITY COMMISSION FOR NORTHERN IRELAND

W www.charitycommissionni.org.uk

T +44 28 3832 0220

Description. The Charity Commission for Northern Ireland is the statutory regulator of charities in Northern Ireland, and was established under the Charities Act (Northern Ireland) 2008. Charities established in Northern Ireland must register with the Charity Commission, and submit financial information to it, and so on.

The website provides the register of charities in Northern Ireland, guidance and information.

COMPANIES HOUSE

W www.gov.uk/government/organisations/companies-house

T +44 303 1234 500

Description. Companies House is an executive agency sponsored by the Department for Business, Innovation & Skills. It incorporates and dissolves limited companies, registers the information companies are legally required to supply, and makes that information available to the public.

REGISTRAR OF INDUSTRIAL AND PROVIDENT SOCIETIES

W www.economy-ni.gov.uk/topics/credit-unions-and-societies

T +44 28 9052 9544

Description. Part of the Department for the Economy, the Registrar is responsible for the registration of credit unions and industrial and provident societies and maintaining the public record.

HER MAJESTY'S REVENUE AND CUSTOMS

W www.gov.uk/charities-and-tax

Description. This provides the official online process for seeking recognition by HMRC for tax purposes to claim entitlement to tax reliefs.

UK (SCOTLAND)

Gavin McEwan, TURCAN CONNELL

OVERVIEW AND MAIN TRENDS

1. WHAT IS THE HISTORICAL BACKGROUND TO CHARITY LAW AND CHARITABLE ORGANISATIONS IN YOUR JURISDICTION?

For many centuries, Scots law treated the concept of charitable trusts as a subset of public trusts, with no special treatment for trusts which were charitable in nature. A key change came about through the recognition of charities for tax purposes in 1891 thanks to the case of *Special Commissioners of Income Tax v Pemsel [1891] AC 531*. That case was considered to apply in Scotland, a point confirmed in the subsequent case of *Inland Revenue Commissioners v Glasgow Police Athletic Association [1953] AC 380*. In effect, the English law definition of charity was applied in Scotland as a result of these court decisions.

Charitable status in Scotland therefore became synonymous with the recognition of bodies as charitable for tax purposes. The Board of Inland Revenue (the precursor to today's HM Revenue & Customs, HMRC) effectively served as the registrar of Scottish charities and was the authority which could grant or deny charitable status for tax purposes.

Some limited regulation was introduced by the Law Reform (Miscellaneous Provisions) (Scotland) Act 1990 (the 1990 Act). The 1990 Act imposed regulations on charities recognised by the Inland Revenue and which were controlled or managed in or from Scotland. The system of regulation created under the 1990 Act included statutory powers granted to the Lord Advocate, exercised primarily through the Scottish Charity Office, which was a department of the Crown Office (the body responsible for the prosecution of crime in Scotland). The Scottish Charity Office's role was very limited and was generally reactive. Investigations would be raised when matters of concern were brought to the Office's attention, but there were additional powers of enquiry and an ability to bring actions in the Court of Session with a view to suspending charity trustees where there had been misconduct.

The 1990 Act also created a basic system of charity accounting and provided the public with rights to request copies of charities' constitutions or their most recently prepared financial accounts, but the overall regulatory system remained extremely basic and was considered inadequate. There were no annual reporting obligations and most charities had no form of interaction with the Scottish Charity Office whatsoever. After a series of fundraising scandals, and following the creation of the devolved Scottish Parliament, greater demand for formal regulation grew.

The report of the Scottish Charity Law Review Commission (known as the McFadden Commission) in May 2001 produced numerous recommendations for detailed legislative reform, including the creation of a regulator and registrar of Scottish charities, a Scottish definition of charity, a public benefit test and other regulatory provisions to help promote public confidence in the Scottish charity sector. The report was taken up by the Scottish Government and resulted in the passing of the Charities and Trustee Investment (Scotland) Act 2005, which forms the foundation and primary source of Scots charity law.

2. ARE INDEPENDENT CHARITABLE ORGANISATIONS COMMON AND SIGNIFICANT IN YOUR JURISDICTION? WHAT IS THE CURRENT SIZE AND SCOPE OF THE SECTOR AND THE MAIN TRENDS?

There is a long tradition of charity and philanthropy in Scotland, and the charity sector has a relatively high profile and public visibility for such a small legal jurisdiction. As of summer 2016, there were estimated to be around 45,000 voluntary organisations in Scotland, of which a total of 24,100 were registered charities listed on the Scottish Charity Register. An estimated 183,000 people serve as charity trustees, which is about 4% of the adult population.

Charities are especially important in rural areas, where there can be a higher concentration of charities per head of population. This emphasises the role which smaller charities play in the country generally, including village halls, social clubs and recreational organisations. Many of these smaller charities have very modest incomes and are run entirely by volunteers. Some studies suggest that there are more charities per head of population in Scotland than there are in any other of the countries which make up the UK.

Of the total number of charities registered in Scotland, about 800 (3.3%) are cross-border charities whose lead regulator is based outside Scotland. The vast majority of those cross-border charities are established in England and Wales. The remaining 96.7% of registered Scottish charities are bodies created in Scotland.

The total turnover of the Scottish charity sector is roughly GB£5 billion, with the largest 100 charities accounting for half of that turnover. Those largest 100 charities also employ 42,500 staff, about a third of the total number of people employed by the Scottish third sector. The total of nearly 140,000 third sector employees (on a headcount basis) has been compared to the 153,000 people employed by Scotland's biggest employer, the National Health Service. The sector is further bolstered by an estimated 1.3 million volunteers, who contribute an estimated 126 million hours of support each year.

Voluntary sector research suggests that around a third of all Scottish charities are engaged in the provision of social care (34%). Community, social and economic development bodies comprise around 16% of Scottish charities, with a further 14% focused on culture and recreation. At the opposite end of the spectrum, only 1% of Scottish charities by number (but not by turnover) operate in each of the fields of housing and advocacy.

The main trends in the Scottish sector in recent years show marked growth in the social care and housing association fields. This is likely to be a reflection of changes in government funding in those areas, and additional reliance on the third sector to fill the resulting service gaps.

Securing funding has become more difficult over the last five years, and most charities now rely on a more complex stream of funders and donors than ever before. Many charities have to look to innovative ways to raise the income they require to sustain their work, including loans and other forms of social investment. Average income growth is typically less than 1% per year across the sector, with the greatest levels of growth found in the very largest charities. Nearly half of the sector reportedly spends more than it raises, suggesting that reserves are being used up to fund charitable activity.

LEGAL FRAMEWORK

3.   IS THERE A LEGAL DEFINITION OF A "CHARITY"? WHAT ARE THE PRINCIPAL SOURCES OF LAW AND REGULATIONS RELATING TO CHARITABLE ORGANISATIONS AND ACTIVITIES?

Definition of charity

A body can refer to itself as a charity in Scotland if it meets the terms of the charity test set out in section 7 of the Charities and Trustee Investment (Scotland) Act 2005 (2005 Act). A body will meet this test if its purposes consist only of one or more of the charitable purposes set out in the 2005 Act and if it provides or intends to provide public benefit. Public benefit need not be provided in Scotland: public benefit provided in any part of the world is sufficient to meet the test.

Charitable purposes. The charitable purposes set out in the 2005 Act are:

• The prevention or relief of poverty (which the regulator considers to include the relief of unemployment).
• The advancement of education.
• The advancement of religion.
• The advancement of health (including the prevention or relief of sickness, disease or human suffering).
• The saving of lives.
• The advancement of citizenship or community development (including rural or urban regeneration and the promotion of civic responsibility, volunteering, the voluntary sector or the effectiveness or efficiency of charities. The regulator considers this also to include increasing or improving the efficiency of the emergency services and the armed forces of the Crown).
• The advancement of the arts, heritage, culture or science.
• The advancement of public participation in sport (that is, sport which involves physical skill and exertion).
• The provision of recreational facilities, or the organisation of recreational activities, with the object of improving the conditions of life for the persons for whom the facilities or activities are primarily intended (that is, recreational facilities or activities primarily intended for persons needing them due to their age, ill-health, disability, financial hardship or other disadvantage, or which are available to members of the public at large or to male or female members of the public at large).
• The advancement of human rights, conflict resolution or reconciliation.
• The promotion of religious or racial harmony.
• The promotion of equality and diversity.
• The advancement of environmental protection or improvement.
• The relief of those in need due to age, ill-health, disability, financial hardship or other disadvantage (including relief given by providing accommodation or care).
• The advancement of animal welfare.
• Any other purpose that can reasonably be regarded as analogous to any of those purposes (the 2005 Act declares specifically that the advancement of any philosophical belief whether or not involving belief in a god is analogous to the advancement of religion).

Public benefit. The public benefit test is set out in section 8 of the 2005 Act. It consists of a series of factors which must be weighed in balance. However, section 8 makes it clear that no particular purpose is to be presumed to be for the public benefit. Instead, there has to be a deliberate demonstration that public benefit will be, or is intended to be, provided.

The factors in assessing whether public benefit will be provided are:

- How any benefit gained, or likely to be gained, by members of the organisation or any other person (other than as members of the general public) compares with the benefit which will be gained, or is likely to be gained, by the public.

- How any disbenefit incurred, or likely to be incurred, by the public compares with the benefit which will be gained, or is likely to be gained, by the public.

In addition, where a benefit is, or is likely to be, provided only to a section of the general public, regard must be had to whether any condition applied before the benefit can be obtained is unduly restrictive. Such a condition is specifically stated to include charges or fees payable to obtain benefit from the organisation.

In other words, the test seeks to weigh up the varying degrees of public benefit, private benefit, public disbenefit, and restrictive conditions which will be imposed by the organisation, or which will arise as a result of the organisation's activities.

The notion of disbenefit did not occur in Scots law before the 2005 Act. It is considered by the regulator to mean something more than a mere lack of benefit. Instead, it is viewed as the opposite of benefit. In essence, it is the equivalent of detriment or harm.

Charities can, due to their activities, provide public disbenefit. They can also provide private benefit. The critical issue is whether the public benefit provided outweighs the public disbenefit and private benefit. That is what is meant when the regulator speaks of weighing these matters in balance.

Unduly restrictive conditions. It is also clear that charities can impose a condition (for example, a fee or charge) before their benefits can be accessed. The condition imposed can be restrictive, in that not every member of the public is able to meet the terms of the condition. What will cause a charity to fail the test is where the condition is unduly restrictive. In any one case, this will be a matter of degree.

Conditions are considered unduly restrictive if they are unreasonable, unjustifiable or unlawful. Unlawful conditions include conditions which are discriminatory against any person covered by one of the protected characteristics in UK equality law, unless the charitable or religious exemptions set out in the equality legislation are met.

Additional requirements. Even when the conditions relating to charitable objectives and public benefit are met, a body can still fail the charity test if:

- Its constitution allows it to distribute or apply any of its property (whether on a winding up or at any other time) for non-charitable purposes. Scottish ministers have power to disapply this provision.

- Its constitution expressly permits the Scottish ministers or a minister of the Crown to direct or otherwise control its affairs. This particular provision has been disapplied under secondary legislation for particular bodies, where the Scottish Parliament considers it justifiable for them to retain their charitable status. Disapplications primarily relate to national collections institutions, universities and colleges.

- Its purposes include the advancement of a political party, or the organisation is itself a political party. There is no power to Scottish ministers to disapply this provision.

Principal sources of law

The principal source of charity law in Scotland is the 2005 Act. This was amended by the Public Services Reform (Scotland) Act 2010, which introduced greater flexibility and corrected some unintended consequences of the original legislation.

The vast majority of the 2005 Act is in force. A key exception is in relation to public benevolent collections, where the existing law remains in full force and effect. The relevant provisions are in the Civic Government (Scotland) Act 1982 and the Public Charitable Collections (Scotland) Regulations 1984, as amended.

Secondary legislation supplements the 2005 Act. The principal statutory instruments are the:

- Charities Accounts (Scotland) Regulations 2006 (amended a number of times since 2006).
- Charities References in Documents (Scotland) Regulations 2007, as amended.
- Charities Reorganisation (Scotland) Regulations 2007, as amended.
- Charities and Benevolent Fundraising (Scotland) Regulations 2009.
- Scottish Charitable Incorporated Organisations Regulations 2011.
- Scottish Charitable Incorporated Organisations (Removal from Register and Dissolution) Regulations 2011.
- Charities Restricted Funds Reorganisation (Scotland) Regulations 2012.

A full review of the existing charity legislation has been encouraged by the regulator, to take place ten years after the introduction of the 2005 Act. Despite Scottish Government indications that such a review would take place, no review has yet been instigated.

LEGAL BODIES

4. WHAT ARE THE FORMS OF ORGANISATIONS THAT ARE USED FOR CHARITABLE PURPOSES? WHAT ARE THEIR ADVANTAGES/DISADVANTAGES?

Charitable companies limited by guarantee

The charitable company is, as in England and Wales, one of the most suitable forms of organisation for Scottish charities where they intend to enter into contracts, employ staff or carry out operational activities. The key features, advantages and disadvantages of charitable companies limited by guarantee are set out in the chapter for England and Wales, with references to the Charity Commission being replaced by references to the Office of the Scottish Charity Regulator (OSCR) (*see chapter, UK (England and Wales)*). The law across Scotland, England and Wales on companies is in the same legislation, primarily the Companies Act 2006.

Scottish charitable companies (that is, any company registered with OSCR as a charity in Scotland) can only wind up through insolvency proceedings or through dissolution with the prior permission of OSCR. Such permission must be sought at least 42 days before any steps to dissolve or commence insolvency proceedings.

Charitable trusts

Charitable trusts can be established in Scotland in broadly the same manner as in England and Wales (*see chapter, UK (England and Wales)*), but Scottish trusts are subject to a separate body of legislation and common law. For grant-making charities, the trust remains the most popular structure adopted.

The principal Scottish legislation is in the Trusts (Scotland) Acts 1921 and 1961, as amended. A major review project to revise trust law in Scotland has been under way under the Scottish Law Commission, but no time has yet been made available at the Scottish Parliament to take forward any of the many recommended reforms.

Advantages. Although a Scottish trust does not have legal personality and is not technically a limited liability structure, trustees of Scottish trusts generally avoid personal liability for their actions if they make it clear that they are acting in a trustee capacity, and that they are signing as trustees. Provided that there is no breach of trust, trustees are generally protected from unlimited liability, but in cases of breach of trust liability is joint and several. Assets held by individuals as trustees are held distinctly from the trustees' personal assets, so trust assets are not available to personal creditors.

Disadvantages. Immunity clauses in Scottish trust deeds are construed strictly by the Scottish courts. Trustees relying on immunity clauses to avoid particular forms of liability must be aware that they may have limited effect.

Unless there is a mechanism for amendment in the trust deed itself, it is likely that changes to purposes or powers will require a reorganisation application to OSCR, provided that the relevant reorganisation conditions are met. In cases where there is some legal or technical difficulty, it is possible for trusts to be amended through a more formal court process, although that will be considerably more expensive and time consuming than an OSCR reorganisation.

Unincorporated associations

The method of establishing an unincorporated association and the rationale for doing so are the same in Scotland as in England and Wales (with references to the Charity Commission being replaced by references to OSCR) (*see chapter, UK (England and Wales)*).

Unincorporated associations are the most common form of charitable structure in Scotland but they are not always suitable, particularly if the charity employs staff and engages in contractual obligations. It is increasingly common for unincorporated associations to convert to incorporated models, to secure the benefits of limited liability and legal personality.

Where a Scottish unincorporated association holds land, the property is (unlike in England and Wales) held by the office bearers of the charity *ex officio*, and title typically transfers to new office bearers automatically. However, land and other property can be vested in trustees of a separate trust on behalf of the members of the association. Much depends on the age of the association, the normal practice at the time of its establishment, and the style of constitution used to create it.

Advantages. The unincorporated association is the lightest touch structure available for Scottish charities, with minimal external regulation. The degree of informality implicit in the structure will not suit all forms of charity.

Disadvantages. There remains a considerable lack of clarity around a number of legal aspects, including where liability rests in an association. The best available authorities point to initial liability resting with the committee members (charity trustees). Some authorities suggest that only those committee members who sanctioned a course of action giving rise to liability will bear any risk.

Equally, there is authority to suggest that all members of an association can bear liability, particularly if the assets of the charity trustees have been exhausted by a claim. However, once the group of liable individuals has been ascertained, it is fairly clear that liability will be joint and several in almost every case. A proposal from the Scottish Law Commission to provide legal personality to unincorporated associations was published some years ago, but the matter is reserved to the UK Parliament and there is no indication yet that the proposal will be given legislative effect.

Scottish Charitable Incorporated Organisations (SCIOs)

The SCIO is the Scottish equivalent of the Charitable Incorporated Organisation (CIO) in England and Wales. SCIOs came into operation as legal forms for charities on 1 April 2011. OSCR has published detailed guidance on how SCIOs are created, managed and dissolved, and SCIOs are governed by key legislation (*see Question 3, Principal sources of law*).

By the early part of 2016, over 2,200 SCIOs had been created in Scotland, representing almost 10% of the entire Scottish charity sector. Initial concerns about the popularity of SCIOs appear to have been put to rest. However, there is still some concern about SCIOs that intend to operate primarily abroad, and possible difficulties in securing their recognition in some foreign jurisdictions.

SCIOs can be single tier structures, similar to a charitable trust, or a two tier structure similar to a charitable company (with the equivalents of members and directors/charity trustees). In either case, a SCIO must have at least two members and three charity trustees, although the same individuals can act in both roles. In addition to the normal legal duties imposed on charity trustees, the members of SCIOs are subject to duties under section 51 of the Charities and Trustee Investment (Scotland) Act 2005, including a duty to ensure, in good faith, that the SCIO acts consistently with its purposes.

Advantages. SCIOs are viewed as a light touch form of limited liability vehicle. They provide the benefits of legal personality and limited liability, but only require to be registered with OSCR, unlike companies which are also subject to registration with and regulation by Companies House. The structure of a SCIO's constitution in Scotland is extremely flexible. Statute sets out the minimum requirements but there is total flexibility about the overall content, provided that the minimum requirements are covered.

Disadvantages. Insolvent SCIOs are subject to a formal sequestration process through OSCR and the Accountant in Bankruptcy. A SCIO can submit an application for its own dissolution when it is clear that it is insolvent, and creditors can also apply for sequestration. For these purposes, an insolvent SCIO is defined as having debts of at least GB£1,500. Where a SCIO is apparently insolvent but has debts of less than GB£1,500, there is no formal process for sequestration and a SCIO would probably have to negotiate with its creditors to reach a resolution. How well these provisions operate in practice remains to be seen.

Other structures

Registered societies (formerly known as industrial and provident societies) are reasonably common in Scotland and some older and larger charities are established as Royal Charter bodies, with their constitutions contained in a charter granted by the Queen. Educational endowments are also common, many of which are created by Royal Charter, as trusts or as statutory bodies under the Education (Scotland) Acts.

Other not-for-profit structures include community interest companies which, by definition, cannot be registered as charities, although they may have objects which are considered to be charitable. A number of community amateur sports clubs, which carry special tax treatment, also exist in Scotland.

5. WHAT ARE THE QUALIFICATION REQUIREMENTS/FORMALITIES TO SET UP THESE ORGANISATIONS?

The process for establishing a charity in Scotland is broadly similar to the process set out in the chapter for England and Wales (*see chapter, UK (England and Wales)*), with references to the Charity Commission substituted by references to OSCR, subject to the following additional information.

Charitable companies limited by guarantee

The normal approach in Scotland is to submit a proposed company's articles of association to OSCR in draft for comment and approval. This avoids the need for members' resolutions to amend the articles of association if OSCR asks for particular changes to be made. Incorporation normally follows after OSCR has provided informal charitable clearance.

Applications to OSCR consist of:

- An application form.
- A form of business plan (there is no fixed template, but it should include some commentary on the proposed activities, including information on funding sources).
- A copy of the draft articles of association and signed declarations from the charity trustees.

If a company already exists and is seeking charitable status, the latest set of accounts is also required.

OSCR aims to deal with all applications for charitable status within three months. Straightforward applications are often processed within about six weeks, depending on workloads at OSCR and whether any additional information is required from the applicants.

Where informal clearance from OSCR is sought before incorporation, the intended directors proceed to incorporate the company at Companies House once OSCR has given an informal indication of charitable status. Once a certificate of incorporation has been issued by Companies House, it is necessary to obtain formal charitable clearance from OSCR, including allocation of a Scottish charity number. Once this is obtained, charities must apply to HM Revenue & Customs (HMRC) to secure recognition of the charity for tax purposes, in the same way as charities in England and Wales.

Charitable trusts

The process is broadly the same as in England and Wales but managed through OSCR instead of the Charity Commission, and as set out above for charitable companies in Scotland (*see above, Charitable companies limited by guarantee*).

Applications can be submitted to OSCR with a draft trust deed, which allows for some flexibility if OSCR asks for changes to the deed.

Unincorporated associations

Applications follow broadly the same pattern as in England and Wales but managed through OSCR instead of the Charity Commission (*see above, Charitable companies limited by guarantee*). Submitting a draft constitution is advisable, as constitutions which have already been adopted may be tricky to amend, depending on how they are worded. In the absence of a clear mechanism, changes to some unincorporated associations' constitutions can only be made by a unanimous vote of the association's members.

Scottish Charitable Incorporated Organisations (SCIOs)

The process is similar to the OSCR application process for charitable companies (*see above, Charitable companies limited by guarantee*). The draft constitution must contain regulations under certain pre-defined headings as set out in the Charities and Trustee Investment (Scotland) Act 2005 and the SCIO Regulations, but there is no fixed style for the constitution overall and applicants have a considerable flexibility over style and content. There are model constitutions from third sector bodies (including the Scottish Council for Voluntary Organisations) and professional advisers are often able to provide styles of their own.

The OSCR application form is specific to the SCIO vehicle, and care should be taken to lodge the correct form when applying.

ONGOING REGULATORY REQUIREMENTS

6. WHAT ARE THE MAIN REGULATORY AUTHORITIES FOR CHARITABLE ORGANISATIONS? WHAT ARE THEIR POWERS OF INVESTIGATION/AUDIT/SANCTIONS?

Regulatory authorities

The main registrar and regulator of charities in Scotland is the Office of the Scottish Charity Regulator (OSCR), a non-Ministerial Department and part of the Scottish Administration. OSCR is independent of the Scottish Government, but reports to the Scottish ministers annually.

HM Revenue & Customs (HMRC) also exercises regulatory authority over the granting of recognition of charities for tax purposes. Its role is the same as in England and Wales. The definition of charity used for tax purposes is governed by English law (even in Scotland) and it is different to that in the Charities and Trustee Investment (Scotland) Act 2005 (2005 Act). Most Scottish charities have charitable objects which reflect a convergence of the Scottish and English legal definitions.

Powers

OSCR's main roles are defined in the 2005 Act. They are to:

- Determine whether bodies are charities.
- Keep a public register of charities.
- Encourage, facilitate and monitor charities' compliance with charity law.
- Identify and investigate apparent misconduct in the administration of charities, and to take remedial or protective action accordingly.
- Give information or advice, or make proposals to the Scottish ministers on matters relating to OSCR's functions.

In carrying out its statutory functions, OSCR must have regard (as relevant) to a number of principles, including that:

- Its regulatory activities should be proportionate, accountable, consistent, transparent, and targeted at cases in which action is needed.
- Notice should be taken of any other principle which OSCR considers best regulatory practice.

As there is no *de minimis* level of income or capital for registration with OSCR, its powers are exercised against all organisations operating in Scotland that wish to refer to themselves as charities in Scotland, regardless of where they are established.

All charities registered with OSCR must file an annual return and annual accounts with OSCR. Aside from that, OSCR's role is generally less interventionist than its English and Welsh counterpart. For example, it is not required or able to sanction property transactions or ex gratia payments.

OSCR's prior consent is required if a charity wishes to change its name, amend its charitable purposes, amalgamate with another body, wind up, or apply to the Court of Session to take any of those actions. In addition, OSCR must be notified within three months of any of the following being taken:

• Change in principal office or principal contact.

• Change in any other details set out in the Scottish Charity Register.

• Change to a charity's constitution.

• Change of name, purposes, amalgamation, winding up or application to the Court of Session, following the granting of OSCR consent.

Charities must also notify OSCR within one month of any administration order being made by a court, or the appointment of a receiver for any of the charity's assets.

OSCR's regulatory powers are wide and extend to charities, bodies controlled by charities (including trading subsidiaries) and organisations and people representing themselves as charities or as acting on behalf of a charity. Inquiries can be started by OSCR of its own accord or in response to representations made by a third party. OSCR has wide information gathering powers for the purposes of such inquiries.

If OSCR discovers evidence of misconduct, or concludes that steps are required to protect a charity's property or secure the proper application of property for a charity's purposes, OSCR has a number of powers, including to:

• Suspend any person concerned in the management of an organisation.

• Direct a body or person to stop representing itself as a charity or a charity representative.

• Restrict the transactions which can be entered into without OSCR's consent.

• Direct an institution or person holding property on behalf of a charity not to part with it without OSCR's consent, or to pay over such sums to the charity.

Where it appears to OSCR that a charity no longer meets the charity test, it must direct the charity to take steps to meet the charity test, or remove the charity from the Scottish Charity Register. Other than this last power, OSCR's powers tend to be restricted to periods of up to six months, although the Court of Session can make similar orders on a more permanent basis.

OSCR must prepare reports on any formal inquiries made under section 28 of the 2005 Act which result in OSCR taking sanctions against an organisation or individual, or where the subject of the inquiry requests that a report be prepared. OSCR can publish such reports in such manner as it thinks fit. OSCR has also developed a practice of issuing regulatory guidance based on its inquiries from time to time, especially where the outcomes may contain lessons of wider use to the charity sector.

7.   WHICH BODIES OR PERSONS MANAGE CHARITABLE ORGANISATIONS AND WHAT GENERAL REQUIREMENTS MUST THEY MEET?

Charity trustees

There are no distinctions in Scots law between natural persons and incorporations when serving as charity trustees (provided that requirements prohibiting corporate directors of charitable companies under the Companies Acts are complied with once fully in force). A person can manage a charity (that is, serve as a charity trustee) provided they are not disqualified. Disqualification arises if an individual:

- Has been convicted of an offence of dishonesty or an offence under the Charities and Trustee Investment (Scotland) Act 2005 (2005 Act).
- Is an undischarged bankrupt.
- Has been removed under the 2005 Act or under the Law Reform (Miscellaneous Provisions) (Scotland) Act 1990, from being concerned in the management or control of any body.
- Has been removed from the office of charity trustee by the Charity Commission for England and Wales or by Her Majesty's High Court of Justice in England, on the grounds of misconduct in the administration of a charity.
- Is subject to a company directors' disqualification order.

A charity trustee who continues to act in that role despite being disqualified commits an offence, and is liable to punishment by a fine, imprisonment, or both.

8.   WHAT ARE THE ACCOUNTING/FINANCIAL REPORTING REQUIREMENTS?

All charities in Scotland must maintain financial records and lodge with OSCR an annual statement of account and trustees' report on their activities. The format of accounts must follow that in the Statement of Recommended Practice for Charity Accounts, devised jointly by OSCR and the Charity Commission for England and Wales.

Where a charity has an income of under GB£250,000 in any one year it can prepare a simplified receipts and payments account. Fully accrued accounts are necessary where a charity has an annual income of GB£250,000 or more. The exceptions are in relation to charitable companies and registered societies, where fully accrued accounts are always required.

Examination requirements also vary depending on income and capital levels. A full audit is required where a charity's income exceeds GB£500,000 and where there is a gross capital asset value exceeding GB£3.26 million. Where income levels are between GB£100,000 and GB£500,000 an independent examination is permitted, with a reduced version of independent examination applicable to charities with incomes below GB£100,000. If a charity's constitution requires a full audit, that requirement overrides the accounting regulations.

TAX

Provided that Scottish charities are recognised by HM Revenue & Customs (HMRC) as charities for tax purposes, they will generally qualify for all standard tax reliefs for charities in the UK. For the basic position on income and capital gains tax and value added tax (VAT), see *chapter, UK (England and Wales)*.

The Scottish Parliament has been given limited control over income tax rates with effect from 6 April 2016, but this does not extend to control over charity tax relief in relation to income. Further devolution of income tax powers applies from 6 April 2017. It is possible that there will be adjustments to the way charity tax reliefs are calculated through the devolution of additional powers to the Scottish Parliament, but for the time being the overall UK position applies in Scotland.

Tax on property used by the organisation

Non-domestic rates are devolved to the Scottish Parliament. Charities receive 80% mandatory relief from non-domestic rates, where property is used wholly or mainly for charitable purposes. Local authorities can top up this relief with up to 20% discretionary relief, which can therefore relieve a charity of all non-domestic rates.

Other

Land and Buildings Transaction Tax (LBTT) is a distinctly Scottish tax levied on the purchase of property in Scotland. There is a total exemption from LBTT for charities where the property purchased is to be used wholly or mainly for charitable purposes.

The taxation benefits for donors in Scotland are the same as those which apply in England and Wales (*see chapter, UK (England and Wales)*). It is possible, but not certain, that further devolution of income tax powers to the Scottish Parliament will result eventually in varying rates of Gift Aid relief for Scottish taxpayers, but this is unlikely to apply until April 2017 at the very earliest.

DISADVANTAGES

The principal disadvantages of charitable status in Scotland are the burden of regulation, the degree of public scrutiny and additional legal requirements to which charities are subject compared to non-charities. For some of those additional regulatory burdens, see *Question 6*.

There are limits on the amount of remuneration which can be paid to charity trustees in Scotland, and these limits extend to persons connected to a charity trustee. Charity trustees or those connected to them can only be remunerated for services they provide if a number of conditions are satisfied:

- At any time, only a minority of the charity trustees can receive or be entitled to remuneration, or be connected with a trustee who receives or is entitled to remuneration.

- The maximum amount of the remuneration must be set out in a written agreement and must be reasonable in the circumstances.
- The other charity trustees must be satisfied before entering into the agreement that it is in the charity's interests for the services to be provided by the relevant individual for the maximum amount stated.
- The charity's constitution must not prohibit the payment of remuneration.

However, if a provision in a charity's constitution was in force on 15 November 2004 which authorises remuneration in different circumstances from those set out above, the charity's constitution will prevail.

OVERSEAS CHARITIES

12.   IS IT POSSIBLE TO OPERATE AN OVERSEAS CHARITY IN YOUR JURISDICTION? WHAT ARE THE REGISTRATION FORMALITIES? HOW (IF AT ALL) ARE OVERSEAS CHARITIES TREATED DIFFERENTLY IN YOUR JURISDICTION FROM CHARITIES SET UP UNDER DOMESTIC LAW?

It is possible for foreign charities to operate in Scotland. Foreign for these purposes includes charities established in parts of the UK other than Scotland. All foreign charities must register with OSCR unless they can satisfy the statutory exception, which requires satisfying all of the following:

- The charity is established under the law of a country or territory other than Scotland, and is entitled to refer to itself as a charity in its home jurisdiction.
- It is managed or controlled wholly or mainly outside Scotland.
- It does not occupy land or premises in Scotland.
- It does not carry out activities in any office, shop or similar premises in Scotland.
- When referring to itself as a charity, it states that it is established under the law of another country.

Detailed guidance is available on OSCR's website on each of these criteria, in its publication *Seeking Charitable Status for Cross Border Charities*. If the exception set out above is satisfied, a foreign charity can operate in Scotland without meeting the Scottish charity test. If the exception is not satisfied, the Scottish charity test must be met, which typically involves amending the charity's constitution to ensure that its charitable objects are consistent with Scots law.

Once entered onto the Scottish Charity Register, a foreign charity must comply with all aspects of Scottish charity law, including annual reporting to OSCR and applying to OSCR for consent for certain actions (*see Question 6*). They must also notify OSCR of other actions taken, and generally comply with fundraising regulations in force in Scotland from time to time.

A cross-border charity registered with OSCR is entitled to refer to itself as a charity, charitable body, registered charity or charity registered in Scotland, but cannot refer to itself as a registered Scottish charity. This term is reserved for charities established under Scots law, or which are controlled wholly or mainly in or from Scotland.

13. IS IT POSSIBLE TO REGISTER A DOMESTIC CHARITY ABROAD, AND HAS YOUR JURISDICTION ENTERED INTO ANY INTERNATIONAL AGREEMENTS OR TREATIES IN THIS AREA?

It is possible for a Scottish charity to register with a foreign regulator, but there are no formal international treaties in place between Scotland and any other nation dealing with charity registration.

REFORM

14. ARE THERE ANY PROPOSALS FOR REFORM IN THE AREA OF CHARITY LAW?

OSCR has recommended to the Scottish ministers that the Charities and Trustee Investment (Scotland) Act 2005 should be reviewed and has proposed a number of changes, including:

- OSCR should have the ability to make positive directions (rather than simply directing a charity not to take particular actions).
- Scottish charities should have a connection with Scotland, including potentially at least one Scots-resident trustee.

Further devolution of tax powers to the Scottish Parliament is also likely to involve increasingly devolved Scottish tax reliefs for charities.

ONLINE RESOURCES

OFFICE OF THE SCOTTISH CHARITY REGULATOR

W www.oscr.org.uk

Description. Up-to-date source of all guidance available from the Scottish Charity Regulator, the Scottish Charity Register, some accounting styles and templates, and links to current primary and secondary legislation.

REGULATORY AUTHORITY

OFFICE OF THE SCOTTISH CHARITY REGULATOR

W www.oscr.org.uk

T +44 1382 220446

Description. Official website of the Office of the Scottish Charity Regulator, established under section 1 of the Charities and Trustee Investment (Scotland) Act 2005.

UNITED STATES: CALIFORNIA

Ingrid Mittermaier and Shirley McLaughlin, ADLER & COLVIN

OVERVIEW AND MAIN TRENDS

1. WHAT IS THE HISTORICAL BACKGROUND TO CHARITY LAW AND CHARITABLE ORGANISATIONS IN YOUR JURISDICTION?

Both the scope and depth of charitable activity in the US are rooted firmly in its history. From the period of early European settlement and colonisation, activities that (in an older, more established society) might have been performed by government were instead taken up by communities, which urgently needed to provide their members with essential social services.

Many Americans tended to be wary of, if not hostile to, perceived encroachments by government (whether the English monarchy or emerging American democracy) on individual rights. Many Americans came to value a pluralistic society that, however imperfect, encouraged diversity of experience and perception, along with the development of active, engaged individuals uniting to work in many ways for the common good.

Today, non-profit organisations of all types, including charities, play a key role in US life, comprising an independent or third sector (after government and commerce) providing an alternative path to a better society.

2. ARE INDEPENDENT CHARITABLE ORGANISATIONS COMMON AND SIGNIFICANT IN YOUR JURISDICTION? WHAT IS THE CURRENT SIZE AND SCOPE OF THE SECTOR AND THE MAIN TRENDS?

As of 2015 there were about 1.41 million tax-exempt non-profit organisations in the US. Donations to charities by individuals, foundations and corporations totalled more than US$358 billion in 2014. Of these, the largest (about 32%) went to religious organisations, while the second-largest (about 15%) went to educational institutions.

Independent Sector, a network of more than 600 US charities, describes the non-profit sector as including a wide range of organisations (including religious organisations, private colleges and schools, foundations, hospitals, day-care centres, environmental organisations, museums, symphony orchestras, youth organisations, advocacy groups, and neighbourhood organisations). They are linked by their mission to serve a public purpose and their voluntary and self-governing nature. In addition, all are prohibited from distributing profits to shareholders (see *www.urban.org/sites/default/files/alfresco/publication-pdfs/2000497-The-Nonprofit-Sector-in-Brief-2015-Public-Charities-Giving-and-Volunteering.pdf*).

LEGAL FRAMEWORK

Definition of charity

The traditional common law definition of charity, as derived from English common law, sets out four charitable purposes: the relief of poverty, the advancement of education, the advancement of religion, and other purposes beneficial to the community (*Commissioners for Special Purposes of Income Tax v Pemsel, AC 531 (1891)*). This tradition has influenced the American law of charities (see generally *AW Scott, WE Fracher, and Mark L Asher, Scott and Asher on Trusts (5th ed., 2006)*).

In the modern era, the traditional definition has been largely superseded in the US by the tax law definition of charity, that is, an organisation that pays no tax on its income and whose donors derive a tax benefit due to their charitable donations.

Principal sources of law

Federal tax law is in the Internal Revenue Code 1986, as amended from time to time. The Internal Revenue Code (IRC) cannot be understood without reference to the Income Tax Regulations issued by the Department of the Treasury. The Internal Revenue Service (IRS) administers the federal tax system.

In addition, states have legal frameworks that apply to certain non-profit legal entities and/or provide tax exemptions for certain types of legal entities. This chapter focuses on California law. The Franchise Tax Board (FTB) is the tax authority in California. The California Revenue and Taxation Code, which provides tax exemptions for certain types of non-profit organisations, mirrors in large part federal tax law in this area.

In addition, California common and statutory law referred to as charitable trust law applies to charities. Extensive provisions on the role of the California Attorney General in regulating charities are set out in the Supervision of Trustees and Fundraisers for Charitable Purposes Act (Charity Act) (*sections 12580 to 12599.7, California Government Code*).

The Uniform Prudent Management of Institutional Funds Act (UPMIFA) (*sections 18501 to 18510, California Probate Code*) also applies rules on endowments, restrictions on use of grants, and investments, to institutions holding funds for charitable purposes.

The Uniform Prudent Investor Act (UPIA) (*sections 16002(a), 16003, and 16045 to 16054, Probate Code*) applies to investments by charitable trusts.

LEGAL BODIES

A charity or other non-profit entity's tax status is mainly a matter of federal law, but its existence as a legal entity and its internal governance are matters of state law. In California a non-profit organisation can be a non-profit corporation, charitable trust, unincorporated non-profit association, or limited liability company (LLC). Each entity can, but is not required to, apply for exemption from federal income tax.

Non-profit corporations

Non-profit corporations are governed by the Nonprofit Corporation Law, in sections 5000 et seq. of the California Corporations Code (the Nonprofit Law and the Corporations Code). The Nonprofit Law distinguishes between three types of non-profit corporations: non-profit public benefit, non-profit mutual benefit, and religious.

Charities can be established as nonprofit public benefit or religious corporations. This section focuses on nonprofit public benefit corporations, the most common structure used for charities.

There are three possible control structures for nonprofit public benefit corporations:

- No members, and the directors elect their own successors (a self-perpetuating board).
- Members (individuals or entities) that elect the directors and have other statutory approval rights.
- Other specified individuals or entities that appoint the directors.

The Nonprofit Law provides an extensive statutory framework governing California non-profit corporations. There are detailed rules, especially for membership corporations, regarding:

- Calling, notice requirements and holding member and director meetings.
- Nominating and electing directors.
- Inspection rights.
- Termination of members or directors.

Advantages. The corporate form of organisation provides two principal advantages: familiarity and clarity. A corporation is a recognised and well-understood legal entity governed by relatively clear statutory norms, in such important areas as:

- Permitted activities.
- Director and member liability.
- Director standards of conduct.
- Indemnification of agents.
- Internal governance.

Importantly, the corporate structure is well-understood in limiting liability for both its members and its directors (see Question 7). The extensive statutory default and mandatory provisions provide a solid internal governance framework and can assist in resolving disputes among directors, officers and members.

In addition, the corporate structure is relatively flexible, allowing directors, as well as members, if any, to adapt to changing circumstances. This can be done by amending the charity's governing documents to restate its purposes and accomplish other changes, such as the size of the board, officer positions, or use of committee structures.

Disadvantages. Potential disadvantages of the corporate form include:

- Ongoing filing requirements with the California Secretary of State (including filings to effect amendments of the articles of incorporation, a merger, and dissolution).
- The need to observe corporate formalities and comply with internal governance provisions.
- Flexibility can be a disadvantage, if the founder wants to permanently impose certain purposes and control structures.

Trusts

Trust law is a matter of state law. The Restatement (Third) of Trusts serves as a codification of the common law of trusts. California also has detailed trust statutes, in the California Probate Code (*sections 15000 to 19405, Prob C*).

Like other charitable legal entities, charitable trusts are subject to the California Attorney General's jurisdiction, and so are also governed by the Charity Act. Therefore, among other things, charitable trusts must be registered with the Attorney General's Registry of Charitable Trusts, and are subject to the Attorney General's continuing supervision. However, unlike nonprofit public benefit corporations, charitable trusts do not need to provide notice or receive approval from the Attorney General before engaging in a merger, transfer of assets, or dissolution, if such actions are taken under the terms of the trust document.

A trust is not a separate legal entity. A trust is a fiduciary relationship with respect to property, arising from an intention to create that relationship, that subjects the person holding title to the property to duties to deal with it for the benefit of charity or one or more persons (*section 2, Restatement (Third) of Trusts, 2003*). In a charitable trust, the trust property is vested in and managed by one or more trustees (who hold the legal title, as trustees).

Instead of having specifically ascertained beneficiaries, the beneficiaries must consist of a class of person selected from the public, and the class must be large enough so that a public interest is served. The trust provisions are typically set out in the trust document executed by the person contributing the property to the trust (settlor).

In California, a trust can be created for any purpose that is not illegal or against public policy (*section 15203, Probate Code*). Charitable purposes include (*section 18502, Probate Code, tracking section 28, Restatement (Third) of Trusts*):

- The relief of poverty.
- The advancement of education or religion.
- The promotion of health.
- The promotion of a governmental purpose.
- Any other purpose, the achievement of which is beneficial to the community.

Advantages. While non-profit corporations are the most common legal entity for a charity, a trust should still be considered, especially if the main activity of the charity is to hold and invest assets and make charitable distributions, which does not require a particularly complex or flexible governance structure.

There are considerably fewer statutory formalities for trust operations than for corporations, which can be a real advantage. The settlor can also be more restrictive in establishing the purposes of the trust.

A trust can also allow a smaller group of designated individuals, such as family members, to retain control. The settlor can irrevocably provide for the initial trustees and successor trustees, or set out how successor trustees are selected. Trusts are not subject to the section 5227 limit on interested directors applicable to corporations (*see Question 7*), and so are not limited in paying compensation to some or all of their trustees, even if they are members of the same family.

Disadvantages. The disadvantages of trusts are that they lack the familiarity, clarity and flexibility provided by corporations (*see above, Non-profit corporations*).

Unincorporated associations

The law of unincorporated associations is a matter of state law. Unincorporated associations, unlike corporations, are not created by filing a formation document with the Secretary of State. They are simply established by the mutual consent for a common lawful purpose of two or more persons (*section 18035(a), Corporations Code*).

Non-profit associations must be established with a primary common purpose other than to operate a business for profit (*section 18020(a), Corporations Code*). There are also only very few statutory requirements applicable to non-profit associations. Therefore, there is a high degree of flexibility in their governance structure.

A non-profit association's governing documents, which can include articles of association, bye-laws, and/or other documents, set out the association's governing principles. Depending on the nature of their activities, some non-profit associations may be subject to California Attorney General supervision and the reporting requirements of the Charity Act (for instance, an unincorporated association that raises donations for charitable purposes).

Unincorporated associations are entitled to general recognition as separate legal entities, and can therefore:

- Enter into contracts.
- Acquire and hold interests in real or personal property.
- Sue and be sued in their name.
- Register and protect trade marks and service marks.

The law generally provides for limitation of the liability of members, directors, officers, and agents of non-profit associations. Among other things, except for payroll taxes, members, directors, officers, and agents of non-profit associations are not individually or personally liable for the association's debts or liabilities on the basis of their relationship with the association (*section 18605, Corporations Code*).

Advantages. The major advantages of an unincorporated association are the relative ease with which it can be organised, the informality with which it can act, and the relatively few statutory requirements.

Disadvantages. Certain disadvantages make the unincorporated association less than desirable for most non-profit enterprises. Despite some relatively recent statutory provisions, associations still face a degree of legal uncertainty in California because the statutory provisions define some, but not all, of the rights, duties and liabilities of the association and its members, directors, officers and agents. Also, as existing law does not provide a standard of care for a director of an unincorporated association, directors are left unsure of their duties and potential liability.

Limited liability companies

A California LLC can engage in any lawful business activity, whether or not for profit. An LLC can therefore operate as a non-profit entity. There is no specific non-profit LLC form.

An LLC can choose to be governed by its member(s) only. Alternatively, an LLC can appoint an individual or entity (which may or may not be a member) to act as manager. In addition, an LLC can, but is not required to, appoint officers.

A properly organised LLC is normally treated for federal income tax purposes as a partnership with no entity-level tax, and taxes passed through to the members. A single-member LLC is typically completely disregarded for federal income tax purposes. An LLC that is classified as a partnership or a disregarded entity for federal income tax purposes must pay an annual franchise tax and an annual fee to the FTB, even if its only members are tax-exempt charities. The only exception is for an LLC that has received California tax exemption as a title-holding company.

Alternatively, an LLC can elect to be treated for tax purposes as a corporation. A non-profit LLC that has elected corporate tax treatment can apply for federal tax exemption as a charity. However, it will only be recognised as tax-exempt by the IRS if, among other things, its members are themselves exempt organisations, governmental units, or wholly-owned instrumentalities of a state or its political subdivisions (see *Private Letter Ruling (PLR) 200827041* which, while non-precedential, lists the 12 factors the IRS considers for LLC exemption). This significantly limits the uses of an LLC that has elected corporate tax treatment.

Advantages. The key attraction of the LLC for charitable activities is similar to that in the for-profit sector. Most LLCs elect for pass-through tax treatment, and so do not need to pay federal income tax. In the charitable context, an LLC is not required to file the fairly complex Form 1023 tax exemption application or separate annual information returns. At the same time, the LLC provides its members with a personal liability shield similar to that given to corporate shareholders.

In taking advantage of these characteristics, non-profit LLCs are mainly used by exempt organisations for managing subsidiary and joint-venture activities, and for holding title to property.

Another advantage for LLCs, both with pass-through and corporate tax treatment, is the flexibility in drafting governance provisions, instead of being constrained by corporate law.

Disadvantages. LLCs lack some of the familiarity and clarity of corporations. The lack of applicable corporate law can also be a disadvantage, with less structure and guidance for the members and managers. In most cases a pass-through LLC still has to pay California franchise tax and fees, even if its members are tax-exempt charities.

5. WHAT ARE THE QUALIFICATION REQUIREMENTS/FORMALITIES TO SET UP THESE ORGANISATIONS?

Non-profit corporations

One or more persons, known as incorporators, can form a non-profit corporation, by filing articles of incorporation with the California Secretary of State and paying a modest filing fee.

To qualify as a California nonprofit public benefit corporation, the articles of incorporation must comply with the Corporations Code, including that the articles must:

- State that the corporation is not organised for the private gain of any person.
- Describe the corporation's charitable purposes, although the description can be, and often is, very general.

To qualify for tax-exempt status, the articles must also include dissolution procedures and certain restrictions on activities.

Bye-laws establish the procedures by which the corporation governs itself. Once a charity is incorporated, it must register, within 30 days of receiving assets for charitable purposes, with the California Attorney General's Registry of Charitable Trusts. Registration is straightforward, involving the provision of basic information about the charity's organisation and operations.

Trusts

A charitable trust is generally created by a trust agreement or declaration of trust, under which the donor (trustor or settlor) transfers certain specified assets to one or more trustees named in the trust document. The settlor executes the trust, and the trustee indicates acceptance of the property and the terms of the trust. Notarisation is optional. The trust agreement both establishes the trust and sets out governance provisions.

The essential elements to create a valid trust, which typically must be stated in the trust document, include (*sections 15201 to 15205, Probate Code*):

- The intention to create a trust.
- Identification of trust property.
- Setting out the trust purpose.
- Designation of the beneficiary.

Successor trustees can be named. The settlor is typically given the power to remove trustees and appoint successor trustees during the settlor's lifetime. A trust must also register with the Attorney General and apply to the IRS and FTB for tax-exempt status.

Unincorporated associations

An unincorporated association is established by the mutual consent for a common lawful purpose of two or more persons (*section 18035(a), Corporations Code*). A non-profit association's governing documents, which can include articles of association, bye-laws, and/or other documents that govern the association's purpose or operations, embody the association's governing principles.

Associations are extremely flexible legal forms. They do not even need to have written governing documents, although associations wanting to receive tax exemption from the IRS need to meet the organisational requirements imposed by the IRC. Non-profit associations holding assets for charitable purposes must register with the Attorney General's Registry of Charitable Trusts and comply with the reporting requirements of the Charity Act.

Limited liability companies

LLCs are formed in California by filing articles of organisation with the Secretary of State (Corporate Division). The articles, which are submitted on a pre-printed form, provide for an initial agent for service of process and state whether the company will be managed by its member(s) or by one or more managers.

The member or members must adopt an operating agreement, a hybrid document combining elements of corporate bye-laws and (for multi-member LLCs) a partnership agreement.

Depending on whether the LLC chooses pass-through or corporation tax treatment, the LLC can apply for recognition of tax-exempt status with the IRS and/or the FTB. If the LLC has elected tax treatment as a corporation and is seeking federal tax-exempt status, additional language must be added as an attachment to the articles, to comply with the legal requirements for this status.

Establishing tax-exempt charitable status for a legal entity

A charity in any form (except for a pass-through LLC) must apply to the IRS for recognition of tax-exempt status, under IRC section 501(c)(3), using Form 1023 (*see Question 9*). It must also establish tax-exempt status in California (*see Question 9*).

ONGOING REGULATORY REQUIREMENTS

6. WHAT ARE THE MAIN REGULATORY AUTHORITIES FOR CHARITABLE ORGANISATIONS? WHAT ARE THEIR POWERS OF INVESTIGATION/AUDIT/SANCTIONS?

Regulatory authorities

Federal level. The IRS supervises the operations of charities in three ways:

- Information provided by charities in their annual returns.
- Its power to audit the finances and operations of charities.
- Its power to assess penalties and fines and, in extreme cases, to revoke a charity's tax exemption for abuses and violations of law.

IRC section 4958 gives the IRS power, with regard to public charities, to impose penalties on individuals who benefit from, or approve, certain private inurement transactions, including potentially the charity's directors. At the same time, the law provides that if a disinterested board or board committee approves a transaction with an insider after appropriate investigation and review, the transaction is entitled to a presumption of reasonableness.

The practical result is that an insider, and any board that approves any transaction with an insider, especially without following the prescribed review procedures, risk personal liability, if the IRS later determines that the insider received excessive benefits from the charity.

Private foundations are subject to the technical and often counter-intuitive rules of IRC sections 4940 to 4946, in addition to the general legal rules applicable to all charities. The rules include:

- Strict prohibitions on many financial transactions between a private foundation and certain insiders to the foundation.
- Annual minimum distribution requirements.
- Restrictions on the ability of a foundation to hold interests in a for-profit business (IRC section 4943 generally provides that a private foundation and certain insiders cannot hold more than 20% of the voting or ownership interest in a business enterprise).
- Restrictions on investment activity (IRC section 4944 prohibits a private foundation from investing in a manner which is likely to jeopardise its ability to carry out its exempt purposes, given the risk of losses from the investments).
- Stricter rules for grant making.

To enforce these rules, the IRS is authorised to impose significant excise taxes. The annual tax return submitted by private foundations to the IRS is intended to help it identify any areas where such taxes could be assessed.

State level. Most California charities, as well as foreign charities operating in California, are subject to the jurisdiction of the California Attorney General. In addition to filing a straightforward initial registration form (Form CT-1) with the Attorney General's Registry of Charitable Trusts, charities must also file the one-page Form RRF-1 annually with this Registry.

The charitable trust doctrine, despite its name, applies to non-profit corporations, unincorporated associations and limited liability companies, as well as to trusts. The central principle is that charity assets are, by law, impressed with a charitable trust, that is, they can only be used for particular charitable purposes. Although the charity can hold legal title to its assets, it holds them in trust for charitable beneficiaries. The specific charitable purposes of the trust can be defined by the donor at the time of donation, or by the charity's governing documents.

The Attorney General can bring legal action on behalf of a charity against directors and officers for breaching the charitable trust, and can hold directors personally liable for any harm to the charity that resulted. Lawsuits are brought most commonly in response to situations involving a manager's breach of the charitable trust, coupled with the directors' negligent inattention or intentional abdication of responsibility.

In California nonprofit public benefit corporations, the charity's directors are responsible for:

- Preserving the corporation's charitable assets.
- Using those assets only in a manner that satisfies the terms of the charitable trust to which the assets are subject.
- Operating the organisation to further its charitable purposes.

The Attorney General has plenary power to investigate and bring legal action if he or she determines that there has been a breach of the charitable trust or misuse of charitable assets (see *section 5250, Nonprofit Law*).

Under the California Nonprofit Integrity Act 2004, charitable corporations, unincorporated associations, and trusts that must file reports with the Attorney General and have annual revenue over US$2 million must prepare and disclose on request (from the Attorney General, or any member of the general public) annual financial statements, audited by an independent certified public accountant in accordance with generally accepted accounting principles.

In addition, covered charitable corporations (but not trusts) must put the selection, compensation, and supervision of the auditor under the control of an audit committee appointed by the board, separate and independent from any finance committee and staff members, and subject to other rules to ensure the independence of the committee.

The Nonprofit Integrity Act also requires the board of directors (or an authorised committee) of all public benefit corporations to periodically review and approve as just and reasonable the compensation packages of the president or chief executive officer, and of the treasurer or chief financial officer.

Franchise Tax Board

Like the IRS, the FTB requires the filing of an annual return.

The FTB can audit California charities, and has power to revoke exemptions for violations of the exemption requirements in the Revenue and Taxation Code.

State Board of Equalization and county assessors

Property taxes in California are administered jointly by the State Board of Equalization (BOE) and the county assessors (*see Question 9*).

7. WHICH BODIES OR PERSONS MANAGE CHARITABLE ORGANISATIONS AND WHAT GENERAL REQUIREMENTS MUST THEY MEET?

Non-profit corporations

While members can have powers to elect or remove directors, the board of directors is the key body that manages and is responsible for the affairs of a California non-profit corporation. The Nonprofit Law permits a board to delegate its responsibilities to committees, officers and staff, but ultimate authority remains with the board.

Section 5231 of the Nonprofit Law sets out the basic fiduciary duties applicable to directors. It imposes on all directors a two-fold duty:

- To act with the best interests of the corporation in mind (duty of loyalty).
- To act with such care, including reasonable inquiry, as an ordinarily prudent person in a like position would do under similar circumstances (duty of care).

The Corporations Code addresses more specifically the duty of loyalty. Under section 5227 of the Corporations Code, no more than 49% of a public benefit corporation's governing body can be composed of interested directors, defined as:

- Any person who has been compensated by the corporation for services in the last 12 months, excluding any reasonable compensation paid to a director as director.
- Any member of such a person's family (including brother, sister, ancestor, descendant, spouse, brother-in-law, sister-in-law, son-in-law, daughter-in-law, mother-in- law, or father-in-law).

The effect of this provision is to limit the number of directors who are compensated by the corporation, or who are related to a person who is compensated by the corporation.

California's insider transaction statute, section 5233 of the Corporations Code, uses the term self-dealing to describe a transaction to which the charity is a party, and in which one or more directors has a material financial interest. Under section 5233, a self-dealing transaction is only proper if all the following conditions are met:

- The charity entered into the transaction for its own benefit.
- The transaction was fair and reasonable as to the charity at the time it entered into the transaction.
- Before implementing the transaction or any part of it, all material facts regarding the transaction and the director's interest in it were disclosed to the board, and a majority of the directors then in office (without counting the vote of the financially interested director) determined, after reasonable inquiry under the circumstances, that the charity could not have obtained a better arrangement with reasonable effort, and formally approved the transaction.

Trusts

In a charitable trust, the trust property is vested in and managed by one or more trustees (who have legal title, as trustees) for the benefit of the public. The initial trustees are named by the settlor. It is also important for the trust instrument to provide how successor trustees are to be appointed.

There are considerably fewer statutory provisions applying to the formation and operation of charitable trusts than apply to corporations. For example, there are no statutory requirements applicable to trusts regarding a governing body or officers, their terms, calling or holding meetings, or the addition or termination of a governing body member. The default requirement for trustee decisions is unanimous voting. This can be changed in the trust document.

In California, the general standard of care imposed on trustees is that they must administer the trust with reasonable care, skill, and caution under the circumstances then prevailing that a prudent person acting in a like capacity would use in the conduct of an enterprise of like character and with like aims to accomplish the purposes of the trust as determined from the trust instrument (*section 16040, Probate Code*). Additionally, the Probate Code contains a detailed list of a trustee's duties (*section 16000 and following, Probate Code*).

Unlike corporate directors, trustees can have a limited scope of responsibility. For example, one trustee can be responsible for grantmaking, and the other trustee for administration and investments.

However unlike in corporations, where directors are expressly allowed to rely on information and reports provided by others and to delegate tasks to others, trustees have no express statutory reliance protection, and their ability to delegate can be more limited. Except for investment decisions, the Probate Code states that a trustee cannot delegate acts that the trustee can reasonably be required to perform personally (*section 16012(a), Probate Code*).

Further, where a trustee has properly delegated a matter to an agent, the trustee has a duty to exercise general supervision over the agent (*section 16012(b), Probate Code*).

In relation to investment decisions, delegation is allowed if the trustee exercises prudence in selecting the agent and the scope and terms of the delegation, and reviews the agent's performance (*section 16052, Probate Code*).

California trusts are governed by the Uniform Prudent Investor Act (*section 16045, Probate Code*). This is one area where trust law contains more useful direction than corporate law. Additionally, the Uniform Prudent Investor Act presents a relatively modern view of investment theory, focusing on the total investment portfolio and the entity's overall investment strategy.

A trustee has a duty not to use trust property for the trustee's own profit or to take part in any transaction in which the trustee has an interest adverse to the beneficiary (*section 16004, Probate Code*). There is no provision for balancing conflicts of interest, as in the corporate context (*see above, Non-profit corporations*). On the other hand, unlike a nonprofit public benefit corporation, in which directors' compensation is limited, all trustees of a charitable trust can receive reasonable compensation for their services to the trust.

Unincorporated associations

Apart from the requirement that an unincorporated association be established by mutual consent for a common lawful purpose of two or more persons (*section 18035(a), Corporations Code*), there is a high degree of flexibility in establishing the governance structure of an association.

Limited liability companies

An LLC can choose to be governed by its member(s) only. Alternatively, an LLC can appoint an individual or entity (which may or may not be a member) to act as manager. In addition, an LLC can, but is not required to, appoint officers.

8.   WHAT ARE THE ACCOUNTING/FINANCIAL REPORTING REQUIREMENTS?

Annual IRS return

Based on their type, tax-exempt charities must file Form 990, Form 990-PF or Form 990-EZ, Return of Charity Exempt from Income Tax, with the IRS. These forms ask for information about the charity's gross receipts and expenditures.

Public charities must include reporting on expenditures that the IRS characterises as lobbying. A charity that does not regularly generate more than US$50,000 in annual gross revenues does not trigger a Form 990 filing requirement and must instead submit an annual electronic filing with the IRS, called a Form 990-N or an e-Postcard, providing information such as:

- The organisation's mailing address, website address (if any), and taxpayer identification number (EIN).
- The name and address of a principal officer.
- Evidence of why the organisation is not required to file a Form 990.

Churches, governments and instrumentalities are not required to file the annual return, but can do so voluntarily. If an organisation that is required to file an annual return fails to file for three consecutive years, the organisation will automatically lose its tax-exempt status, as of the date the third annual return or notice is due. There is a process for reinstatement.

All section 501(c) and (d) organisations, not just charities, must publicly disclose their applications for tax exemption, and their federal annual information returns for the three most recently completed years with schedules.

An organisation can claim relief from the requirement to provide copies of its forms if it shows to the IRS that it is the victim of a harassment campaign. The regulations also allow an organisation to disregard requests for copies exceeding two per month or four per year, made by a single individual or sent from the same address.

Annual FTB return

California law requires each exempt organisation to file an annual information return, California Form 199, with the FTB if its income exceeds US$50,000.

Small organisations with gross receipts normally equal to or less than US$50,000 must instead file a Form 199N online (California e-Postcard). An organisation that fails to file the required California e-Postcard for three consecutive years will automatically lose its California tax-exempt status.

If a charity carries on any lobbying or other political activities, it must attach a Form 3509 to its FTB Form 199, and may have to file reports under the California Political Reform Act 1974 and the lobbying registration rules.

Registry of Charitable Trusts Filing

Form RRF-1 is designed to assist the Attorney General's Registry of Charitable Trusts in supervising charitable organisations, to ensure that funds and assets held for charitable purposes are actually so used. This short form is due annually and covers the charity's prior fiscal year. Along with Form RRF-1, charities must file a copy of its annual IRS return with the Registry of Charitable Trusts. Failure to file either form could cost the charity its state tax exemption, as well as result in the Attorney General suspending or revoking the registration of the charity and other penalties.

In certain situations, a charity may need to file Form 990 with the Attorney General, even when it is not required to file an annual return with the IRS.

Audited financials

Certain charitable corporations, unincorporated associations, and trusts that must file reports with the California Attorney General and have annual revenue over US$2 million must prepare annual financial statements audited by an independent certified public accountant, in accordance with generally accepted accounting principles.

When calculating the US$2 million threshold, grants or contract income from government agencies are not included, as long as the governmental entity requires an accounting of those funds. If an organisation does have audited financial statements (as required by California law, or if prepared for charitable organisations required to file reports with the Attorney General, even if not required by law), it must make the audited financial statements available to the Attorney General and the public, within nine months after the close of the fiscal year.

TAX

9.   HOW ARE CHARITIES TAXED, AND WHAT (IF ANY) ARE THE PRINCIPAL EXEMPTIONS AND/OR RELIEFS FROM TAXATION THAT THEY ENJOY?

Tax on income

A charity in any form (except for a pass-through LLC) must apply to the IRS for recognition of tax-exempt status, under IRC section 501(c)(3), using Form 1023.

To qualify for federal tax-exempt charitable status, an organisation must satisfy the requirements of IRC section 501(c)(3). An organisation must satisfy the following six requirements:

- Have an exempt purpose, that is, one or more of the purposes listed in IRC section 501(c)(3).
- Be organised exclusively for exempt purposes.
- Be operated primarily for that purpose.
- No inurement, that is, no improper benefit to anyone in a position to control the charity or exert substantial influence over it.
- No candidate activity, that is, no support or opposition to any candidate for public office.
- No substantial lobbying activity, that is, no substantial support or opposition to legislation.

The IRS exemption application involves completing a lengthy form, which includes questions about:

• The charity's actual and planned activities, governance procedures, and compensation policies.

• The qualifications of, and relationships between, directors, officers and key employees.

Financial data and governing documents must also be provided. The IRS typically takes from six weeks to six months to issue a determination of tax-exempt status. The process can take longer if the IRS identifies significant issues in the application, and/or requires changes to the organisation's governing documents. Certain small charities can use a much simpler Form 1023-EZ for their application.

Federal tax law divides charities into two categories: public charities and private foundations. A private foundation is typically supported by one family or individual, or by the income the foundation receives from investing its endowment. Public charities include religious institutions, schools and universities, hospitals, and charities that are supported by a broad base of donors or consumers. This distinction is not related to the civil law distinction between associations and foundations. Further, having the word foundation in the charity's name does not make it a private foundation. Private foundations are more heavily regulated than public charities, and certain tax rules differ depending on whether a charity is a private foundation or a public charity.

A charity that has gained exemption under section 501(c)(3) is generally exempt from income tax, except for unrelated business taxable income generated by the regular conduct of a business that is not significantly related to the exempt purposes of the charity.

California law mirrors in most respects federal tax law in relation to charity qualification requirements. California Revenue and Taxation Code section 23701(d) charities under California law are, for example, the equivalent of IRC section 501(c)(3) charities under federal tax law. To obtain recognition of tax-exempt status in California, a charity typically files a simple form with the FTB, once the charity has obtained its federal tax exemption letter from the IRS.

Tax on capital gains

Generally, charities are not taxed on capital gains (unless the property generating the capital gains was acquired with debt financing, as defined in IRC section 514).

Tax on property used by the organisation

Churches, schools and museums are eligible for certain specific exemptions from California property taxes. Other charities may also be eligible for complete or partial property tax exemption, under what is known as the welfare exemption. To claim this exemption, charities must obtain an organisational clearance certificate from the State Board of Equalization, and must make an annual filing by 15 February of each year with the county tax assessor in the county where the property is located.

Value added tax (VAT)

There is no federal VAT, and California does not have VAT.

Other

A variety of state-level taxes can be imposed on a charity, including property taxes and sales and use taxes.

10. WHAT, IF ANY, ARE THE TAXATION BENEFITS FOR DONORS TO CHARITIES?

Both individuals and businesses are eligible for significant tax benefits through their donations to charities. Those benefits vary, depending on whether the charity is a public charity or private foundation, and on the nature of the property donated.

The amount of the tax deduction that a donor can claim in the year of a gift to a public charity is capped at 50% of the donor's adjusted gross income, and can be reduced to 30% of the adjusted gross income in some circumstances (*IRC section 170(b)(1)*). Adjusted gross income is a technical concept defined in IRC section 62, and amplified by the Regulations. Generally, adjusted gross income includes all wage income, net investment income, and net business income.

A corporate donor can claim a tax deduction of no more than 10% of its taxable income in any year. It can carry forward any excess donations for up to five years (*IRC section 170(b)(2)*). As with individual donors, some donations result in a fair market value deduction, and some only in a basis deduction.

California law regarding charitable contributions conforms to federal law in many respects. However, California does not automatically adopt the federal tax rules in this area, so it is important to confirm the California tax treatment of charitable contributions, especially for larger or non-standard gifts.

DISADVANTAGES

11. WHAT ARE THE MAIN DISADVANTAGES OF CHARITABLE STATUS?

The main disadvantage of becoming a tax-exempt charity is that to qualify for tax benefits, charities must comply with the detailed requirements applicable under federal tax law and state law. The primary activity of the charity must meet the definition of charity for federal tax purposes. Even if charities meet this requirement they are, among other things, limited in the amount of compensation they can pay, so as not to breach the prohibitions on private inurement and private benefit imposed on them. Private foundations, in particular, are completely prohibited from engaging in many financial transactions with insiders. As another example, section 501(c)(3) charities are subject to extensive limits and rules on lobbying and election-related activities. All of these rules are enforced by a variety of agencies, including the IRS, the FTB, and the California Attorney General.

Another possible disadvantage is that charities must make extensive information about their operations publicly available on their annual returns, including data on the compensation of their highest-paid officers and staff, and detailed income and expense information.

OVERSEAS CHARITIES

12.   IS IT POSSIBLE TO OPERATE AN OVERSEAS CHARITY IN YOUR JURISDICTION? WHAT ARE THE REGISTRATION FORMALITIES? HOW (IF AT ALL) ARE OVERSEAS CHARITIES TREATED DIFFERENTLY IN YOUR JURISDICTION FROM CHARITIES SET UP UNDER DOMESTIC LAW?

Giving to overseas charities

The tax laws of the US, like those of most other industrialised nations, reflect an intent to encourage domestic rather than international philanthropy. Since 1938, the IRC has contained a place-of-organisation requirement for charitable gift recipients. US taxpayers are only entitled to a charitable deduction for gifts to charities that are created or organised in the US or any of it possessions, or under the law of the US, any state, the District of Columbia, or any US possession (*IRC section 170(c)(2)(A)*). Tax treaties between the US and Canada, Mexico and Israel include limited exceptions to this rule, if the donor to a foreign charity has income from sources within that country, and the foreign-source income exceeds the amount of the donation.

Under IRC section 170(c), corporate contributions to be used outside the US are not tax deductible, unless the donee is a US corporation (and not a trust or unincorporated association).

Overseas charities operating in the US/California

Due to the above restriction on making donations to foreign charities, while foreign charities can operate in the US and conduct activities there, foreign charities often determine that they need to establish a related charity in the US, so that they have an entity that can accept tax-deductible contributions from US residents. Alternatively, foreign charities can identify an existing charity in the US that can accept donations from US citizens. This existing charity can then be used to support the foreign charity.

In all cases where donations are made to a US charity to ultimately support a foreign charity, the governing body of the US charity initially receiving the donations must show that it has full discretion over their use, even if the US charity then decides to re-grant the money to the foreign charity. If the donor irrevocably restricts a gift to the US charity for specific use by the foreign charity and no other use, the IRS will view the transaction as a conduit, and deny the charitable deduction to the donor.

13.   IS IT POSSIBLE TO REGISTER A DOMESTIC CHARITY ABROAD, AND HAS YOUR JURISDICTION ENTERED INTO ANY INTERNATIONAL AGREEMENTS OR TREATIES IN THIS AREA?

US charities can conduct charitable activities outside the US directly through their own employees and contractors, and can register abroad to facilitate such operations, if permitted by the laws of the foreign country. They can also make grants for activities outside the US, to US charities with activities in other countries or directly to foreign organisations for charitable purposes. For compliance with US laws, no tax treaty is required to permit a US charity to take these steps.

REFORM

14. ARE THERE ANY PROPOSALS FOR REFORM IN THE AREA OF CHARITY LAW?

In the US, the charitable sector is large and active. As a result, there tend to be at any given time a number of reform proposals affecting charities. In recent years, there have, for example, been proposals to strengthen or weaken the prohibition on charities engaging in lobbying and/or electioneering. Another area that has attracted attention and in which guidance is due is the operation of donor-advised funds, essentially charitable accounts established by donors as existing charities, for which the donors or other named advisers can provide ongoing advice.

ONLINE RESOURCES

INTERNAL REVENUE SERVICE

W www.irs.gov

Description. IRS Publications and Forms are available from the IRS website. Some of the most helpful publications include:

- Charitable Contributions Deductions (IRS Publication 526).
- Tax-Exempt Status for Your Organization (IRS Publication 557).
- Compliance Guide for 501(c)(3) Public Charities (IRS Publication 4221-PC).
- Public Inspection of Tax Exempt Application and Annual Information Returns (IRS Notice 88-120, 1988-2 Cum. Bull. 454).

LEGAL INFORMATION INSTITUTE, CORNELL UNIVERSITY LAW SCHOOL

W www.law.cornell.edu/uscode/text/26

Description. Unofficial listing of the US Code, including the Internal Revenue Code, Title 26.

CALIFORNIA NONPROFIT PUBLIC BENEFIT CORPORATION LAW

W http://leginfo.legislature.ca.gov/faces/codes.xhtml

Description. Official Codes of California.

CALIFORNIA ATTORNEY GENERAL'S GUIDE FOR CHARITIES

W http://ag.ca.gov/charities/publications/guide_for_charities.pdf

Description. Published in 2006, and currently under revision, this guide offers information on running a public benefit corporation in California.

CALIFORNIA SECRETARY OF STATE GUIDE TO CORPORATE FILINGS

W www.ss.ca.gov/business/corp/corporate.htm

Description. Many of the forms for filing with the Secretary of State are available online.

REGULATORY AUTHORITIES

INTERNAL REVENUE SERVICE

W www.irs.gov/charities

T +1 800 829 4933

Description. The IRS is a bureau of the US Department of the Treasury, responsible for collection of federal tax revenue and enforcement of the Internal Revenue Code. The Exempt Organizations division administers tax law governing charities, private foundations and other entities exempt from federal income tax.

OFFICE OF THE ATTORNEY GENERAL OF CALIFORNIA

W www.oag.ca.gov/charities

T +1 916 445 2021

Description. Part of the State of California Department of Justice, the Attorney General is the chief law enforcement officer in the state. The Attorney General regulates charities and professional fundraisers who solicit on their behalf.

CALIFORNIA FRANCHISE TAX BOARD

W www.taxes.ca.gov/exemptbus.shtml

T +1 800 852 5711

Description. The FTB is responsible for administering several taxes, including personal income tax and corporation tax. The FTB makes determinations on non-profit exemption from certain taxes.

CALIFORNIA STATE BOARD OF EQUALIZATION

W www.boe.ca.gov

T +1 800 852 5711

Description. The BOE administers tax programmes, along with county assessors, to collect sales and use taxes, property taxes, and special taxes, and serves as the appellate body for contesting tax decisions.

CALIFORNIA SECRETARY OF STATE

W www.sos.ca.gov

T +1 916 653 6814

Description. The Secretary of State's office maintains business filings. The Attorney General is the chief law enforcement officer in the state. The Attorney General regulates charities and professional fundraisers who solicit on their behalf.

CONTACT DETAILS

GENERAL EDITOR
Anne-Marie Piper
Farrer & Co
66 Lincoln's Inn Fields
London WC2A 3LH
England

T: +44 20 3375 7462
E: anne-marie.piper@farrer.co.uk
W: www.farrer.co.uk

AUSTRALIA
Vera Visevic
Mills Oakley
Level 12, 400 George Street
Sydney, NSW 2000

T: +61 2 8289 5812
E: vvisevic@millsoakley.com.au
W: www.millsoakley.com.au

BELGIUM
Philippe Malherbe
Liedekerke Wolters Waelbroeck Kirkpatrick
boulevard de l'Empereur 3 Keizerslaan
B-1000 Brussels

T: +32 2 551 15 77
E: p.malherbe@liedekerke.com
W: www.liedekerke.com

BRAZIL
Flavia Regina de Souza Oliveira & Michelle Baldi
Ballon Sanches
Mattos Filho, Veiga Filho, Marrey Jr. e Quiroga
Al. Joaquim Eugênio de Lima, 447
São Paulo - SP
01411-001

T: +55 11 3147 7600
E: flavia@mattosfilho.com.br
E: msanches@mattosfilho.com.br
W: www.mattosfilho.com.br

CANADA
Robert B Hayhoe & Sarah G Fitzpatrick
Miller Thomson LLP
Scotia Plaza
40 King Street West, Suite 5800
Toronto
Ontario M5H 3S1

T: +416 595 8174
T: +1 604 643 1272
E: rhayhoe@millerthomson.com
E: sfitzpatrick@millerthomson.com
W: www.millerthomson.com

GERMANY
Dr Andreas Richter & Dr Anna Katharina Gollan
P+P Pöllath + Partners
Potsdamer Platz 5
10785 Berlin

T: +49 30 25353 132
E: andreas.richter@pplaw.com
E: katharina.gollan@pplaw.com
W: www.pplaw.de

GIBRALTAR

Peter Montegriffo
Hassans International Law Firm
57/63 Line Wall Road
GX11 1AA

T: +350 200 79000
E: peter.montegriffo@hassans.gi
W: www.gibraltarlaw.com

IRELAND

John C O'Connor & Helen McGrath
O'Connor, Solicitors
8 Clare St
Dublin 2

T: +353 1 6764488
T: +353 1 6764488
E: john.oconnor@oclegal.ie
E: helen.mcgrath@oclegal.ie
W: www.oclegal.ie

ISRAEL

Asher Dovev
Herzog Fox & Neeman
Asia House
4 Weizmann Street
Tel Aviv 64239

T: +972 3 692 7424
E: doveva@hfn.co.il
W: www.hfn.co.il

ITALY

Francesco Facchini, Giacomo Ficai & Alessia
Vignudelli
Studio Tributario Associato Facchini Rossi & Soci
Foro Buonaparte 70
20121 Milan

T: +39 02 89013228
E: f.facchini@frstax.it
E: g.ficai@frstax.it
E: a.vignudelli@frstax.it
W: www.frstax.it

LUXEMBOURG

Eric Fort & Guy Harles
Arendt & Medernach SA
41 Avenue J-F Kennedy
L-2082

T: +352 40 78 78 306
T: +352 40 78 78 204
E: eric.fort@arendt.com
E: guy.harles@arendt.com
W: www.arendt.com

MEXICO

Daniel Del Río, Julio J Copo Terrés,
Mariana Arrieta & Eduardo Ramos Parra
Basham, Ringe & Correa S.C.
Paseo de los Tamarindos No 400-A, Piso 9
Bosques de las Lomas
Mexico City
05120

T: + 52 55 5261 0432
T: + 52 55 5261 0411
T: + 52 55 5261 0518
T: + 52 55 5261 0424
E: delrio@basham.com.mx
E: jcopoter@alumni.nd.edu
E: marrieta@basham.com.mx
E: eramos@basham.com.mx
W: www.basham.com.mx

THE NETHERLANDS

Reinier W L Russell
Russell Advocaten
Reimersbeek 2
1082 AG
Amsterdam

T: +31 20 301 55 55
E: reinier.russell@russell.nl
W: www.russell.nl

SINGAPORE

Elaine Seow E-Lin
Braddell Brothers LLP
11 Beach Road #04-01
Singapore 189675

T: +65 6499 9490
E: elaine.seow@braddellbrothers.com
W: www.braddellbrothers.com

SOUTH AFRICA

Shirley Fodor & Tatyana Radebe
Werksmans Attorneys
155 5th St
Johannesburg, 2196

T: +27 11 535 8316
T: +27 11 535 8312
E: sfodor@werksmans.com
E: tradebe@werksmans.com
W: www.werksmans.com

SWEDEN

Michael Karlsson & Gustav Engvall
Mannheimer Swartling Advokatbyrå
Södra Storgatan 7
Box 1384
251 13 Helsingborg

T: +46 42 489 22 22
T: +46 42 489 22 37
E: michael.karlsson@msa.se
E: gustav.engvall@msa.se
W: www.mannheimerswartling.se

SWITZERLAND

Benoît Merkt
Lenz & Staehelin
Route de Chêne 30
1211 Geneva 6

T: +41 58 450 70 00
E: benoit.merkt@lenzstaehelin.com
W: www.lenzstaehelin.com

UK (ENGLAND AND WALES)

Anne-Marie Piper & Philip Reed
Farrer & Co
66 Lincoln's Inn Fields
London WC2A 3LH

T: +44 20 3375 7462
T: +44 20 3375 7112
E: anne-marie.piper@farrer.co.uk
E: philip.reed@farrer.co.uk
W: www.farrer.co.uk

UK (NORTHERN IRELAND)

Jenny Ebbage
Edwards & Co. Solicitors
28 Hill Street
Belfast, BT1 2LA

T: +44 28 9032 1863
E: jenny.ebbage@edwardsandcompany.co.uk
W: www.edwardsandcompany.co.uk

UK (SCOTLAND)

Gavin McEwan
Turcan Connell
Princes Exchange
1 Earl Grey Street
Edinburgh EH3 9EE

T: +44 131 228 8111
E: gavin.mcewan@turcanconnell.com
W: www.turcanconnell.com

UNITED STATES: CALIFORNIA

Ingrid Mittermaier & Shirley McLaughlin
Adler & Colvin
235 Montgomery Street
Russ Building, Suite 1220
San Francisco, CA 94104

T: +1 415 421 7555
E: ingrid@adlercolvin.com
E: smclaughlin@adlercolvin.com
W: www.adlercolvin.com